CROSS CURRENTS
A Yearbook of Central European Culture

1982

Edited by Ladislav Matejka and Benjamin Stolz

Ann Arbor

Michigan Slavic Materials, No. 20
© 1982 by University of Michigan
International Standard Book Number: 0-930042-43-3

Front Cover: *Kaddish* by Aleš Veselý

The most breathtaking sculpture I have ever seen stood in 1978 (and maybe stands now) in Středokluky, a village less than ten miles from Prague. It is erected in open air in a somewhat fenced-off area next to a ramshackle barn filled with other welded but smaller-scale sculptures, all created by Aleš Veselý, who also owns the property. His large construction was made around 1968 in the iron works of Ostrava under a government program. Veselý named the work *Kaddish*, the Jewish Prayer for the Dead, in memory of his recently deceased father. It was supposed to have been incorporated in a memorial for the victims of German concentration camps, but those plans were shelved after the Soviet occupation. Instead, the sculpture was shipped to Středokluky to be hidden from the general public. In fact, while small bands of initiated art lovers make pilgrimages to it, the ordinary citizens seem indifferent . . . Actually, the rural location seems strangely fitting. At dusk, the headlights of vehicles moving on the horizon along the Prague—Kladno road add an eerie halo to the sculpture set off against the darkening sky . . .

From a letter by an American visitor

Tortured and beaten in the skull—What mad hallucinations of the damned that drive me out of my own skull to seek Eternity till I find Peace for Thee, O Poetry—and for all humankind call on the Origin

Death which is the mother of the universe!—Now wear your nakedness forever, white flowers in your hair, your marriage sealed behind the sky—no revolution might destroy that maidenhood—

Allen Ginsberg, *Kaddish*

Back Cover: *A Masque* by Eva Kmentová

Department of Slavic Languages and Literatures
The University of Michigan

CONTENTS

Looking for a Center: 1
On the Poetry of Central Europe
Czesław Miłosz

Letter from Budapest   12
George Konrad

Milan Kundera Interview   15
A. Finkielkraut

Defining "Central Europe":   30
Power, Politics, and Culture
Roman Szporluk

East Europe? West Europe? Both? Neither?   39
Jan Triska

Ivan the Terrible as the Gentry's Candidate for the Polish Throne: 45
A Study in Political Mentality
Wiktor Weintraub

The Independent Publishing Movement in Poland: 55
Its Past and Future Perspectives
Stanisław Barańczak

Samizdat: A Return to the Pre-Gutenberg Era?   64
H. Gordon Skilling

Conversation with Tadeusz Konwicki   81
A. J. Liehm

Czesław Miłosz and the Landscape of Exile   89
Harold B. Segel

Who is Elias Canetti?   107
Ingo Seidler

Krleža's Glembay Cycle in its European Context   125
Ivo Vidan

American Motifs in the Work of Bohumil Hrabal   207
Josef Škvorecký

Slovak Surrealism as a Parable of Modern Uprootedness   219
Peter Petro

Contemporary Poetry in Poland, Hungary, and Czechoslovakia   233
(with selections in English)
Emery George

Jiří Orten's Elegies   243
(with selections in English)
George Gibian

Rilke's Early Contacts with Czech and Jewish Prague   255
Daria A. Rothe

Kafka's Milena as Remembered by Her Daughter Jana   267
Jana Černá

Spellbound by Prague   289
(with samples of modern Czech visual art)
Jindřich Chalupecký

Béla Bartók as a Collector of Folk Music   295
Albert B. Lord

Béla Bartók and Slovakia   305
Michal Željar

Hába's Microtonal Theory in Yugoslavia   309
Jelena Milojković-Djurić

The Liberated Theatre of Voskovec and Werich   315
Jarka M. Burian

Andrzej Wajda: Film Language and the Artist's Truth   339
Herbert Eagle

The Swell Season Comes to an End: 353
Sad Autumn Blues
Josef Škvorecký

LOOKING FOR A CENTER:
ON THE POETRY OF CENTRAL EUROPE

Czesław Miłosz

The title of my paper may suggest something profound, perhaps a metaphor referring to the psychology of modern man. But I intend to speak on earth of earthly matters, namely geography. Whoever pronounces the word "center" implies another word, "periphery," and a relationship between the two, either centrifugal or centripetal. Also, a center implies two crossing lines, vertical and horizontal. These few elementary notions about space should be present in our mind when we deal with the geography and history of Europe taken as a whole, and particularly of so-called Eastern Europe. Perhaps, coming from an area which for a long time has been considered the Eastern marches of Rome-centered Christendom makes one more sensitive to shifting points of gravity, symbolized by the very fluidity of such terms as "the West" and "the East." Though my subject is the twentieth century, when such shifts have been accelerated, I feel I must first make a brief historical survey. My examples will be taken from the history of Polish letters, with which I am best acquainted, but I do not doubt that students of Czech or Hungarian or Baltic literatures will easily find analogies.

Human imagination is constantly busy with organizing geographical space. A village or town where we live is "here," while many important events take place "over there," at a distant, more or less definite point. For a medieval clerk the West-East axis was perhaps less tangible than the North-South axis, as the countries situated north of the Alps directed their longing toward Italy and the capital of the Christian world, Rome. In Poland for a couple of centuries medieval Latin was the only written language, as opposed to the spoken vernacular, and, as a consequence, literary models were brought from *outside*. Even Polish syllabic verse was invented in imitation of the medieval Latin syllabic verse. More or less at the same time the marvels of Italy of the Quattrocento began to acquire a legendary dimension. A Polish poet writing in Latin around 1500, Janicius, while staying on scholarship in Italy, sang the beauty of that country, though he was wary to moderate the extent of his "Italinization" for fear that his scholarship wouldn't be renewed. The most important Slavic poet to appear before the nineteenth century, Jan Kochanowski, spent ten years in Italy as a student of humanities. And a curious anecdote might be recalled concerning his time, namely the sixteenth century. Readers of French poets of La Pleiade are familiar with a poem *On the Ruins of Rome* by Joachim du Bellay. However, an identical poem is found among the works of his Polish contemporary, Mikolaj Sep-Szarzyński. What is more, an identical poem exists in Spanish under the name of a famous Spanish poet, Francisco Quevedo. It is quite probable that the same poem exists in other European languages, always presented as an original product. To my knowledge, nobody solved that puzzle with the exception of a Polish gentleman-scholar, the late Jerzy Stempowski, who told me about the results of his detective work in a private letter. He discovered the source of all those poems—an original written in Latin by an Italian humanist, Ianus Vitalis of Palermo, who is today forgotten. Many similar examples of Italian influence can be found in poetry, painting, architecture and music.

The seventeenth century not only initiated a scientific revolution but also gradually moved the cultural center of continental Europe from Rome to Paris. Baroque architecture, Italian opera, and Italian dance tunes competed for a while with French classical tragedy, but the name of René Descartes explains why Paris proved to be victorious. The French language was becoming a language of letters and sciences as well as of the literary salon in a more and more cosmopolitan Europe, and it preserved that position till the outbreak of World War I.

My paper could as well be entitled, "What Happened in Our Time to Paris, Once a Mecca of Poets and Painters?" A student of modern poetry in whatever language must invariably go back to Charles Baudelaire, Arthur Rimbaud and Stéphane Mallarmé. Those were also the patron saints of bohemian groups of poets around 1900 in Cracow, Warsaw, Prague or Budapest. The claims of Berlin, Munich and Vienna to the position of cultural capitals of Europe were short-lived in spite of ties between such groups as "Young Scandinavia" and "Young Poland" meeting and influencing each other in Germany. For poets and painters to be "in" meant to be "in" artistic Paris. Bołeslaw Lésmian, the most accomplished poet of the Polish "Moderna," went through several years of Parisian apprenticeship. The roster of the Society of Polish Artists active in Paris in 1910 reads like a list of the most eminent names in Polish arts and letters of that period. The mythological aspects of Paris and the birthplace of everything new and daring was enhanced of course by the fact that great Polish romantic poetry had been written there and a nineteenth-century precursor of modern Polish verse, Norwid, had lived there. (In parenthesis, he was as much Italy-oriented as was Robert Browning. One of the most interesting Polish long poems of the nineteenth century, *Quidam* by Norwid, deals with Rome at the time of Emperor Hadrian.)

The legends surrounding a center of attraction travel with a variable speed, and it may happen that the glow of a star is strong while its source is fading. Paris after World War I, the Paris of Gertrude Stein, Hemingway, Fitzgerald and so many other American expatriates, was still aglow, but signs of decline appeared. Probably one spot in Paris could be indicative of the last acme and of the fall—this was the Café La Coupole at Boulevard Montparnasse which together with Café Dôme reached its peak of fame in 1926 and started to fade in 1930, never to recover, or, what amounts to the same, it acquired a different, less colorful public. Paris of the 1920's and 1930's still was sending abroad its inventions: surrealism, even new phases of Picasso, *Le Cimetière Marin* of Paul Valery, the Neo-Thomistic philosophy of Jacques Maritain. Yet for poets in Warsaw or Prague the City of Lights remained primarily the home of nineteenth-century genius, above all of symbolist poetics, much as for their painter contemporaries everything received a new beginning with the paintings of Cézanne. Two main schools of poetry in Poland of the interwar period, Skamander and the Avantgarde, even if hostile to each other, continued, each in its own way, different aspects of the poetics to be found in the poems, notes, and letters of Stéphane Mallarmé. Native roots in the past of Polish poetry should not be neglected by a student of that period, nor the affinity with Russian Acmeism bypassed, but the French contribution probably outweighs others.

Similarities among poets of the Renaissance, whether French or Polish or Croatian, were due to their common models taken from Italy. Similarities among modern poets of various languages were due to their openness to French influence. However, it would be a mistake to reduce this to the question of fashion and of imitation. Rather, French men of letters succeeded in imposing everywhere their own conviction that what was French was universal, i.e., a norm for the whole civilized world, while the particular, different in every country, constituted so many deviations. Such a view can be traced back to the French Revolution, with its ambition of delivering a message to the whole of humanity. And undoubtedly, a certain political mythology of liberty, then of Napoleon, helped in sustaining the authority of French thought and literature in my part of Europe. If the attitude of the nineteenth-century Russians toward France was one of love-hate, the countries situated between Russia and Germany represented another nuance of feeling, close to unhappy love.

Only someone who, like myself, witnessed in 1940 the reactions of the Polish population to the news of the fall of France, realizes the extent of their shock and despair. Instinctively it was taken as even more significant than Hitler's victory over Poland—in fact, as the end of Europe. And it was. After the first tentative partition of Europe by the Ribentropp-Molotov Pact, the second partition in Yalta sealed Europe's fate. An enigmatic new era emerged for some hundred millions of Europeans who were then officially relegated to "the East"—and also for their poets.

Moscow, the capital of the Empire, aspired now to the title of the center of Communism and, potentially, of the planet Earth. The premise of its precedence as a model for the future had to be universally accepted. The first decade after the war saw a gradual implementation of that premise as political institutions, the economic system, philosophy, art, and literature, first elaborated in Moscow, were imposed and copied in the newly conquered countries. Then something strange happened: a clash between two forces opposed to each other, between the traditional pull of Mediterranean civilization and of France on the one hand, and of the new center of political power in Moscow on the other. Nowhere was that clash more obvious than in literature, especially in poetry. As a result, Moscow completely failed in its attempt to establish its cultural pre-eminence; on the contrary, it came to be regarded as backward and barbarian. Yet since it exerted complete political control, a curious and ominous dichotomy made its appearance, consisting in rule by a party which hadn't conquered the hearts and minds of the people. The dichotomy was kept in check as long as Western imports in styles and ideas were strictly forbidden and branded as decadent and bourgeois. The relaxation of control after the turbulent year 1956 in Poland and Hungary brought about a true invasion of everything Western, in thought, art, literature, music, even women's dresses: a sufficient demonstration that there was a vacuum to be filled. Since that moment Polish and, as far as I know, Hungarian or Czech poetry has been in form as "Western," or, if you prefer, "postmodern," as one could desire.

Such facts are usually told with a kind of glee or with a self-congratulatory smile and presented as a victory of freedom. In my opinion the matter is made a little more complex by the rather illusory existence of the Western half of Europe. Amid prosperity and technical progress it has been losing its power to inspire arts and letters and its once famous center, Paris, has been touched by a progressive eclipse of vigor.

The military impotence of Western Europe thus mysteriously parallels or follows the weakening of its spirit. Avid for Western models, people of the Eastern half of Europe have been discovering the illusory character of Western promise. One could write a whole book on Polish poetry of the last two decades as a history of the gradual realization that former centers of attraction do not offer much in terms of values, and that a poet from the East must rely upon his own resources.

There is a curious poem by Zbigniew Herbert, "Mona Lisa." Leonardo's painting in the Louvre symbolizes the Europe of supreme cultural achievements, but a Europe that was for many years forbidden to the inhabitants of countries behind the Iron Curtain. Images of war and annihilation are the background for the representation of a dream about going one day to Paris. The narrator obviously is a survivor with obsessive memories. Those very memories make a mockery out of a meeting with Mona Lisa, an inert object. Let me quote a few fragments:

> Through seven mountain frontiers
> barbed wire of rivers
> and executed forests

LOOKING FOR A CENTER 5

and hanged bridges
I kept coming—
through waterfalls of stairways
whirlings of sea wings
and baroque heaven
all bubbly with angels
—to you
Jerusalem in a frame

. . .

So I'm here
You see, I am here
I hadn't a hope
but I'm here

Laboriously smiling
resin colored mute convex

As if constructed out of lenses
concave landscape for a background

between the blackness of her back
which is like a moon in clouds

and the first tree of the surroundings
is a great void froths of light

so I'm here
sometimes it was
sometimes it seemed that

don't even think about it

only her regulated smile
her head a pendulum at rest

her eyes dream into infinity
but in her glances snails are asleep

so I'm here
they were all going to come
I'm alone

when already
he could no longer move his head
he said
as soon as all this is over
I'm going to Paris
between the second and the third finger
of the right hand
a space
I put in this furrow
the empty shells of fates
so I'm here
it's me here
pressed into the floor
with living heels*

    A chapter in a hypothetical book on Polish postwar poetry should be dedicated to irony and even derision in the treatment of the Western European and particularly French intellectuals. Paris in the 1950's exported a desperate vision of man's condition in the writings of its existentialists. Though Albert Camus didn't want to be called that name, he, more than any of his colleagues, caught the imagination of Polish poets who engaged in polemics with him in poetry and prose. Camus' short novel *The Fall* provoked Jarosław Iwaszkiewicz to answer in a story entitled "The Ascent." The narrator is an average Pole who has lived through the horrors of the Nazi occupation and later of the Stalinist terror. By implication Camus is accused of contriving sufferings for his hero in a century when *real* sufferings abound. In other words, a *real* hell is opposed to a *literary* hell. Yet in my opinion, the scorn with which Iwaszkiewicz treats Camus is unjustified and the story may be called an exercise in self-pity. Nevertheless it merits mention as it is highly characteristic.

    Some Polish critics have considered Tadeusz Różewicz as the most important voice among poets who made their debut after the war. If this is true, then a tone of derision, especially when he speaks of Western thinkers and artists, deserves particular attention. Różewicz's nihilistic poetry seems to be built upon several layers of anger and disgust, perhaps disgust with the pretense of Western Europe to exist, while its time is over. In any case, such a meaning may be read into a polemic with *The Fall* of Albert Camus. I quote from Różewicz's poem entitled "Falling":

    Camus
    La Chute the Fall

---

*Translated by Peter Dale Scott.

LOOKING FOR A CENTER

Oh, my dear fellow, for a man who is alone, without
God and without master, the weight of days is dreadful

that fighter with the heart of the child
imagined

that the concentric canals of Amsterdam
were a circle of hell
the hell of solid citizens
of course

"here we are in the last circle"
the last moralist
in French literature
was saying to a chance acquaintance
in some joint

he inherited from his childhood
a belief in the bottom
he certainly had a deep love of Dostoevsky
he certainly suffered because
there was no hell no heaven
no Lamb
no lie
it seemed to him he had discovered the bottom
that he was lying at the bottom
that he had fallen

Meanwhile
there was no longer any bottom
instinctively this was understood by
a certain young miss from Paris
and she wrote a composition
about copulation bonjour tristesse
about death bonjour tristesse
while grateful readers
on both sides
of the formerly so-called
iron curtain
bought her . . .
for its weight in gold
the young miss that lady
that young miss that lady
understood that there is no Bottom

no circles of hell
no rise
and no Fall
that everything is played out
in the familiar
none-too-large area
between
Regio genus anterior
Regio pubice
and regio oralis
and what was once
the vestibule of hell
has been changed
by the fashionable lady of letters
into the vestibulum
vaginae*

I do not share Różewicz's philosophy. I think his mistake consists of exaggerating the predicament of contemporary man. Certainly, our century is not a serene one. But problems confronting our ancestors were not easier to cope with, even if we today witness the fulfillment of Nietzsche's prophesy, namely the rise of "European nihilism." Not very much comes out of wailing over the human condition as Różewicz does. Intellectually crude, he may be interesting only if we regard his poetry as a code for an obsession of a political nature, what I would call a complex of betrayal by the West. That complex may express itself sometimes as a rejoicing over the universal decay of values.

It would be wrong to underestimate the subtle and hidden relations between poetry and politics. And the intellectual Paris of the 1950's and the 1960's turned with expectation to the East, masochistically assigning itself the role of a periphery of Moscow. A poem written decades earlier by the Greek poet Cavafy, "Expecting the Barbarians," acquired a new poignancy and was particularly liked by the Polish poets as an indictment of their Western European brethren. The poem is famous and I am sure many people in the audience know it, but let me recall it here once more. It tells the story of how a center, by losing faith in itself, changes through resignation into a periphery.

What are we waiting for, assembled in the public square?
The barbarians are to arrive today

*Translated by Magnus J. Krynski and Robert Maguire.

LOOKING FOR A CENTER

Why such inaction in the Senate?
Why do the Senators sit and pass no laws?

Because the barbarians are to arrive today.
What further laws can the Senators pass?
When the barbarians come they will make the laws.

Why did our emperor wake up so early,
and sit at the principal gate of the city,
on the throne, in state, wearing his crown?

Because the barbarians are to arrive today.
And the emperor waits to receive
their chief. Indeed he had prepared
to give him a scroll. Therein he engraved
many titles and names of honor.

Why have our two consuls and the praetors come out
today in their red, embroidered togas;
and rings with brilliant glittering emeralds;
why are they carrying costly canes today,
superbly carved with silver and gold?

Because the barbarians are to arrive today,
and such things dazzle the barbarians.

Why don't the worthy orators come as usual
to make their speeches, to have their say?

Because the barbarians are to arrive today;
and they get bored with eloquence and orations.

Why this sudden unrest and confusion?
(How solemn their faces have become.)
Why are the streets and squares clearing quickly,
and all return to their homes, so deep in thought?

Because night is here but the barbarians have not come.
Some people arrived from the frontiers,
and they said that there are no longer any barbarians.

And now what shall become of us without any barbarians?
Those people were a kind of solution.*

---

*Translated by Rae Dalven.

In recent decades, American, not French, poetry has entered the countries of Eastern Europe as an active force. And yet, it had been to a large extent shaped by Europe-oriented expatriates, like Ezra Pound, or T. S. Eliot. Thus, we may speak of American poetry of our century as undergoing a rather belated transformation from a dependent into an autonomous organism, if not a center. There are signs indicating that a similar process has been taking place in my area of Europe. Its poetry has been recognized as a specific component of the international literary scene. When in the 1960's I translated a number of poems from Polish and published them under the title *Postwar Polish Poetry*, I had a very vivid response, especially among young American poets, many of whom told me later that poems from my anthology influenced their own writings. They sensed in those poems something different from what they had found in Western European poets read in translation, perhaps more vigor, clarity, and sensitivity to historical situations. Yet poets whom I translated, whether Herbert or Różewicz or others, were still in the phase of bitter accounts with Western Europe because of its failure to continue to exist as a *subject,* not an *object,* of history.

A visible change occurred in the 1970's, as if a new generation assumed the decline and fall of the Western center as self-evident and decided to tackle their own problems in their own way, which, in poetry, meant giving a growing role to Polish poets of the past and a priority to the moral choices of the individual in the Communist system. Such for instance is the poetry of Barańczak, Krynicki, Kornhauser, Zagajewski—committed, not expecting anything from outside and fostering the development of the new power: public opinion.

The present cultural set-up in Europe is strange indeed and its future, enigmatic. It is not probable that Moscow will emerge as a center of attraction. On the contrary, every year seems to advance its sclerosis in philosophy, art, and literature, while only its military power is growing. The inhabitants of the Empire, if they look for an inspiration from *outside,* may follow fashion that favors America; and of course the English language has been doing well all over Europe, at the expense of French. However, the differences in the political and economic systems are so great that affinities must be superficial, often based upon misunderstanding, much as the Polish independent trade unions have little in common with American unions, except for the name. One may submit the thesis that we are moving toward a pluralistic, multi-centered world without a clear-cut North-South or East-West axis. Then the name "East-Central Europe" would receive a new legitimacy as a certain cultural unit, placed in the Eastern orbit by force of arms and by pacts between the superpowers, but maintaining its own identity. Poetry of that part of the world, always registering the moods of a given country through a tangle of hints and allusions, may provide many insights in that respect.

And yet, if we take such an outcome as probable, we are confronted with many unknowns. Standing on one's own feet, liberating oneself from the vestiges of unhappy love for the West is a good thing, provided it doesn't lead to entrenching oneself in a morbid nationalism. An East-Central Europe composed of closed national compartments hostile or indifferent to each other would be against the vital interests of its nations. The remedy for such a division is a clear understanding of the past which, in spite of national differences, is common, for East-Central Europe was ruled by the North-South axis and the East-West axis. It is quite a task, the task of bringing to light what unites those countries in their present struggle for cultural identity, and it also awaits their poets, whether they are Polish, Lithuanian, Czech or Hungarian. A sense of history is a specific contribution of our geographic area to world literature; and if a poet must sometimes turn against the nationalism of his compatriots to remain faithful to his historical imagination, he will be vindicated sooner or later.

LETTER FROM BUDAPEST

George Konrad

It's here in East Central Europe that Eastern and Western culture collide; it's here that they intermingle. Here we see side-by-side the physical and psychic baggage of industrial and preindustrial civilizations. Our heads, like old radios, hiss and buzz with the claims of Soviet-style state socialism and Atlantic liberalism; we try to adjust the tuner, but get the same static again and again. As intellectuals we groan under, and revel in, our own authority. Personified contradictions, we'd like to see ourselves in a clearer light. But that's hard and risky to do. So we drink instead. Nowhere in the world are there as many drunken thinkers as in Eastern Europe.

Neither Westerners nor Russians, we Middle Europeans never became true bourgeois, and it seems we never will. The answer to what we really are is forever stuck in our throats. Even our status in society doesn't reveal much about us: whether we are on the top or the bottom of the social scale, the state hangs over us, and always has. We have been under pressure so long, the constant, senseless weight has conditioned our feet to giving way. We have been argued over, agreed upon, traded, sold, dismembered; we have been the subject of peace conferences and settlements. The First World War began in Sarajevo, the Second in Gdansk; the world had better pay attention to us.

We are all unresolved, still pending questions, "popular democrats," which means neither one nor the other, but something else. We are not liberal democrats and we are not Soviet communists; we are not even social democrats. That would be too rational for us, we are much crazier than that. There have always been too many secret anarchists among us: rebels, outlaws, partisans, insurgents, terrorists. We've had more than our share of murderers and suicides, and we never lacked for gendarmes and political prisoners either. We cursed our kings under our breath, then one day we stung them. The truth is, we became sneaky—it would do us good to be treated like human beings for a change. However, we do not want kind words wedded to loaded guns.

When we Eastern Europeans arrive in the West, we stick together and protect our own. We listen to what our Western friends have to say, but don't believe half of it; and when alone, we have a good laugh. We are bad boys, skeptics, rogues, con artists, wheeler-dealers, survivors. Deep down we love destruction and derision; our historical legacy, our stock in trade, is

*Reprinted with the kind permission of *The New York Review of Books*.

cynicism. We are always thinking of ways to clear out, or show up, if we must, with one foot in the door. How could we not be artful dodgers, long-shot players, sneaky idlers, rascals? We paid a price for being honest more than once. Those of my gnereation who respected the law had a much smaller chance to stay alive than those who broke it. We'd be crazy to give ourselves away; where would we be if we didn't have alternate strategies up our sleeves?

We learned in school, from our history books, how to respect rebels: those who would take it no more, who would jeer at liars and fight with bare hands, who, even when backed up against a wall, would say what they thought. Breakout, riot, getaway: in our countries these are beautiful words. Rebellions are holiday revels with us; we know better not to rebel on weekdays.

The communist world is highly sensitive to ideas. Here religious, meditative, critical attitudes carry more weight. The ideas in whose names the rulers rule and the people obey, or grumble, or criticize, are of paramount importance. The mainstay of the system is the prevailing written and unwritten ideology, which the people are cajoled or coerced into supporting. And they support it not only by casting a ballot for it, but by learning the strange and complicated rules of the game. State ideology creates, and conforms to, its own mores. Thus from the point of view of both the state and its citizens it is as risky to sing loudly on the street as it is to question the leading role of the Party.

Westerners are untested and may therefore be more fragile than Eastern Europeans. They have more possibilities, which doesn't necessarily mean they are freer. Daily training for grimmer times keeps us in shape; we are consoled by our pessimism.

Capitalists and state bureaucrats have a monopoly on decision making; how nice it would be to break up this monopoly and socialize the centers of power. Western officialdom brings up the horrors of the Eastern secret police, and Eastern officialdom the dire prospect of unemployment, in order to frighten those who demand more democracy in both the economic and political spheres. With moralistic scare tactics they discourage an objective comparison of capitalism and state socialism. But we must persist in asking: which are the institutions that allow us to worry least about dismissal notices and police summonses?

Hard dictatorships are out, soft dictatorships are in. Gradually, the state phases out its harsher means of persuasion. If it doesn't herd people in camps, it has to begin making concessions. Suddenly people appear for whom not being able to say what's on their minds is a greater loss than not being able to count on privileges. Such people are liberated rather than intimidated by punishment. They really have nothing to lose: they'll find well-wishers wherever they end up, and will get by, if need be, on their own.

If I write what I think; if I am not afraid of what people are usually afraid of; if my book interests me more than its reception; if I don't mind that my opinions do not remain confidential; if I don't confuse a slightly milder form of oppression with freedom, and know that my freedom will never be presented to me as a gift, then, chances are, some people will hate me and consider me crazy, others will like me but consider me crazy, and still others might like me and not even think me crazy. It's possible, of course, that this last group of people are themselves crazy.

We Eastern Europeans should be long-distance runners, with stamina enough to declare at the end of each race that our countries need us, we need our countries, and we won't be excluded from their affairs. Eastern Europeans conservatives would love to export their independent-minded intellectuals to the West. They no longer wish to lock them up, but simply send them where they feel they will blend in. If they do, then the conservatives are right and the dissidents belong elsewhere. The guarantee of our independence is that we won't become export commodities and we won't blend in anywhere.

We need those patient, long-term strategies. Things will work out eventually; and whoever is freer has a better chance of winning. The state and we are not adversaries but partners in a game. Our lives are played out in stadiums, not combat zones, though sometimes we do get kicked around in the field. The oppressor is in love not with oppression but with the oppressed. He puts his subjects out of commission so he can function that much more smoothly. Of course he wants to seduce us, get us into bed; he wants us to praise him, pet him; he gives us a whack to get us to give him a kiss. He could be more refined and more generous, but he could also be rougher and pettier. Even in civilized games it's not just sportsmanlike respect that keeps the players going. Power politics, like sexuality, has a metaphysical dimension. In Eastern Europe abstinent cardinals and lascivious heretics keep laughing at each other's face.

Freedom can be practiced wherever you are. Talk to others and don't dissemble; go public. You are surrounded by secretive section chiefs, department heads, assistant heads. The lowliest official is proud of his secrets, even kindergarteners learn to watch what they say. In our region a revolutionary is one who shuns secrets. So go public, be naive, and catch your friends at their naive best. Choosing between two aging, self-satisfied gentlemen every four years does not make you free. Whether you are free or not will always be decided in the very next minute. You could be on a street corner waiting for a bus, in your room waiting for a telephone call, in bed waiting for a dream.

The complacent citizen, just because he lives undisturbed, is not free. Our freedom is an impatient master; it doesn't give us much time to rest. It likes to see inspired, rather than sensible, acts. "This is what I am; this is what I can do," we complain. "You are more, you can do more," the master says calmly. Make room for light in you, for you are the room and you are the light. When you get tired, the room grows dark.

Translated by Ivan Sanders

MILAN KUNDERA INTERVIEW

Alain Finkielkraut

Alain Finkielkraut: *To the best of my knowledge, you are the only Eastern European writer in the emigration to the West who objects to the term "dissident." Why?*

Milan Kundera: I am allergic to today's political terminology and I don't make use of it.

A.F.: *But it certainly seems that public opinion, which for a long time remained cold toward critics of the East, has been warmed up so to speak by the word "dissident." In France, one even has the impression that the success of dissidence is primarily due to the name it has been given. The word is as popular today as militant and guerilla were in the past.*

M.K.: Yes, words act more through their magic than through their rational content. Before the election, I saw the debates on French television: the Left sang the praises of Socialism and defended its desire to set up a collective system. The Right set everyone on guard against collectivism, and was careful not to attack the untouchable word Socialism. Actually, these two words mean the same thing and the politicians were behaving like magicians: they hid behind the sacred word and tried to label the other word evil.

For—you are right about this—words are important: every historical event begins with a struggle centered on naming. The South Vietnamese who fought against the Americans were called patriots. The Afghans who opposed the Russian invasion were called rebels. As far as naming is concerned, one finds a world-wide consensus about the future of an event, and this is how the Afghans came to be forsaken in advance: it is nearly a foregone conclusion that the patriots will one day regain control of their country while the rebels will lose their rebellion.

A.F.: *It is the magical nature of political vocabulary which offends you then?*

M.K.: Political thought is capable of rendering only a very small part of reality. And given its present vocabulary, it is not even able to understand the political events themselves. Russia and Hungary are two Communist countries. But one wants to dominate the world, while the other is dominated. The regime of one is supported by the population, the other is almost unanimously contested. Political thought, clouded by the idea of political system, credits this substantial difference with no more than parenthetical significance. It sees nothing of what goes on behind the scenes in political systems: not the concrete life of the individual, the destinies of nations, not the cultural transformations, nor the great collisions of civilizations—Moslem, Russian, Chinese, Western, etc.—which have different visions of man and the world, of time and of death.

A.F.: *You are surely thinking of what is happening in Iran. I agree that our usual analyses—poverty, exploitation, the class struggle—cannot explain very much.*

M.K.: Certainly not. But one can look back to Europe for an example. I could point to the popular sentiment of the Czechs on the first day of the Russian invasion in 1968 for instance: that visceral horror did not come from the fact that Dubček's reforms were finished, but from that infinite void that could be sensed behind the faces of the Russian soldiers, from that strangeness of a civilization that thinks differently, feels differently, has a different destiny, lives in a different historical time—a civilization that came to swallow us up into its own eternity. Political regimes are ephemeral, but the frontiers of civilizations are traced by centuries.

A.F.: *But wasn't the fate of Czechoslovakia sealed twenty years earlier, in 1948, when the pro-Soviet regime was set up?*

M.K.: Certainly. But little by little, our life force itself, the originality of the country, the traditions of its millennial history—a western history—began to break down the system that had been imported from Russia, to transform it inwardly.

A.F.: *And it culminated twenty years later in the famous reformism of Dubček.*

M.K.: Politicians played a secondary role in this process. The best one might say about the most attractive among them is that they were sincerely though awkwardly attentive to the popular movement. The greatness of the era of the '60's and the Prague Spring does not lie in the politics of the times (which were incompetent and destroyed everything in the end), but with the culture. Culture in the broadest sense of the term: not only the arts and sciences, but the overall behavior of the people, its tradition of tolerance, of humor and of freedom. This culture attacked the imported political structure in order to fill it with its own contents, to invest it with another meaning. The social organizations (unions, professional organizations, the writers' union, etc.), originally set up to communicate the will of the party, liberated themselves and constituted a very original democratic system which functioned without planification. These years marked an extraordinary flowering of Czech culture. The West, which is no longer capable of conceiving of this culture as anything other than an appendage to the political system, never understood what happened in Czechoslovakia before 1968. It never understood the *massacre of Czech culture* that was the most incredible consequence of the Russian invasion in 1968 either.

A.F.: *In any case, a liquidation of the rebel culture, a disciplining of the opposition has been referred to. You do not agree with this analysis then?*

M.K.: No. It wasn't the culture of the opposition that was killed; it was culture in general. Everything that was important, authentic and of value had to be destroyed. A half million Czechs were put out of jobs. About two hundred writers, including the very best, were not only prevented from publishing, but their books were taken away from all public libraries and their names were erased from history books. One hundred forty-five Czech historians were removed from their posts. Instead of forty literary and cultural journals, there was only one. The great Czech cinema disappeared. Political and cultural history was rewritten: there are no traces of Franz Kafka left, nor of T. G. Masaryk, who in 1918 founded the Czechoslovakian Republic— there is nothing left that Russian totalitarianism would find hard to swallow. If we consider the '60's as the period of the progressive westernization of a Socialism imported from the East, then the Russian invasion of '68 marked the definitive moment of cultural colonization of a western country. All that has characterized the West since the time of the Renaissance (yes, that Renaissance that Solzhenitsyn disliked so)—tolerance, a methodical doubt, a plurality of thought, the personal nature of art (and of man too, of course)— all this is destined to disappear there. And all this brain-washing, far from being simply a provisional measure, is part of a long-lived, patient and coherent strategy designed to move a country into the sphere of another civilization.

A.F.: *Right now, it is as if the West believed it was born with the Industrial Revolution. Capitalism, consumer society—Westerners always describe themselves in terms of political economics. For you, the West is not reducible to this definition then?*

M.K.: My country is not capitalist, nor do I think it wants to become so again. And yet, it is an old Western European country and it wishes to retain this identity. The West constitutes a common history, a common culture. But the cultural dimension has dropped out of the contemporary vision of the world. In the ridiculous theater of allegory that today's political thinking represents, it is the West that plays the role of the colonialist. That is why the idea of a colonized West does not enter into the current system of symbols, and why this idea is poorly grasped today and refused. Not only is my country a colonized form of Western Europe, but it is even a colonized West that has in turn never colonized anyone else.

A.F.: *Colonized West: these are two words which I have in fact never seen joined. We have grown so accustomed to equating the West with Power, the West with Imperialism, that the concept of a colonized West is almost unthinkable for us.*

M.K.: The big western countries identify themselves too easily with the values belonging to the entire West, and they also attribute their own sins too easily to the entire West. But the West is also made up of little nations who have no reason to feel guilty for the crimes of the larger countries and who have the right to defend their western culture without remorse.

In 1956, just a few minutes before his office was destroyed by artillery, the director of the Hungarian news agency sent a desperate telex message out to the world telling about the Russian offensive that had begun that morning. The communication ended with these words: "We will die for Hungary and for Europe."

No one grasped this pronouncement less well than Europe itself. In the non-occupied West, it is not understood that Europe is capable of standing for values that one can still die for.

A.F.: *You have written somewhere that the Prague Spring was a "popular revolt of the moderates." Yet among intellectuals, for whom moderation—as a synonym for inertia or middle-of-the-road—is above all a bourgeois virtue, this idea cannot help but cause a scandal.*

M.K.: After awhile, the European Left accepted the Prague Spring and listed it along with its other positive symbols. In order to do this, it was invested with a lyrical aura borrowed from Paris' May. This was a very generous offer, but it covered over the originality of the event.

What we saw in Paris was a fascinating burst of revolutionary lyricism, still being nourished by the beauty of the images and slogans of the Surrealists. The Prague Spring on the other hand was the explosion of a post-revolutionary skepticism. In the course of this movement, which was not just the spark of a springtime, but of the entire period of the '60's, the rigid power structures were taken apart, the lyrical demagogy of the ideologues was ridiculed, all that was hard was softened, all that was too heavy was lightened. This is why the popular climate in Prague during the '60's was so very much more tolerant, antidoctrinaire, ironic, gay and libertarian than what I find today in the West, which is humorless, serious, susceptible to all the formal temptations and all the lyrical demagogy.

A.F.: *Everyone in the West will be asking you if this was a movement of the Left or the Right.*

M.K.: The division between Left and Right does not make a great deal of sense when you are confronted with a totalitarianism that is the negation of pluralism—of the pluralism of the Left as well as of the Right, that is. This is why the Marxists and the anti-Marxists, the Christians and atheists worked together so well in the popular resistance to events in Czechoslovakia.

It often seems to me that the Czechoslovakian situation represents a magnification of the situation in the West in general: the Left fights the Right, the Right fights the Left, but it is in fact their commonly-shared civilization, founded on tolerance and open dialogue, which will be mortally endangered in the world of tomorrow.

What I experienced in Prague represented for me an enormous demystification of the symbols that dominate our century and a rejection of the vocabulary that kept us under its spell.

A.F.: *Does this apply only to you? Not to us?*

M.K.: You are included too, certainly. But you do not rid yourselves of these things so easily. I have the experience of Stalin behind me and this shocked me into understanding that ideological language is a mystification. The linguistic revolt, the suspicion about words has come from this. I would never say "Afghan rebels." I know all of these language tricks far too well. I don't even like to say "the Soviets." What are the Soviets? A nation? A religion? A race? And what do they have in common with the Soviets who are not in their own country? It is a cover-word to make us forget about the nations that have been Russified name and all. Every evil comes from the moment when a false word is accepted. Capitulation begins there. One can make compromises with people, but never with words!

A.F.: *The demystification you speak of was especially connected to Marx, wasn't it?*

M.K.: More with the spirit that results from the everyday language of Marxism: *the total reduction of the world to its political signification alone.* Interestingly, the so-called Right participates in this Marxist heritage as much as the so-called Left does.

One month after the Russian invasion of 1968, I came to Paris where *The Joke* had just appeared. I had lunch with a well-known intellectual whom I admired very sincerely because of the violent and brilliant articles he had written about the occupation of my country. He was a bit astonished to learn that I would be ready to return to my country in a few days. He found this courageous of me, and after thinking for a few seconds, asked me a strange question: "Are there forests in Czechoslovakia?" I said: "Yes, there are." He said: "Well then you can live in the forests. During the German Occupation, our Maquis lived in the forests too."

I don't know how well you can appreciate the absurdity of his thought. At the time, Dubček was still in power, though his power was precarious, and we wanted to stay and support him. We didn't want to run into the forests. But above all, the thought that in a small, overpopulated Czechoslovakia, occupied by the army and the Russian police, a resistance movement could have been formed in the forests revealed such ignorance that it seemed incredible to me coming from a man who gave me political lessons about what was happening in our homeland and about the importance of those events.

Actually, there are a great many articles on the Prague Spring, but they lack historical, sociological and cultural knowledge—they lack all knowledge of reality. One of the lyric illusions of our time is that political discussion leads directly to the heart of the real. This is not true. Political thought such as it is today is the new ivory tower.

A.F.: *But this ivory tower is also a tower of power.*

M.K.: And that's where the problem lies. The real problems of this planet (problems of food, population, nature, overwhelming technology, problems of cultures and the dialogue between them) remain untouched, while the pseduo-problems (of ideology and doctrine), manufactured in the tower, are taking over the world. As a result, we have the impression of being at the mercy of a false history based on false problems, while the true history remains by the wayside, forgotten and unrealized.

A.F.: *But to look at the distance between us now and the '60's, can we continue to criticize politics as if it were still the primary principle of existence? What seems to be the catalytic principle now is not Marx's "change the world"—it's the more timely and prosaic "right to" principle. For several years, it's been as if the cult of politics had been replaced by manifestations with more precise objectives: the right to abortion, to refuse the construction of nuclear plants, the right to better working conditions, the right to allow foreign students to study in France, etc.*

M.K.: In France, perhaps. But even in France, if there is a demonstration today to have the "right to," there is just as much pathos as if the demonstration were for large changes. What remains of Marxism, and what will remain for a long time, is not the rational thought of Marx, but the *system of symbols* which acts unconsciously like archetypes and which is not easily gotten rid of. There is a well-known term: class struggle. It points to a social fact and at the same time sanctifies the verb "to struggle." We can forget the class struggle more easily than we can forget our admiration of struggle itself. Struggle has become a value, so much so that it is through fighting that people want to accomplish their lives: women struggle, high school students struggle, we all struggle for self-realization, we struggle with blisters that come from sitting through boring meetings, we have replaced dialogue with ideological struggle, etc. . . . The lyric aura surrounding the word struggle adds an irrational and impotent form of aggression to attitudes that are relatively rational. In Prague, members of Chapter 77, who have been heavily persecuted, try in vain to persuade the government to *talk* with them. Western intellectuals refuse to speak with their democratically-elected government, because they are *fighting.*

A.F.: *What you are saying makes me think of a youth's remark at Sartre's funeral. It was reported with a great deal of fervor by a journalist: "We've hardly read his books. But we know his work must be continued; we must hold on to hope and fight." Fight what? Nothing: just fight. Nothing counts aside from this urgency: not even reading the immense works of the person being honored counts.*

M.K.: Marxism was the grandiose attempt to explain the world in terms of total rationality. Having failed, it picked up a lyre and descended into the irrational, just as Orpheus did. It has become a symbolic system, a kind of poetry, of beauty.

A single stanza of this poetry has hypnotized our entire era: the idea that the human era is divided into two parts—prehistory (the realm of necessity where man is at the mercy of unknown laws) and true history beginning with the proletarian revolution (when man finally becomes master of his destiny). Throughout half a century, we have lived under the spell of this very beautiful, very attractive idea: the entire artistic avant-garde, with its dream of complete liberation from tradition, was born in the light of this great image of Marx.

But the little tricks that history plays are nasty: at the time of their prehistory, man and the nations enjoyed a certain possibility of mastering their destiny. On the other hand, from a time coinciding more or less with the October Revolution, we entered the age of determinism and of total dependence.

Man learns that he is master of neither nature nor his civilization, of neither history nor himself. But if man is not the master, where then is the master? The happy atheism of the past is replaced by the melancholic atheism of our own time.

A.F.: *You have mentioned the word "lyric" several times in a negative context. And this seems to me to be the heart of your own, very original contribution to the critique of totalitarianism. Traditionally, criticism has developed along two lines: criticism of the totalitarian practices carried out in the name of the true principles of Communism; criticism of the Communist philosophy itself seen as totalitarian monster. Trotsky or Solzhenitsyn. But you say: there is also a poetry of totalitarianism. In your novel* La Vie est ailleurs [Life Is Elsewhere], *you speak of Stalinism as if it were an era where "the poet reigned along with the executioner." If the New Philosophers find the roots of the Gulag in Fichte and Hegel, you yourself find them in poetry. Isn't that so?*

M.K.: No civilization and no ideology has a monopoly on totalitarianism. Its roots are anthropological. Each of us has had the experience of totalitarian practice within the social microcosms (the family, the army); each of us knows the totalitarian temptation. The dream of a community where everyone is moved by one and the same desire, one and the same faith, where no one keeps a secret from anyone else, is an archetype that is found in all religions and in each one of us. André Breton sang the praises of the house of glass where all that is private is public. Franz Kafka created the world where K. loses all that is intimate; he is even followed and scrutinized in his bed. The abolition of the private realm is paradise for Breton; it looks more like hell in Kafka's world. But we are dealing here with two faces of a single archetype, which is paradisiacal and hellish at the same time.

What I hold against the critique of totalitarianism is its simplistic Manicheanism. Totalitarianism is seen solely as the embodiment of evil. This critique leaves all the "poetry" that is linked to this evil and constantly engenders it intact. The Gulag is condemned and a new house of glass is sought elsewhere. But when it is located, there will still be people who do not want to live there and consequently a new little camp for them to one side. Totalitarianism is not a Gulag; it is an idyllic house of glass, with the Gulag put to one side.

Totalitarianism is the fruit of Manicheanism, and the preachers of Manicheanism are angels, not devils. That is why I am distrustful of the pure ones who criticize the diabolic side of totalitarianism and forget about its angelic side.

Since the Romantic era and particularly since the time of Surrealism, the idea of poetry has become a sacred, inviolable value. No human attitude lacks a substantial dose of ambiguity. Jaromil, the hero of *Life Is Elsewhere,* denounces his girl friend to the police, not as a devil, but as an angel. His is the most authentic form of lyric exaltation: he has the impression of going beyond himself, of identifying himself with something that is greater than he is. Paul Eluard publicly and solemnly approved the death sentence of his friend Zavis Kalandra, the Czech Surrealist. He did this with all the pathos of an archangel of poetry.

A.F.: *But wasn't it the party that was speaking in him rather than poetry?*

M.K.: Eluard's murderous proclamation is linked to all the poetry he wrote at this time—poetry exalting peace, the future, and the angelic nature of the society's house of glass. The totalitarianism of the '50's was not just oppression alone. It was not by means of its execution posts that it attracted the masses, the young, the intelligentsia. It was by its smile. We tend to forget this today; we are ashamed of this. We no longer say: the bloody totalitarianism of the '50's had a poetry that we succumbed to. If we blame it on the Gulag, we feel pardoned. If we speak of the poetry of totalitarianism, we remain implicated in the scandal.

A.F.: *Was the verdict of Eluard known in Czechoslovakia at the time?*

M.K.: Zavis Kalandra was hung in 1950. A few days before, Eluard approved his execution. It was then that I met Konstantin Biebl, the great Czech poet of Surrealist inspiration, for the first time. It was he who told me, with a horrified look in his eyes, about Eluard's declaration. One year later, Biebl could no longer put up with the burden of Stalinism and he threw himself out a window. In 1952, I published my first volume of poetry, *In Memory of Konstantin Biebl*, and there my long dispute about the angels and the pure ones began. In 1978, I returned to the story of Eluard and Kalandra in my novel *Le Livre du rire et de l'oubli [The Book of Laughter and Forgetfulness]*. My citizenship was taken away because of this book. The circle was completed.

A.F.: *Konstantin Biebl must have been a different kind of poetic ideal for you, an anti-Eluard.*

M.K.: Biebl was also a Communist and at the time he wrote poetry that had about the same orientation as Eluard's. But the horrifying and direct experiences of someone coming from Prague (experiences that Eluard could not have had) woke him up and crushed him. Understand me well now: if I speak of this episode now, it is not to blacken the name of Eluard, but to understand more fully the lyrical dimension of man. It isn't the story itself that is of interest to a novelist; it is the human condition unmasked in the course of an historic situation.

A.F.: *You have showed how lyrical enthusiasm is an integral part of the totalitarian sickness. But you seem to contradict yourself in* Farewell Waltz, *since it is Jakub, the sceptic, the wise one, the one who has survived all, the man who is disgusted by the aggression of the world, who commits a strange murder.*

M.K.: Jakub is a sceptic; he knows that those who are persecuted become the persecutors and that it is easy to imagine this role reversal; lyric gestures do not move him; he has seen too much and lived through too much to be able to love people. It's a matter of just a split second when his reason falters, when his unconscious disgust and hatred of people wells up: an innocent young girl dies.

A.F.: *It seems to me that intellectuals today are leaning more toward Jakub than toward Jaromil. They total up all their disillusionments, and announce that they will not be caught off guard again. Jakub didn't consider himself a hero, but these sceptics have added the same love of system to their new incredulity as they did to their former religion.*

M.K.: There are some people who raise their fists, take everything seriously, and open themselves to the idea of sacrificing the life of another in the name of the sacred cause. And there are others who, observing their agitation, see only senseless pantomime in it. This is what Jakub does. Remember that he experiences the *unbearable weightlessness* of all things, including murder. You can see how it is that the two extremes (lyricism and scepticism, the angelic and the diabolical, seriousness and non-seriousness) in certain circumstances become accomplices of death. There is no path that man can choose which will allow him to avoid this complicity for sure.

A.F.: *But it seems to me that the "melancholic atheism" of Jakub is very close to you on a personal level.* Laughable Loves, *which you wrote when you were still in Prague, bathes in this kind of melancholy— one in fact that seems rather joyous to me. Your characters take nothing seriously and live through some beautiful adventures, as if they owed their scepticism to the richness or the gayness of their erotic lives.*

M.K.: The erotic climate in Prague is certainly more intense than here. There, eroticism has become the only arena for freedom and self-realization. Politics, with its interminably futile aura of seriousness, has acted like a vaccine. The habit of taking seriousness seriously has been undone, and beneath the cover of official mortality, a hedonism and a wise light-heartedness reign. I know you are going to smile at this, but when I left Czechoslovakia, I had the impression that I was leaving an erotic paradise that I would never find again. Here, eroticism is much more conventional and prudish, the family more sacred, despite the appearance of much-proclaimed liberated mores. This liberalization is hardly hedonistic at all. It is ideological. It is demonstrative, a verbal tic. The more one claims pleasure as a motto, as a plan, as a concept, the less one finds it in life.

A.F.: *What you are saying makes me think of Jakub again. Doesn't he leave his country, just as you did, with feelings of both regret and relief?*

M.K.: I finished the novel at a time when I hadn't the slightest thought of leaving Czechoslovakia, and Jakub is not a self-portrait. But it is true that his scepticism is closer to me on a personal level than the faith of his rival, Bertleff. And even so, in the course of my work on the text, Jakub became continually more problematic, and Bertleff more likeable. I wrote this novel counter to myself, so to speak. Moreover, I believe that this is how one writes novels. If the novel is successful, it must necessarily be wiser than its author. This is why many excellent French intellectuals write mediocre novels. They are always more intelligent than their books. The novel either outdoes its author or it is worthless.

When Tolstoy began writing *Anna Karenina,* he wanted to condemn this adulterous woman. Fortunately, the wisdom of the novel greatly surpassed its author's.

A.F.: *You speak of the wisdom of the novel. This means that the novel, for you, is more than one genre among many, doesn't it?*

M.K.: The novelistic exercise consists in creating characters. Therefore, it is a confrontation between different value systems, between different visions of the world; it is a reconstruction of the substantial relativity of the human world, of that rich, enigmatic and marvelous relativity which is constantly being negated by the ideological spirit and its single form of truth.

A.F.: *You feel that the novel cannot be in service to a form of truth that goes beyond it, that is more important than it then?*

M.K.: I have never come across this truth.

A.F.: *I might bring to mind for you André Gide's line: "I think that this is a time when such important events are developing that one is almost ashamed to devote oneself to literature."*

M.K.: This is the well-known complex suffered by people in the arts when confronted by politics.

A.F.: *You do not suffer from this complex?*

M.K.: How could I? My books are banned from the Elbe all the way to the Pacific Ocean. Nothing frees you of this kind of complex better than persecution. I would like to paraphrase Gide: if such important events are developing, there is nothing more urgent than to prolong the life of literature and its complete independence. Otherwise, one will be crushed by the machine of political and ideological simplification—a machine which runs terribly rapidly in times of such great events.

A.F.: *But aren't your books themselves crushed by this machine when they are simplified through interpretation?*

M.K.: Of course. In the West, my first novel, *The Joke,* was clearly understood to be a denunciation of Stalinism. I have too much respect for the novel to use it as an illustration of such a truism. But literary criticism is almost non-existent these days, and novels are at the mercy of the journalists and the minor ideologues of the day—at the mercy of these workers of reduction.

A.F.: *Is it entirely political reduction you are speaking of?*

M.K.: Man is reduced to his social function; the work of art is reduced to its meaning; the history of humankind is reduced to a series of events, which are in turn reduced to a preconceived interpretation. This institutional reduction which neither the East nor the West escapes from, finds its companion piece in the reduction that becomes a part of the human condition; the greatest love ends up being reduced to a skeleton of puny memories; a miracle of the concrete realm vanishes behind an abstract résumé. Life is constantly chipped away by these *reductive forces,* and the work of the novelist is a Don Quixote-like effort to defend man from reduction, to recreate the small imaginary world that has the freshness of an unexpected question.

A.F.: *For you, the novel is a question that is addressed to the world. You do not wish to answer the question. But who will answer instead of you?*

M.K.: Idiots. They are always ready to answer. Idiocy is the total inability to frame a question; it's the total ability to answer all.

A.F.: *But the texts that you write are related to both the novel and the essay. An essay, however, even if it strives toward subtlety and nuance, can never avoid dogmatism or assertion. Doesn't that contradict the primary task of the novel, which is, as you have said, to express the substantial relativity of the world? Why have you wanted to combine these two kinds of writing, which are a bit like water and oil, and how do you go about reconciling the unreconcilable?*

M.K.: The desire to incorporate reflections of great intellectual significance in the novel is as old as the novel itself. You find it in Cervantes, you find it in Robert Musil or Thomas Mann: the thoughts of their characters are often excellent essays. But this method presupposes characters of an exceptional intellectual level. Hermann Broch, who concentrated instead on the irrational forces that guide people's behavior as if by remote control, could not follow the same path. His intellectual ambition manifested itself differently: in the third part of *The Sleepwalkers* (one of the novels that I admire most), he included an essay on the *degradation of values,* written in difficult and theoretical language. It is a magnificent essay, but I am not sure that it is an integral part of the rest of the text; as you were saying, it constitutes a dogmatic component of the novel, representing the truth of the author. Personally, I think that intellectual reflection (essay) can be an organic part of the novel if it remains respectful of the substantial relativity of the novelistic world—or to put it another way, if it replaces dogmatism with irony, if it plays the role of buffoon rather than sage, if the reader never knows for sure what is being said seriously and what is not, whether the remarks are hypothetical or thetical, if they resemble more closely the aphorisms of Lichtenberg or the reflections of Jaspers.

A.F.: *This seems to be the case in your latest book. But what about the musicological passages in* The Joke? *Couldn't we speak of thesis in regard to them?*

M.K.: These pages represent neither the truth of the author, nor the résumé of the book, but they do tell the paradoxical story of folk music in the context of Utopian Socialism. Ideas, ideologies, concepts, utopias have stories which are hardly less grotesque, odd, bizarre, and romanesque than the stories of men. This is why I could hardly imagine a novel without a scientific or philosophic component.

A.F.: *In the course of our conversation, you have mentioned Hermann Broch and Robert Musil. I know how much you love Bartok, Gombrowicz, and Italo Svevo. I could add Jaroslav Hašek or Milos Forman, your student in Prague, to the list. There are several things you all have in common, particularly the same allergic reaction to the hero. And you all come from the same part of Europe. Does this constitute a specific tradition for you?*

M.K.: Gustav Mahler wrote a farewell song to a world that was disappearing. Musil, in *The Man without Qualities,* speaks of a society that, without knowing it, has no future. Hermann Broch understood contemporary history in terms of a breakdown of values. Kafka conceived of the world as an infinite bureaucratic labyrinth, in which man is hopelessly lost. Jaroslav Hašek's brave soldier Šveik imitates the ceremonies of the surrounding world with such zeal that he transforms them into an enormous joke. In this activity, which could hardly be less heroic, Hašek finds a last trace of freedom.

It is from Central Europe that a lucid form of scepticism has arisen in the midst of our era of illusions. It is a scepticism that is attributable to the experience of an extremely concentrated history: we have seen the collapse of a great empire in the course of our century, the awakening of nations, democracy, fascism, we have seen the Nazi occupation, the glimmer of Socialism, massive deportations, the Stalinist reign of terror and its downfall, and finally, we have seen the most essential thing of all—the death throes of the West within our own countries and before our own eyes.

This is why I am always shocked by the perfidious vocabulary that has transformed Central Europe into the East. Central Europe represents the destiny of the West, in concentrated form.

A.F.: *It also represents the cradle of all the great cultural experiments of modern times: psychoanalysis, structuralism (born in Prague), the twelve-tone system, Bartok, Kafka, Witkiewicz' theater of the absurd....*

M.K.: Yet Central Europe no longer exists. The three wise men of Yalta split it in two and condemned it to death. They didn't give a damn about whether it was a question of a great culture or not.

A.F.: *A great culture... and you feeling like one of its last survivors?*

M.K.: Yes.

Translated by Susan Huston

DEFINING "CENTRAL EUROPE": POWER, POLITICS, AND CULTURE

Roman Szporluk
University of Michigan

It is common to define "Eastern Europe" as a region comprising those lands of Europe which are ruled by Communist parties and which have (or had, as Yugoslavia and Albania) a close political, military and ideological relationship with the Soviet Union. This definition includes Poland and Hungary and excludes Finland and Greece; Prague is in, while Vienna, actually located farther east than Prague, is out. Among its drawbacks this concept of "Eastern Europe" as an appendage of the USSR leaves rather unclear the proper designation of the Soviet Union's western republics, such as Latvia and Ukraine, as well as Russia proper: what are *they* if the lands to the *west* of the Soviet Union's European boundary are *Eastern* Europe?

The term "Eastern Europe" has not enjoyed popularity among those to whom it claims to apply. Yet, the idea that there is a distinct zone on the European continent called Central or East Central Europe is not new and, in fact, seems to be in special vogue among the intellectuals of Czechoslovakia, Poland and Hungary today. In the 1940s and 1950s the Polish Catholic historian, Oscar Halecki, writing in exile, advanced the idea of a special East-Central European zone which he called the "borderlands of Western Civilization."[1] Thirty years before Halecki, the Czech scholar and politician Thomas G. Masaryk, working during World War I for the destruction of the Habsburgs and the founding of Czechoslovakia, used a similar concept in support of his program for a "New Europe." According to Masaryk, that particular geographic and cultural area comprised the peoples who lived between the Germans and the Russians. The recent publication of *The Making of a New Europe*, which is both a biography of Robert William Seton-Watson, one of the men who played a role in the destruction of Austria-Hungary, and a study in the politics of World War I, brings the ideas of Masaryk to public attention again: as could be expected Masaryk is a major presence in *The Making of a New Europe*.[2]

What did Masaryk understand by "East Central Europe"? His first public pronouncement on this subject came in the inaugural address which he delivered at the School of Slavonic Studies at the University of London in October 1915. Masaryk noted "a striking difference" between the western and eastern parts of the European continent: in the west there were many nations and states, of different sizes, large, small and medium, but together forming a "kind of national equilibrium." The east was quite different:

there was only one large nation and state there—Russia—while all the other nations and states were small, except for Germany and Austria which were only partly eastern because the other part of each was western. In fact, Masaryk continued, the east and the west were not separated by a sharply drawn boundary; between them lay "a peculiar ethnological zone," extending from Trieste-Salonica-Constantinople in the south to Danzig and Petrograd in the north, in which a number of smaller nations had lived or still lived under the domination of Germany, Austria, Turkey and Russia.[3] This zone, comprised of the eastern parts of Prussia, the Balkans, Austria-Hungary, and "the West of Russia," was the center of national antagonism — the conflict between the principle of the state and the principle of nationality. It was here that the demand for a political restructuring of Europe arose and the question of nationality and the language question became "the political *vis metrix*."[4] In a later, even more representative and influential statement of his position, *The New Europe*, printed in 1918, Masaryk defined this zone as the lands "between the East and the West, more particularly between the Germans and the Russians."[5]

As Masaryk saw it, the nationality question in Central Europe was made especially acute because the large states such as Austria and Russia oppressed smaller nations that were nationally and socially conscious and educated and that had a history of political independence. What was in evidence was not simply a conflict between different ethnic groups, but rather the incongruity between the cultural level of a number of nations and their political status as dependencies of politically reactionary states.[6] When viewed from this perspective, Masaryk's anti-Austrian work during the war appears as an implementation of his long-held political beliefs regarding the nature of the monarchies of Central and Eastern Europe. He considered them reactionary and "theocratic" and accordingly denied their legitimacy not simply on national grounds (that is because they were German or Russian while their subjects included non-German and non-Russian peoples), but also because they were cultural and political obstacles to the free development of their subjects.

This interpretation is supported by Masaryk's comments on Russia in writings that are primarily known as pieces of anti-Austrian and anti-German propaganda during the war. Masaryk explicitly included Russia in the same category as Austria-Hungary and Germany, and he supported national freedom for the "civilized" nations of Russia, just as he advocated freedom for the peoples of Austria-Hungary. However, he considered the great majority of the peoples of Russia (he noted that the Russian empire comprised multitudinous peoples in Asia, not only in Europe) as "uneducated and lacking in national consciousness"; "the Russians themselves have not developed to the point of national consciousness; the masses of the people have their religious viewpoint, and the intelligentsia, as far as it is Socialistic, does not feel nationally."[7] Masaryk was highly critical of the record of tsarism in Russia's history: "Russia does not lack natural and historical variety of cultural forces, but tsarism was unable to stir up and organize these forces; that was the cause of its breakdown and disappearance." It was because of the negative record of tsarism, Masaryk felt, that the revolution in Russia itself was "so negative, so lacking in constructive force." Tsarism did not prepare the Russians for self-government.[8]

The "excessive negativeness" of the Russian revolution would also weaken its potential impact in Europe, Masaryk felt, writing in late 1917—early 1918. Yet he expected the fall of tsarism to speed up the fall of "the tsarism of Vienna and Berlin." To have a positive impact beyond its boundaries, the Russian revolution would have to become a "revolution of hearts and heads." But Masaryk was not very optimistic in this regard: "The tsarism of the Russian masses and revolutionaries is worse than that of the Romanovs themselves; they rid themselves of the Tsar, but they have not yet rid themselves of tsarism."[9] While he was critical of the Russian revolution, Masaryk was confident that Russia would not play a major role in the affairs of Europe. "Napoleon's prophecy of a Cossack Europe has not been fulfilled," he commented. Europe was marching toward "liberty and humanity."[10]

The "New Europe" Masaryk and his friend Seton-Watson helped to build collapsed after a mere twenty years. In 1938 it was deeply wounded by Nazi Germany, and in 1939-40 it was completely subjugated by Germany in concert with Soviet Russia. After the Second World War, all of it lay in the sphere of power of Moscow. While primary responsibility for the destruction of an independent East Central Europe lies with its two powerful neighbors, the nations of the region themselves were not without blame. As the Seton-Watsons put it:

> After sixty years it is easy to see what went wrong with the order established in Central and Eastern Europe by the victory of the Allies and the disintegration of the Habsburg monarchy. In each of the new states there prevailed a narrow official nationalism. . . . Every state was on bad terms with most or all of its neighbors. . . .[11]

Whatever their past errors and faults may have been, the nations of the area did not surrender to external force. The national consciousness of the Central and East European nations has remained "unvanquished by either Nazi German or Soviet Russian imperialism." Democracy as it had been understood in Robert William Seton-Watson's time has not been secured, and democratic liberties have proved to be "frail, precarious and temporary blessings," but, the authors state, "national cultures are virtually indestructible."[12]

Milan Kundera, the contemporary Czech writer living in Paris, obviously shares the position of Masaryk on the key role of culture in the survival of nations threatened by political oppression. He would probably agree also with the conclusion of the Seton-Watsons that culture offers a powerful counterforce to externally imposed political systems. As he put it, an alien political system was forced upon Czechoslovakia in 1948, but "little by little, our life force itself, the originality of the country, the traditions of its millennial history — a western history — began to break down the system that had been imported from Russia. . . ." The origins and the greatness of the "Prague Spring" lie in culture, not politics. "This culture attacked the imported political structure in order to fill it with its own contents, to invest it with its own meaning." [13] Kundera argues that the language of politics is not a proper key to an understanding of a country like Czechoslovakia. He thinks that in general the concepts of political thought are of limited use even for an understanding of political systems. Even if both Russia and Hungary are Communist, and thus supposedly alike, what matters is that at present the former "wants to dominate the world, while the other is dominated;" in the former the population supports the regime, and in the other the regime is universally opposed. Political thought is incapable of looking through the political into what really matters: the life of the individual, "the destinies of nations," cultural transformations, "the great collisions of civilizations. . . which have different visions of man and the world, of time and death."[14]

In the 1968 Soviet invasion of Czechoslovakia, Kundera sees one such great collision. The horror of the Czechs who witnessed the invasion, he says, came from "that infinite void that could be sensed behind the faces of the Russian soldiers, from that strangeness of a civilization that thinks differently, has a different destiny, lives in a different historical time. . . . Political regimes are ephemeral, but the frontiers of civilizations are traced by centuries." [15] What matters to Kundera is not the question of choosing capitalism versus socialism — socialism is acceptable to him — but the fact that Czechoslovakia is a western country colonized by an eastern power from which it is separated by a barrier of civilization.

The idea that Czechoslovakia belongs to a cultural sphere which is importantly different from the cultural sphere to which Russia belongs is a frequent theme in Kundera. In his interview with Philip Roth, for example, Kundera declared that Russia, with a history "anchored in the Byzantine world," is the real "Eastern Europe." Bohemia, Poland, Hungary, Austria have never been part of that Eastern Europe: they are central Europe and belong to Western civilization. However, Central Europe (with the exception of Austria) was annexed by "Russian civilization" after World War II. As a result Western culture has lost its "vital center of gravity." This fact inspires in Kundera the gravest pessimism as to the future of Europe as a whole. [16]

Kundera accuses the West of having failed to understand the cultural revolution in Czechoslovakia that preceded the Spring of 1968 (for the West culture is a mere "appendage of the political system") and of having equally failed to understand that *"the massacre of Czech culture. . . was the most incredible consequence of the Russian invasion in 1968."* [17] The aftermath of 1968 taught Kundera that culture is extremely vulnerable and that the very survival of his nation is no longer secure:

> If someone had told me as a boy: One day you will see your nation vanish from the world, I would have considered it nonsense, something I couldn't possibly imagine. A man knows he is mortal, but he takes for granted that his nation possesses some kind of eternal life. But after the Russian invasion of 1968, every Czech was confronted with the thought that his nation could be quietly erased from Europe, just as over the past five decades 40 million Ukrainians have been quietly vanishing from the world without the world paying any heed. Or Lithuanians. Do you know that in the 17th century Lithuania was a powerful European nation? Today the Russians keep Lithuania on their reservation like a half-extinct tribe; they are sealed off from visitors to prevent knowledge about their existence from reaching the outside. I don't know what the future holds for my own nation. It is certain that the Russians will do everything they can to dissolve it gradually into their own civilization. Nobody knows whether they will succeed. But the *possibility* is here. And the sudden realization that such a possibility exists is enough to change one's whole sense of life. Nowadays I even see Europe as fragile, mortal.[18]

It is significant that Kundera should cite the fates of the Ukrainians and the Lithuanians to illustrate the danger which he thinks the Czechs are facing: do we find here the suggestion that the Czechoslovaks and those western nations of the USSR live in one zone even though the former are a formally independent state while the latter constitute republics of the USSR? Whether he remembers the Masaryk conception or not, Kundera is obviously thinking along the same lines as Masaryk had done: he includes the western peoples of the Soviet Russian state in a zone that also encompasses the peoples of central Europe.

This inclusion is not based only on geographical considerations. Rather, Kundera recognizes a community of fate of certain nations which are threatened with the loss of their cultural and spiritual identity. The main difference between them is that some have been exposed to the process of liquidation for decades while others are still in the initial stages. Thus, according to a recent study, not a single school in the capital city of Belorussia, Minsk, uses Belorussian as the language of instruction anymore. In the Ukrainian capital, Kiev, Ukrainian schools are in the minority, despite the Ukrainian majority in the city's overall population. The teaching of Russian has now been introduced even in some kindergartens attended by non-Russian children, and the authorities are planning to expand the use of Russian in pre-school facilities in non-Russian areas.[19] Understandably, these plans and prospects are creating intense anxiety among the intelligentsia in the non-Russian republics of the Soviet Union. In a recent article entitled "Memory of the Heart," the Belorussian scholar and teacher,

Fedar Yankausky, makes a plea for the preservation of the Belorussian language. His sentiment has been echoed in other republics.[20]

It is not accidental that the Belorussian linguist should speak about "memory" of the heart. For Kundera, too, the struggle for survival is "the struggle of memory against forgetting";[21] "the first step in liquidating a people is to erase its memory."[22] Nor is the question of memory as a mainstay of national identity and culture of concern to the Czechs (or Belorussians) alone. The Warsaw historian Marcin Król wrote recently about "ideologically motivated destruction of the past" practiced in the schools and literature of Poland.[23] According to another contemporary Polish historian, Bohdan Cywiński, the aim of the officially-produced school curricula in Poland has been "to disarm national consciousness."[24]

There is ample evidence to support this interpretation. Documents published in 1980 by an independent Warsaw journal provide a clear insight into the official program of rewriting Polish history. These documents include secret reviews of Polish history textbooks written by the experts from the Soviet Academy of Pedagogical Sciences in Moscow to instruct the Polish authors and educational administrators in their work. What the Moscow critics especially disliked (and let us remember that Polish textbooks under consideration had gone through official screening before their publication in the first place) were the negative references to Russia, even when the Russia in question had been the tsarist oppressor of Poland. They were annoyed that "much is being said, often needlessly, about the policy of Russification" practiced by the Russians in nineteenth-century Poland.[25] In official terminology, as another independent source recently revealed, the rewriting of Polish history in the spirit of love for Russia is considered "internationalist education." The teaching of the Russian language, too, promotes "internationalism" among young Poles.[26]

These examples suggest that Kundera may have been right, after all, in seeing the condition of his own nation as a part of a larger complex including the Ukraine, Lithuania, and, as we now see, also Belorussia and even Poland, although individual peoples find themselves at rather different stages of "internationalization." What exactly is this "internationalism" which threatens their survival? According to a recent scholar, Kenneth C. Farmer, the official ideology — or the "political myth" — of "proletarian internationalism," as espoused within the USSR, holds that "the principal political entity with which Soviet citizens identify is the class, not the nation, and that indeed, national characteristics will become increasingly less important as the society evolves toward communism." At the same time, Farmer notes, this myth contains "an important subcategory" which is "the myth of Russian patrimony of the former Tsarist empire." This "submyth" provides that "the international culture that will emerge with the building of communism will in fact be Russian culture."[27]

It is customary to discuss the status of the independent nations of the "Socialist Community," as distinct from that of the constituent republics of the USSR, in terms of the "Brezhnev doctrine," which asserts the right and duty of all socialist states jointly to protect socialism when socialism is in danger in any one of them. While the goal of economic, political, and even ideological integration of all socialist states is openly upheld under this doctrine, it is not equally openly admitted that the Socialist Community is also supposed to become integrated linguistically—on the basis of the Russian language—or that the histories of all of its component nations are to be rewritten—the memories recreated—in the spirit of "friendship" for Russia, old and new. There is growing evidence, however, suggesting that this is a goal, albeit a very long-distance goal, of Moscow.

However, this official identification of "communism" with Russian ethnicity (if not as an immediate reality then as a real prospect for the future) helps to build defense mechanisms on the part of its intended victims. According to Allan Janik and Stephen Toulmin, the Communist Party of the Soviet Union

> by its claim to the "leading role" as historic spokesman for the international proletariat . . . confers on itself the same cosmic right to govern, and grants itself the same immunity from criticism and judgment, that the claim to divine right implied on behalf of the Habsburg emperors. [28]

This claim makes it impossible for the citizens to articulate publicly "the authentic needs, interests and conflicts" emerging in society and to seek their resolution through the constitutional machinery of the state. All issues have to be formulated in ideological categories that conform to the principle of party wisdom and authority. In order to overcome this "divergence between constitutional appearances and political realities," the non-Russian nationalities resort to nationalism which interprets the real problems of life as *national* (for example, Georgian) problems, and thus "provides a natural and easy way out" of those contradictions by attributing "the artificialities of official Soviet life" to "arbitrary, external impositions by a stupid, Russian-speaking officialdom. . . ."[29]

There are reasons to think that the same mechanism is at work in Soviet-dominated East-Central Europe: do not all conflicts and crises emerging there sooner or later acquire a "nationalist"—i.e. anti-Soviet or anti-Russian—coloring? (The Polish crisis of 1980, which began as labor protest against government-imposed price increases but was rapidly transformed into a political crisis and a *national* revolution, provides the latest illustration of how this happens.)

If things do stand this way, then there is an additional reason to question the narrow "power-politics" criterion in defining "East" or "East-Central" Europe. Instead, we might go back to the Masaryk formula which transcended any particular political boundaries or spheres of influence and defined the area ethnically, culturally, and politically at the same time.

Masaryk, as we recall, defined nations linguistically and endorsed their aspirations toward *cultural* self-realization and *political* self-rule in opposition to the reactionary regimes of Vienna, Berlin and St. Petersburg. In his understanding of the problem, under the conditions of oppressive authoritarian regimes (Masaryk saw "tsarism" in all three capitals) cultural nationalism was a force working for cultural pluralism and thus for greater political liberty.[30]

NOTES

[1] Oscar Halecki, *Borderlands of Western Civilization: A History of East Central Europe* (New York: Ronald Press Company, 1952).

[2] Hugh and Christopher Seton-Watson, *The Making of a New Europe: R. W. Seton-Watson and the Last Years of Austria-Hungary* (Seattle: University of Washington Press, 1981).

[3] Thomas G. Masaryk, "The Problem of Small Nations in the European Crisis," reprinted in R. W. Seton-Watson, *Masaryk in England* (New York: Macmillan, 1943), pp. 139-40.

[4] "The Problem of Small Nations," ibid., p. 140.

[5] Thomas G. Masaryk, *The New Europe (The Slav Standpoint)*, ed. by W. Preston Warren and William B. Weist (Lewisburg: Bucknell University Press, 1972), p. 52.

[6] *The New Europe*, p. 96. For the same point see also "The Problem of Small Nations," *Masaryk in England*, p. 140.

[7] *The New Europe*, p. 118.

[8] Ibid., p. 117.

[9] Ibid., p. 123.

[10] Ibid.

[11] Seton-Watson and Seton-Watson, *The Making of a New Europe*, p. 435.

[12] *The Making*, pp. 435-36.

[13] Alain Finkielkraut, "Milan Kundera Interview," *Cross Currents* 1, 1982.

[14] Ibid.

[15] Ibid.

[16] Ibid.

[17] Ibid.

[18] Philip Roth's interview with Milan Kundera, *The New York Times Book Review*, November 30, 1980, p. 7.

[19] Roman Solchanyk, "Russian Language and Soviet Politics," *Soviet Studies*, vol. 34, no. 1 (January 1982), pp. 27, 37-38.

[20] Ibid., pp. 36-37.

[21] Milan Kundera, *The Book of Laughter and Forgetting* (New York: Knopf, 1981), p. 3.

[22] *The Book of Laughter*, p. 159.

[23] Marcin Król, "A Frozen Image of the Past," *Survey*, vol. 25, no. 1 (Winter 1980), p. 104.

[24] Bohdan Cywiński, "The Poisoned Humanities," *Survey*, vol. 25, no. 1 (Winter 1980), p. 97.

[25] "Recenzja z Moskwy o polskich podręcznikach historii," *Zeszyty historyczne*, no. 57 (Paris 1981), pp. 73-91.

[26] Jan Nowicki, "Internacjonalizm puka do szkół,"*Głos*, no. 5, reprinted in *Głos, Niezależny miesięcznik społeczno-polityczny* (Paris: Instytut Literacki, 1981), pp. 154-57.

[27] Kenneth C. Farmer, *Ukrainian Nationalism in the Post-Stalin Era: Myth, Symbols and Ideology in Soviet Nationalities Policy* (The Hague, Boston, London: Martinus Nijhoff, 1980), p. 30.

[28] Allan Janik and Stephen Toulmin, *Wittgenstein's Vienna* (New York: Simon and Schuster, 1973), p. 271.

[29] *Wittgenstein's Vienna*, pp. 271-72. Since the Russians, just as the Viennese in the pre-1918 days, do not have the escape route of nationalism, "any thoroughgoing attempt they make to deal with these actual realities in public, instead of tolerating the Soviet establishment's insistence on 'keeping up appearances,' is once again liable to erupt into an 'affair.' Where Austria-Hungary had its Friedjung and Redl Affairs, the Soviet Union has been afflicted similarly by its Pasternak and Solzhenitsyn Affairs, its Medvedev and Sakharov Affairs." (Ibid., p. 272.)

[30] Multinational states understand the danger which the rights of nationalities pose to their integrity. In 1969, shortly after the suppression of the Prague Spring, a Czech historian, Milan Svankmajer, published an article on Tsar Nicholas I and his struggles against the revolutionary movements in Europe in 1848-49. According to Svankmajer, the Russian empire was "constantly exposed to the danger of disintegration, which can be prevented only by a strong central government. . . . Civil rights threaten not only the individual and peripheral interests of multinational empires but also their very existence." Russia intervened in 1849 to suppress the Hungarian revolution against Vienna because civil rights and national self-determination "threatened the very foundations of Russian autocracy." (Quoted by Antonin J. Liehm, "East Central Europe and the Soviet Model," *Problems of Communism*, vol. 30, no. 5 (September-October 1981), p. 52, from Milan Svankmajer, "The Gendarme of Europe," *Dějiny a současnost* (April 1969).)

EAST EUROPE? WEST EUROPE? BOTH? NEITHER?

Jan F. Triska
Stanford University

The imposition of martial law in Poland is not only a powerful signal that the Soviet bloc is antiquated, economically inefficient, politically unresponsive and socially harmful; it is the best evidence to date of the bankruptcy of the communist system of government. The Polish Communist Party (PCP) could not survive the challenge of the workers, the proletarians on whose behalf it was supposed to rule. Its legitimacy was destroyed, its monopoly of power broken. If not propped by the military, the Party would have been forced to accept a pluralistic political system, sharing its power with labor, the Church, the intellectuals and possibly the Parliament. The Party collapse, its disintegration and abdication of power to the military, showed that a managed, Stalin-type communist economy can no longer accommodate the demands of modern society.

The military occupation of Poland, however, is only a temporary respite, a measure "to normalize" the bankrupt economic, social and political conditions in Poland. It is not a permanent device. Not only is it extravagant economically, but it goes against the grain of communist thinking. Military dictatorship smacks of suspect "Bonapartism;" the military is and always has been viewed as a supreme danger to Party rule, a genie to be safely kept in its proper bottle until needed, and then used only under controlled conditions.

So what will happen when martial law ends? The Polish Communist Party will have to cope with the same people and the same problems it could not cope with before. Supposedly the country will have learned its lesson. But there has been no change in the obsolete political, economic and social structures and institutions, and no major changes are contemplated. Martial law was invoked to prevent the economy from collapse, to save the communist system, to buy time. While it is true that strikes were forbidden, harsher laws were enacted, more stringent controls were imposed, and intimidation and police brutality became the order of the day, all that had happened before, in different variants, in the 1956 crisis, in the 1970 riots and in the 1976 strikes and demonstrations. The activists were beaten (and sometimes killed), arrested, tried, sentenced and jailed. It is nothing new to the Poles. And it is nothing new to the rulers. They were able to cope with past social upheavals. Their so-called "crisis management" consisted of emergency measures which were identical: punish the guilty, give the population — with Soviet emergency help — as much as possible of what they want, *but do not rock the boat*.

The present Polish crisis management, however, is different from the past in two important respects: first, its scope is broader, its intensity higher and its direction more diffuse—a clear testimony of the cumulative effects of the past as well as of the escalation of severity in social turbulence. And second, the workers discovered something they never knew before: they learned that they have power. If they deny the political system their labor, the government collapses. Three party leaders were deposed in this way: Gomulka in 1970, Gierek in 1980 and Kania in 1981. The workers discovered that with courage they can be masters of their own destiny. They have been socialized into a new important role they did not know they could play. And this is a hard thing for them to forget.

This is the lesson of Poland in 1982. A deep, progressive alienation between social forces on the one hand and antiquated political structures on the other hand has culminated in the present situation. The Polish Communist Party has not learned how to cope with social change. It fears it, and that is its downfall. There is no indication that General Jaruzelski's government is any different in this respect from his predecessors. Like them, he is treating the symptoms, not the malady. The workers have emerged as a social force with an occupational solidarity of their own unknown in the past. Unless the government accommodates at least their basic demands on an institutional, permanent basis, the stagnation and decay of the Polish political system is inevitable. And yet, such accommodation appears unthinkable to the Jaruzelski government. This development, in turn, leads to deep, progressive destabilization of Soviet-controlled Eastern Europe.

With the possible exception of Hungary, all East European economies are in bad shape, not just Poland's. Growing labor shortages due to a slowdown in population growth; disappointing technological progress; antiquated industry; inefficient agriculture; the rising cost of imports; and large hard currency trade deficits (about 60 billion in 1981) are bringing Eastern Europe rapidly to a serious economic crisis. The East European dependency on the USSR is approaching welfare status. If the West decides, as it well may, not to send good money after bad, there is nothing the East Europeans can do, short of a substantial Soviet subsidy. This time the Soviet Union may be hard pressed to bail out East Europe once again. A cut in Soviet supplies and credits to East Europe, coupled with a reduction in import levels from the area, would bring about certain economic collapse.

The USSR itself appears to be at a critical turning point. The Soviet economy, the second largest economic system in the world, is seriously ill. Soviet oil wells east of the Urals are drying up; Soviet manpower is declining; labor productivity is decreasing; technological backwardness outside of the industrial-military complex is continuing; and agriculture is ailing. Chronic crop failures have led to sharply higher grain imports (about 7 billion dollars worth in 1981). Moscow now owes the West close to 20 billion dollars, about one billion dollars more in short-term debt than it can afford (*Wall Street Journal*, Feb. 8, 1982). It sold almost 10 tons of gold in December 1981 and January 1982, as well as large quantities of diamonds and oil, a sign of distress because large quantities dumped on the market depress prices. To finance its extension beyond its own borders—in Eastern Europe, in Cuba, in Afghanistan, on the Chinese border, in its support of Vietnam, in Kampuchea and in the Third World—the USSR needs a sound economy, which it does not have.

As a consequence, the future looks bleak for Eastern Europe. In the competition for increasingly scarce Soviet resources with such powerful Soviet claimants as the defense establishment, Eastern Europe will largely lose out.

At the same time, the developments in Poland have exacerbated problems in Western Europe. The Atlantic Alliance, a U. S.-West European coalition of almost a half billion people and of almost forty years' standing, has been experiencing a difficult period. Disagreements between Washington and its NATO friends have included such crucial issues as détente, East-West trade, the economy, arms control, and defense expenditures. With the crisis in Poland, new divisive problems emerged, such as the Western response to martial law in terms of sanctions, the large Polish indebtedness to Western creditors, and the building of the natural gas pipeline from Siberia to Western Europe. Thoughtful analysts worry about the increasingly sharp divergencies of political, economic and military interests and perceptions between the U. S. and Western Europe. The differences are leading some observers to ask how enduring the Western alliance is, or should be. Might not changing conditions and increasing instability in Eastern as well as Western Europe demand a rethinking of the post-World War II order, and perhaps a political reconceptualization of Europe as a whole?

To answer this question we must begin by looking at Europe as it stood at the end of World War II. Europe was divided into two parts, West and East, at Yalta in February 1945. It was not a conscious decision. The formal plan for Allied occupation zones of Nazi Germany agreed upon at Yalta, however, became the effective instrument of East-West division. The Russian zone of occupation became East Germany, and the three western zones—American, British and French—became West Germany. Berlin was divided the same way. The Soviet Union later added countries to the East that lay on their side of the (agreed-upon) line of occupation—Poland, Czechoslovakia, Hungary, Romania, and Bulgaria. Albania and Yugoslavia joined Soviet Eastern Europe as well. Outside of West Germany and West Berlin, the new "Western Europe" which emerged from World War II was ratified as a friend and ally of the United States through the Truman Doctrine in Greece and Turkey in 1947 ("the turning point in America's foreign policy, which now declared that whenever aggression, direct or indirect, threatened the peace [and] security of the United States," action would be taken to stop that aggression [H. S. Truman, *Memoirs*, vol. 1, 456, pp. 103-9]) and through the Marshall Plan west of the new East European boundary line in 1948. The Warsaw Pact and NATO formalized the two groups as Soviet and American alliances. The division of Europe into East and West was cast and, over the decades, legitimized; the 1975 Helsinki Agreement confirmed it.

Zbigniew Brzezinski, the national security advisor in the Carter Administration, wrote recently (*Wall Street Journal*, February 19, 1982) that the time has come for the U. S. "to disassociate" itself from the Yalta order, a symbol of "American-Soviet collusion" to divide Europe. W. W. Rostow, the national security advisor to Presidents Kennedy and Johnson, has argued (*The San Francisco Chronicle*, January 28, 1982) that what we need is a "farsighted plan to end the confrontation in Central Europe that for 35 years has passed for normality." Joseph C. Harsh questioned the Yalta legacy in a thoughtful analysis (*The Christian Science Monitor*, January 8, 1982). Mark Hopkins, reflecting on the fact that solidarity in Poland upset the old European balance imposed at Yalta, pointed out that "a new arrangement must be worked out, in the Soviet national interest, not to please the Americans" (*The New Leader*, January 11, 1982, p. 5). And Hodding Carter, official spokesman for the State Department in the Carter Administration, wrote (*The Wall Street Journal*, March 11, 1982) that "what is desperately needed is a trans-Atlantic 'Great Debate' similar to the one that preceded America's decision to promote and join the alliance in the late 1940's."

Perhaps the time has come, as Charles Gati argues, "to put the issue of Eastern Europe, and not just Poland, on the agenda of the forthcoming Reagan-Brezhnev summit meeting. . . . Given the region's chronic instability, the economic and political costs of maintaining the empire, combined with internal needs and problems, the Soviet leaders may be tempted to negotiate — as long as they can hope to obtain implicit Western support for a new concept of stability in Europe and economic support for themselves and their allies" (from a private memorandum, March 1982).

Why not indeed? The major interests of the two superpowers, U. S. and USSR, are global — their overwhelming concern is the security of the world, a world of which Europe is but a single, though important, part. NATO and the Warsaw Pact, on the other hand, are concerned only with the security of Europe. Only a superpower can contain another superpower and deter nuclear war. But alliances such as NATO and the Warsaw Pact "tend to exacerbate danger by multiplying the ways war could start without offering the means for tomorrow's commensurate benefit: deterring nuclear war and preventing nuclear blackmail" (Ronald C. Nairn, "Why NATO Doesn't Work," *The Wall Street Journal*, March 26, 1982).

Since World War II, the nature of world military and strategic change has been crucial in rate, volume and direction. NATO and the Warsaw Pact have been left behind by this extraordinary developmental metamorphosis in technological breakthrough. What was once essential to world security interests has shrunk to merely regional importance—significant but not vital. Perhaps the time has come to take Europe out of the superpower game, where it no longer belongs, not only for the sake of world security but for the sake of the Europeans themselves. After almost four decades of division, the 420 million Europeans (250 million in Western Europe and 170 million in Eastern Europe) can look after their own destiny. It would be in their own interest to control and direct their own affairs, while freeing the superpowers to worry about each other, their own global roles, and their own world interests. The interests of Europe and the interests of the superpowers have never been as divergent and heterogeneous as they are now, and they will grow more so with time.

The major argument against this kind of analysis is that the Soviet leaders, traditionally obsessed with security to a degree approaching paranoia, would never voluntarily agree to a Soviet withdrawal from Eastern Europe, their *cordon sanitaire*. And indeed they may not. But this is an empirical question. We may never know unless we put the issue on the table. With an appropriate set of guarantees making Soviet security in Europe inviolable, with balanced military disengagement, with neutral zones and atom-free zones (as proposed to the United States by Polish Foreign Minister Adam Rapacki in 1958), the Russians may consider a comprehensive peace plan for Europe worthy of at least tentative consideration. After all, there is a precedent. The Soviets did agree to withdraw from Soviet-occupied Austria in 1955 in exchange for Austrian neutrality. The negotiations would be difficult, long and frustrating. But the possible benefits would make the necessary costs the best possible investment to all concerned—the Americans, the Russians and, of course, the Europeans.

Would West Europeans welcome such a development? With its high techno-economic and managerial capability, diplomatic skills, cultural assets, large markets, energy supplies and working connections to former colonies, Western Europe could easily forge ahead on its own. The only worry all around may be a reunited, unified Germany.

Admittedly, that would be a problem. East Germany would probably gravitate to West Germany. No one wants German reunification—not the West Europeans, nor the East Europeans, nor the USSR, nor the U. S. The memories of pre-war Germany are still vivid, and a unified Germany would disturb the balance of power in Europe as it has since the reunification of Germany in the nineteenth century. And neutralization of Germany à la Austria is not realistic; the largest country in Europe with eighty million people, united Germany would hardly be a candidate for neutrality. Germany would probably have to remain divided.

East Europeans would welcome the new development whole-heartedly. It would give them a freedom of maneuver they never dreamt of. They would still live in the shadow of the USSR, however, just as Finland does. Soviet troop withdrawal from Eastern Europe would not mean Soviet disappearance from the European continent. The USSR still would be the only superpower in Europe; its capability, influence and leverage would remain. But just as the West Europeans fear Finlandization, East Europeans would rejoice in it. They would keep their healthy respect for their neighbor, the Soviet Union. But at home, they could experiment in many ways, all worthwhile.

Undoubtedly, many other problems would have to be considered, debated, and resolved. But as Zbigniew Brzezinski argues, American-Soviet relations are at a critical turning point. They may go either way, up or down: "Both sides are becoming prisoners of a dangerous dynamic, with [Poland] serving as a catalyst for escalating enmity." What may be needed now is a bold, imaginative, broad strategy rather than the usual tinkering with the margins. What is there to lose?

IVAN THE TERRIBLE AS THE GENTRY'S CANDIDATE FOR THE POLISH THRONE: A STUDY IN POLITICAL MENTALITY

Wiktor Weintraub
Harvard University

The reign of the last Jagiellonian king of Poland, Sigismund August, was a relatively peaceful one, except for the eastern borderlands. From time to time, Tartar inroads devastated Podolia. And from 1561 on, the Polish-Lithuanian commonwealth was engaged in a protracted war with Muscovy over the dominion of Livonia. The Tsar who waged that war earned the appellation "the Terrible," so notorious was his cruelty. He ruled over his subjects with an iron hand, and the class that particularly suffered during his reign were the boyars, the Muscovite counterpart of the Polish landed gentry.

Thus, we are amazed to learn that after the death of King Sigismund August in 1572, there emerged among the gentry a party that wanted to elect this very Ivan the Terrible, or his younger son, Fedor, to the Polish throne. How the devil was it possible?

No wonder that most Russian historians thought that the "candidacy" of Ivan the Terrible was nothing more than a clever stratagem of Lithuanian magnates who through such a device wanted to prevent the Tsar from breaking the truce concluded in 1570 and starting a new military campaign during the troubled time of the interregnum. Polish-Lithuanian diplomacy could *also* have had such an aim in mind. But there can be no doubt that, at the beginning of the interregnum, a considerable segment of the gentry genuinely wanted to put Tsar Ivan on the Polish throne. Quite recently, a Soviet historian, Boris Floria, has convincingly proved that that was the case.[1] To the data he marshalled one can add more proofs. One of them is especially telling. It comes from the pen of a contemporary historian, Reinhold Heidenstein, who in his work *Rerum Polonicarum ab excessu Sigismundi Augusti libri XII* states in unambiguous terms that at the beginning of the interregnum "the majority of the gentry leaned towards the Tsar."[2] Heidenstein was employed in diplomatic service by King Stephen and was close to the Chancellor Jan Zamoyski. He is the author of an "official" history of King Stephen's war against Ivan the Terrible, *De bello moscovitico commentariorum libri sex*, published in 1584, a work as fiercely critical of Tsar Ivan as any historical work could be. Thus, he cannot be accused of any pro-Muscovite bias. Of course, it would be difficult nowadays to prove or disprove Heidenstein's statement that "a majority" of the gentry was for the Tsar. There can be no doubt, however, that at first a substantial segment of the gentry was prone to vote for the Tsar or his son.

The present paper is not interested in the vicissitudes of that strange candidacy or in finding out what particular circles or regions were for the Muscovite elect. Neither is it interested in retelling the story of how the Tsar forfeited whatever chances he had to the Polish throne by treating the Polish offer with diffidence and discourtesy—he must have been as perplexed by it as any modern historian. The aim of this paper is different. It tries to penetrate the mentality of those of the gentry who considered the Tsar to be the proper candidate for their ruler and to reconstruct their ratiocinations.

Fortunately, we have at our disposal texts that give us insight into that mentality, tracts written during the interregnum which try to sell the Tsar or his son to Polish voters. Five such pamphlets have survived and are available in an old but good critical edition.[3] They make fascinating reading.

The first three pamphlets have been preserved in manuscript copies only; the fourth, both in an printed version and in a manuscript copy; and the last in a printed version only. We know for sure the name of the author of that last pamphlet. Its author, like the authors of other tracts, did not sign it, but he preceded the actual tract with lengthy and awkward rhymed compositions. The first of them, entitled "The Author," gives us in acrostic the name and patronymic (in the Muscovite manner) of its author, "Piotr Mycielski Tomasowic."[4] It is dated *"de domo cuiusdam equitis districtus Calisiensis."*[5] Since the preceding tract was dated *"de domo nobilis districtus Kalisiensis"*[6] as well, and since both of them were written in a similar type of Polish interspersed with frequent Latin locutions, the editor of the collection, Czubek, argues, quite convincingly, that both pamphlets came from the same heavy pen of Mycielski. We know little about him, except that he belonged to the Reform camp and joined the Czech Brethren who had settled in Wielkopolska,[7] a circumstance that might have some bearing on his opting against the Catholic frontrunners, the Habsburg and the Valois candidate.

Aleksander Brückner suggested in his review of Czubek's edition that the first of our pamphlets, *Zdanie o obieraniu nowego króla*, might have been written by Augustyn Rotundus, a burgher raised to the rank of nobility, a Protestant who turned Catholic, an intellectual prominent in Lithuanian political life, although not a Lithuanian by origin.[8] Brückner did not insist on his attribution, and later, in her study on Rotundus, Maria Baryczowa rejected it as improbable: elsewhere Rotundus spoke harshly of Tsar Ivan.[9] From the text of the pamphlet we can infer that its author considered himself to be a Lithuanian and spoke in terms of the specific interests of Lithuania.

We are in the dark as to the authorship of the writers of the two remaining tracts.

When we peruse these pamphlets, one common feature strikes us above all. Their writers try to persuade Slavic voters that they should elect a Slavic candidate, but they don't play up the Slavic card; they don't insist on common Slavic ties. Of course, Poles knew very well that the Slavic languages were close to each other and they were conscious of the common origins of Slavic nations, but, as concerned Muscovy, the great divide, denominational, political and cultural, proved to be much stronger than the consciousness of common Slavic ties.

Kochanowski's poetry is a good case in point. In his *Epinicion*, a Latin poem praising King Stephan's victory over Tsar Ivan, he states that Poles are of the same origin as Muscovites, but that religion divides them as it can divide even brothers:

> Moschis genus atque Polonis est idem
> Slavicum, dispar scindit uniter aptos
> religio, unanimes quod scindit et fratres malum.[10]

Muscovites are branded in his poem as "foes," "wild and horrid foe," or an "insane foe." [11] Elsewhere, in a much earlier poem, a Latin elegy written in 1563, the Muscovite is presented as a "barbarous foe." [12]

It is true that at the end of his pamphlet Mycielski mentions that Muscovites and Poles are "one nation" ("*gdyż to jest jedna nacja z nami*") and that the Sarmatians, a popular synonym for Slavs, never swore allegiance to Alexander the Great or to the Romans.[13] He does it in a casual way, however; he does not dwell upon the subject. The Slavic argument is for him of marginal value only.

More telling in this respect is another tract, *Sententia de eligende novo rege ex duce Moschorum* (No. XXIV). Its author stresses the point that a Habsburg candidate cannot be trusted, that he would like to curtail the privileges of the gentry, and he refers to the Czech precedent, to "what they did to the Czechs, our brethren." [14] Czechs are a kindred nation but not the Muscovites. Speaking of the latter, the writer is cold and detached.

It is not difficult to find in sixteenth-century Polish rhetorics phraseology extolling Slavs, or for that matter, Sarmatians. All five tracts, however, prove eloquently that such a Slavic phraseology did not engage the Polish gentry deeply. From the Polish perspective, there were close and distant Slavs, and an appeal to Slavic solidarity was of no avail when applied to a Muscovite candidate.

Free of Slavophile accents, the tracts try to capitalize on mistrust of Western foreigners. One cannot, they argue, rely on these Westerners, because they are treacherous and contemptible of things Polish. An anti-German note is especially strong in our pamphlets,[15] and they evoke as well the French massacre of the Huguenots, St. Bartholomew's Eve.

In the second half of the sixteenth century, the Commonwealth was more open to Western influences than ever before. Every year, hundreds of students registered at Western, mostly Italian, universities. Rich noblemen liked to travel abroad. The Commonwealth was open to foreign merchants. These contacts with the West left a strong impact on Polish culture and were changing its very style of life. Of course, this does not mean that every country squire could afford expensive foreign trips or acquire the polish that went with them. Those squires resented the changes in the style of life; they saw in them so many marks of corruption. Xenophobia became their natural defense mechanism against an inferiority complex. Stanisław Kot in his study on Polish attitudes towards the West in the sixteenth century noticed that in the literature of the interregnum period such a critical attitude towards Western nations became especially articulate.[16] This does not mean that it did not exist before. It came into the open during the interregnum: because most of the candidates to the Polish throne were from the West, it became an important political issue then. Quoting from one of the pro-Muscovite pamphlets the statement that it would be easier to handle "Vassily than Hans, our natural enemy," Kot concluded that such an anti-Western attitude had been generated by pro-Muscovite sympathy among a part of gentry society.[17] Most probably, we are dealing here with an inverse process: the author of the tract tried to graft a sympathy for the Muscovite candidate onto anti-Western feelings.

Above all, however, the writers of our pro-Muscovite pamphlets tried to be matter-of-fact and hardheaded, and they stressed the political and economic profits such a choice would bring with it. They argued that the election of Tsar Ivan or his son would put an end to protracted wars, open vast lands of Muscovy to Polish-Lithuanian colonization and enrich the nation. One of the pamphleteers expresses himself in an amusingly enthusiastic way about these bright economic prospects: "Then millions shall stand wide open for us, virtuous, rich, inexhaustible."[18]

Most remarkably, these tracts do not try to idealize Tsar Ivan, to defend his character or praise his kind of rule in Muscovy. A few years later, during the war of King Stephen against Muscovy, Polish propaganda would try hard to depict the Tsar as a monster of tyranny and cruelty.[19] But Tsar Ivan became notorious in Poland long before that war. After all, the Commonwealth was a neighbor of Muscovy and Prince Andrey Kurbsky fled to Poland as early as 1564.

The pamphlets do not fight the negative image of the Tsar. They freely admit that he is a tyrant. "All nations have the Muscovite for a tyrant," writes one of them.[20] "Other people understand that the Muscovite is a tyrant and a brute," chimes in another writer.[21] The third, Mycielski, also admits that the Tsar is a tyrant but exculpates his tyranny by two considerations: it is due to the "brute nature" (*fera natura*) of the Muscovites and it is not directed against "virtuous" people, although even those virtuous subjects, as he freely admits, have no legal defense against the Tsar, ale "*exleges*."[22] In his second pamphlet Mycielski equally freely admits that the Tsar is "an obvious tyrant."[23]

Neither are our tracts kind towards the Muscovites. As we have already seen, Mycielski explains lack of constitutional guarantees in Muscovy by the "wild nature" of its population. People there would not understand such guarantees, and the Tsar must treat them like wild animals. It is "a simple nation, one can say, crude," states another writer.[24] One pamphlet defends the Muscovites against the accusation of crudeness. After all, we read there, they don't serve any foreign masters and "probably" at the court one can find more refined people.[25] Mycielski, in his second pamphlet, asserts that Muscovites excel Poles in prowess and military skill.[26] Common to all these opinions, whether critical or laudatory, is a deepseated conviction that Muscovites belong to a different world, that they differ vastly from Poles.

Does Tsar Ivan's candidature mean that our pamphleteers would like to sell the political liberties of the gentry for economic advantages? Not in the least. All of them are convinced that the Tsar, once in Poland, on the Polish throne, would behave differently. Mycielski in one place argues that the election of a king with such tyrannical proclivities would put an end to dissentions among Poles, because they would have to present a united front against such a dangerous ruler.[27] Even such an admission of the potential danger of King Ivan is countered by the conviction that the gentry, if united, would be able to avert it. Our pamphleteers draw their confidence from a historical precedent. Already in the past, they argue, Poles called to the throne a barbarous and bloodthirsty ruler and their choice proved to be highly fortunate for the country: it opened a new and splendid era of Polish history. They refer, of course, to the union with Lithuania and the call to the Cracow throne of the Lithuanian prince Jagiello.

Even a contemporary historian, Heidenstein, mentions the example of the Jagiellonian precedent as a reason for the popularity of Tsar Ivan's candidature, together with the vastness of his state and the prospects for a lasting peace in the east.[28] Our pamphlets bear out the aptness of his observation. Over and over again, the Lithuanian precedent is recalled. The author of the first pamphlet affirms that the ruler of Muscovy must be a tyrant, because the regime of Muscovy is "pagan" like that of Lithuania of yore.[29] One should notice the author's sleight-of-hand: by declaring Muscovy's autocratic regime to be "pagan," he can equate the Muscovite polity with that of old pagan Lithuania. The unsaid but quite obvious premise of such an argument is that once a Muscovite ruler is brought to a country with a Christian, constitutional regime, he shall comply with it, his tyrannical rule having its source not in his temper but in the nature of his regime.

The second tract (XXIV) starts with an evocation of the union of Poland with Lithuania. Poles preferred a pagan to a German prince on their throne and their choice proved to be providential: Jagiello's reign was a happy one and under his rule and that of his descendants Poles managed to secure their freedom. Then he goes on: "There is no doubt that would the Tsar or his son become the king of Poland, in the process of time that would lead to one monarchy," as powerful a monarchy as that of ancient Assyria, Persia or Rome.[30]

The third author dwells primarily on the dire consequences of a "German"—read: Habsburg—choice. He does not fail, however, to mention that just as Poland was all the better for the union with Lithuania, so would it gain by a union with Muscovy. Numerous Poles had settled in Lithuania. In the future they would be able to settle in Muscovy as well, that country being depopulated.[31]

Nor does Mycielski, the author of the fourth pamphlet, miss the union with Lithuania. Poles, he argues, should not fear the Tsar's tyrannical nature; Jagiello had been worse than a tyrant—he was a parricide.[32] And once elected, the Tsar would "incorporate" his state into the Commonwealth, as Jagiello had done.[33]

No wonder that we find the same note in the second paper by Mycielski, the last one in our collection. Jagiello, we read there, was not only a pagan but also a tyrant in Lithuania, and how useful he had turned out to be for Poland.[34]

As we see, the Jagiellonian precedent serves as a trump argument for all our pamphleteers: the Poles had once elected a cruel tyrant and that tyrant had proved to be a humane ruler in Poland; moreover, his election turned out to be a happy turning point in the history of the country. It is obvious that all the authors were acting under the influence of a powerful historical myth. Seen through the prism of that myth, even the Tsar's bloodthirsty, tyrannical nature seemed to acquire a positive character, offering almost a challenge: so much was he like his predecessor, the pagan Jagiello.

We can trace the origins of that myth. It was Długosz's portrait of King Ladislas Jagiello in his *Annales seu cronicae inclyti regni Poloniae* that made possible such a presentation of the Jagiellonian precedent. It was a highly subjective, obviously prejudiced portrait. Długosz's venerated patron was Zbigniew Oleśnicki, bishop of Cracow and cardinal, who became a powerful political figure during the last years of the reign of Jagiello and was a virtual ruler of the country during the reign of Jagiello's son, Ladislas II (1434-44), who ascended the throne at the age of ten. Oleśnicki was then brutally deposed from power by the younger brother of Ladislas II, King Casimir IV. Because of this, Długosz felt a grudge against King Casimir as well as against his father. In his *Annales* he settled Oleśnicki's old score with the Jagellonian dynasty.

Długosz told the story of King Ladislas Jagiello at great length in books X and XI of his work. At the end of that story he gaves a character sketch of the King or, strictly speaking, two character sketches.

We read in the *Annales* that a few weeks before Jagiello's death in 1434, the Bishop, who was about to leave Cracow for the Council of Basel, decided to upbraid the King in public. Długosz regals us with Oleśnicki's solemn, adhortatory speech. The Bishop recognizes the King as a "kind, pious, generous, patient, meek and merciful" person.[35] In spite of all this, he is a weak and bad ruler. He spends nights at revels, the Church suffers from his taxes and levies, his courtiers oppress people, he is remiss in redressing grievances and allows bad money to be minted. The Bishop's speech, set in high-flown, rhetorical phrases, serves two purposes. It underscores the King's serious shortcomings and presents the Bishop as his moral judge, as the representative of moral standards in the country.

A few pages later, after having told the story of the King's death and funeral, the historian gives his own, quite detailed character sketch, presented in a different, homely, down-to-earth style. Like the Bishop he admits that the King was kind, humane, generous, not prone to shed blood, but presents him as a rather ineffectual and lazy ruler and a superstitious man. He liked, we learn, to spend long periods in the privy and received people while sitting there. We learn as well that the King was "prone to sex," licit as well as forbidden.[36] This is said in a few words, as if *en passant*, but the damage is done.

The general impression of Jagiello from both character sketches — the one put into the mouth of the Bishop and that in which the historian speaks directly — is that of a good-natured but somehow weak, primitive and slightly ridiculous human being. These, however, are Jagiello's features after he had been baptized and had become the King of Poland. The pagan Jagiello, the ruler of Lithuania, cuts a completely different figure. He is a cruel, treacherous and bloodthirsty tyrant. Długosz brings home these features by telling the story of Jagiello's treatment of his paternal uncle, Kiejstut. Kiejstut was the Prince of Samogitia and contested Jagiello's exclusive rule over Lithuania. When he and his son Witold were preparing for a military campaign against Jagiello, the latter, assuring them of their safety, invited both for negotiations to his camp, imprisoned them and ordered Kiejstut to be strangled. In order to underscore the enormity of Jagiello's parricidal crime, Długosz, in summing up the episode, stresses that "from among all the sons of Prince Gedymin [Kiejstut was] the wisest and most diligent and shined above all with the virtues of being polite, humane and trustworthy." [37]

How was it possible that the monstrous Lithuanian Mr. Hyde changed into a humane Polish Dr. Jekyll? Długosz does not give us any explanation of this miraculous development except for a telling sentence with which he introduces the story of Jagiello's conflict with Kiejstut and in which he states that the story illustrates the maxim that "in barbarous countries, deprived of the knowledge of Divine laws, no covenant can be kept. There is no faith, no oath, no decency or conscience there." [38] A barbarous country breeds a barbarous ruler, but that same ruler transferred into a civilized surrounding can blossom into a decent, if otherwise far from perfect, man.

On account of Długosz's hostile attitude towards the ruling dynasty, his *Annales* could not be published in sixteenth-century Poland and the ban was in force even afterwards. When in 1614, Szczęsny Herburt started printing the *Annales*, he could not go beyond book VI, because of royal interference. It does not follow, however, that Długosz's work was inaccessible to sixteenth-century readers. The *Annales* offered the best and the fullest presentation of early Jagiellonian times and the prohibition had its publicity value; it whetted the appetite. More than eighty manuscript copies of that big book have been preserved, thirty-six of them coming from the sixteenth century.[39] Moreover, for the Renaissance historians *Annales* served as the main source, and sometimes the only source, for the history of Poland in the late fourteenth and fifteenth centuries. Sixteenth-century historians avoided the offending details but still looked through Długosz's eyes at the early Jagiellonian times. This held true as well for the presentation of the pagan Lithuanian Jagiello. With what a naive insistence, for instance, does Maciej Stryjkowski try, in his history of Lithuania (published in 1582 in Königsberg), to emotionally involve the reader when recounting the tragic end of Kiejsut whom, on the one hand, he calls a "dear old man" (*staruszek*) and, on the other, "the second Achilles, Hector, Ajax, Ulysses and Hercules of Lithuania and Samogitia."[40]

Seen through such a prism, Tsar Ivan's notoriously tyrannical rule seemed to be a "natural" phenomenon in a "barbaric" country, something not to be bothered about. That is why while advocating the election of Tsar Ivan to the Polish throne, some of our pamphleteers did not hide the fact that he was a tyrant in Muscovy. The tracts bear witness to the superb political self-confidence of the gentry. They believed that they would be able to keep the Tsar in check, to civilize him and, with him, Muscovy. Above all, however, they bear witness to the power of a historical myth which originated with Długosz. The myth could the more easily exert an influence on the Polish imagination because of the Union of Lublin, which shortly before the death of the last Jagiellonian king in 1569, completed the task of soldering together Poland and Lithuania. It made of the Commonwealth a great power, the largest state in Europe after Muscovy. The idea of the election of the Tsar was a bold attempt at making the cumbersome institution of elective monarchy an instrument of peaceful Polish imperialism. It seemed to promise to move the frontiers of the state far to the east again, to offer dazzling prospects of economic and cultural penetration. It disregarded the fact that, unlike Jagiello, Tsar Ivan was not fighting with his back to the wall against a powerful military order bent on conquest. It overlooked as well the circumstance that Muscovy was not, like Jagiello's Lithuania, a pagan relic, but belonged to a different—and hostile—Christian world. It is for this reason that those attempts were chimerical. One cannot, however, deny them boldness or imaginative sweep.

The union idea was very attractive to the Poles. No sooner had the newly elected King Henry Valois fled Poland in 1574, then another pro-Muscovite party emerged and again advocated the election of Tsar Ivan to the Polish throne.[41] Even more telling is another, later initiative. In 1586, after Ivan the Terrible had been succeeded by Tsar Fedor, King Stephen sent to Moscow Michał Haraburda—the same Haraburda who had acted as an envoy to the Tsar in 1572-73—with a new project for union. King Stephen, like Tsar Fedor, was childless, and he suggested that whoever of the two survived would rule over both Muscovy and the Commonwealth. It was an open secret that Tsar Fedor was of poor health, and nobody would guess at that time that King Stephen's days were numbered. But the boyars would have nothing to do with such a plan.[42] Finally, one can consider Piłsudski's plans for a federation of nations situated between Russian and Germany under Polish guidance as a new, modernized version of the old union idea, this time with an anti-Russian thrust.

NOTES

[1] Borys Floria, "Wschodnia polityka magnatów litewskich w okresie pierwszego bezkrólewia," *Odrodzenie i reformacja w Polsce*, XX (1975), pp. 45-67.

[2] "Majoris partis nobilitates in Moscum fere propensa studia erant." Reinholdi Heidensteinii *Rerum Polonicarum ab excessu Sigismundi Augusti libri XII*, Francoforti ad Moenum 1672, p. 28.

[3] *Pisma polityczne z czasów pierwszego bezkrólewia*, Jan Czubek ed., Cracow 1906, pp. 349-97; later quoted as *Pisma polit.* The pamphlets form Nos. XXIII-XXVII of the collection. The initial, "poetic" part of pamphlet No. XXVII was published by the editor separately as No. XXVIIa, pp. 705-26.

[4] *Pisma polit.*, p. 705.

[5] *Pisma polit.*, p. 397.

[6] *Pisma polit.*, p. 381.

[7] See his biogram by Włodzimierz Dworzaczek in *Polski Słownik Biograficzny*, XXII (1977), pp. 345-46.

[8] See Aleksander Brückner in *Pamiętnik Literacki*, VI (1907), pp. 408-409.

[9] See Maria Baryczowa, "Augustyn Rotundus Mieleski, pierwszy historyk i apologeta Litwy," *Ateneum Wileńskie*, X (1935), p. 93.

[10] Joannis Cochanovii *Carmina latina*, Josephus Przyborowski ed., Varsaviae 1884, p. 313.

[11] "Hoste indomitoque, trucique," "demens /. . . / hostis." *Op. cit.*, pp. 320, 329.

[12] "Barbarus hostis." *Op. cit.*, p. 120. A detailed analysis of Kochanowski's attitude towards the Muscovites is to be found in Tadeusz Ulewicz's book *Swiadomość słowiańska Jana Kochanowskiego*, "Prace z historii literatury polskiej" No. 8, Cracow 1948, pp. 134-149.

[13] *Pisma polit.*, p. 396.

[14] "Jako uczyniono Czechom, braciej naszej." *Pisma polit.*, p. 357.

[15] *Pisma polit.*, pp. 354-55, 364.

[16] Stanisław Kot, "Polska Złotego Wieku wobec kultury zachodniej," in the collective *Kultura staropolska*, Cracow 1932, p. 701.

[17] S. Kot, *op. cit.*, p. 702.

[18] /. . . / dopiero sie nam otworza miliony, cnotliwe, bogate, nigdy nie przebrane." *Pisma polit.*, p. 354.

[19] See A. Kappeler, *Ivan Groznyj im Spiegel der ausländischen Druckschriften*, Bern 1972.

[20] *Pisma polit.*, p. 354.

[21] *Pisma polit.*, p. 356.

[22] *Pisma polit.*, p. 377.

[23] "Jest tyranem jasnym." *Pisma polit.*, p. 395.

[24] "Naród prosty, a może się rzec, że gruby." *Pisma polit.*, pp. 356-57.
[25] "Podobno też i ćwiczenie lepsze." *Pisma polit.*, p. 361.
[26] "Nas dziś /.../ męstwem i biegłością przewyszszają." *Pisma polit.*, p. 395.
[27] *Pisma polit.*, p. 395.
[28] "/... / nondum obsoleta in animis hominym memoria Jagellonis, qui pari ratione ex barbare christianus, ex hoste Rex factus, cum Lithuaniae magnum ducatum regno adjunxerat, tum firmam in hunc usque diem pacem eidem peperat." Heidenstein, *op. cit.*, p. 28.
[29] "/... / musi tam być tyraństwo, mając R. P. obyczajem pogańskim jaka była i w Litwie za pogaństwa." *Pisma polit.*, p. 354.
[30] *Pisma polit.*, p. 356.
[31] *Pisma polit.*, p. 361.
[32] *Pisma polit.*, p. 378.
[33] *Pisma polit.*, p. 379.
[34] *Pisma polit.*, p. 390-93.
[35] "Scio quidem te mansuetum, devotum, liberaliem, patientem, humilem et clementem esse." Joannis długosz, *Opera omnia*, cura A. Przezdziecki, V. XIII, Cracoviae 1872, p. 523.
[36] "In Venerem proclivus, non permissam modo, sed etiam prohibitem." *Ibid.*, p. 536. The whole character sketch, pp. 533-38.
[37] "Inter omnes Gedimini Ducis filios magis prudens, magisque industrius, et quod illum plurimum honestabat, civilis et humanus et verax in sermone." Długosz, *Opera omnia*, V. XII, Cracoviae 1871, p. 411.
[38] "Neque enim inter barbaros tuta et sincera possunt durare foedera inter quos verus ignoratur Deus: nulla quoque viget fides, nullum sacrosanctum iusiurandum, nulla legitima religio." *Ibid.*, p. 405.
[39] See Wanda Semkowicz-Zarembina's introduction to Jana Długosza *Roczniki czyli kroniki sławnego królestwa polskiego*, Books I-II, Warsaw 1961, p. 13.
[40] *Kronika* Macieja Stryjkowskiego (*Zbiór dziejopisów polskich*, V. II), Warsaw 1766, p. 432.
[41] See Wincenty Zakrzewski, *Po ucieczce Henryka. Dzieje bezkrólewia 1574-1575*, Cracow 1878, pp. 226-32.
[42] See Kazimierz Lepszy's biogram of Haraburda in *Polski Słownik Biograficzny*, IX (1960-61), pp. 289-90.

THE INDEPENDENT PUBLISHING MOVEMENT IN POLAND: ITS PAST AND FUTURE PERSPECTIVES

Stanisław Barańczak
Harvard University

The unprecedented development of events in Poland beginning in August, 1980 does not cease to amaze Western observers. As a matter of fact, Poles themselves are equally amazed. However, I believe that it is considerably more difficult, from a Western perspective, to become conscious of the fact that what happened in August, and after August, had already been unfolding for a long time. The fact that everything happened so rapidly — the lightning-swift tempo at which events evolved — caught everyone, not excluding the most insightful specialists of political prognoses, by surprise. On the other hand, the direction taken by developing events could have been, to a certain extent, foreseen.

By stating this, I have several phenomena simultaneously in mind. First of all, one could have realized the dimensions and nature of the growing crisis. Western observers are frequently not fully aware of the fact that the workers' riots of 1956, 1970, 1976, and 1980 only ostensibly had an economic base — in reality, they were an external expression of a growing political need within the society for mutual participation in the decision-making processes affecting the country's fate. This demand was formulated ever more clearly, especially in the seventies, and despite appearances of stagnation or discouragement, sufficiently broad segments of society were conscious of the actual nature of the crisis and its sources in the years directly preceding August, 1980.

From where, however, did this consciousness arise? We are here encroaching upon another realm of problems, not always comprehended and appreciated by the West. I believe that only someone who spent the years 1976 to 1980 in Poland can fully appreciate the colossal, although not always self-evident role of the "unofficial education of society" which developed in those years on an unprecedented scale. This education appertained to various realms of knowledge — political, social, economic, and cultural — and reached society by various routes. As always in postwar Poland, Western radio programs broadcast in Polish enjoyed universal popularity. On a smaller scale, publications of Polish emigré publishing houses reached a reading audience mainly as copies smuggled across the border in the suitcases of tourists returning from the West.

These two methods of unofficial and uncensored instruction of society were nothing new. On the other hand, what was novel in the second half of the seventies was the fact that initiatives which came into being within the country itself and not in the West, began to play an increasingly greater role. Besides this, they were carried out in an unprecedented manner—once again this adjective must be used—unprecedented, because the principle of complete independence from government control was coupled with the principle of complete openness. I have in mind here undertakings such as the so-called "Flying University" (*Uniwersytet Latający*) —its real name, the Society of Scholarly Courses (*Towarzystwo Kursów Naukowych*)—which organized lectures on history, social studies, literature, and so on, in private apartments. Numerous similar efforts at organizing an independent cultural life, in the form of uncensored exhibitions, performances, concerts, literary readings, etc., can also be mentioned. Unquestionably, however, the pioneering and most important role was enacted by yet another form of activity —the independent publishing movement.

This last phenomenon is peculiar to Poland and actually has no counterpart outside of Poland. It will suffice to become aware of several basic facts to realize the importance of the turning point which was brought about by the inception of the independent publishing movement. In countries such as Poland, government censorship exerts a rigorous and severe control over all forms of publication. Concurrently, all attempts at bypassing the censorship are immediately punishable by diverse forms of repression, from the informal (various types of petty annoyances) to legal proceedings (fines, jailings, and the like). In countries of this sort, the phenomenon of "samizdat" can —and as a rule does—appear. It must pay a double price for its existence, however. In the first place, anxiety in the face of repressions forces the publishers, and frequently the authors, to conceal their names. In the second place, the necessity of a conspiracy precludes the utilization of a more complicated technical support system (the basic "means of production" of a typical samizdat publishing house is an ordinary typewriter), which, in turn, results in minimal output and difficulties with circulation. In other words, the typical samizdat which has been in existence for years, as, for example, in the USSR or in Czechoslovakia, has—in spite of its heroic character and inestimable role—several fundamental shortcomings. While giving authors the opportunity to freely express themselves, it is not in a position to ensure them participation in normal political, scholarly, or literary life and enable them to reach a wider public.

In Poland individual examples of this type of samizdat existed before 1976, but their social role was insignificant. The turning point, which was achieved in the years 1976-77, was made possible in equal part by the farsighted and bold initiative of a certain small group of people, as well as by several particular historical coincidences. To the latter category, above all, belonged two facts. In the mid-seventies, government censorship pressures became, to put it briefly, so overpowering, that they surpassed the tolerance threshold of many authors. The unusually narrow framework delimited by the censors' decisions, which practically eliminated any bolder thought, was unable to contain the creative output of numerous authors, journalists, and scholars. In addition, beginning in 1976, many authors were included in a complete publication ban by way of reprisal for their political views of one sort or another. In this manner, to use a Marxist slogan, quantity, at a certain point, turned into quality: all of a sudden there were so many writers who either could not reconcile themselves to the censorship, or were banned by the censors, that there appeared a demand, on their part, for a form of publishing activity oriented more towards mass production and at the same time, more overt than samizdat.

The second historical circumstance alluded to earlier, coincided with this demand. The year 1976 was the birth date of an organized democratic opposition in Poland. I have in mind here, above all, the first historical attempt at the creation of a link between specific social strata, particularly between workers and intellectuals, as witnessed by the formation of the Workers' Defense Committee (KOR—*Komitet Obrony Robotników*). KOR's example proved to be infectious. In a short period of time, a whole series of other groups and social enterprises arose, linked not only by slogans relating to the battle for democracy and human rights, but also by the basic tenet of their activity: overtness. KOR and other similar organizations were based on the premise that their activity was legal in the light of both national law, as embodied, first and foremost, in the Constitution, as well as regarding those international agreements signed by the Polish People's Republic (above all, the Human Rights Accords). This being so, conspiratorial activity became needless and harmful. Openness was not merely the natural consequence of legalities, but it was also the best defense against accusations of anti-state or subversive goals. All this seems obvious. One must, however, keep in mind that in countries such as Poland, the authorities are rather unconcerned with constitutions or legal codes and with all due ruthlessness persecute even the most legal independent enterprises. The rise of KOR and other related groups, therefore, entailed considerable risk. The fact that they were able to survive can only be explained by the rapidity of the movement's growth. In a short period of time it became too all-encompassing to be stifled by arrests and repressions (circumstances of an international character also played a certain role here: Poland's growing debts forced its leaders to avoid any notorious actions that could endanger their relations with the West.) In addition, the development of the movement was made possible thanks to the fact that from the very beginning the democratic opposition was conscious of the colossal importance of information—authentic and detailed information about events within the country and its own activities. It is not coincidental that the rise of KOR concurred with the birth of the first uncensored periodical, the "Informational Bulletin" (*Biuletyn Informacyjny*) and that from the first days of its existence, KOR published communiqués about current political events and about its own actions. At first, these publications had a limited reach. However, in 1977 a fundamental transition occurred in both quantity and quality with the implementation of better technology (screenprinting machines and xeroxes in the place of typewriters) and the training of a semi-professional cadre of printers—mostly young intellectuals and students.

From that time on, one could talk about a situation that was genuinely without precedent. For the first time in the history of the Eastern bloc, three different factors were combined. First, there appeared a circle of authors interested in the possibilities of publishing outside of the censorship. In the second place, a publishing movement arose which offered such possibilities. And finally, there arose an audience of readers who both participated in and sympathized with the opposition movement and who were eager to take advantage of the results of such publishing activity.

At this point, however, one must go back in time and note that this combination of factors had its roots in a longstanding Polish tradition of protest against the institution of government censorship. Already at the time of the partitions, during a period of lost sovereignty lasting over 120 years, Polish political thought and literature were forced to struggle against the limitations of a censorship imposed by the three invading countries. This censorship was particularly severe in the part annexed by Russia. The situation underwent a radical change for the better in 1918, after Poland regained independence, even though in the thirties, efforts to introduce an informal preventive censorship grew in strength (never legalized, however, by any law.) In 1944, together with the imposition of a Communist regime, a rigorous preventive government censorship was introduced into Polish life. Censorship, as an institution, became legalized by decree in 1946 and remained virtually unchanged and binding up to 1980. The whole postwar period could be described as a dramatic history of the suppression of culture by the censorship. At the same time, mutual relations between cultural life and the censorship were dependent upon the evolution of the general political situation. For example, the control of censorship became weakened in an obvious manner during the successive political "thaws" (the period lasting several years following the events of October, 1956 and the even shorter period following December, 1970). On the other hand, the so-called Stalinist period (1946-53) and the latter part of the "Gierek epoch" (1976-80) were synonymous with the strongest censorship. The so-called "Black Book of Censorship of the Polish People's Republic," containing secret documents brought out of the country in 1977 by one of the professional censors, and brought to light by KOR, revealed that in the second half of the seventies the activities of the censorship took on appalling and simultaneously grotesque dimensions. In this period, not only all possible publications (including, for example, printed wedding invitations or rubber stamps) underwent preventive censorship, but also various other forms of unofficial and supplementary censorship appeared. Editors of magazines and publishing houses, for example, were required to evaluate texts from the point of view of their political "correctness." The effect of all this was a dreadfully sterile and lackluster "propaganda of success" which in those years completely supplanted not only social criticism, but also all objective information about the actual state of the country.

Already in preceding years, such a state of affairs had evoked the frequent protests of intellectuals (for example, the famous "Letter of the Thirty-Four" in 1964); however, these protests proved to be isolated, weak and ineffectual. Only the above-mentioned combination of factors led to a situation in which it became possible to oppose the censorship with the sole truly effective solution: a publishing movement that was completely independent of the censorship, as well as overt and (at least theoretically) legal.

This movement obviously did not at once take on the mass character it has today. As I have already mentioned, its beginnings did not differ significantly from the traditional forms of samizdat. The first communiqués of KOR, for example, and the first issues of the "Informational Bulletin" were simply copied by typewriter and passed around from hand to hand. Each reader was obligated to "multiply" his copy or simply to rewrite it and pass it on to the next reader. This primitive method undoubtedly had one virtue — it developed a feeling of participation and cohesiveness in its readers and created an audience of readers who were at the same time co-workers in the publishing effort.

A real breakthrough was achieved in 1977, when the first real uncensored publishing house arose: the Independent Publishing House (*Niezależna Oficyna Wydawnicza* — NOWa). According to the founder of NOWa and its director of many years, Mirosław Chojecki, "The founders of NOWa . . . had a vision of a quasi-normal publishing house, related to the market and with a regular output of books and periodicals with a circulation running into thousands of copies, but in contrast to official publishing houses they lacked not only the necessary infrastructure (printing, storage, bookshops, etc.), but also the very means of printing." This obviously was a very basic lack. One must remember that in a country such as the Polish People's Republic, access to the simplest screenprinting or xerox machine is made immensely difficult. An ordinary individual, to all intents and purposes, cannot own these machines and their use at a place of employment requires special permission, including control over the texts of the duplicated materials, and so one. This, at least, was the situation preceding August, 1980. In light of this situation only two possibilities existed: either to construct simple homemade screenprinting machines or to import them from abroad. The first method had the merit of being cheap (possible confiscation of the equipment, therefore, would not entail serious losses). The printed matter produced by this method was, however, of second-rate quality, as well as limited yield. That is why increasingly the technical base of the independent publishing houses (in a short period of time, following the example of NOWa, more have arisen) has been brought from abroad, bought with funds provided by Western sympathizers. It need not be added that the importation of such equipment poses considerable problems due to customs checks, but even this difficulty can be surmounted. From a technical point of view, the output of contemporary independent publishing houses is developing ever more efficiently and their editions do not differ much from the official editions (also in terms of the number of printed copies); moreover, the type quality is often impressive.

During the initial years, however, there were enormous difficulties which did not concern mere typographical problems. Equally problematic was the acquisition of various materials indispensable for production—paper, cardboard for covers, metal staples—since purchasing large quantities in stores aroused immediate suspicions. Certain products, as, for instance, printing ink, are anyway, as a rule, completely unavailable in Polish stores, and, again, they had to be homemade or else smuggled from abroad. The personal safety of the printers constituted another problem since they were subject to (in spite of the complete legality of their work) searches, confiscation of their equipment and paper, and arrest by the police. This was the sole sphere of activity in which the opposition movement had to work under conspiratorial conditions. In the case of the printers, apart from the risk of "normal" repressions, the risk of losing priceless equipment also came into play. Therefore, printers worked under conditions almost reminiscent of the Nazi occupation. Locked away in private apartments or basements, they did not exit at times for several days and nights, and the need for frequent changes of locale required skill in the swift transport of the whole set-up from one place to another. Distribution problems were similar in many respects and led to the creation of a whole complicated network of mutual contacts. Distributors of NOWa and other publishing houses travelled all over the country, delivering copies of periodicals and books to previously appointed places. The principle behind the relative openness of their activity (that is, so that a public craving reading matter could be reached and at the same time the police could be kept off their trail) also required an equally high degree of skill in throwing off police pursuit. This was not always successful. Actually the distribution stage was the point at which the secret police most frequently hit upon the trail of the independent publishing houses. Apart from various repressions, this ended in the painful confiscation of copies produced with such labor.

From today's point of view, it may seem that the activity of NOWa and other independent publishing houses developed under astounding conditions of freedom—for a totalitarian state—as compared with the conditions under which, for instance, the publishing house Petlice in Czechoslovakia or other forms of samizdat operate in the Eastern bloc. Let us not forget, however, that this freedom was only relative (whenever the police had an opportunity to make use of repressions it exercised that right). In the second place, it was a hard-won freedom. The use of repression by the authorities was maximally hindered every step of the way, for example, by organizing immediate social protests, whenever some form of police coercion was used. As in the case of the whole democratic opposition movement, the independent publishing houses survived the worst period thanks to a complicated combination of favorable circumstances, among which growing social support, as well as Poland's international position due to its economic straits, played the most important role.

All of this led the publishing houses to produce genuinely impressive results. Taking a look at the output of NOWa, one must remember that at the present time it is only one of about nine other publishing houses of a similar type. In the course of the four years of its existence, NOWa has undergone a noticeable evolution. In the beginning, to quote Mirosław Chojecki again, the publishing house aimed to function primarily "as a sort of rescue service for Polish culture," filling in the gaps that existed in general information, literature, and social sciences due to the interference of the government censorship. It soon became apparent that this program had to be broadened. A well-known example is the first uncensored literary journal *Zapis* (*The Record*). According to the original plans of the editorial staff, *Zapis* was to be a periodical in which writers would be able to publish works of theirs that had been modified or banned by the censorship. When the first issue appeared, however, many authors who did not in fact have concrete problems with the censors, but who simply wanted to publish in a journal in which, as a rule, such problems would not be encountered, applied to the editorial staff. In this manner, the second issue of *Zapis* included quite a lot of material that had been written specifically for the journal, and successive issues evolved more and more clearly towards a model of a "normal" literary periodical, differing from others only by the fact that it was published outside of the scope of the censorship.

Similarly, the complete activity of NOWa and other publishing houses depends not only upon "filling in the gaps" caused by the censorship, but also in creating new cultural values. Let us take note that NOWa by itself has by now published over 150 books, among them the already classic, although continually banned, works of Stefan Żeromski, Kazimierz Wierzyński, and Witold Gombrowicz. Only NOWa among all the other publishing enterprises released several books by Czesław Miłosz before 1980, against the background of official silence in Poland surrounding his work, before he was awarded the Nobel Prize. Leading comtemporary prose writers, poets, and critics have published in NOWa. The publishing house has also printed the books of foreign authors banned in the Polish People's Republic (among others, those of Solzhenitsyn, Mandel'shtam, Orwell, Hrabal, Joseph Brodsky, and Günther Grass), as well as collections of historical documents, scholarly books (a separate series of brochures compiled by the Society of Scholarly Courses), appeals and leaflets, and, finally, periodicals, which, in fact, began the tradition of the independent publishing movement. At least forty periodicals appeared before 1980, published both by NOWa and other publishing houses. Today, the number of titles is difficult to establish, although with all certainty, it is several times greater. The "Informational Bulletin", which does not exist anymore, belongs to the oldest and most meritorious periodicals. Others include the literary quarterlies *Zapis* (*The Record*) and *Puls* (*Pulse*), the political periodicals *Krytyka* (*Criticism*) and *Opinia* (*Opinion*); the periodical of young Catholics, *Spotkania* (*Meetings*); the political cultural quarterly, *Res Publica*; the agricultural publication, *Placówka* (*Outpost*); and one of the oldest periodicals, *Robotnik* (*Worker*), which played a fundamental role in what I earlier termed the "unofficial education of society". *Robotnik*, which addressed itself to the workers and was co-edited by them, propagated the ideas which achieved expression in the historical "Twenty-one Postulates" announced in August by the striking workers in the Gdansk shipyards.

The mention of August leads us into the latest phase of activity of the independent publishing movement, which differs quite significantly from that of the preceding years. One of the most important postulates set forth in August by the striking workers was the demand for a normalization and limitation of legal censorship. Many months of struggle between the newly-formed Solidarity and the authorities, unusually stubborn in this case, led to a new law regarding censorship that has recently been ratified by the Sejm (Diet). Polish society pinned great hopes on this law, and it must be said at once that it did not fulfill expectations. Alongside a series of points which are undoubtedly a step forward in comparison with the previous state of affairs (for example, the possibility of petitioning a decision of the censorship in court, the permission to mark deleted passages in a published censored text, and so on), one comes across formulations that without question constitute a step backwards. The ambiguous wording permitting the authorities to take punitive sanctions against individuals not in conformance with the censorship, and consequently against independent publishing houses, belongs to the latter category. These types of threats can not obviously frighten anyone today. Since the birth of Solidarity, the activity of the independent publishing houses has been growing at a doubled rate. All attempts at repression against independent printers or publishers have been met with an immediate and effective answer in the form of strikes or the threat of strikes. Moreover, the books and periodicals of NOWa and other publishing houses are reaching (thanks to, among other things, a network of libraries set up by local chapters of Solidarity) incomparably broader circles of readers than before August. Solidarity itself has become the most influential of all independent publishers, since under its sponsorship and editorship a multitude of uncensored newspapers, bulletins and brochures is appearing. In summation, as a result of independent publishing, large-scale segments of society have become conscious of the primary importance of a free flow of information and the circulation of cultural values, and in case of need, they will, by all possible means at their disposal, defend these achievements. It is common knowlege that the good will of those in command cannot be depended upon. Neither can one count on any sort of "thaw" sanctioned from above. As long as the present political system continues to exist in Poland, censorship will continue to safeguard this system. And as long as censorship continues to exist, so will the need to fill in gaps in the social consciousness, in national culture, or at the very least, in basic, current information. Irrespective of far-reaching plans which recently have begun to appear, publishing houses acting beyond the reach of the censorship seem, at present, to be the sole possibility for fulfilling this need.

Afterword

Several days after this article was completed, there came the news from Poland of the institution of martial law and of a government takeover by a military regime. Soon this news was augmented by additional information that brutal repressions and police terror were being used not only against striking workers, but also against representatives from the fields of culture, science and communications.

The words "It is common knowledge that the good will of those in command cannot be depended upon. . . " have been unexpectedly and startlingly confirmed.

But conclusions regarding society's stand are also being confirmed. General Jaruzelski's regime is striving to stifle completely all forms of information beyond the most strictly official, to say nothing of other forms of terror. In spite of this, in spite of the fact that under a state of martial law, uncensored publishing activity is subject to Draconian penalities, we hear of bulletins, appeals, and leaflets appearing. It can be foreseen that for the near future, activity of this sort will be forced to operate under conditions of absolute conspiracy and will be severely weakened in a quantitative sense. One can, however, be equally certain that even under these extremely difficult conditions, society will not abandon its chief weapon—the free word and authentic information. In a situation where all "social contracts" —including those concerning the limitation of the censorship—were crushed in the course of one night by tank treads, the role of publishing houses outside the censorship will, with all certainty, be even greater than heretofore.

Translated by Anna Peć

SAMIZDAT
A RETURN TO THE PRE-GUTENBERG ERA?

H. Gordon Skilling
University of Toronto

On 22 December 1848 Dostoevsky was sentenced to death for having associated with a circle which met to talk of socialism and to criticize conditions in Russia, for having circulated a letter by the journalist Belinsky to Gogol which was extremely critical of the Orthodox Church, and for having attempted to circulate anti-Government writings with the aid of a private press. Although the sentence was in fact "only" eight years of penal servitude, this was concealed from the prisoners until the time of their "execution"; it was later commuted to four years in jail, and four more as a private soldier. Dostoevsky served his full sentence and dropped out of Russian literature for some nine years.[1]

This may be considered an early example in Russian history of what we would now call "samizdat," the distribution of uncensored writings on one's own, without the medium of a publishing house and without permission of the authorities. Although this is not an entirely new phenomenon, and in varied forms has been the very stuff of revolutionary movements throughout history, in its modern form of samizdat it is a new medium of communication, emerging on a large scale in Soviet Russia in the mid-sixties, and in Poland, Czechoslovakia, China and other communist countries in the mid-seventies.

The action of Dostoevsky in circulating illegally a private letter and anti-Government writings was not the first such case in Russian history. As far back as 1790 a famous anti-serfdom book by Aleksandr Radishchev, *A Journey from Petersburg to Moscow*, after being confiscated by the police, was passed around, in the few remaining copies and in manuscript form, among educated circles—"an eighteenth-century example of *samizdat*," writes the historian Isabel de Madariaga.[2] Before and after the Decembrist Revolt in 1825, Pushkin and Griboedov circulated manuscripts privately to avoid the censor. Aleksandr Herzen's journal *Kolokol* (The Bell) was printed in London and copies were smuggled back into Russia. During later decades of the nineteenth century, many unpublished manifestoes and tracts, usually produced on illegal printing presses or abroad, were distributed in Russia, although this was strictly circumscribed and severely punished by the police. Lenin's Bolshevik party and other revolutionary movements depended on such underground publications to propagate their views and to advance the cause of revolution.[3]

This phenomenon did not disappear under communist rule. During the early twenties the typewritten works of Osip Mandelshtam and other writers were passed around in what was then called "Underwood" after the typewriter used. Mandelshtam was in fact arrested and eventually died in prison, his crime having been to write an anti-Stalin poem which circulated only by word of mouth and in a few manuscript copies.[4] The author Marina Tsvetaeva recalled that in the 1920's: "I copy out poems sewn together in notebooks and sell them. We call this 'overcoming Gutenberg.' "[5] She also spoke of memorizing her own work or that of others for eventual publication. During the years of Stalinst terror, small groups of intellectuals passed around typed literature which was forbidden or "was not publishable."[6] At this time, however, most literary works which could not be published were written "for the desk drawer" (*v yashchik*), to use a phrase which had long been used in Russia.[7] In fact, however, such manuscripts had to be hidden in the safest possible place, somewhere far more secure than an ordinary drawer. Solzhenitsyn, for instance, reported the difficulties facing an "underground writer," including the constant effort to conceal the very existence of his writings and to hide the actual manuscripts. He also wrote of memorizing his writings while imprisoned in a labor camp, where he committed many thousands of words to memory in the hope of eventually recording and even publishing them.[8] It was only after Stalin's death that manuscripts began to pass from hand to hand and were copied, without permission of the author, by editors and by others anxious to read them. In the late fifties and early sixties this became increasingly the pattern of distribution of unpublished manuscripts, and several typewritten magazines, notably *Syntax, Phoenix and the Sphinxes*, were issued and disseminated surreptitiously.[9] These were but "timid shoots" of what later became the massive production of samizdat as "a self-contained and singularly original sphere for the realization of society's spiritual and intellectual life."[10]

The Meaning of Samizdat

The term samizdat is said to have emerged in the late fifties, when a Moscow poet described the bound, typewritten publication of his poems as "Samsebyaizdat," i.e., "publishing house for oneself."[11] This was derived by analogy from the acronyms used for official publishing houses, such as Gosizdat (State Publishing House), Politizdat, Voenizdat or Gosmedizdat (publishing houses for politics, military affairs, and medical writings). The same poet coined the term samizdat with the same meaning. It was the latter word which came into general usage to refer to unofficial publications of all kinds (not limited to those by an author himself) and to the entire process of unofficial publication.[12] There is no English equivalent other than the awkward "self-publication." In French and German the Russian word is normally used, although there are the alternatives *auto-édition* and *Selbst-verlag*.[13] Samizdat is a nonword in the official Soviet vocabulary (except for the occasional scornful reference to "so-called samizdat" in Russian newspapers[14]) and does not appear in Soviet dictionaries.

For the sake of completeness in this etymological interlude, one might mention other Russian acronyms, none of which is officially recognized in Soviet dictionaries or reference books. Although at first most items of samizdat appeared separately, on an individual basis, and many still do, the practice of publishing a number of them together in a typewritten journal or book later developed and was soon nicknamed "kolizdat," i.e., publication in quantity.[15] Another term, "radizdat," refers to books and other materials, as well as music, which are broadcast by foreign radio and copied by listeners. Two other terms, "magnitizdat" or "magnizdat," are used to cover materials, especially music and verse, reproduced by tape recorder, either from foreign broadcasts or from reading and playing at home.[16] Finally, the word "tamizdat" was coined to denote books published "over there," i.e., abroad, which often find their way back to Russia in printed form or are reproduced in samizdat form.

A turning point in the development of samizdat was the decision of Boris Pasternak in 1958 to publish his book *Doctor Zhivago* abroad after he had failed to get it published at home through official channels.[17] Other authors had entertained some hope after the death of Stalin that their work would be published officially at home, for instance, in the magazine *Novy mir*, edited by Aleksandr Tvardovsky. Some, including Solzhenitsyn, had succeeded to a limited extent, although always after great difficulty and with substantial emendation at the editors' request. As long as this hope existed, publication in samizdat or abroad was avoided lest it jeopardize the chance of publication at home. After the fall of Khrushchev, however, when the chances of domestic publication declined, the only alternative seemed to be samizdat or tamizdat.[18]

The term samizdat therefore does not have a precise and unambiguous meaning, having gradually extended from its original meaning of an author's publication of his own works to encompass unofficial dissemination not only of any books in typewritten form within Russia, but also copies (typewritten or printed) of books published abroad by émigrés or by Russians still living in Russia.[19] It could also include books written in an earlier period, which were either not published at the time or were later banned under Stalin, or even foreign literature which could not be translated and officially published in the USSR. Samizdat has been defined succinctly as "typewritten copies, transferred by hand,"[20] or more fully, as "unapproved material reproduced unofficially ... by hand, typewriter, mimeograph or occasionally by Xerography."[21]

Development of Russian Samizdat

The evolving content of Russian samizdat has been fully analyzed by the Russian emigre and former samizdat author Michael Meerson-Aksenov. [22] The first phase, already referred to, was mainly literary in character, beginning with Boris Pasternak's *Zhivago*, and comprising eventually books by Solzhenitsyn, A. Sinyavsky, and Juri Daniel (who wrote abroad under the pseudonyms Abram Tertz and Nicholai Arzhak); the memoirs of N. Mandelshtam; the novels of V. Maksimov; earlier works which had never been published in Russia by M. Bulgakov, O. Mandelshtam, and A. Akhmatova; and contemporary poets such as Josef Brodsky, Bulat Okudzhava, and others. As another émigré wrote, there could be no doubt that "the real 'specific gravity' of Russian literature was now to be found jointly in samizdat and tamizdat." [23]

This "literary samizdat," which was in a sense removed from politics, was followed and supplemented by a second phase of "social samizdat," which was more political in content and consisted of letters, appeals, declarations, etc. This began to "fulfill the function not only of a book but of a newspaper," especially with the publication of *The Chronicle of Current Events* from 1968 on. This bulletin, which appeared every two weeks or so, became the main organ of the human rights movement in the Soviet Union and reported on violations of human rights, house searches, arrests, trials, and imprisonments. The documents included were almost always signed, with addresses given, and represented therefore, it was said, "the greatest internal freedom, a complete independence, not only from government, but from various groups which ... determine limits of press accessibility in the West." [24] Although interrupted by severe repression for a year and a half, the *Chronicle* reappeared in 1972 and came out so regularly that it was published abroad in English translation and could be ordered on subscription. It was joined by other bulletins with national and religious emphasis, notably the Ukrainian Herald (*Ukrainsky Visnyk*), [25] the Zionist Herald of Exodus, the Chronicle of the Lithuanian Catholic Church, and the Herald of the Evangelical Christian Baptists.

Finally there emerged a third phase of samizdat in which varied social programs and expositions of independent social and political thought appeared in Meerson-Aksenov's words as "the foundation of a growing independent consciousness in the intelligentsia and as an emancipation from party-government ideology." [26] Outstanding examples were the legal writings of A. Sakharov, V. Chalidze, and I. Shafarevich, the political works of Solzhenitsyn, and the historical studies of Roy Medvedev.

It could be said that by 1967 samizdat had started to become "the mainstream of independent thought and opinion, of free uncensored Russian literature." As the writer Georgii Vladimov wrote to the Writers Union in that year, "Creative freedom ... is being realized ... in the activity of the so-called samizdat." He went on: "There are now two kinds of art in the country. One is free and uninhibited . . . whose distribution and influence depends only on its genuinely artistic qualities. And the other one, commanded and paid for . . , is badly mutilated, suppressed, and oppressed. It is not hard to predict which of these two arts will be victorious." [27]

In 1974 Aleksandr Sinyavsky, in exile, wrote of "a literature which had not long ago appeared in our country . . . modestly and simply called samizdat . . . the second literature." "It is difficult to think of a more precise and inoffensive name than samizdat, which says only that a man has sat down to write everything he wants, as he sees fit . . . We are already witnessing the planning of something great, fantastic, and incomparable: the beginnings of Russian literature, which once before in the nineteenth century enriched mankind. Now once again it is going through its birth pangs." [28]

A more detailed analysis of the content of samizdat, together with the texts of important items, can be found in several places. F.J.M. Feldbrugge, in a book of over 250 pages, makes a thematic analysis of samizdat as a form of "political dissent" or "opposition." [29] Meerson-Aksenov and Shragin, in a volume of more than 600 pages, give the texts of important items of political, social, and religious thought in Russian samizdat.[30]

The rise of samizdat can also be roughly measured in terms of the quantitative growth of the material known in the West. According to estimates given by Feldbrugge, the various types of dissent documents began with a modest forty-seven items in 1965, doubled in number in 1966, and doubled again in 1968, when it reached 220 items. It remained at that level until 1974, when it jumped to 362 items. The total over the first decade (1965–1974) was about 2,000. [31] It might be added that a complete archive of Russian samizdat (*Arkhiv Samizdata*) is located at Radio Liberty in Munich, and has been published under the title *Sobranie Dokumentov Samizdata* (Collected Samizdat Documents) (Munich, 1972–). [32]

The Samizdat Process

The process of producing samizdat has often been described and need not be repeated here in detail. [33] The basic requirements are simple enough—a typewriter, thin paper, and carbon paper, together, of course, with an author anxious to express his thoughts freely, without censorship, and willing to run the risk of putting them in writing. After this initial step the author types, or has typed, a number of copies, probably no more than five to fifteen, on onion-skin paper. The last copies are often almost illegible. The copying is usually done in single space and covers the entire page, with almost no marigns and little space at the bottom, and often on both sides of the page. The typists are usually volunteers, or are paid for the work involved. Copies are given to those who supplied the item in the first place and are passed on to others who may make copies on their own. Since the original author soon loses touch with the process, as in a chain letter in the West, it is impossible to know how many copies are eventually made; they may amount to several hundreds, or even a thousand or more. Occasionally photographic methods are used for reproduction, thus speeding it up, and eliminating variations and inaccuracies. Other methods such as hectograph or mimeograph (sometimes on homemade machines), are rarely used in the Soviet Union, and still less frequently the printing press.

Dissemination of samizdat is equally difficult and fraught with danger. Most samizdat documents are signed by the author, with his address, although some are written pseudonymously. Sometimes, for instance in the case of novels or collections of essays or poems or periodicals, the material is bound, but it is often disseminated unbound, which has the advantage that a group of people can read them together, passing each page around separately. The copies are usually distributed by hand, not by mail, and are sent abroad through foreign correspondents, foreign embassies, travelers, or by more conspiratorial means. The process of diffusion is as spontaneous as the initial production, and has a number of disadvantages, such as the irregularity of the process, the difficulty of getting hold of specific items, lack of contact with readers, and hence an absence of follow-up and criticism. Moreover, since the materials are liable to confiscation by the police, there are problems of safe-keeping and storage. A pseudonymous writer, S. Topolev, outlined some of these disadvantages in 1971 and urged a transition to kolizdat, i.e., the publication of journals which would have the advantages of greater regularity of appearance, wider opportunity for contact with readers and the exchange of opinions, and more assurance of accessibility to back numbers. Moreover, the costs would be covered through a kind of subscription. Kolizdat had its own problems, however, such as getting the journal started, raising the initial funds, distributing a bulkier product, and if mimeographing or other machines were used, the problem of securing (or making) them and concealing them.[34]

Returning to Gutenberg

It has sometimes been suggested that samizdat in the Soviet Union and other communist countries represents a return to the period prior to the invention of printing—a kind of pre-Gutenberg process of communication.[35] Certainly the medieval scholar, like the samizdat author, was his own polygrapher, editor, and publisher of the author he read or of his own work.[36] The samizdat copiers, too, resemble the medieval scribes, whether he was a monk in a monastery or a paid copier in a lay stationery store.[37] The number of copies is strictly limited in both cases, although samizdat is perhaps more limited than the manuscript or even printed works (*incunabula*) in the first decades after Gutenberg. McLuhan writes of a handwritten book by Pliny which circulated in 1,000 copies in the second century A.D. and argues that few *incunabula* before 1500 had such a large circulation.[38] A medieval historian, Eisenstein, while casting some doubts on McLuhan's estimates of the number of manuscripts, agreed that the number both of manuscripts and of *incunabula* was relatively small. She estimated that the average production of a printed book between the years 1450 and 1500 was between 200 and 1,000 — a figure almost precisely equivalent to the estimates of the average samizdat product today.[39]

Although the analogy between samizdat and the pre-Gutenberg manuscript is tempting, it should not be pressed too far. In a sense the typewriter is a form of printing, and not to be identified, or even compared, to the handwritten process of "scribal culture." Like printing, the typewriter can reproduce a number of copies simultaneously, far more than the medieval scribe could by hand, although fewer than the developed printing press. With the more recent development of electronic forms of typesetting, printing has in fact come more than ever to resemble the typewriter. In other words printing and typing may be conceived of as merely two kinds of reproduction in printed form, not essentially different from each other. The process of samizdat therefore is not a reversion to the pre-Gutenberg manuscript, a reversal of the revolution wrought by the invention of movable type, but more simply, a reversion to a less efficient form of printing.

It is none the less paradoxical that five hundred years after the invention of printing and at the beginning of the electronic revolution, samizdat writers have had to go back to less advanced methods of reproduction. This transformation in the media of communication has been due not to technological factors — the result of a new technology or the decline of an old, but to political factors: the attempt in totalitarian and authoritarian countries (communist and others) to control the written and spoken word by state and party management of publishing and by means of censorship. The only way to "publish" a freely written and uncensored work is by samizdat, usually in typewritten form. Only if samizdat were to utilize Xerox methods of reproduction (as to some degree has occurred in Poland) would this represent, although on a small scale, a kind of "miracle" equivalent to Gutenberg's invention.[40]

Samizdat in Other Lands

Although samizdat is Russian in origin and in name, a similar phenomenon manifested itself in other communist countries, particularly in Czechoslovakia, Poland, and China. The Czechs, Poles, and Chinese had no doubt heard of Soviet samizdat through Western radio and other Western sources of information and were to some degree following the Soviet example. In large part, however, this was, in each country, a spontaneous development evoked by the same restrictions of censorship and state control, and expressing the same desire for freedom of expression. The means of reproduction used are similar, primarily the typewriter and carbon copies, although in Poland other methods such as mimeographing and even Xerox and photography have been employed, and in China the printed leaflet or booklet has been supplemented by the unique medium of the wall poster. Uncensored material in each country had, too, its own distinctive origins and special features and should therefore be examined separately.

Samizdat Czech Style

"If the Russians invented samizdat," wrote Pavel Tigrid, Czech émigré publicist and editor, "it is undoubtedly the Czechs who perfected the system and made it an art."[41] Tigrid had in mind the book series *Petlice* (Padlock) which began to produce typewritten, bound books in 1973 under the general editorship of the novelist Ludvík Vaculík, and had issued some two hundred volumes by 1980. These included novels, short stories, poetry, plays, literary criticism, historical and philosophical essays, and more rarely, political essays or studies. Strictly speaking, these books were not regarded as samizdat since the author signed each of the few copies personally for distribution to friends and expressly forbade on the title page further duplication. The volumes were prepared by typists, who were usually compensated for their work and produced several carbon copies, most of which were quite legible. The books were professionally bound, sometimes simply in cardboard covers, but occasionally with more elaborate linen covers and with illustrations and photographs, and are often genuinely handsome in appearance. The readership has been variously estimated at several hundred or even several thousand, but it cannot be accurately measured due to unofficial copying and unknown circulation. The authors were the cream of the Czech literary profession—including many outstanding authors who were unable to publish in the normal way, as well as some younger writers who chose to be published, without censorship, in a series such as this.[42]

Other book series began to appear in the late seventies, for example *Expedice* (Despatch) under the general editorship of the playwright Václav Havel, who signed each volume himself and assumed the responsibility of selecting books for inclusion. It may be roughly estimated that some four hundred to five hundred samizdat books appeared during the decade in these and other series. There can be little doubt that this "second" or underground literature was of much higher quality than the output of the official publishing houses, and many individual works were published abroad in Czech or in foreign languages.[43]

Also noteworthy was the proliferation of feuilletons and of periodicals or journals. The feuilleton, a traditional form of Czech journalism, was initially stimulated by Vaculík, who wrote and encouraged others to write these light, somewhat humorous essays on serious subjects. He was able to publish an entire volume of them each year in *Petlice*, and these were in turn published abroad in German.[44]

Periodicals began to appear in the wake of Charter 77 and soon included journals in the fields of history, economics, foreign affairs, religion, Polish affairs, music, as well as several devoted to philosophy and literature. One of the latter was republished abroad, in printed form, by Index on Censorship in London under the title *Spektrum* and smuggled back into Czechoslovakia.[45]

Charter 77 gave birth to a substantial diffusion of typewritten materials including "authorized" materials signed by the Charter spokesmen, as well as unofficial materials circulated by individuals. The authorized materials included numbered documents—twenty-eight items in the first three years—many of which were systematic studies of violations of human rights in specific spheres, such as freedom of thought, freedom of literary expression, popular music, nuclear plants, the gypsy community, etc. In addition the spokesmen issued dozens of letters and appeals addressed to organs of the Czechoslovak government or to international institutions or personages describing the situation of human rights in the country. In the spring of 1978 a newsbulletin, *Informace o Chartě 77* (Information on Charter 77) began to appear, published by a group of Chartists under the leadership of Petr Uhl. This bulletin, typewritten and from twenty to thirty pages in length, appeared every three weeks or so and was comparable to the *Chronicle of Current Events* in the USSR.[46]

Charter 77 was also a catalyst for a large-scale production of uncensored materials by individuals and groups which is too voluminous to describe. It included, inter alia, letters to the Czechoslovak authorities and to foreign bodies, religious documents (both Catholic and Protestant), historical and political essays as well as documents relating to the purposes and methods of the Charter. The Committee for the Defense of the Unjustly Persecuted (VONS), which was loosely associated with Charter 77 but acted independently, issued regular communiques on individual arrests, trials, and imprisonments, and other forms of persecution. Some 225 of them had been issued by the end of 1980.[47]

This system of unofficial communications constituted "a parallel information system," parallel that is to the official media of communications.[48] This "free journalism," as Vilém Prečan called it, was "born of the will for free expression" and published "everything which the official information monopoly of a totalitarian regime conceals and keeps secret from the citizen, reader, or concerned person, and the publication of which, or accessibility to the public, is prevented and suppressed."[49] This political samizdat, wrote the pseudonymous writer Josef Strach (the name means "fear" in Czech) is "a medium of communication which looks poor and miserable beside the fantastic rotary press and color television, but which in fact is an unusually powerful and indestructible force.... It is written only by someone who has something to say.... When I take it in my hand, I know that is cost someone a good deal to write it—without an honorarium and at no little risk . . . And it cost someone to devote his time and energy to copying it. This is something I cannot say of any newspaper, any journal, or any broadcast." [50]

Petr Pithart, one of these "pre-Gutenberg scribes," as he called them, spoke in similar terms: "When the work is finished it is copied by others, once again in their spare time, and with no assistance from either the mail or the telephone; it is passed on to a few friends and acquaintances, and thus ultimately to hundreds and perhaps even thousands of readers. All of them share the additional worry of being possibly summoned to confess whether they have read it, from whom they received it, and to whom they lent it, who talked them into doing it, and who paid them for doing it, and how much.... Thus, entirely through the dedicated effort and expense of the people addressed, a work is published which cannot possibly lie idle, unwanted and superfluous. Are these circumstances really abnormal, when the extent to which the written words get circulated depends upon nothing more than the urgency of its message, moderated, let us admit, by the author's fear of trouble? How difficult and exhausting it all is!" [51]

Another prolific samizdat author Milan Šimečka (now in prison) has written of these "homemade books": "concealed in attics and in various absurd hiding places, they are passed secretly from hand to hand. Some of them are in safes, secured with ridiculous bits of string and plasticine. Some of them have been paid for dearly, by imprisonment, humiliation, and anxiety. But one thing is certain: whatever the future may bring, it will be those homemade books which will provide a testimony of the time in which we live, for the language which sounds like falling gravel will not interest anyone." [52]

A Polish Version

In Poland it was the formation of the Committee for the Defense of the Workers (KOR) in 1976, its transformation in 1977 into the Committee for Social Self-Defense (KOR), and the founding in the same year of the Movement for the Defense of Human and Civil Rights (ROPCiO) which produced a veritable flood of samizdat materials, more immense than in Czechoslovakia or Soviet Russia. Beginning in September 1976 KOR issued a bulky bi-monthly *Biuletyn Informacyjny*, and also *Kommunikat*, which contained communiqués on cases of persecution. KOR was also responsible for issuing *Robotnik* (The Worker), based on material from worker correspondents, which appeared in offset form in some 40,000 copies and was read by four to five times as many. Other important KOR publications were the *Black Book* on censorship, based on secret official documents and instructions, and *Document on Lawlessness* (April 1978).

The two organizations, Committee for Social Self-Defense and ROPCiO, together with other associations, produced some thirty or more newspapers or periodicals, ranging from one or two sheets to voluminous texts, usually produced in large quantities with the use of mimeographing machines and by more advanced techniques of duplication, including even printing. Among the papers produced by KOR were *Glos* (The Voice) and *Krytyka*; by ROPCiO, *Opinia*, its official organ; *Gospodarz* (The Farmer); *Droga* (The Way); *Gazeta Polska*; and *Bratniak* (a student paper produced in Gdansk). Catholics relied mainly on long-established, legally published newspapers such as *Tygodnik Powszechny*, a weekly, and *Wiez*, a quarterly, both of which were subject to censorship. In addition there was a samizdat journal for young Catholics published in Lublin under the name *Spotkanie* (Encounters).

Polish literary and scholarly publications were not as numerous as the Czech counterparts, nor as handsomely turned out. There were, however, several samizdat publishing houses, notably NOWA in Warsaw, which issued the literary journal *Zapis*. This was republished in printed form in England (a forerunner of *Spektrum* in Czech), and was smuggled back into Poland. Some fifty books had appeared under NOWA auspices by 1980. There were other literary journals such as *Puls* in Lodz, and political journals such as *Res Publica*, *Merkuryusz* (Cracow), *Postep* (Progress), *Indeks* and *Sygnal* (both student papers in Cracow), *Przeglad* (Review) which published Western articles, and *Wiadomosci Naukowé* (Scientific News).[53] In the words of one writer, literature was enriched by a new literary circuit entirely independent of party-state license and the eye of the censor—"a publishing network which attempts to be a conscious, consistent, and permanent alternative to the official, monopolized, and state-controlled circuit of literary publications," and which has among its authors and editors "writers who constitute the forefront of contemporary Polish culture." [54]

The momentous strike movement in Poland in the summer of 1980 and the wave of reform which followed cannot be ascribed only, or even mainly, to the human rights movement and its samizdat publications. The latter, however, helped to create an atmosphere of civic freedom and to prepare the ground for the process of "renewal." Many of those actively involved in samizdat publication became associated as advisers or editors of Solidarity, the free trade union. With the launching of the latter's own organ, *Solidarity Weekly*, and the much freer tone and content of the official newspapers and other media, the need for samizdat was reduced, and some of the uncensored publications no longer appeared. Others continued to perform their special functions in the literary or journalistic spheres, and were able greatly to increase their production and circulation.

Uniquely Chinese Forms

In China after the death of Mao and the fall of the Gang of Four there emerged a democratic movement and an equivalent of Soviet samizdat in the form of many uncensored journals and of the uniquely Chinese form of *datzepao*, which literally means "paper of big letters or bold characters." A *datzepao* is simply a large sheet of cheap paper (or even old newspaper) on which large Chinese characters, more than an inch high, are painted with a brush, and which is then posted in a prominent place, usually on the walls within an institution or on outside walls within a city. It has no fixed format, length, or style, and might consist of slogans, satirical prose, comic strips, cartoons, letters, reports, tables, graphs, or songs, or even long essays. It could also be written on any kind of surface, including floors and sidewalks, or even hung on clotheslines in offices or institutions. Because of its character it is inexpensive and can be produced by anyone.[55]

The origins of the *datzepao* can be traced back to the precommunist era when imperial edicts were posted on city walls. Mao Tse Tung posted his first *datzepao* at age seventeen, and wall newspapers were used in Red Army camps during the years prior to the communist takeover. Once established, the communist regime borrowed and extended the established Soviet institution of the wall newspaper in factory, farm, and institution and used them as a medium of official propaganda but also of limited public criticism of persons and practices. During the period of the Hundred Flowers and the subsequent anti-rightist campaign in 1956–57, and again during the Cultural Revolution in 1966, millions of *datzepao* appeared in major cities throughout China, serving as a massive medium for the diffusion of both official and unofficial views and also as an instrument of factional struggle, as many posters were directed at individuals.[56]

An early dramatic use of *datzepao* as a medium of authentic democratic protest occurred in November 1974 in Canton when a huge series of wall posters, 20,000 Chinese characters long and extending along 100 yards of wall, appeared under the title, "On Socialist Democracy and the Legal System," signed Li-Yi-Zhe. This was a pen name for three authors who were at once arrested.[57] A new wave of democratic expression and protest in the form of wall posters began in 1976 after the suppression of the April 5th demonstration in support of the deceased Zhou Enlai, and crested for a few months after November 1978.[58] This was tolerated, and indeed for a time encouraged by the now dominant Vice-Premier Deng Xiaoping, who saw in it a source of support for his more pragmatic course. The movement was largely spontaneous and led to a spate of *datzepao* throughout China in almost every town and city. In Peking, the Xidan or Democracy Wall on

Changan Avenue in the center of the city became the focal point of this extraordinary outpouring of free expression. On November 27th and 29th thousands of people (not less than 10,000 on the latter day) gathered at Xidan Wall to read posters and to listen to speakers.[59] For several months the Wall remained a center of poster activity and of heated debate and mass meetings. As the Human Rights League stated in January 1979: "Putting up big-character posters in itself is not only legal but glorious. It shows that we are exercising a right to which we are entitled as citizens. It also indicates... that putting up big-character posters is fulfilling a citizen's glorious obligations—such as showing real courage in being concerned over the future of the motherland and the destiny of the nation and over the unhappiness or happiness of the whole body of citizens."[60]

The posters had in fact the endorsement of the Constitution of 1975 which, in Article 13, established the right of citizens to use big-character posters.[61] By March 1979, however, the authorities began to consider it a dangerous phenomenon going beyond the limited purposes envisaged officially and threatening the established order. The authorities in Peking and elsewhere started to crack down on the entire *datzepao* movement, as well as on the uncensored journals, arresting some of the leading figures and imprisoning them for long terms. At the end of the year the Peking authorities issued a decree banning the use of the Xidan Wall entirely and limiting the *datzepao* to a more remote wall, where each one had to receive official permission from a special office. In 1980 the Constitution was amended to remove the right of citizens to issue big-character posters.

Another element of the democratic movement closely connected with the *datzepao* was the uncensored journals which began to appear, often with the same editors. Many organizations were formed to defend civil freedom and to press complaints on the authorities. Although the most visible medium was the wall poster, most of these organizations issued their own publications, sometimes in mimeographed form prepared from handwritten stencils, and in some cases even in printed form.[62] No less than eighty-two organizations and journals have been identified.[63] The journals were often affixed to the Xidan Wall or were sold by vendors in the neighborhood. The *Masses' Reference News*, for instance, was published in 20,000 copies, others in more limited runs. The most militant was *Exploration*, published by Wei Jingsheng, an electrician by trade, who was eventually (29 March 1979) sentenced to fifteen years in prison for his activity. The most broadly based organization was the Chinese Human Rights League, led by a woman, Fu Yuehau, who was also later given a long prison term. More moderate journals were the *Beijing Spring*, published in 10,000 copies, the *April 5th Forum*, *Enlightenment*, and the aforementioned *Reference News*, as well as *Today*, a literary review, and student journals such as *Voice of the People* (Canton). By the end of 1979 most of these journals had been forced to suspend publication, and several of their editors received severe prison sentences.

Significance of Samizdat

Samizdat has emerged in some form or other, and in varying extent, in almost all countries of the communist world and in other countries with authoritarian systems such as Chile and Iran. Only in the countries discussed above, where an organized dissent or human rights movement has come into being, has samizdat assumed substantial dimensions.

In its simplest form it is a means of expressing one's thought and feelings openly and honestly and of communicating these to others of like mind. It offers a way in which the individual can maintain his identity and intellectual integrity and achieve a certain degree of freedom under repressive conditions. No less important, samizdat serves as a vehicle of cultural expression, assuring the continuity of national culture at a time when it is threatened by repression and censorship. Samizdat joins independent activity in other spheres—painting, sculpture, music, and drama—in helping to protect and develop a second or independent culture, and contributes to the preservation and extension of free and unrestrained scholarship. Finally, it serves as a channel for the expression of political dissent and opposition and points a way for a possible transition to a freer and more human society and polity. In addition, samizdat provides an important source of information, at home and abroad, about the real conditions within a country, countering domestic propaganda and misinformation. It thus aids foreign governments, the media abroad, international organizations, and individual scholars and journalists in their efforts to understand and interpret the society concerned.

Needless to say, samizdat has been seen as a dangerous threat to the authoritarian regimes whose control of information and culture are challenged by this competing force and whose very nature has given rise to this challenge and is threatened by it. The ruling powers have used every provision of the criminal code and every means of police harassment to discourage people from writing samizdat and from copying and passing it on, or even from storing it in their dwellings. In spite of intense efforts, however, the state and the ruling party have not been able to stamp out this medium of free expression and at best have made its continuance more difficult and more painful for those who seek to use it. Even in the Soviet Union and Czechoslovakia, where the repression has been most severe, samizdat and the human rights movement have survived. It seems doubtful that the Chinese authorities will do any better. Deng Xiaoping, as late as December 1980, complained in a speech of "counter-revolutionary leaflets," "illegal organizations," and "illegal journals." In Poland, at least, where repression has been less severe and samizdat more widespread, free dissent has helped to create an atmosphere and prepare the ground for a genuine movement for social and political reform. Elsewhere, it may be hoped, it holds the door open for such an eventuality in a more distant future.

NOTES

[1] D.S. Mirsky, *A History of Russian Literature, From its Beginnings to 1900* (New York, 1958), pp. 182-83.

[2] Isabel de Madariaga, *Russia in the Age of Catherine the Great* (London, New Haven, 1981), p. 545.

[3] Gayle Durham Hollander, "Political Communication and Dissent in the Soviet Union," in Rudolf L. Tökès, ed., *Dissent in the USSR: Politics, Ideology and People* (Baltimore, 1975), pp. 263-64. On the dissemination of "secret" works by the young Pushkin and Ryleev, see N. L. Stepanov, in *Ocherki po istorii russkoi zhurnalistiki i kritiki* (Leningrad, 1950), I, p. 194. Other writers refer to the letters of Prince Kurbskii to the Tsar during the reign of Ivan the Terrible, unpublished letters of Chaadayev, and in the 1820's the dissemination among the peasants of a handwritten text of the New Testament in Russian (instead of the usual Chruch Slavonic) (Michael Meerson-Aksenov and Boris Shragin, eds., *The Political, Social, and Religious Thought of Russian 'Samizdat': An Anthology* (Belmont, Mass., 1977), pp. 25, 439. Another example of early "proto-samizdat" is the encyclicals of Patriarch Tikhon which the government printing establishments refused to print (D. Pospielovsky, "From *Gosizdat* to *Samizdat* and *Tamizdat*," *Canadian Slavonic Papers*, XX, no. 1 (March 1978), p. 46.

[4] Cited by Hollander in Tökès, *Dissent*, p. 264, from N. Mandelshtam, *Hope Against Hope*.

[5] This phrase she took apparently from G.K. Zaitsev; see Julius Telesin, "Inside 'Samizdat,'" *Encounter*, Feb. 1973, p. 25.

[6] Meerson-Aksenov, p. 25.

[7] F.J.M. Feldbrugge, *Samizdat and Political Dissent in the Soviet Union* (Leyden, 1975), p. 4.

[8] A. Solzhenitsyn, "The Writer Underground," in *The Oak and the Calf: A Memoir* (New York, 1979-1980), pp. 3, 5.

[9] Hollander, in Tökès, *Dissent*, p. 264.

[10] Meerson-Aksenov, pp. 25-26.

[11] Telesin, p. 25.

[12] Feldbrugge, pp. 3-4.

[13] In Ukrainian *samvydav* is used. There is no Polish or Czech equivalent.

[14] Feldbrugge, p. 4.

[15] For a discussion of kolizdat, see Meerson-Aksenov, pp. 446 *et seq*.

[16] Feldbrugge, p. 4; for a full discussion of musical magnitizdat by Gene Sosin, see Tökès, pp. 276-309.

[17] Pospielovsky, pp. 48, 50; Meerson-Aksenov, pp. 57-58.

[18] For a full discussion, see Solzhenitsyn, "Out of Hiding," *Oak and Calf*, pp. 18 *et seq*. On the relationship of samizdat and tamizdat, see Pospielovsky, pp. 44 passim.

[19] Meerson-Aksenov, pp. 28-29n; Feldbrugge, pp. 3-4; Telesin, p. 26.

[20] Feldbrugge, p. 1.

[21] Pospielovsky, p. 44. The Oxford Russian-English dictionary defines samizdat as "unofficial reproduction of unpublished MSS."

[22] Meerson-Aksenov, Part I, Introductory, pp. 28-30, esp. n. 19.

[23] Pospielovsky, p. 51.

[24] Meerson-Aksenov, pp. 33-34, pp. 228-29. For an analysis of the Chronicle, see Peter Reddaway, ed., *Uncensored Russia: The Human Rights Movement in the Soviet Union* (London, 1972), Introduction and pp. 350-51.

[25] For Ukrainian human rights documents, see *The Human Rights Movement in Ukraine: Documents of the Ukrainian Helsinki Group 1976-1980*, eds. L. Verba and B. Yasen (Baltimore, 1980).

26 Meerson-Aksenov, pp. 35-37.
27 Cited by Pospielovsky, pp. 58-59.
28 Abram Tertz (pseudo.), "Literarnii protses v Rossii" (The Literary Process in Russia), *Kontinent*, I (1974), pp. 154-55, cited in English in Leonid Vladimirov, *Soviet Media and Their Message* (The American Bar Association, 1977), p. 37.
29 Feldbrugge, with a summary of the main themes on pp. 7-10. For similar lists of categories in general, see Tökès, p. 265; Telesin, pp. 26-27.
30 Meerson-Aksenov.
31 Feldbrugge, facing p. 12.
32 Ibid., p. 7.
33 For a full description, see S. Topolev (pseudo.), in Meerson-Aksenov, pp. 489-501; see also Feldbrugge, pp. 15-19; Tökès, pp. 226-68; Telesin, pp. 30-33.
34 Topolev, in Meerson-Aksenov, pp. 496-501.
35 Feldbrugge, p. 18.
36 Marshall McLuhan, *The Gutenberg Galaxy: The Making of Typographical Man* (Toronto, 1962), p. 95.
37 Elizabeth L. Eisenstein, *The Printing Press as an Agent of Change* (Cambridge, 1979), I, pp. 11, 37, 91n.
38 McLuhan, p. 78.
39 Eisenstein, esp. pp. 37, 45.
40 Meerson-Aksenov, p. 40.
41 "Quinientos anos despues de Gutenberg . . . " (typewritten).
42 H. Gordon Skilling, *Charter 77 and Human Rights in Czechoslovakia* (London, 1981), Chap. VI.
43 See Jiří Gruša's interesting discussion of this "unpublishable literature," as he called it, as an integral part of Czech literature as a whole, including that which was published abroad (Gruša, et al., eds., *Stunde namens Hoffnung, Almanach tschechischer Literature 1968–1978* (Lucerne, 1978), pp. 47-56. See also the essay by Jan Lopatka on the "literature of the catacombs," ibid., pp. 300-10.
44 Skilling, Chap. VI.
45 Ibid., Chap. VI.
46 Ibid., Chap. V; in spite of the imprisonment of Uhl in 1979, the bulletin continued to appear under his name and that of his wife.
47 Ibid., Chap. VI.
48 Vilém Prečan, *Kniha Charty* (Book of the Charter) (Cologne, 1977), p. 13.
49 Ibid., p. 10.
50 Typewritten, April 1977, also in *Listy* (Rome), VII, no. 3-4 (July 1977), p. 26.
51 "Onion-skin paper, white, 30 gr/m^2," typewritten, Prague, n.d., published later in Czech in *Spektrum*, no. 1 (Index on Censorship, London, 1978), no. 1.
52 Typewritten, Bratislava, 20 February 1979, published in English under the title, "Home-made Books," *Index on Censorship*, Vol. 8, no. 5 (Sept., Oct. 1979), pp. 24-25.
53 For the above, see special issue on Poland, *Survey*, Vol. 24, no. 4 (109) (Autumn 1979), in particular Lidia Ciolkosz, "The Uncensored Press," pp. 56-57, and passim, pp. 9-10, 18, 37, 46-47, 55. The issue also contains the texts of many items published in these journals. See also the regular summaries of "Poland's Uncensored Publications," *Radio Free Europe, Research Reports*, beginning with 3, no. 16 (Feb. 9-15, 1978), and continuing in subsequent issues in 1978, 1979, and 1980.
54 Stanislaw Baranczak, "The Gag and the Word," *Survey*, special issue on Poland, Vol. 25, no. 11 (110) (Winter 1980), pp. 66-67. Another Polish writer expressed the opinion that the level of this uncensored material was no higher than that of the better "normal" publications, for instance, the Catholic monthlies *Znak* and *Wiez* and that the main responsibility still rested with the majority of writers in the latter (Ryszard Kowalski,

"Polish Literature Today," Ibid., pp. 86-87).

[55] David Jim-tat Poon, "*Tatzepao*: Its History and Significance as a Communication Medium," Chap. 7 in Godwin C. Chu, ed., *Popular Media in China:Shaping New Cultural Patterns*, pp. 184, 187, 201. This chapter gives a full analysis of the role of *datzepao* (modern spelling) in communist China.

[56] Poon, pp. 189ff., 193ff. resp. See also B. Michael Frolic, *Mao's People: Sixteen Portraits of Life in Revolutionary China* (Cambridge, Mass., 1980), p. 169ff.

[57] Roger Garside, *Coming Alive: China after Mao* (London, 1981), p. 102.

[58] James D. Seymour, ed., *The Fifth Modernization: China's Human Rights Movement, 1978-1979* (Stanfordville, N.Y., 1980), esp. the Introduction by Mab Huang and Seymour. The volume contains the texts of many documents of the democratic movement.

[59] Seymour, 12-13. For a vivid personal account of the events at the Xidan Wall, see John Fraser, *The Chinese: Portrait of a People* (Toronto, 1980), Chap. 12. See also Garside, *Coming Alive*, Chap 10.

[60] *U.S. Joint Publications Research Service* (JPRS) 73421, 10 May 1979, p. 66.

[61] Poon, p. 221.

[62] For a survey of these journals, see Seymour, Introduction. Seymour lists thirty organizations and periodicals in an appendix, p. 291. See also Garside, Chaps. 11, 12.

[63] *Freedom Appeals*, no. 9 (March-April 1981), pp. 21-24. This includes seventeen in Beijing and eleven in Shanghai.

This article is based on a paper presented to the Royal Society of Canada at its annual meeting in Halifax, Nova Scotia, June 2, 1981.

CONVERSATION WITH TADEUSZ KONWICKI

A. J. Liehm
University of Pennsylvania

The leading Polish writer and filmmaker Tadeusz Konwicki [Dreambook for Our Time, Penguin Paperbacks] has not published a novel in Poland for many years. He has, however, completed two novels in the last five years, The Polish Complex *and* The Little Apocalypse, *which will be published next year by Farrar, Strauss, and Giroux. Considered too dangerous by the authorities, they are both widely circulated in Poland in copies published by the underground press NOVA. The Little Apocalypse is, to say the least, unusual in its subject matter: a member of the dissident movement is selected by his comrades to set himself on fire on the day of the proclamation of the annexation of Poland by the USSR. But what is even more unusual is the devastatingly ironic picture Konwicki gives not only of those he opposes, not only of Poland in the seventies, but also of the dissident movement and its followers, among whom he himself has been from the outset.*

Visiting with his daughter who lives in New York, Konwicki talked to a Czech writer in exile, A. J. Liehm, before returning to Poland.

A.J.L.: *Your last novel,* The Little Apocalypse, *is soon to be published in the United States, as well as the novel you wrote earlier,* The Polish Complex. *Both of them have been published in Poland only by the unofficial presses.*

T.K.: On the surface, *The Little Apocalypse* appears as a kind of science fiction: it takes place some time in the future. But in reality it is a contemporary realistic novel. I wrote it in 1978 and I assure you that it corresponds to reality even in its smallest details: though perhaps it was not a bridge that had collapsed, but instead a building that had exploded, etc. In my opinion it is simply a realistic novel about a time before an explosion—about a time of pessimism and despair when nobody believed any longer that anything could change.

A.J.L.: *It is obviously a book not easy to accept: its irony does not spare even those who believed in a change and worked for it....*

T.K.: In Poland they always say that one must write to strengthen the heart and spirit. This is of course nonsense. A curse. It is damaging for literature. Stefan Żeromski did not become a world writer for the very reason that he was so tied to the Polish situation of his time. The feeling that one must serve leads directly into provincialism. I refused to submit, I did not wish to write patriotic literature. Literature is the expression of discontent, of indignation. A hole in the whole.

Every unofficial opposition carries within itself a virus of intolerance and totalitarianism, a danger of demoralization. Dostoevsky showed it so well in *The Possessed*. I started having the feeling that the regime influences the opposition directly and negatively. The opposition becomes the image of a regime. One must very carefully choose the weapons to be used against the regime. Our opposition was for a long time isolated and this had a bearing on its morals. But the leitmotiv of my novel can be found already in Wyspiański: a cry against passivity and lethargy.

True, the book glosses over nothing and is altogether non-propagandistic. Its irony has its roots in my attitude toward surrealism. The Polish tradition in this respect is rather weak; we are more inclined toward bathos. And it is exactly this kind of predilection for bathos which leads to the kind of humor so typical for our surrealist poets, Witkiewicz and Gombrowicz. Schulz too, but he was more under the influence of German literature.

I come from Wilno, the capital of Lithuania. Thus I grew up very close to Russian influences and that is why I am so sensitive toward the danger of a Sovietization of Poland. Of a Sovietization of our daily life. At work, people speak kindly of the USSR and of socialism, while at home they do not have enough dirty words for them. A double morality. Russification means for me corruption, fear of the West. It is the superimposition of another civilization, with its messianistic characteristics: the Russian man is just, he will save the corrupt Western world. For centuries Poland has been exposed to a pressure from Russia which deprives it of its individuality. I come from the frontier, and so perhaps I feel this more strongly than others. Miłosz described it beautifully in his *Native Realm*.

A.J.L.: *And* The Polish Complex?

T.K.: When I was writing this book, I still thought that it might be published by an official publishing house. When I wrote *Apocalypse,* I no longer thought of this at all. This is probably why *Complex* is more agreeable and pleasant to read.

We must always keep in mind, and so must our friends, that a Soviet writer has to struggle with his own regime, while a Polish, a Czech or a Hungarian writer has to fight two of them. And as our regime is not an independent one, our own books will sooner or later touch upon certain subjects that will allow them to be labeled 'anti-Russian,' even though there may be nothing anti-Russian about them. This simply results from the fact that socialism, our type of socialism, was imposed on us by force.

Complex takes place in a surreal situation, in a line of people waiting in front of a jewelry shop. Everybody has money, but there is nothing to buy. There are rumors that Soviet rings are being imported. It is Christmas eve, and in this one line everything happens that can happen among Poles today. Within this framework two independent stories are told. They both take place in the year of the Polish uprising of 1863; The hero of the first story after long sufferings joins the uprising and is almost immediately defeated. The hero of the second is the real dictatorial leader of the uprising—Romuald Traugutt—whom we meet on his way from Galicia. He spends a passionate night with his wife and does not yet know (as does the reader) that he will be captured and hanged. And there is also a third kind of a story, an apocryphal letter supposedly written to me by a friend who lives in a country dominated by a brutal dictatorship. Everybody in Poland immediately recognizes of course our own way of surviving. I believe that all these defeats have paved the way to victories, that all these defeated uprisings were necessary, that they strengthened our protest, our feeling that we shall not be defeated.

Complex was printed by the underground presses in approximately 3000 copies, *Apocalypse* in 10,000. I believe that both are honest books, and they have been accepted as such by the readers. Maybe I have contributed in my own way to what is happening now. The opposition did not react badly, it did not feel offended. It was searching for a moral way, and as I have already said demoralization may become the fate of any conspiracy, because there is no public control. One must think about these things, and the opposition has discussed them very seriously. This problem of course does not concern only the Poles; it is in the air. The Czechs in Czechoslovakia, for instance, are today obviously facing the same problems and issues. We follow their struggle very closely and CHARTER 77 has been documented in Poland perhaps better than it ever could be in Czechoslovakia. I personally was always very close to Czech attitudes in art, to Czech surrealism, Czech irony. But my work is sometimes invaded with bathos, and this is my Polish trademark. I do not mention the Czechs because you happen to be one of them, I sincerely believe that they had and have an enormous influence on all of us and everybody in Poland feels it. It is really a culture of a great nation.

A.J.K. *Ironically enough, the Czechs seem today to feel exactly the opposite. In defeat they tend to denigrate their own contribution and often they cite the Poles as an example.*

T.K.: This is all right. And it should be so. We also have important qualities—our spontaneity, our gift for improvisation, a certain kind of emotional madness. Our literature is characterized by a kind of graphomaniacal chaos. The Czechs tend toward order, toward perfection. However, this chaos of ours is also very important; it gives birth to life, to form.

A.J.L.: *What is the situation of Polish literature today?*

T.K.: Right after I left for my American trip, the underground publishing house NOVA organized a small banquet to celebrate the publication of its 100th book. This is already a real breakthrough, a breach in the internal barriers. I would have never written *Apocalypse* had I not known that my friends would help to publish it. In a moment of utter Sovietization, when we ourselves had fallen victim to barbarism, this publishing activity weakened our inner mechanism of self-censorship and started bringing us back to Europe. We can begin to think of ourselves as a nation no longer in prison, as a nation living in some minimal conditions of freedom. We can even afford such a luxury as a free culture.

It is very important that the whole opposition, including its publishing house, tries to behave as normal as possible, including the payment of honorariums to published writers. For *Apocalypse* I even received an award from a private citizen, a relatively well-off small entrepreneur. Thus the *samizdat* itself produces patrons of art and culture in an inofficial way. We used to have these things in the 19th century, but they disappeared. Thus, society begins to relearn a different attitude toward culture. NOVA has published an important essay by Brandys, Strzyjkowski's *Great Fear* (about the occupation of Eastern Poland by the Red Army in 1939), Woroszysky reports from Budapest in 1956 (as they had been published in *Nowa Kultura* in 1956, but never since), and Andrzejewski's novel *Myazga* (The Essence of Wood), the work of his life, which he tried for years to have published officially. This last book was a real event.

There are good writers who are still publishing officially, however: Panicki, Kusniewicz, Lem, and some new talented writers. It is a strange situation: we have two literatures, which are both well read. And as there is not enough paper, there is a black market for books published unofficially as well as officially.

A.J.L.: *What about the role of the Polish literary tradition?*

T.K.: The 1970s turned the attention of literature toward social problems. But literature by its very essence revolts against provincialism; it tends to become world literature. Our young poetry and literature thus deal with the same problems as young literature and poets elsewhere in the world.

Basically we and our culture belong to the West. From the inside, from our inner self. We are a part of the western world, even though on its periphery, nonetheless we are an internal part of it. That is why for me it is hard to be objective toward it. The West often annoys me with its lack of consequence, its formlessness, its support of dictatorships, its passivity, etc. etc., but at the same time I know that even all this ties me to it. I am its child. And I know that in the confrontation between totalitarianism and democracy, democracy will win. Russia's strength lies in the possibility of rapid decision-making. Democracy is slow, but this slowness is its force. It sometimes irritates me, but it is always something I feel very close to.

A.J.L.: *For years there was a barrier between Polish intellectuals and Polish workers.*

T.K.: In the last months a new social institution came into existence. The experts. All strike committees had their "experts," recruited among the oppositional KOR, the Catholic intellectuals and the members of the group Experience and Future, formed by reformist Party members. These are all groups of intellectuals, academics, writers, journalists, and they take active part in the workers' movement. This new situation profits both sides. The workers formulate more precisely (the experts helped to write all the documents), and the intellectuals feel stronger, less isolated.

Between 1970 and 1980 the workers and the intellectuals appeared to be two separate armies. Now they are converging, coming together, joining forces. This is the great merit of KOR and also the flying university contributed in an important way. The society as a whole, including the bureaucracy and the technical intelligentsia, started taking interest in the fate of the country. A psychological climate emerged which benefitted those who were bearers of and spokesmen for discontent.

This is, it seems to me, the moment to say a good word about Gierek, who is now out—perhaps precisely because it does not seem altogether fashionable. Gierek was a Western man, with some of the best Polish qualities deeply implanted in him: a deep dislike for bloodshed and brutal violence. During his rule the police harassed the opposition, but the opposition could continue to work, to publish, to take stands on the problems of the country. KOR was carrying out all its activities exclusively in public. It was a great school of courage for the society, which was also learning that the police are not omnipotent.

We, as Poles, now feel, above all that the society as a whole is basically sound, that as a whole it has achieved something, that it has expressed its will and its ideas. We have independent unions, the government has accepted the public role of the church, and censorship is being publicly discussed (before its existence was never even publicly mentioned). This is what has happened.

Now, what is happening. The honest people in the Party try to adapt to the changed situation—in spite of the tradition of intolerance and dictatorship. The Party might even reform itself, but it is not so entirely free, and the question remains whether its older brother will allow this.

What will happen? With the Poles you never know. I hear every day how rationally, how thoughtfully the Poles behave. But I still don't know whether we are already enough "Czechs," or whether we shall tomorrow begin to act absolutely irrationally again. In the last 40 years the entire nation went through enormous changes, structural, tectonic changes, and none of these have yet been properly examined. We just do not know well enough who we are today and what exactly we want.

A.J.L.: *What about the relationship toward the Germans? And toward the socialist countries?*

T.K.: The aversion toward the Germans subsists. There is much admiration for what they have.

About the other socialist countries, we can say that there is obviously a 'divide and rule' policy. There is always great danger when the serfs begin to shake hands. Then you have an opposition between Latin and Byzantine cultures. The Poles, the Czechs, the Hungarians, are three nations with a specific tradition. And what did Mandelshtam give his life for? Mediterranean culture? There is a European solidarity against Byzantium.

Elsewhere Protestantism was the school of democracy. Catholic Poland was a country of tolerance. Catholicism was often the harbinger of the intellectual opposition. In the last many years it was always during the great Catholic holidays that Catholicism was recognized for all its strength. It was on Corpus Christi day that television broadcast almost without interruption the most popular American films (Westerns, etc.), rarely seen otherwise. People had only the church to thank for it. During the recent strikes, the same thing happened: Nothing but the most recent American entertainment films on TV screens.

I believe that the role of the church will be positive and progressive. The purpose is not to replace state censorship with censorship by the church. But the church will always have to watch closely its main rival. This strengthens the hope that it will not return to its past methods.

A.J.L.: *What about Catholic literature?*

T.K.: Catholic poetry is better than Catholic prose. In general its level is equal to that of European Catholic literature. Many Catholic intellectuals today are more intellectuals than Catholics. But it may happen that some of them will now return to an ideological, more militant Catholicism.

However positive the role of Catholicism is in today's Poland, a part of the overall crisis of Catholicism at the center of which stands the Pope himself. The Catholic church is today just one among many churches, maybe the first among equals, maybe not. This changes a lot. Religion will have to come to an agreement with science, and science with religion.

A.J.L.: *Is there any Jewish problem in Poland today?*

T.K.: Here I can only give my personal opinion. The insinuations about antisemitism in Poland hurt Poland very much in the eyes of the world community. This by itself should make us think about it. I believe that there are some forces whose interests are served by these insinuations. It is all a part of a political game. If there is some antisemitism, it comes from the upper and not from the lower levels of society. There is no physical ground for antisemitism; there are practically no Jews. There remains only the tragic memory of tragedies of the past. Thus, all these insinuations are a part of a game, of a political game played on Poland's account. And because of censorship, the society is neither in the position to air the problem publicly, nor to come to grips with it. (Very few people acknowledge for instance that the minister of finance in the uprising of 1863 was a Jew, Wohl.) Briefly, there is not enough freedom which would make it possible to do away with the problem once and for all.

If the censorship does not allow articles about the uprising in the Warsaw ghetto, it is not the Poles, who are guilty, but the regime. This is one of the enormous and painful problems for all of us. It is not a question of telling, but of honoring in an appropriate way the memory of our concitoyens. Let me give you one example: While I was working as literary manager for one of the production groups of the Polish film industry, I conceived a large project based on Jewish folklore. We had everything, authors, actors, directors, costumes, locations. . . . But all these films were never made, and it was not my fault. Nobody must identify the Polish nation with the people who are responsible.

A.J.L.: *Just one last question: After the Polish Pope, a Polish Nobel Prize winner, the poet Czeslaw Miłosz.*

T.K.: It seems like a Polish wave, doesn't it? Almost as if it all had a magic meaning. As if a sort of Polish climate was coming into being, just at a moment of a difficult trial for my country.

I was overwhelmed and my joy was the greater, because Miłosz also comes from Vilno, as do I. From a land of poets, the land of Mickiewicz. As a writer and as a man, he seems to represent this frontier region, this culture of the boundary, which was always a culture of great tolerance, of a place where East meets West. He represents the culture to which I am tied by all those invisible links, the culture that made me. I recognize in him my own conscience, my own philosophy, my own culture.

For all these years he was not published in Poland. But his work was circulated, it was read, and even published underground. I spoke before of NOVA's celebration of the publication of its 100th volume. This volume was a collection of Miłosz's poems. We even used to listen to his voice on innumerable tapes. Once an official newspaper organized a poll about the best and most beloved Polish writers. And this unpublished poet came on quite high. The censorship, of course, had his name deleted from the results. Just now naturally his popularith in the country almost touches on hysteria.

What did his poetry bring, what did it add to the art of poetry? Well, he writes intellectual poetry. But the more he tries to be, to sound intellectual, the more emotional he becomes. Among Polish poets he counts as one of the intellectual ones, but he is unable to close himself to the emotionality of the Polish poetic tradition.

He is, with no doubt, the greatest living Polish poet and thus the Nobel price is and will be of enormous importance for our young, contemporary poetic generation.

But let us not forget that Miłosz was and is a poet living in exile. Together with an emigré poet, a whole cultural emigration was honored. An emigration which was scandalized, went through difficult times, and now is being vindicated. And that again means a lot for the entire polish society. And not only for the Poles. For the Czechs, for the Hungarians, who had to go the way of exile and whose creativity is also being honored in Miłosz.

CZESŁAW MIŁOSZ AND THE LANDSCAPE OF EXILE

Harold B. Segel
Columbia University

> *Is there such a world*
> *over which I rule sole and absolute?*
> *A time I bind with chains of signs?*
> *An existence perpetuated at my command?*
>
> *The joy of writing.*
> *The power of preserving.*
> *The revenge of a mortal hand.*
>
> Wisława Szymborska, from
> "Radość pisania" (The Joy of Writing)[1]

In his Nobel lecture, Czeslaw Miłosz speaks of what "seeing" means to the poet:

"To see" means not only to have before one's eyes. It may mean also to preserve in memory. "To see and to describe" may also mean to reconstruct in imagination. A distance achieved thanks to the mystery of time must not change events, landscapes, human figures into a tangle of shadows growing paler and paler.[2]

To a writer like Miłosz who has spent the past thirty years in a self-imposed estrangement from his own land "to preserve in memory" has a profound personal meaning. Although the interpenetration of past and present has long been among the poet's dominant concerns, the marked autobiographical element in his work can be related, in large measure, to the experience of exile. But Miłosz's exile has more than a single facet to it. The more obvious, and familiar, political exile, entered into when the writer abandoned his diplomatic post at the Polish Embassy in Paris in 1951, had been preceded by the definitive loss of his true homeland when an independent Lithuania, once a part of the old Polish Commonwealth, was incorporated into the Soviet Union in 1940 and the city of Wilno, where he went to the University and which he loved, ceased being Polish. Moreover, the suspicion with which he was long regarded in Polish emigre circles after his defection, despite the publication of *The Captive Mind* in 1953, created a gulf between him and the Polish community in Western Europe capable only of intensifying feelings of alienation.

Miłosz's attachment to his native Lithuania informs much of his writing, but nowhere with greater sense of purpose than in his autobiographical work *Rodzinna Europa* (Native Europe, 1959; translated into English under the title *Native Realm*) or more lyrically than in his thinly disguised autobiographical novel *Dolina Issy* (The Issa Valley, 1955). These sentiments about Lithuania were also voiced in his Nobel lecture, lending them still greater prominence:

> It is good to be born in a small country where Nature was on a human scale, where various languages and religions cohabited for centuries. I have in mind Lithuania, a country of myths and of poetry. My family in the sixteenth century already spoke Polish . . . so I am a Polish, not a Lithuanian, poet. But the landscapes and perhaps the spirits of Lithuania have never abandoned me.[3]

The Nobel laureate's emphasis on his Lithuanian roots in his Stockholm lecture underlines the importance for his cultural and intellectual development with which he invests them. To Miłosz, Lithuania represents a particular interplay of heterogeneous forces of the greatest impact on the poet in the all-important formative years of his youth. But in the light of this "Lithuanian-ness," what then of Miłosz is Polish? The product of a long process of social and cultural polonization, Miłosz defines himself as a Polish writer less by virtue of ethnic origin (the German and Lithuanian sources are equally significant) than by his use of the Polish language. And by writing in Polish, Milosz has become a part of a literary culture that is as much European as it is Polish.

The evidence of Miłosz's abiding interest in those factors which, in his judgment, formed his view of the world and his art is ample in his writings and public utterances. But if we examine his literary career from the time of his defection in 1951 to the present, we find that works of the greatest autobiographical character cluster in the ten years he lived in France following his break.

Although his career began with poetry and has been distinguished above all by poetry, the post-defection 1950s marked a period of Miłosz's most concentrated prose writing to date. This is not to say that Miłosz at any time abandoned poetry for prose—the very important, in part autobiographical, *Traktat poetycki*, Treatise on Poetry, in verse, was published in 1957—but only that the circumstances of his life in the 1950s seemed to create an imperative for prosaic expression not subsequently experienced to the same degree despite the large number of essays he has written on an extraordinary range of topics. This inclination to prose in the 1950s finds a ready explanation in the autobiographical nature of major works produced during those years and Miłosz's need to communicate thoughts and ideas more easily accommodated in prose.

The defection in 1951 took the form of a rejection of a recall to Warsaw from his cultural attaché's position at the Embassy of the Polish People's Republic in the French capital, followed by a severance not only with the Polish diplomatic service but with People's Poland itself. The reasons for the rupture came, explicitly and implicitly, in his first major prose work, *Zniewolony umysl* (The Captive Mind), first published by the Paris-based Polish emigre publishing house Instytut Literacki, the publishers of the well-known monthly *Kultura*. A sensation when it appeared soon afterward in translation into all the major European languages, including English, the book has lost none of its power as a compelling analysis of the ensnarement of the minds and talents of artists and intellectuals in Eastern Europe. The articulation of a sense of outrage as well as of artistic, intellectual, and moral claustrophobia, *The Captive Mind* was no hasty post-defection self-vindication, but the fruit of a long gestation. That it came soon after Miłosz's decisive break with People's Poland only attests to the poet's inner compulsion to communicate, both for himself as well as for the outside world, his perceptions of a political and intellectual climate now wholly inhospitable to him.

Two years after *The Captive Mind*, Miłosz published another political prose work, this time in the form of a novel, *Zdobycie wladzy* (The Seizure of Power), and animated by the same fervent desire to vent feelings about Communist tyranny. To the international acclaim won by *The Captive Mind* there was now added the distinction of the Prix Littéraire Européen accorded the new publication.

The same year that saw the publication of *The Seizure of Power* also brought forth yet another major work in prose, *The Issa Valley*. Although Miłosz's most engaging and artistically appealing prose effort, *The Issa Valley* tended to be overshadowed by his political works. Given, however, the world political climate of the mid-1950s in which *The Captive Mind* and *The Seizure of Power* appeared, the inattention to a novel as remote from politics as *The Issa Valley* is hardly difficult to understand. But whatever the logical explanations, the publication of the first English translation of the novel in 1981, twenty-six years after its original appearance in Polish, underscores the dimensions of the neglect. Yet, though only now becoming known, *The Issa Valley* can no more be separated from the circumstances of Miłosz's life in the first few years of the 1950s than the political prose writing that made him an overnight literary celebrity.

In his Nobel lecture and several of his prose essays Miłosz has given voice, clearly and eloquently, to the pain, indeed the anguish, of permanent dislocation from one's native land and one's native culture. Typical are the remarks in his essay "O pewnej chorobie trudnej do nazwania" (On a Certain Malady Difficult to Name) in his collection *Widzenia nad zatoką San Francisco* (Views from San Francisco Bay, 1969):

> No Gypsy could have prophesied that I would leave my native regions forever. And those, among whom I now reside, cannot imagine that I come from a place where there were no automobiles, bathrooms, telephones, where on roads covered with dust in summer and mud in spring and fall five miles was no mean distance, where the populace managed to get along without doctors, trusting instead in home cures, magic, and charms. The scope of the cataclysms which destroyed traditional ways of life and drove people from their homes and native lands has already become assimilated, recognized as an accomplished fact, but from time to time the thought of it makes my head spin.[4]

It is against the background of Miłosz's experience of the trauma of exile and emigration, entered into some thirty years ago, and his consideration of the psychic impact of the phenomenon of dislocation in his writing, that such prose works as *The Issa Valley* and *Native Realm* must be observed.

Although a novel in design, *The Issa Valley* is patently an attempt by Miłosz to reconstruct the temporally and spatially distant landscape of his Lithuanian childhood and adolescence. For the English reader who comes to the translation only in the 1980s, lacking the ability to situate the work in its proper chronological frame, the novel might appear to be a latter-day reflective glance back at lost youth. But seeing it distinctly as a product of the 1950s enables us the more easily to relate it to Miłosz's major prose works of the period—as well as to certain of his poems—and to better understand its genesis.

Once Miłosz had satisfied the compulsion to establish his political identity in the international community, another impulse, no less urgent, manifested itself. This was the need to delineate a personal and cultural identity. As if in response, at least partially, to demands for more information about the Polish writer whose defection and subsequent political books catapulted him beyond the ghetto of the Polish emigré literary community in the West (with which his relationship was anything but comfortable), Miłosz wrote the work known as *Native Realm* in English translation. Here, in straightforward expository prose, he recreates the geographical, demographic, social, and cultural milieu from which he emerged and which shaped him as a man and as an artist. While not an autobiography in the strict sense— which allows Miłosz the freedom to distribute emphases as he chooses— *Native Realm* is, nevertheless, the closest he has yet come to writing a full-scale autobiography.

The Issa Valley, however, is much more a response to a psychic urgency on the part of the recent political exile facing the anxieties and uncertainties of a life in emigration to find a certain sustenance, both spiritual and psychological, in a vivid recreation of that segment of the past obviously dearest to him. In view of the likelihood of never being able to return to a homeland to which his emotional ties remained firm, acutely aware of the power of distance in time and space to efface the memory of the past, to change, as he declared in the Nobel lecture, "events, landscapes, human figures into a tangle of shadows growing paler and paler," Miłosz set out in *The Issa Valley* to spare his Lithuanian boyhood further erosion by reconstituting it in a striking exercise of memory and art.

Miłosz's concentration on his early youth is neither unique nor surprising. On the threshhold of a life in emigration—with all its uncertain tomorrows despite the sudden acquisition of international literary fame—and after the severe dislocations and shocks of war, occupation, underground activity, the political transformation of Poland after 1945, the long night of Stalinism, and the anguish of defection, the past of childhood and adolescence in rural Lithuania must have seemed a carefree period of tranquility, happiness, and stability. So evoked in *The Issa Valley,* the rural Lithuanian boyhood becomes the almost timeless poetic landscape of childhood, hence of innocence, a magical realm, as it were, in which the way of life appears immutable.

The Lithuania conjured up with such obvious warmth and specificity in *The Issa Valley* comes into focus virtually as a pastoral landscape, cozy, secure, visited by few perturbations from the greater world beyond. That outside world is not, to be sure, entirely absent from view. The temporal setting is the late teens and early 'twenties of the present century and allusions are made to World War I, the toppling of the Romanov dynasty in Russia, the creation of an independent Lithuania and the subsequent conflict with Poland, and the Polish-Soviet war of 1920. But the allusions are few and far between, barely mentioned in passing, and little developed in the novel's narrative structure. It is as if they are interpolated from time to time merely to establish a certain chronological framework and also to prevent the poet's Lithuanian boyhood from projecting itself as wholly mythic. The only episode related to "outside" events dwelt on to any extent involves the forester Baltazar's killing of a Russian P.O.W. trying to escape through the woods from a German prison camp. And even here the focus is not so much on the murder of the Russian as some war-related incident as on the toll the senseless act takes of Baltazar's psyche and his desperate attempts to end his torment.

The town of Gine, the principal locus of *The Issa Valley,* is not without its tensions. But these are primarily social—between the Polish landowning class and the Lithuanians of lower social station resentful of longstanding Polish privileges, especially at a time of growing Lithuanian nationalism. And even here, where the potential for the dramatic surely existed, Miłosz never allows the tensions to become paramount in the narrative, to gain any ascendancy over the affectionate and goodhumored depiction of the flora and fauna of the valley of the Issa River and the traditional mores of its inhabitants. Again, only on one occasion, do the social antagonisms between Lithuanians and Poles erupt into anything dangerous: that is when the young

Lithuanian peasant Wackonis vents his anger at everything Polish by tossing a grenade at the house of the Surkonts. The grenade lands in the room of the boy Tomasz, the Surkonts' grandson and Miłosz's fictional self in the novel. Fortunately, the grenade fails to explode, but Miłosz's account of the episode consciously eschews the dramatic:

> The grenade had not exploded, but it might have, in which case Tomasz would have been laid to rest under the oak trees, a stone's throw from Magdalena's grave. The world would have gone on as before; swallows, storks, and starlings would have winged their way back from their annual migrations beyond the seas; wasps and hornets would have gone on sucking pears for their sweet juice. Why it had failed to explode is not for us to judge. It had hit a wall, bounced to the floor, and rolled over to Tomasz's bed, where the decision to explode or not to explode had ripened inside it.[5]

True, a greater response comes from Tomasz's grandparents who feel unjustly wronged by the assault in view of grandfather Surkont's long advocacy of Lithuanian independence. But the shock waves emitted by the incident are few and the opening of Miłosz's account of it has already defused the explosive potential.

Apart from such occasional ripples, the surface of the life in and around Gine is comfortingly serene. The pursuits of the Polish gentry are traditional with hunting taking up the lion's share of the men's time—and a good part of the book. And the objects of the hunt are as varied as the animal life of the region: snakes, hare, wood grouse, snipe, ptarmigan, duck, blackcock, buck. Although anxious to demonstrate his prowess as a hunter and so establish his credentials as a man in a male-dominated society, Tomasz functions poorly under pressure and fails miserably. Since his education lacks any formal structure at this time, his discovery of the world of books and especially those on Polish and Lithuanian history in grandfather Surkont's library comes as a revelation in more than one sense and ultimately of greater delight than the hunter's pursuit of animals the boy does not really enjoy killing in any case.

If Tomasz necessarily engages the reader's interest, it is not because he stands at the center of a novel with any well-defined architectonic structure. *The Issa Valley* is hardly a novel in a conventional sense, but instead a series of slow-moving pictures of Polish gentry life in the early twentieth-century Lithuanian countryside. In this sense, the work is aptly named for its true center of gravity is the valley of the Issa. The characters about whom the novel's episodes cluster are no more or less important to the author's purpose than the lengthy descriptions of flora and fauna, all interrelating as components of a way of life already radically altered by the time the novel came to be written.

Partly out of a longstanding interest in the mystic and supernatural[6] and partly out of a desire to illuminate the tenacity of pre-Christian pagan beliefs and practices in his native provincial Lithuania, Miłosz introduces several episodes in the novel reflective of this pagan subculture: the consuming passion for magic of Tomasz's grandmother Michalina, the weaver Pakienas's encounter with a shepherd's ghost, the appearance of the servant girl Magdalena's ghost to Father Monkiewicz and the subsequent ritualistic mutilation of her exhumed corpse by the townspeople, Dominik Malinowski's attempt to prove the existence of God by driving a knife into the host, and the counsels of the wizard Masiulis.

The prominence of folk beliefs and practices of a pagan character among the people of the Issa valley Miłosz attributes to the fact that the valley itself "has the distinction of being inhabited by an unusually large number of devils. It may be that the hollow willows, mills, and the thickets lining the riverbanks provide a convenient cover for those creatures who reveal themselves only when it suits them."[7]

Miłosz's writing about the devils of the Issa is believing but playful, a measure of the extent to which pagan attitudes were woven into the fabric of everyday life of rural Lithuania. But if he faithfully portrays popular concepts of the devil, the wry humor with which his account is informed harbors an element of affectionate mockery:

> Those who have seen them say that the devil is rather short, about the size of a nine-year-old; that he wears a green frock coat, a jabot, his hair in a pigtail, white stockings, and tries to conceal his hoofs, which are an embarrassment to him, with high-heeled slippers. Such tales should be treated with a certain caution. It is possible that, knowing the superstitious awe in which the Germans are held—they being people of commerce, inventions, and science—the devils seek to lend themselves an air of gravity by dressing up in the manner of Immanuel Kant of Königsberg. It's no coincidence that along the Issa another name for the Evil Spirit is the "Little German"—implying that the devil is on the side of progress. Still, it's hard to believe they were in the habit of wearing such a costume for everyday. If one of their favorite pasttimes was dancing in the empty scutching sheds near the farm buildings, how could they possibly kick up clouds of grain dust without showing due regard for their appearance? And why, if they are endowed with a certain immortality, would they be apt to choose a costume from the eighteenth century?[8]

The powerful act of recall from which *The Issa Valley* arose is perhaps nowhere more strikingly demonstrated than in Miłosz's descriptions of nature, beginning with the very opening of the novel:

I would begin with the Land of Lakes, the place where Tomasz lived. This part of Europe was long covered with glaciers, and the landscape has much of the severity of the north. The soil is sandy and rocky and suitable only for growing potatoes, rye, oats, and flax. This explains why such care was taken not to spoil the forests, which helped to soften the climate and offered protection against the Baltic winds. The forests are predominantly of pine and spruce, though birch, oak, and hornbeam are also in abundance, but not beech, the border of its domain running farther to the south. . . . From almost any hilltop you can glimpse a blue sheet of lake with a white, barely perceptible smudge of grebe, with a string of ducks winging over the reeds. The marshlands abound in every species of waterfowl, and in spring the pale sky reverberates with the whir of snipe—a *whew-whew-whew*—made by the air in their tail feathers as they perform their monotonous acrobatics, signifying love.[9]

To see Miłosz very much in his element here is to recognize the importance of nature in his creative writing as a whole. His poetry, above all, is a record of a great sensitivity to the beauty, the subtlety, and especially the infinite variety as well as eternality of nature. To a poet as poignantly aware as Miłosz of the ephemerality of human constructs and designs, a poet who has expressed uneasiness over attachments because of the transience of so much in life, the meaningfulness of nature as timelessness more than compensates for the threat from forces (for Miłosz, demonic) ever lurking to disfigure its beauty. Perhaps a single small lyric poem, "Dar" (Gift), from the collection *Gdzie wschodzi słońce i kędy zapada* (Where the Sun Rises and Whither It Sets, 1974), can be cited as encapsulating in just a few lines Miłosz's reaction to nature:

> Dzień taki szcześliwy.
> Mgła opadła wcześnie, pracowałem w ogrodzie.
> Kolibry przystawały nad kwiatem kaprifolium.
> Nie było na ziemi rzeczy, którą chciałem mieć.
> Nie znałem nikogo, komu warto byłoby zazdrościć.
> Co przydarzyło się złego, zapomniałem.
> Nie wstydziłem się myśleć, że byłem kim jestem.
> Nie czułem w ciele żadnego bólu.
> Prostując się, widziałem niebieskie morze i żagle.
>
> (A day so happy.
> Fog lifted early, I worked in the garden.
> Hummingbirds were stopping over honeysuckle flowers.
> There was no thing on earth I wanted to possess.
> I knew no one worth my envying him.

Whatever evil I had suffered, I forgot.
To think that once I was the same man did not embarrass me.
In my body I felt no pain.
When straightening up, I saw the blue sea and sails.)[10]

Considering the importance of nature for his view on life and for his art, Miłosz's emphasis on it in *The Issa Valley* is fitting, for if the novel is read as illuminating the poet's youth, then the impact on his consciousness of the Lithuanian countryside deserves the prominence given it. It is also in the context of his treatment of nature in the novel that Miłosz tips his hand as to its underlying autobiographical character. The young boy Tomasz, the reader learns, loved and responded to nature and at one point

> began compiling a notebook, or rather a scrapbook, having the shape and feel of an actual book. Cutting sheets of paper to size, he glued the margins together and bound them with a cardboard cover inscribed with the word *Birds*. Anyone taking the liberty to pry . . . would have found a series of headings, capitalized and underlined, followed by ornithological descriptions in small-case letters. . . . He had no way of knowing, of course, that the *L.*, or Latinized "Linni," was in honor of the Swedish naturalist Linnaeus, the first bird taxonomist. Yet he scrupulously guarded against allowing any discrepancies between other taxonomies and his own, the Latin names appealing to him because of their sonority: *Emberiza citrinella* for yellowhammer, *Turdus pilaris* for fieldfare, *Garrulus glandarius* for jay, and so on. Some of the names were conspicuous for their proliferation of letters, forcing his eyes to jump continuously from his notebook to the antiquated ornithology at his elbow. Even the longer names, if repeated often enough, acquired a pleasant lilt, one of them, that of the common nutcracker, being absolutely magical: *Nucifraga caryocatactes*. . . . The notebook proved that Tomasz had the gift of concentrating on things that excited him. To name a bird, to cage it in letters, was tantamount to owning it forever. The endless multiplicity of colors, shadings, mating calls, trills, wing sounds. . . . Turning the pages, he had them all before him, at his command, affecting and ordering the plenitude of things that were. In reality, everything about birds gave rise to unease. Was it enough, he wondered, to verify their existence? The way the light modulated their feathers in flight, the warm, yellow flesh lining the bills of the young feeding in deeply sequestered nests, suffused him with a feeling of communion. Yet, for many, they were little more than a mobile decoration, scarcely worthy of scrutiny, whereas, surrounded by such wonders on earth, people should have consecrated their whole lives to contemplating only one thing: felicity.[11]

The similarity with Miłosz's accounts of his own youthful fascination is anything but coincidental. "As a child," he writes in *Native Realm,* "I safeguarded myself against grownups by my passion for nature, my aquariums, my ornithological books."[12] This passion forms the subject of his essay "Wspomnienie pewnej miłości" (Recollection of a Certain Love), included in *Views from San Francisco Bay*. Recalling his excitement over the varieties of shapes and colors in nature, especially of insects and birds, Miłosz remembers how enthusiastically he responded to colored illustrations in nature books and atlases and how his desire to make his own everything he saw in pictures could be gratified only through the special magic of names. Hence,

> In thick notebooks I designed rubrics and pedantically made lists of order, family, species, and genus, until the name composed of a noun to indicate species and an adjective to indicate genus fused into a single entity with that to which it always belonged and the *Emberiza citrinella* did not inhabit a thicket but rather an ideal expanse, beyond time. In this impulse to classify there was a furious Aristotelianism. I repeated early procedures for the ordering of the world around us, as if it was true that childhood, boyhood, and maturity correspond to phases through which mankind passes. And I might add that my frenzy had distinctly masculine features. Expressed in it was the same greed for delimitations and definitions, stronger than the actuality of concepts, that armed some with swords, threw others into dungeons, and drove the faithful to holy religious wars.[13]

As a practical consequence of these enthusiasms, Miłosz continues, he retained an impressive vocabulary of the names of the plants, animals, and birds of his native northern country, a lexical storehouse, one might add, that he was able to put to good use in *The Issa Valley*.

Self- or imposed exile and emigration are not phenomena of Polish experience unique to the twentieth century. The Partitions, the failure of the Napoleonic campaigns, and the insurrections of 1830 and 1863 created a tradition and, in a certain sense also, a legend of Polish exile and emigration. Polish Romantic literature, in its fullest flower and most consequential expression, was almost wholly a creation of both exile and emigration. Miłosz's own literary career over the past thirty years legitimately can be viewed, therefore, within the framework of a long and extremely important Polish tradition. But there is more linking Miłosz to this tradition than merely his exile and the theme of emigration in his writing. With *The Issa Valley* as the principal frame of reference, certain parallels can be found in the careers of Miłosz, the greatest living Polish poet, and his great predecessor in the nineteenth century, Adam Mickiewicz.

Both Mickiewicz and Miłosz have their origins in polonized gentry of the Lithuanian region of the former Polish Commonwealth. Both graduated the University of Wilno and both have articulated a very strong, almost palpable, attachment to their native land. It was in the spirit of this attachment that Mickiewicz began his monumental epico-lyric poem *Pan Tadeusz* (Master Thaddeus, 1834) with the Invocation: "O Lithuania, my country, thou/ Art like good health; I never knew till now/ How precious, till I lost thee. Now I see/ Thy beauty whole, because I yearn for thee."[14]

After an exile of some five years in Russia, Mickiewicz found himself an emigre in Western Europe in 1829. A desultory effort to return to Poland during the November Insurrection of 1830 proved fruitless and after the suppression of the uprising in 1831, Mickiewicz joined the Great Emigration that had resettled in the West, primarily in France, and remained an emigre the rest of his life. When Miłosz walked away from the diplomatic service of the Polish People's Republic in 1951, he spent nearly a decade in France and might have remained there indefinitely had he not received an invitation to join the faculty of the University of California at Berkeley as a professor in the Department of Slavic Languages and Literatures. While careful to keep a certain distance between himself and the established Polish emigre community in Paris, among whom his post-defection works aroused no little controversy, Miłosz's retention of Polish as the language of his creative writing and the printing of his Polish works by a Polish emigre publishing house in Paris replicate the pattern of the Polish emigre Romantics of the nineteenth century, including and above all Mickiewicz. But the parallels with Mickiewicz can yet be extended.

Among Mickiewicz's greatest works are the three written between 1832 and 1834 in response to the challenge of divisiveness within the post-insurrectionary Great Emigration: *Dziady, część trzecia* (Forefathers' Eve, Part Three), *Księgi narodu i pielgrzymstwa polskiego* (The Books of the Polish Nation and Pilgrimage), and *Pan Tadeusz*.

Of course, no real comparison can be made between Mickiewicz's position in the Great Emigration in Paris in the early 1830s and that of Miłosz at the time of his break with People's Poland in 1951. Yet it would not be an exaggeration to suggest that once the publication of *The Captive Mind* in 1953 transformed Miłosz into an international celebrity, his new fame in the West as a political writer coupled with his already considerable reputation as a poet among Polish readers created an aura around him, at the very least an aura of qualified expectation, in some ways reminiscent of that surrounding Mickiewicz in Paris in the early 1830s. And while *The Captive Mind, The Seizure of Power, The Issa Valley,* and *Native Realm* are, for the most part, quite different literary experiences than Mickiewicz's great works of the period 1832-1834, there are a few points of contiguity worth considering.

Driven by an overpowering sense of mission in the Emigration as the foremost poet of the Polish language and, by definition, the voice by which the entire Polish nation itself spoke, Mickiewicz sought, in the works of the early 1830s, to justify himself as worthy of at least the spiritual leadership circumstances seemed to have prepared for him and, at the same time, to shape the ideology of the Emigration. If Miłosz, by contrast, would indeed have been loath to assume the mantle of a latter-day *wieszcz* (or vatic poet) in the Polish emigre community in France in the 1950s, his indictment of Soviet tyranny carried no less authority and had, *toutes proportions gardées,* no less impact than Mickiewicz's denunciation of Russian tsarist tyranny in *Forefathers' Eve, Part Three* and in *The Books of the Polish Nation and Pilgrimage.*

Much of the impetus to the undercurrent of self-definition and self-justification discernible in Mickiewicz's writing of the early 1830s derived from the poet's uneasiness over his failure to participate in the November Insurrection. Until this "lapse" had somehow been rationalized or otherwise overcome, the poet could not hope to assume the leadership role in the Emigration to which he believed himself destined. Again, no real analogy with Mickiewicz in this respect exists in the case of Miłosz. But a parallel of sorts, nevertheless, can be found in that Miłosz's political "exposures" of the 1950s, particularly as they illuminated the situation of artists and intellectuals in Eastern Europe during Stalinism, would have carried less conviction had they not also been informed with a measure of apologia on the part of a major poet of the 1930s and '40s who had survived the war and found an accommodation with the post-war Polish Communist regime sufficient to permit the assumption of diplomatic responsibilities in behalf of that regime from 1946 to 1951.

The most important link with, or reminiscence of, Mickiewicz, however, lies not so much in the realm of the political as in the nostalgia for a homeland and a boyhood identified with that homeland generative of the kind of brilliant recall characteristic of the nineteenth-century poet's *Pan Tadeusz* and Miłosz's *The Issa Valley.* In both works, the poets drew on the immense resources of their artistic gifts to summon an extraordinarily vivid and captivating picture of a traditional Polish gentry youth in rural Lithuania at a time in both their lives when they stood before the chasm of life-long emigration. Whatever the differences between *Pan Tadeusz* and *The Issa Valley* as literature, the similarity of circumstances in which they came to be written and the spiritual and psychological needs the act of their writing fulfilled for both poets cannot be easily dismissed. And, despite the differences between the two works, the correspondences, however, are striking: the rural Lithuanian countryside celebrated by both poets as homeland; the remarkable evocation of landscape, of flora and fauna; the titular or central figure of a youth viewed within the context of the traditional Polish gentry pursuits of the region, above all hunting; the momentous political and military events forming the background but permitted only a barely intrusive or belated presence in the narrative—the eve of the Napoleonic invasion of Russia in *Pan Tadeusz* and World War I, the Russian Revolution, and the Polish-Soviet war in *The Issa Valley.* Both works demarcate a time and a way of life. In *Pan Tadeusz,* a great military campaign carries the implicit danger of irrevocable transformation, while in *The Issa Valley* the carefree, almost idyllic routine of life draws to a close when the young man has to exchange the pastoral landscape for the urban in order to begin formal schooling. A watershed is reached in both works beyond which nothing will ever be quite the same again, except in memory—or art. This same sense of reaching a turning point must have occurred to Miłosz in the immediate aftermath of his break with Poland in 1951, just as it had occurred to Mickiewicz in Dresden in 1832 when he resolved to make the lot of the post-insurrectionary emigration then forming his own and in a frenzy of guilt, atonement, and self-realization composed the dramatic work that heralded the new direction his career would henceforth take, *Forefathers' Eve, Part Three.*

Throughout his thirty years of emigration, Miłosz's appreciation of landscape never dulled, nor did the capacity of nature to provide a spiritual contentment lose its efficacy. As he writes in *Native Realm*:

> The classic result of all sudden ruptures and reversals is the rumination on one's own worthlessness and the desire to punish oneself, known as *delectatio morosa.* I would never have been cured of it had it not been for the beauty of the earth. The clear autumn mornings in an Alsatian village surrounded by vineyards, the paths on an Alpine slope over the Isère River, rustling with dry leaves from the chestnut trees, or the sharp light of early spring on the Lake of the Four Cantons near Schiller's rock, or a small river near Périgueux on whose surface kingfishers traced colored shadows of flight in the July heat—all of this reconciled me with the universe and myself.[15]

Reconciliation with the universe and himself did not necessarily mean, however, a reconciliation as well with the status of a political emigre in Western Europe. If he made a peace of sorts with his life in France where landscape again—whether Paris or the French countryside—proved a saving grace, there was still a sense of strangeness, of alienation which he was never quite able to escape and which he expresses in his writing. No matter how well he spoke French or adjusted himself to French ways, he would never cease being a foreigner, an East European, an emigré.

That this changed, and changed dramatically, when Miłosz emigrated from France to America is evidenced in a number of his poems as well as in the essays in *Views from San Francisco Bay.* America was not, to be sure, a new experience for Miłosz, for he was posted to the Polish Embassy in Washington in 1946 and remained there until reassigned to Paris in the fall of 1950. In discovering the American countryside for the first time he found much that reminded him of the Lithuania of his boyhood. More importantly, in a land where almost all have roots elsewhere, in other lands and cultures, he no longer felt a stranger and the alienation he experienced in France at long last began to fade. "Most of all," he writes in *Native Realm* about his first stay in America,

> I got to know the American countryside, which restored me, after a prolonged interval, to my boyhood. Like all Europeans I had painted for myself a false picture of technology's reign in America, imagining that nothing was left of nature. In reality her nature was more luxuriant than even the wooded regions where I grew up.... I plunged into books on American flora and fauna, made diplomatic contacts with porcupines and beavers in the forests of Pennsylvania, but I was most drawn to the Northern states: Vermont and Maine. Maine spruce trees shrouded in white fog at sundown and sunrise were not, in my eyes, substitutes for my Lithuanian spruce. Had I used them to satisfy my nostalgia, it would have robbed them of their own individual beauty. But the waist-high grass showering me with droplets of dew, the fallen trees with their tangle of roots, the hidden presence of the moss and the bear—what a surprising kinship of emotional tradition! This America of trees and plants, fragrant with the hay reaped on forest meadows, fitted over me smoothly and I ceased to be a foreigner in her. None of us "Easterners," regardless of how long he may have lived in France or England, would ever be a Frenchman or an Englishman; but here, at barn dances where everybody, both grownups and children, danced together, one could forget.[16]

These earlier feelings about America were reenforced when Miłosz's last emigration, from France to the United States, brought him to the state of California which has been his home for the past twenty years. The rugged beauty of the American West and the Pacific coast only sharpened for him the distinction between Europe and America. In his essay "On a Certain Malady Difficult to Name" in *Views from San Francisco Bay,* he perceives this distinction in terms of two metaphors suggested by landscape:

> The landscapes of Europe are a metaphor of its whole past, its particularisms, its emotional attachments to everything stupidly local, its gradual joining of municipalities and petty principalities into larger units. On the other hand, the city-abstraction and the abstract-theater of Nature, as something that passes, are metaphors of America.[17]

Moreover, in Miłosz's view, America as a land of exile *per se* encompasses at the same time a paradigm of all exile, hence the ease with which his integration into American life could occur. But, if ultimately he must ever regard himself as an alien, then in a land of aliens, it is, as he remarks in "On a Certain Malady Difficult to Name," a "privilege to live in California and drink daily of the draught of perfect alienation!"[18]

Views from San Francisco Bay brims with an almost child-like wonderment at the new landscape of the West, and specifically California—Crater Lake, Death Valley, the old Spanish missions, the redwoods, the Monterey Peninsula, Carmel and Big Sur, San Francisco and the Bay area. By the time Milosz left Europe for America his one-time fascination with the names of plants and animals had lost its hold on his imagination. But in California, when he began to encounter new varieties of species familiar to him, his old interests reawakened. With obvious delight he describes in his essay "Recollection of a Certain Love" how his concept of "pine," for example, based on the one type he knew in Lithuania (the Polish *sosna*), enlarged unbelievably in America when he made the acquaintance of the Sugar Pine, the Ponderosa Pine, the Monterey Pine—all told, seventeen different types of pine.

By becoming American in America in the sense of no longer being encumbered by the burden of "differentness," Miłosz succeeded in curing himself of the sickness of unreality afflicting so many of the emigres from Eastern Europe which he describes in one of his most trenchant statements on the psychosis of emigration:

> However great the strength of attachment to one's native land, a person can live far away from it perhaps only for a certain period of time, reacting with distaste to everything he sees daily, lamenting the foreignness of language, customs, and institutions, straining his sight and hearing in the direction of his lost fatherland. We are nourished by our senses and, although we are not conscious of it, a continuous process takes place whereby chaotic perceptions are ordered and placed into certain totalities. A complete *déracinement* is contrary to our nature and the human plant, once torn from its soil, seeks to set down roots in whatever soil it is thrown. This happens because we are corporeal beings, that is, we occupy a place in space and this "place," concealed by the covering of our hide, cannot, however, be "nowhere." Just as the hand reaches out and takes a pencil lying on a table, thereby determining a relationship between the body and that which is beyond it, so too does the human imagination extend us, determining the relationship of sense and image between us and a street, a city, a district, a country. Among displaced persons from the eastern part of Europe one can frequently observe a despairing rejection of reconciliation with this fact. Instead, they try to preserve their homeland like some ideal expanse of space in which they move, but because it exists only in their memories, unfortified by daily impressions, it grows stiff, transforms itself into words which, the more obstinate they are, the more they lose their palpable content.[19]

In his new, perhaps final home, Czeslaw Miłosz has succeeded admirably in achieving the reconciliation with reality, elusive for so many emigres, of which he speaks above. The poet's—and the boy's—delight in landscape was rekindled in America with a fervor unknown since his Lithuanian youth and the revisit of that youth in *The Issa Valley* in the 1950s. But landscape—nature—for Miłosz has never existed as a thing unto itself, an abstract good. In all his observation of and pleasure in nature Miłosz has never lost sight of man and it is in this deep-seated reverence for man that the roots lie of the Polish poet's polemic with the great American poet of the California coast, Robinson Jeffers, above all in the poem "Do Robinsona Jeffersa" (To Robinson Jeffers). Reading Jeffers' poetry of negation in the context of his discovery of the awesome beauty of the Pacific shoreline, Miłosz could not accept the American's celebration of a nature purified of the presence of man. The keener his appreciation of the transcendant majesty of the Western landscape, the deeper Miłosz's feeling of man's integral, humanizing place in it. Hence, his admonishment to Jeffers that "Ziemia uczy więcej niż nagość żywiołów" (The earth teaches more than does the nakedness of elements).[20] Characteristically, in the final stanza of "To Robinson Jeffers," Milosz is again drawn back to the ancient landscape and lore of his far-off native Lithuania, counterposing the symbiosis of man and nature first learned there to the man-denying fearsomeness of Jeffers' vision:

> Raczej wyrzeźbić słońca na spojeniach krzyża
> jak robili w moim powiecie. Brzozom i jedlinom
> nadawać żeńskie imiona. Wzywać opieki
> przeciwko niemej i przebiegłej sile
> niż tak jak ty oznajmiać nieczłowieczą rzecz.[21]

> (Better to carve suns and moons on the joints of crosses
> as was done in my district. To birches and firs
> give feminine names. To implore protection
> against the mute and treacherous might
> than to proclaim, as you did, an inhuman thing.)[22]

NOTES

1. Wislawa Szymborska, *Sounds, Feelings, Thoughts: Seventy Poems,* tr. and intr. Magnus J. Krynski and Robert A. Maguire, Princeton, New Jersey, p. 59.
2. Czeslaw Milosz, *Nobel Lecture,* New York, 1980, pp. 21-22.
3. *Ibid.,* pp. 9-10.
4. *Widzenia nad zatoką San Francisco,* Paris, 1980, p. 32. Translation mine [HBS].
5. Czeslaw Milosz, *The Issa Valley,* tr. Louis Iribarne, New York, 1981, p. 77.
6. On Milosz's mystic and philosophical interests, see especially his (as yet untranslated) *Ziemia Ulro* [The Land of Ulro], Paris, 1977. For the reader of Polish, Stanislaw Barańczak's remarks on the work in his essay "Summa Czeslawa Milosza," in his collection *Etyka i poetyka: Szkice 1970-1978,* Paris, 1979, pp. 56-68, are illuminating.
7. *The Issa Valley,* p. 6.

8. *Ibid.*
9. *Ibid.*, p. 3.
10. Czesław Miłosz, *Selected Poems*, rev. ed., New York, 1980, p. 118. The poem was translated by Miłosz himself. Polish text in Czesław Miłosz. *Utwory poetyckie*, Ann Arbor, 1976, p. 350.
11. *The Issa Valley*, pp. 150-151.
12. Czesław Miłosz, *Native Realm: A Search for Self-Definition*, tr. Catherine S. Leach, Garden City, New York, 1968, p. 272.
13. *Widzenia nad zatoką San Francisco*, pp. 18-19. Translation mine [HBS].
14. Adam Mickiewicz, *Pan Tadeusz*, tr. Kenneth MacKenzie, Everyman's Library, New York, 1966, p. 2.
15. *Native Realm*, p. 293.
16. *Ibid.*, pp. 260-261.
17. *Widzenia nad zatoką San Francisco*, pp. 33-34.
18. *Ibid.*, p. 34.
19. From the essay "O emigracji do Ameryki tudzież jakby podsumowanie" [On Emigration as Well as by Way of Summation], *Widzenia nad zatoką San Francisco*, pp. 155-156. Translation mine [HBS].
20. *Widzenia nad zatoką San Francisco*, p. 75. English translation in Czesław Miłosz, *Selected Poems*, rev. ed., New York, 1980, p. 95. Poem translated by Czesław Miłosz and Richard Lourie.
21. *Widzenia nad zatoką San Francisco*, p. 75.
22. Czesław Miłosz, *Selected Poems*, p. 95.

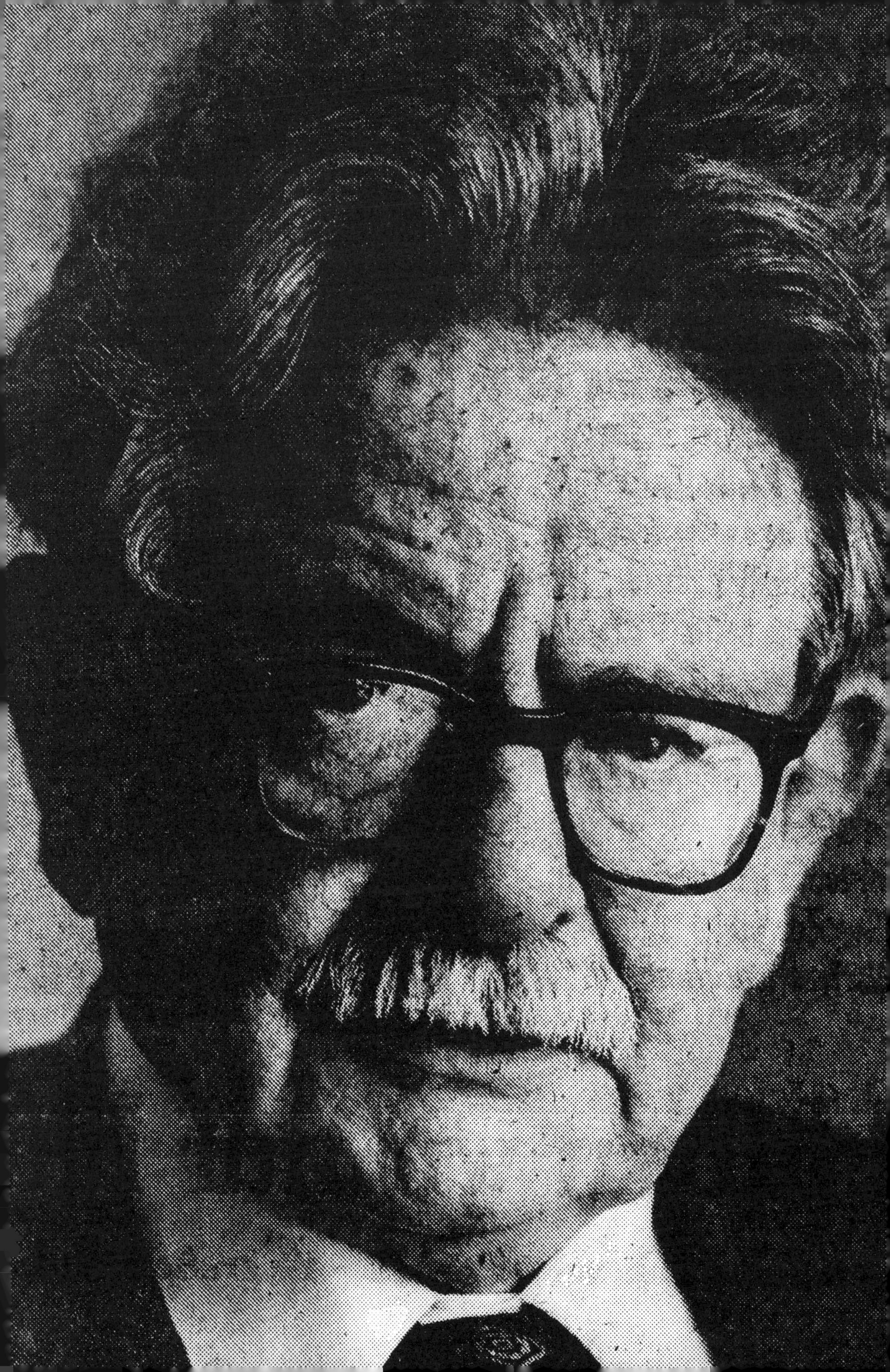

WHO IS ELIAS CANETTI?

Ingo Seidler
University of Michigan

I

Less than two years ago, the German Literature Archives in Marbach am Neckar opened its grand permanent exhibition of modern German literature, "From Nietzsche to the Gruppe 47," covering roughly the period from 1880 to 1950. It is an impressive documentation, well-balanced between what has long been known and what ought to have been. Among the few relevant authors who are conspicuous by their absence is the 1981 Nobel Prize laureate for literature, Elias Canetti—his name is nowhere mentioned in the catalog. Tempting as it might be to accuse the organizers of the exhibition of anti-Austrian bias, anti-Semitic sentiments, or lack of interest in exiled writers, it would not be fair. Austrians are very well represented (Schnitzler, Hofmannsthal, Rilke, Musil, Kafka, Broch, Werfel, Kraus). So are German Jewish authors (Döblin, Feuchtwanger, Wolfskehl, Lasker-Schüler, Toller). In fact, the writers who went into political exile during the period 1933–1945 have two entire sections of the exhibit dedicated to their work. Why, then, is Canetti not at least mentioned as one of them?

The answer to this question has to be sought in Canetti's life and most unorthodox development; his is the life of an outsider *par excellence*. Although German is the only language in which he has written, and the Austrian wing of German literature the only national tradition into which he might, at a pinch, be fitted, he was never either an Austrian or a German citizen, and he has lived the larger part of his seventy-six years outside the German-speaking areas of Europe. Nor is German his first language; the curious fact is that it is the *fourth* of the several languages he acquired during the bizarre Odyssey of his life.

Canetti was born in what is now Bulgaria (Ruse on the Danube, fifty miles south of Bucharest); in 1905 that made him a Turkish citizen. And it was in Turkey, too, that his family had lived for many generations after they had been forced, as Sephardic Jews, to leave their original Spanish homeland in 1492. An archaic sort of Spanish was thus the first language young Elias spoke with his parents. As he observed himself, he is one of probably not very many speakers in whom the two languages of the worst historic expulsions live side by side. In 1911 the family (including the writer and two younger brothers) moved to England, where Canetti's father Jacques joined a brother to run a textile factory in Manchester. Thus the first books young Elias read were in English, with French, his third language, soon being added in school. Shortly after Jacques Canetti's sudden death in 1912, his widow decided to move to Vienna, and by way of preparation taught her eight-year-old son German in one summer. Both parents had learned German during youthful sojourns in Vienna and had used it as a kind of secret language in front of their children. The code thus cracked was to be Canetti's literary medium for the rest of his career: "I will not let anyone tell me what language to write in—least of all Mr. Hitler!"

From 1913 to 1916 Mathilde Canetti and her three sons lived in Vienna, moving to Zurich during the war, and on to Frankfurt/Main in 1921 (Zurich had become "too idyllic"). By 1924 they were back again in Vienna, the city where Canetti was to live from his nineteenth to his thirty-third year and which later he was to call his *real* hometown. It was there that he attended the university, studying (upon his mother's express wish) chemistry, a field in which he obtained a doctorate in 1929, but in which he was never professionally active. He came under the spell ("idolatrous devotion" Canetti himself called it later) of Karl Kraus, the poet, writer, critic, satirist, and one-man opposition to the cultural, literary, political and press establishment in Vienna. He also met other writers and artists both in Vienna and in Berlin, among them George Gross and Fritz Wotruba, Robert Musil and Hermann Broch, Isaak Babel and Bert Brecht. He translated three novels by Upton Sinclair—for money, he later explained—but he also wrote a very perceptive and appreciative little essay on Sinclair's reception in Europe, the Soviet Union, and the USA; this was twenty-three-year-old Canetti's first publication.

In 1930–1931, at the age of twenty-five, Canetti wrote his one and only novel, *Die Blendung* (translated into English under the titles *Auto-da-Fé* [1946] and *The Tower of Babel* [1947]). Two of his three plays followed, *Hochzeit* (The Wedding) in 1932 and *Komödie der Eitelkeit* (Comedy of Vanity) in 1934. In 1934 he also married Veza Taubner-Calderon (1898–1963). During the thirties Canetti became a witness and painstaking observer of the mounting political tensions and violence in Vienna—motivation and materials for his later study on crowds and power. In March 1938 Hitler annexed Austria; Canetti—who was busy studying the behavior of the crowds—and his wife were among the last Jews to leave the city. In November 1938 they moved, first to Paris, and a year later, to London. Since 1939 Canetti has lived in London: "I feel at home only when, pencil in hand, I write down German words and everyone around me speaks English." An odd statement in itself—but how much odder out of the mouth of someone with Canetti's background and roots!

The outbreak of the Second World War also marked the beginning of the twenty years that Canetti was to devote almost exclusively to his ambitious study, *Masse und Macht*, finally published in German in 1960 and subsequently as *Crowds and Power* in England and the USA, as well as in a half dozen other languages. The twenty years of "exile, silence, and cunning" in which Canetti wrote *Masse und Macht* must have been extraordinarily hard for him. These were, after all, the years (from the age of thirty-five to fifty-five) in which, in any writer's halfway normal development, the public begins to take notice and respond to a new, original voice. Canetti, however, wrote few and published no new works during that entire period; even his attempts to republish his novel and the plays failed. The silence around him was almost total. To anybody but himself he must have seemed merely another uprooted expatriate with a modest literary past and no future at all, hopelessly enmeshed in an enormous task that he had precious little chance of ever bringing to a conclusion.

As a sort of "creative counterweight" to the extended studies that went into the writing of *Crowds and Power*, Canetti started, in 1942, to write a continuous series of aphoristic jottings, *Aufzeichnungen*, to which he gave an hour or two every day. Written mainly for Canetti's own use, they have been published thus far only in excerpts (in 1965, 1970, and 1973, as well as in a one-volume English edition entitled *The Human Province* [1978]). These "notations" should not be confused with Canetti's actual diaries, which are, according to the author, most confidential and certainly not for publication in his lifetime, if ever. Also, a third play, *Die Befristeten* (The Numbered), was finished in 1952; and a 1954 trip to Morocco led to the writing of *Die Stimmen von Marrakesch*, an extraordinary travel book that was published only in 1968 in German, and not until 1978 in English (*The Voices of Marrakesh*). Further travels in the fifties and sixties took him to the South of France, Italy, and Greece—but never to the United States. Very sporadically some of Canetti's plays were seeing performances (Oxford, 1956; Braunschweig, 1965, causing a theater scandal; Basel, 1978; Vienna, 1980). In 1963 Veza Canetti died. Canetti married again in 1971, a much younger woman this time, Hera Buschor; a daughter was born to them the next year. In 1971 Canetti also began work on his elaborate autobiography. The first volume, covering the years 1905 to 1921 (*Die gerettete Zunge, Geschichte einer Jugend*, 1977), has also since appeared in English as *The Tongue Set Free: Remembrance of a European Childhood* (1980); the second, covering the Vienna years under the Krausian title *Die Fackel im Ohr* (1980; *Die Fackel* was, of course, Kraus' famous journal published in Vienna, 1899–1936), is presently being translated. Slowly the author acquired a wider public; it was only in the seventies that several highly regarded German and Austrian prizes finally helped spread Canetti's reputation.

At the beginning of October 1981, Mr. Werner Mark Linz, President of New York's Continuum Publishing House, announced that, even though (based on past experience) "financially, Canetti will probably never be a success," Continuum was determined to publish his work in English translation for its intrinsic value and importance. The announcement two weeks later that the Nobel Prize Committee had awarded the annual literary prize to Elias Canetti will probably put an end to the most pressing worries of his American publisher—or so one would hope. The choice of Canetti seems an unusually happy one. It honors a considerable literary achievement, and it should thereby help overcome the historic handicap that has long kept him from reaching the wide audience he deserves.

II

But if Canetti's life refuses to conform to any predictable pattern, so does his work, so does his thought. For one thing, he has never written the one novel—mature, final, representative, and yet translatable and culturally transferable—which could identify him internationally—no *Magic Mountain*, no *Dr. Zhivago*, no *L'Etranger* and no *Faux Monnayeurs*, no (if that's translatable) *Ulysses* and no *The Sound and the Fury*. The one novel he did write at the age of twenty-five was to be one of eight, all satirizing trends of the time and comprising a kind of *Comédie humaine*. Each of the eight was to have a central figure who exemplified a particular trend to the point of near insanity. But only one of these projects was ever completed; its hero, a bookish and misanthropic Sinologist, comes to grief and suicide in his struggle against an exceedingly hostile environment. The tension informing the novel grows out of the rather arid intellectualism of its schemes on the one hand, and on the other, the very amusing but virtually untranslatable surface naturalism of its dialogues. Characters that have clearly been invented—and invented for the purpose of a *demonstratio ad absurdum*—speak in grotesque variations of current cliches, thereby revealing much about the social and cultural problems they represent without being themselves aware of that fact. Though packed with fascinating or amusing perspectives (dependencies, lack of communication, manipulation, aggression, insanity), artistically the novel has never enjoyed a broad success, despite various German reprintings and numerous translation attempts. Even a critic as progressive as Hans Magnus Enzensberger could speak of the book as "a literary monster, painfully elaborate and frighteningly monotonous."

And the fact that the reader encounters similar difficulties with Canetti's three plays suggests his main gift may not lie in mimetic invention at all. It seems likely that the two genres in which, generally, characters interact in time and space and in their own rights and ways, that is, the novel and the drama, require some degree of simple-minded *presence*, at least on the part of the main characters; but such presence Canetti seems either unwilling or unable to establish. Even what he terms "acoustic masks" (an individually recognizable manner of speech) may not suffice to keep the reader's or the audience's interest alive for an evening. Some of these acoustic masks, Canetti says, are modeled after people he has known, others—and most of them—are inventions, but patterned by analogy with the ones taken from life. No one will doubt Canetti's uncanny ear for individual speech habits.

But, as Canetti also said himself, he has never had any practical experience with the *theater*—even though he also (and rightly) claims that all of his writing is dramatic in nature and that (somewhat surprisingly) he enjoys writing *plays* most of all. Two new ones seem to be in the making. Like his former critical idol Karl Kraus, Canetti is fond of reading his plays for an audience; and there are critics who have claimed that this is by far the most convincing manner of having them presented. Canetti's unfailing ability to keep as many as thirty acoustic masks distinct is said to be stunning. But it must also be said that there have been only a few successful stage performances of these plays. Some, to be sure, have failed for entirely the wrong reasons; and it has been observed that after several decades of the Theater of the Absurd, Canetti's plays have become more performable than they were when he wrote them. Still, the fact that all of them essentially work out a certain *aperçu*, a whimsical idea (What if the use of mirrors were forbidden? [*Comedy of Vanity*]; What if people knew from the time of their birth exactly when they will die? [*The Numbered*]) may also have something to do with their limited success. So does the local flavor of the dialogue, at least in the first two plays. Both Canetti's sense of humor and his delight in absurd turns of events have a distinctly Viennese quality; they wither during transport outside Austria, and they may well die during the operation of being translated into another language. The fact that Canetti's plays have not been published in English (despite a successful performance of *The Numbered* in Oxford, 1956) is probably less surprising than it might initially seem.

In one sense, *Crowds and Power* could be considered Canetti's main work, in another, his collection of aphorisms, *The Human Province*, might claim that position. Significantly, neither of them could qualify as mimetic or even imaginary literature. The six hundred pages of *Crowds and Power* are Canetti's contribution to the Second World War, much as Thomas Mann's embarrassing (and still untranslated) *Considerations of a Non-Political Man* were *his* contribution to the First World War. But there the parallel ends. Where Mann's tract is a highly conservative defense of German ways and values against those of the liberal and democratic Western Allies, Canetti's book was written in the spirit of total opposition to the events around him. He himself thought of the work as "a merciless hunt for those in power. How one hated them and how one got used to this hatred!" And in the end he thought he *had* succeeded in "gripping this century by the throat." Such violent metaphors will hardly prepare the reader for what is after all a highly theoretical study. But *understanding*, understanding both the crowds and the rulers better than they had ever understood themselves, was Canetti's only means of combat in this unequal fight, and understanding the roots of totalitarianism, elitist or populist, was his declared aim.

The six hundred pages of the published text represent volumes, entire libraries, in fact, of reading—ethnology and anthropology, sociology and history, mythology and psychiatry. The result is a scholarly work, but also much more; or at least it represents a kind of scholarship that has practically disappeared from the social sciences for being too demanding, too qualitative, and too ingenious. Such scholarship has studied its sources (and some very rarified materials among them), has compared and weighed them, but then it also resolutely pulls the results together to interpret and evaluate them. It may come as a surprise that neither Marx nor Freud are called upon for help in this study of the two poles of political action, the masses and the manipulators of power. Nor are there other major "witnesses" who might do the author's thinking for him. Canetti mixes phenomenological description and etiological tracing of causes, his manner is both critical and brilliant. There are passages where the brilliance comes in somewhat subjective form (as Theodor Adorno, in an interview, observed), but this may be the price to be paid for the many discoveries of hidden or forgotten connections. "Orders," for example, are subtly analyzed, both among humans and among animals (the creature world plays a significant role in all of Canetti's writings), and a connection unearthed between orders issued and judgments pronounced, in the end, between absolute orders and the death sentence. Another important connection which Canetti's study establishes is that between political dominance and paranoia. Here, among many other sources, he uses the very memoirs—by the German parliamentarian Schreber—that Freud had used in *his* discussion of paranoia. But the resulting interpretations are very different. Whereas Freud's reading which links paranoia to homosexuality remains individual-psychological, Canetti points out the *social* roots of the phenomenon: What the paranoic shares with the absolute ruler is the wish to use all others, or, in its most extreme form, to survive them all by eliminating *them* who, in the imagination of the patient, are all trying to eliminate *him*.

Canetti's *Die Provinz des Menschen. Aufzeichnungen, 1942–1972* (1973), published in English as *The Human Province* (1978), consists of those aphoristic jottings to which he gave an hour or two every day after he discovered that the long and intense work on *Crowds and Power* needed a "safety valve." They follow a long tradition of personal and unsystematic, but incisive and illuminating "minimal writing"; the French *moralistes*, G.F. Lichtenberg, and (in method, though hardly in message) Nietzsche, are his most obvious predecessors. Some of the thoughts thus assembled are clearly reactions provoked by specific readings (*Lesefrüchte* they would be called in German); most, however, are the result of much previous reading and of long reflection. A number of themes recur again and again: the war, history, nations and their ways, myths, Jews and their fate, power, fear, faith, language, psychology, and philosophy. But the structures that hold these jottings together are subterranean, the texts themselves, from a line to a page in length, are never developed far beyond the initial flash of insight. It is only by slow accumulation that a perspective emerges, Canetti's perspective, and once that vantage point has been located, most of the aphorisms, despite their originality and frequent elements of surprise, turn out to have a *gestalt*-like coherence after all.

If this perspective is to be given a name, "ethical humanism" might do—except for the fact that, in contrast to most current *liberal* versions of humanism, "humanism" is here radicalized to an unheard-of degree. The assumption, shared with other humanists, that the life of the individual remains the one and ultimate value, leads Canetti to certain conclusions which are for him inevitable and urgent. Most of them have not customarily been faced, let alone been put into practice. Among such convictions are the following. No *power* that metes out death, either in war or in peace, can be supported. No *religion* that accepts, tolerates, excuses, or even glorifies death is in turn acceptable—and that includes, as Canetti is well aware, all the known religions. No *philosophy* that tries to console and reconcile man with death (his own or other people's) can be tolerated. This again applies not only to Canetti's "main enemies," Hobbes, de Maistre, and Nietzsche, but also to Schopenhauer, the Stoics, Freud with his death wish, even to the thinkers of the East—though Canetti seems to have more natural respect for them than for most Western thinkers. Canetti's nonacceptance, his single-minded and intransigent hatred of death, runs through all of his writings; at times it assumes the character of an article of faith, at others, that of an obsession. He advocates a state of permanent revolution (or at least rebellion) against death. "In the most important question of all, in the question of death, I have, among all thinkers, had nothing but enemies." The thought that the explanation for this odd state of affairs might be that they all see something which he is missing never seems to have occurred to him. It is one thing, and easy, to join Canetti's protest against any ready acceptance of death that makes us accomplices of systems of repression or of hollow consolation. But it is another, and much more difficult, to share his utopian vision of a death-free existence to come.

Yet, while Canetti finds himself in rather complete and splendid isolation on the question of death, he does not lack models, allies, and comrades-in-arms in other areas. His essays, collected in English as *The Conscience of Words* (1979), are largely exercises in paying intellectual debts, gracious *hommages* to other writers. None of them enjoys quite the status of Kafka (for Canetti "that purest of all models"), about whom he has written more than once. His most recent effort is a brilliant and sympathetic book-length study of Kafka's letters to his fiancée Felice, and of the implications that painful relationship had for *The Trial*. Other, though less personal role-models include Aristophanes ("I would lose my mind with pride if I had written just *one* of his comedies"), Confucius (Chinese thought in general is central to Canetti; he even detects a "Chinese quality" in Kafka), Stendhal, Büchner, Tolstoy, Gogol, and his fellow Austrians, Karl Kraus, Robert Musil, and Hermann Broch. Almost an afterthought to *Crowds and Power* is Canetti's discussion of the image of Hitler that emerges from Speer's controversial memoirs; and Canetti's account of Dr. Hachiya's Hiroshima diary is a grim case study in support of his radical opposition to death and the powers that perpetrate it.

No more than a curious little interlude is Canetti's *Der Ohrenzeuge. Fünfzig Charaktere* (1974), available in English as *Earwitness* (1979). Modeled, it seems, on Franz Blei's *Bestiarium*, a popular collection in the Vienna of Canetti's youth, the book has misled readers and critics by its subtitle, which seems to conjure up Plutarch, Suetonius, or similarly weighty fare. Nothing of the sort is intended. The "characters" are not even real characters (as Blei's still were), but timely, all too timely *types*; among them are found a "fame tester," a "beauty newt," a "syllable-pure woman," a "fun-runner" (who, it turns out, is not a jogger, but a jet-set tourist), a "sultan addict," a "hero-tugger," and a "never-must." A page or two in length, these witty satirical sketches have more to do with Morgenstern's Surrealist jokes than with their actual forerunners, Theophrastus and La Bruyère; they are also not related to Canetti's most recent work, his massive autobiography.

It is an impressive account of an impressive (though by no means spectacular) life. The first volume (*Die gerettete Zunge. Geschichte einer Jugend*, 1977) is available in English as *The Tongue Set Free: Remembrance of a European Childhood* (1980); the second is being translated. There is hope for at least a third volume, adding the London years. Predictably, the armchair and fireside quality of some memoirs is almost totally absent from this one; there is nothing chatty, quaint, or cozy about this life remembered. It is no more and no less that a careful account of "how one becomes what one is"—if what one is, is Elias Canetti. Few readers are likely to recognize aspects of their own childhood or youth in these pages—the experience seems unique, not only in its hot-house intellectualism, even bookishness, but also in its paradoxical juxtaposition of economic security and ethnic, existential, and political insecurity. A clearly gifted but disturbingly manipulative mother emerges, as well as two brothers who remain fairly pale. The early, traumatic death of the father. Long chains of minor catastrophies, schools, friends, but above all—books. Although this is obviously an imaginative, even poetic, writer's story, it is decidedly in the classical vein, with total recall, clear outlines, unhesitating and apodictic judgments. Since none of the participants had to be invented, and since the perspective *could* only be the author's own, the problems encountered in Canetti's fictional work never arise; the figures are both physically present and understood by a superb and passionate intelligence. Autobiography, and the aphoristic chips off that same block, may be Canetti's most congenial form and his most lasting achievement. If the unexamined life is not worth living, Canetti's is. If many an examined life is not worth reading about—Canetti's is.

III

The following selection of aphorisms comes from *Die Provinz des Menschen. Aufzeichnungen 1942–1972*, and has been translated by Janice Orion and myself. The aphorisms follow the chronological order in which they were written, and no attempt has been made to take them out of the random pattern of the original or to arrange them according to some superimposed principle. Although a selection of a selection, they nevertheless seem to me representative of their author's scope, themes, and manner. Since some of them derive their poignancy from the exact point of history at which they were written, the year of each entry has been provided.

* * *

My greatest wish is to see a mouse eating a cat alive. And the mouse would have to take its time playing with its victim. (1942)

*

Revenge be cursed. Even if they kill my dearest brother, I do not want revenge. What I want is different human beings. (1942)

*

The lowest form of humanity: the person whose every wish has been satisfied. (1942)

*

The various languages you should have: one for your mother, which later will never be spoken again, one you read and never dare to write; one in which you pray and of which you understand not one word; one you count in, everything to do with money belongs to it; one you write in (but not letters); one you travel in—and in that one you may also write letters. (1942)

*

It is a good thing to tempt the gods, the oftener, the better—they shouldn't have a moment's peace. They sleep too much and leave man alone on the raft with his dying brothers. (1942)

*

There will still have to be Jews after the last Jew has been exterminated. (1942)

*

Success, man's rat poison—very few survive it. (1942)

*

Many simple people ask: "Do you think the war will soon be over?" And if you reply naturally, "Yes, quite soon," you suddenly notice, and at first you will hardly believe it, that their faces are suffused with fear and fright. They are a bit ashamed of it and know well enough that they should be happy on humanitarian grounds. But the war has brought them bread and a good income, to some for the first time in their lives, to others again after many years, and so they are plagued by one emotion: If only it would go on a little longer, if only it wouldn't end just yet! Whole peoples, and right down to the lowest classes, have become war profiteers, and with all the reactions to the world that such people have. If I had to say what has brought me to the depths of despair in this war, it would be this daily experience: war in the guise of breadwinner and security. (1943)

*

My whole life is nothing but a desperate attempt to do away with the accustomed division of labor and to think everything through for myself so that it all comes together in one head and becomes one again. I don't want to know everything, only to unite what has been fragmented. It's almost certain that an undertaking of this sort cannot succeed. But the very small hope that it might makes it worth the trouble. (1943)

*

The great aphorists read as if they had all known one another well. (1943)

*

An Englishman wants to arrive at a *single* judgment as dictated by the circumstances; he does not want to line up abstract judgments. For him, thought is a direct exercise of power. Thought for its own sake seems suspect and distasteful, the thinker is for him always a stranger, especially when he uses his own language. An Englishman likes to mark out for himself a small area where his knowledge is superior, and where he need not submit to anyone. Someone who has cast his eye on several such areas is disapproved of by an Englishman; he senses a land-hungry invader in him, and not without justification. People who do not put their knowledge to use are a puzzle to him. Better for them to hide their light than to make themselves a laughing stock. The essence of English life is shared authority and inescapable repetition. Because authority is so important it must disguise its ubiquitous presence and clothe itself in modest phrases. The slightest infringement is immediately picked up by the others, who, for the sake of their own authority, rebuff it matter-of-factly and decisively, but politely. In no other land are the boundaries, as expressions of the permitted, equally secure; and what is an island but a land with clearly marked boundaries? Repetition gives life here its endless security; the years have insinuated themselves into the smallest details of existence, and — not only in terms of time — everything will again be what it has already been a thousand times. (1943)

*

There is an old confidence in language that trusts itself to name things. The poet in exile, and particularly the dramatist, is seriously weakened in more than one direction. Away from the air of his native tongue he is deprived of the familiar nourishment of names. Earlier, he might never have noticed the names he heard every day; but they noticed him and called to him loud and clear. When he sketched his characters, he created them out of the insurance of an immense storm of names, and although he might then use one that meant nothing more in memory's clear light, still it had once been there and had heard itself called. Now the emigrant's memory for his names has not been lost exactly, but there is no longer a living wind that brings them to him. He now protects them like a dead treasure, and the longer he has to be away from his old climate, the greedier are the fingers that slide through the old names. Thus, for the poet in exile, if he does not give up entirely, there remains but one thing: to breathe the new air until it too calls to him. For a long time it won't, it starts out and fades away again. He knows it and is hurt; perhaps he closes his ears altogether and then no name can get to him. The strangeness grows, and when he awakens there is an old, dried-up heap beside him, and he satisfies his hunger with a grain that was grown in his youth. (1943)

*

The meager number of his principal ideas marks the philosopher, also the obstinacy and irksomeness with which he repeats them. (1943)

*

The greatest spiritual temptation in my life, the only one against which I find I must struggle very hard, is to become a Jew entirely. Wherever I open the Old Testament, I am overwhelmed by it. At almost every line I find something that has to do with me. I would like to have been called Noah or Abraham, but my own name too fills me with pride. I try to tell myself, when I am about to drown in the story of Joseph and David, that they charm me in my capacity as a poet, and what poet would not be charmed? But it's not true, there is much more to it. Why did I rediscover my dream of man's future high age in the Bible, as a list of the oldest patriarchs, as part of the past? Why does the psalmist hate death the way only I know how to? I scorned my friends who tore themselves away from the attractions of the various nationalities and blindly became Jews again, simply Jews. How difficult it is now for me not to imitate them. The new dead, dead long before their time, plead with you, and who has the heart to deny them? But are there not new dead everywhere, on all sides, in every nation? Should I turn away from the Russians because there are Jews? From the Chinese because they are distant, from the Germans because they are possessed by the devil? Can I not go on belonging to everyone, as I always have, and yet be a Jew? (1944)

*

The language of my intellect will always be German *because* I am a Jew. As a Jew, I shall preserve in myself whatever remains of that land, now devastated in every way. Their fate is mine also; but I bring with me a common human portion as well. I shall give back to their language what I owe it. I want to make my contribution toward something that other peoples will thank them for. (1944)

*

A serious aim of my life is to know thoroughly all the myths of all the peoples. But I would like to know them as if I had believed in them. (1945)

*

You have remained so naive that you really expect the best from every new person; your greater maturity only expresses itself in that this expectation very quickly turns into doubt and disdain. When all is said and done, everything depends on the strength of this naive hope that finds it so difficult to hold its own against the increasing experience of a lifetime. As long as this hope still exists, everything can still be expected, also from you. (1945)

*

The sorrows of the Jews had become an institution, but it outlasted itself. No one wants to hear about it anymore. With amazement, people have discovered that the Jews can be eradicated; perhaps without being aware of it, they now despise the Jews for a new reason. Gas *has* been used in this war, but only against the Jews, and they were helpless. Even the money that gave them power before was of no use. They were degraded to slaves, then to animals, then to vermin. The degradation succeeded; the others who have heard of it will find it harder to eradicate all traces of this than the Jews themselves. Every act of power is twofold; every degradation increases the pleasure of the one who abuses his power, but it thereby also infects others who want to abuse it. The very old history of the relationship between Jews and other people has changed drastically. They are still despised, but they are no longer *feared*. It is for this reason that their greatest error would be to continue those lamentations in which they have always been the masters and for which there is now more foundation than ever before. (1945)

*

I would like to become tolerant without overlooking anything; to persecute no one, even when everyone persecutes me; to become better without noticing it; to become sadder, but to love life; to become more serene and happier in others; to belong to no one, grow in everyone; to love the best, to comfort the worst; not even to hate myself anymore. (1945)

*

A passion can be unspeakably beautiful if, after control, order, and awareness, it becomes again blind and impulsive. It saves itself by threatening destruction. He who lives without passion is not living, he who always controls himself half lives, he who perishes by passion has lived, he who remembers it has a future, and nothing but past has he who has banished it. (1946)

*

The only interesting thing about translating is that which gets *lost*. One should translate occasionally just in order to find this something. (1947)

*

Exchange of habits: I give you these, you give me those; out of this a marriage is supposed to grow. (1947)

*

It is a pity for everybody. By rights, nobody should ever have died. Even the worst crime was not worthy of death, and without the *acceptance* of death worst crimes would never have been committed. (1951)

*

We must be evil because we know that we will die. We would be more evil still if we knew from the beginning, when. (1951)

*

The satiety of the victor, his overfulness, smugness, his long, luxurious digesting. There are many things one should not be, but the only thing one must *never* be is a victor. Still, one always *is*, and over everyone one knows well and outlives. To win is to outlive. How can one do it: go on living and yet not be a victor? — the moral squaring of the circle. (1952)

*

Is it possible that her death has cured me of jealousy? I have become more tolerant of the people I love. I watch less over them, I grant them their freedom. I think: do this, do that, do what pleases you, as long as you go on living; do, if necessary, all sorts of things against me, annoy, deceive me, push me aside, hate me — I expect nothing, I want nothing, only this: *that you live.* (1953)

*

All intellectuals live also by theft and are aware of it. But they react to this fact in very different ways. Some express their gratitude effusively towards the one they robbed; they proclaim his name to the heavens and mention him so often that he becomes somewhat ridiculous as the object of their overdone cult. Others are *resentful* towards him after they have robbed him; and when he is mentioned by others in their presence, they attack him maliciously. Since, as his personal thieves, they know him intimately, their attack hits home and damages him badly. (1955)

*

These Oxford philosophers — they pare down and pare down until nothing is left. I have learnt a lot from them: I now know that it is better never to start paring down. (1958)

*

The most beautiful thing about *Montaigne* is that he is never in a hurry. Even emotions and thoughts that are full of impatience he handles slowly. His interest in himself is unshakeable, he is really never ashamed of his person, he is not a Christian. Whatever he observes is of importance to him, but his own self, to him, is inexhaustible. He thereby gains a kind of freedom for staying within himself. He is an object which can never be lost, he has himself, always. This one life that he never loses sight of passes by as slowly as his observation of it. (1960)

*

Translation of thoughts that have occupied one for more than twenty years into another language. Their discomfort, because they did not originate in that language. Their daring is dulled, they refuse to radiate. They drag along what does not belong and they drop important things on their way. They turn pale, they change color. They feel cautious and cowardly, the angle from which they approached cannot be recovered. They soared like birds of prey, now they flutter about like bats. They had the gait of leopards, now they creep along like a blind-worm. It is humiliating to think that in this reduction, this moderation and emasculation, they will have a better chance of being understood. (1961)

*

Supposing it were a fact that *everyone* believed what was false? Or supposing that each person caused exactly the opposite of what he believed in? Just look at those powerful fanatics who could so believe that they infected thousands of others with their belief! The Christian belief in love and the Inquisition! The founder of the thousand-year German Reich: their scattering and scrambling! The white saviour of the Aztecs in the shape of the Spaniards who annihilated them. The isolation of the Jews as the Chosen People and the end of their isolation in the gas chambers. The belief in Progress: its completion in the atom bomb. It is as if every belief were its own curse. Would one have to start here, in order to solve the riddle of belief? (1964)

*

The most embarrassing illusion of psychoanalytical therapy is that never-ending listening to the patient. Hours and hours he spends talking, but in reality he is not being listened to, or at least listened to only for things that one knew already before he ever opened his mouth. It would be just as well if he had sat out every session in silence. If it were otherwise, the whole theory of psychoanalysis would long ago have vanished into thin air. For every person to whom one really listens causes one to think completely new thoughts. The accomplishment of the analyst consists, therefore, in resisting his patient, who can say whatever he pleases; the result, as if by an unshakeable verdict of destiny, is already known and long anticipated. The whole listening stance is an act of condescension, nothing else. The changes and splittings away from the dogma are due to the few moments when some therapist forgot himself to the point of actually listening. These changes differ according to the size of the "error" and the nature of the person committing the "error." Freud himself must still have listened quite a bit; otherwise he could not have been so full of errors and of changes. (1965)

*

The one ambition that is always legitimate, keeping people alive longer, has been specialized into a job by which some people make a living: physicians. These are the very people who see the most deaths and they get even more used to death than the rest of us. Because of occasional professional mishaps even their original ambition pales. Thus the people who have always done the most against any religious acceptance of death in the end accept death as natural. One would wish for physicians who emerge from their activity with a change of heart: an unshakeable spite against death which they detest the more, the more frequently they have watched it. Their defeats would be the nourishments of a new faith. (1967)

*

A pain so great that one no longer relates it to oneself. (1967)

*

Every old man sees himself as the sum of ruses that worked. Every young man sees himself as the origin of the world. (1967)

*

To dissect a river into its brooks. To understand a human being. (1967)

*

In every family that is not one's own, one suffocates. In one's own, one also suffocates, but one does not realize it. (1967)

*

With Kafka something new has come into this world, a more precise feeling for its questionable character. Yet this is not tied to hatred, but to reverence for life. The combination of these two attitudes—reverence and ability to question—is unique, and whoever has experienced it once will never again want to do without it. (1968)

*

Self-accusations improve nothing. The deeper they go, the more reliably they will end in self-congratulation. "What a great fellow I am! Even something like that I can say to myself with impunity!" (1971)

*

All the pessimism of the history of mankind is nothing compared to reality. Not one of the old religions will do—they all originated in idyllic periods. (1971)

*

Freud's "death wish" is the descendant of old and sinister philosophical doctrines, but more dangerous than they because it dresses itself in a biological terminology that enjoys the prestige of modernity. Without being a philosophy, this psychology lives off philosophy's worst heritage. (1971)

Ivan Generalić *Scarecrow*

KRLEŽA'S GLEMBAY CYCLE IN ITS EUROPEAN CONTEXT

Ivo Vidan
Zagreb University

"Families, I hate you!" The young André Gide's exclamation in *Les nourritures terrestres*[1] was to ring out across the boundary of the 19th century and strike cords in the avant-garde spirits of later decades in the bourgeois spiritual crisis. "There is nothing more dangerous for you than your family, your room, your past," the poet addresses Nathanael. Let the home fires die out, break through the barred doors, leave everything and teach "the soul to become a wanderer."

In the novel by Roger Martin du Gard (1922-1923), Jacques Thibault, on the threshold of the "beautiful age" in his intensive life, quotes Gide's exclamation and sees it as a programme and the point of departure for his entire generation's active independence. Just a few years later in the novel he dies as a revolutionary of the Internationale in a plane full of socialist proclamations above the trenches of a scarred and war-stricken Europe.

This Nietzschean pure hatred spans, therefore, a broad front, several decades in depth, of rebellion against stagnancy and authoritarianism, from the intoxication with sensual expectation ("It is not enough for me to *read* that the sand on the beach is soft, I want my bare feet to feel it . . .") to radical social criticism of the existing, that is, the bourgeois, traditional and rigid—all that is alien to life's fullest freedom.

The beginnings of *Les Thibault* date back to those same years when Krleža published works which, linking two stylistically distinct periods in his artistic orientation, testify to precisely this same span: from ecstatic dithyrambs to earthly fruits and Pan, to a decisive and vehement incision into the rotting tissue of the anti-human relations which blocked the way for poetic ascent towards the integral man and which in Krleža's case are also moulded into a picture of the family.

As early as 1919 in *Eppur si muove* Krleža, writing about the Hungarian revolution, ponders on the circumstances of the Bolshevik victory in Russia and makes fun of "our Russofile intelligentsia," who think that "Russia is Uncle Vanya" and who "in particular like that cretinous Golovlevian somnolence (. . .) for they themselves are also broken and lazy."[2] Krleža saw the characters in Chekhov and Saltykov-Shchedrin as being profoundly symbolic of the ineffectual nature of an entire attitude towards the course of history, which was condemned to death: the euphonic similarity between *Gospoda Golovlevy (The Golovlev Family)* and *Gospoda Glembajevi (The Glembays)* is quite clearly merely an expression of a deeper link in content.

The essential subject of these two so markedly different works is inescapable in the modern history of every country and it was long since observed that novels such as *Buddenbrooks* by Thomas Mann, *The Forsyte Saga* by Galsworthy and *Decadence* by Gorkiy are near to *Les Thibault* and *The Golovlev Family*. These titles have already been mentioned on several occasions in connection with Krleža's Glembay cycle, and the most exhaustive list of works with which it belongs, with regard to the "subject of the decline of a bourgeois family," is to be found in the essay by Marijan Matković, "Marginalije uz Krležino dramsko stvaranje."[3] The English Slavist Edward Goy also mentions several of these works, underlining in particular *Decadence* (which, he finds, "bears an interesting similarity to the end of the play *Gospoda Glembajevi*"), but does not enter further into the meaning of this analogy, contenting himself with the observation that "this problem may be treated in the most diverse ways."[4]

The question is whether this is always the same "problem" for the circumstances of the decline of a bourgeois family in Germany and Russia or France and Croatia are not the same; and in the material sense is it really a case of decline in Galsworthy's Forsytes? The external circumstances in which the Golovlevs are decaying are set in train by a crisis, and only then by the liberation of the serfs; Gorkiy's Artamonovs at first rise—precisely as the continuation of this same historic process—and then decline in the proletarian revolution. And what shall we say about Faulkner, whom Matković does not mention in his essay and whose works completely correspond to the group enumerated? In his case we are dealing with the specific conditions of the American South and the degeneration which began with the defeat of the South in the Civil War and was the fate of a number of pseudo-aristocratic families dependent on black slavery.

What is common to the history frameworks of each of these family groups is that it is a question of periods of transition and social change, in a word, a process, and that the family's fate is also a process in concrete time. Without more detailed comparison we should not, in view of the historic and social context and individuality of each example, assert in advance that all these works comprise a unified literary phenomenon and even less should we state that influence, if it exists at all, is the dominant reason why we find them in so many literatures.

Whatever the case, it is certainly interesting to compare several such works and endeavour to identify the features common to all or many of them. If such features exist, the literary historical question arises of what category is at issue here. Such a broad perspective also provides new opportunities for evaluating the work of each author individually. Miroslav Krleža will be able to be measured against the well-known European names at this particular level, in the category to which the Glembay cycle belongs.

Such works were probably treated as a category for the first time in the article by A. E. Zucker, "The Genealogical Novel, A New Genre,"[5] but no common characteristics are defined here. These are works dealing with the decline of a family through several generations, this new type having been conceived by Zola and Samuel Butler (in the novel *The Way of All Flesh*). In Butler's novel, Zucker inaccurately observes, there are allusions on almost every page to hereditary influence; this is the only sign that to Zucker's mind heredity is a constitutive feature of the genealogical novel as a type or genre (Zucker does not distinguish between these two terms). Together with *Buddenbrooks* and *The Forsyte Saga,* among the latest works he also mentions *Decadence* (which was translated in 1927 into English; Zucker states that it is "naturalistic in mode and impressionist in style"). He also lists a number of contemporary and now forgotten American novels dealing with relations between the generations in a single family and mentions an English play (*Milestones,* 1922) by Arnold Bennett and Edward Knoblauch. In this itemisation he relies on the superficial subject of the works and fails to examine the principle according to which the attribute "genealogical" acquires its application.

Max Schertel also uses the concept of the genealogical novel in his dissertation (of which only a summary is published), "Thomas Mann and the Genealogical Novel,"[6] which places the tetralogy *Joseph and His Brothers* among the *Buddenbrooks* and the works of Butler and Galsworthy. In contrast to the others, Mann does not stress the demolition of social constraints but, on the contrary, the links and coherence resulting from the force of tradition through several generations. The individuality of the complex central character arises from a profound determinism which Mann bases on the psychological factor of myth, while biological heredity is of secondary importance.

Thomas Mann cannot be avoided when the genealogical subject is under examination and it is lamentable that the bibliography of comparative works on him contains no further discussions of this problem, which is incontestably international, comparative and yet at the same time too narrow to gain a place in the general theories of literature. Although Zucker and Schertel did speak about the genealogical novel, the problem is not related specifically to the genre of the novel—one need look no further than Krleža for proof of this. On the other hand, in Krleža, *Buddenbrooks* and *The Forsyte Saga* this subject appears at one level while in the tetralogy about Joseph it appears at a completely different, mythical-anthropological level, which demolishes the concrete historical milieu and negates it without (as even in Faulkner) forming *in* it a universal symbolism of questions concerning the human condition. There again, the play mentioned by Zucker, *Milestones,* is not a drama of generations as is the case in Krleža's cycle or *The Golovlev Family*: it does not formulate the principle which affords the family its unity and character and does not define it in relation to a historical process but rather remains within the confines of social anecdote showing how three generations (1860, 1885, 1912) look at things.

In the following examination Krleža's work will be traced side by side with corresponding works by seven foreign writers (Emile Zola, M. Y. Saltykov-Shchedrin, Thomas Mann, John Galsworthy, Roger Martin du Gard, Maksim Gorkiy and William Faulkner) in relation to the literary historical and structural problems which concern us here. At the centre of our attention, therefore, will be the singular constitutive form of the genealogical cycles and to perceive it the better we shall demonstrate how it appears in the case of all seven writers. We shall thereby reveal how one common characteristic of our subject is manifested in individual cases. This examination, however, will not proceed with mechanical progression, but rather individual works or a similar phenomenon in individual authors will be compared, related or contrasted. Our aim is to demonstrate a common European literary phenomenon (and the examination of an individual work will be set against what is common) and define precisely Krleža's place among the other writers. This is why we are treating Krleža among the rest, singling out various aspects of his work together with theirs. However, we shall also endeavour to underscore his specific characteristics and those features of his work which show him to be a separate part of a broader group.

This method of exposition has been chosen in view of the goal we are pursuing, but it naturally has its drawbacks. When the works of eight writers are examined with attention being focused on certain aspects which are common to them, then, as in literary cycles themselves, certain motifs crop up in new contexts. Because of this internal link it is impossible to avoid the impression that certain things have already been dealt with, but at every stage in the exposition endeavours are made to grasp the entirety of the matter. Moreover, in some places details must be dwelt on while elsewhere the broader dimensions are important. Sometimes things are anticipated: talking, for example, about Mann's genealogical conception in *Buddenbrooks* we shall have to use our full powers of analysis; on the other hand, talking about Gorkiy, perceiving merely the basic outline will allow us better to grasp his conception of the inner principle of the whole.

KRLEŽA'S DRAMA IN THE LIGHT OF THE NORTH EUROPEANS

The fact that Henrik Ibsen is exceptionally interesting in an examination of the cycle in more recent literary history is testified to by Thomas Mann and Arnold Hauser, while Krleža himself indicated that Ibsen's work is central to an understanding of the genealogical idea and internal structure in the plays about the Glembays. We should, therefore, examine Ibsen's importance to our subject, even if his works do not belong to the group with which we are concerned.

We must, then, follow the Glembay cycle in parallel with seven other individual cycles. However, if we want to link the genealogical theme in him

Ivan Generalić *A Fish in the Air*

with world drama, it is sufficient to follow his own indications on dramatic technique (in the Osijek lecture, April 1927).[7] Having sought dramatic action in the quantitative direction, in the expressionist inspired plays from *Hrvatska rapsodija (Croatian Rhapsody)* and *Galicija (Galicia)* to *Golgota (Golgotha),* he realised that the "power of dramatic action (. . .) is concrete and qualitative in the Ibsen sense and consists of the psychological objectivization of the individual subjects who experience themselves and their fates on the stage." There cannot, therefore, be good drama, Krleža continues,

> without internal psychological volume as the instrument and a good actor as the musician playing this instrument. Having experienced all the external and superfluous gadgetry of the external, decorative and therefore quantitative side of modern dramatic writing, I have decided to write dialogues on the lines of the Nordic school of the nineties with the intention of stretching the internal range of psychological tension to a greater conflict and of moving these conflicts as close as possible to a reflection of our reality. This is how my latest plays came about. They are not, and I do not want them to be, anything other than psychological dialogues, appearing now for the first time in our dramatic literature forty years late.

How is that "internal psychological volume" created in Krleža? What is the content of these psychological dialogues and what is their relation to the Nordic writers, Ibsen and Strindberg?

It is not, of course, a case of external similarities in the sentence structure, imagery or the treatment of thoughts. In Ibsen's prose speeches are short, emotions restrained and—until the culmination—there is no demonstration of strong emotion or long suggestive "stage directions." What they have in common is that the dialogue in *Gospoda Glembajevi* or *U agoniji (In Agony)* directly links the present with the past—in fact, leads the past into the present—and gradually from scene to scene builds up the viewer's knowledge of all the circumstances leading to the situation which is now unfolding before him. If, for example, we divide the first act of *Gospoda Glembajevi* into units of content, we see that following a short introduction, in which Leone experiences Angelika in the rational co-ordinates of a layman but with a painter's sensibility, there follow three short sections: a) the family history symbolised by the portraits on the wall and the story of old Barboczy's curse, the Glembays' many suicides being mentioned here; b) the Rupert—Canjeg scandal and Leone's part in its unfortunate denouement; c) Silberbrandt's attitude towards Leone and his affair with Baroness Castelli. In all three sections past events are talked about, attitudes are established and the already present tensions, which are to take the action further and be resolved in the future, are determined. This technique is continued in the second act, in the dialogue between the father and son where the relationships between the father and mother, son and father, mother and son, and the baroness and each of them are illuminated and linked up. In the third act this family theme, together with the themes from act one, is connected to the hitherto suppressed subject of the reality behind the illusion and façade of the Glembays' prosperity. The familial and the economic, the private and the public, lead to the final series of melodramatic explosions— as they are *already here* and have *already taken place.*

It would be difficult to find an obvious analogy in the plots of Ibsen's dramas but the technique with which he composes his plots is, in fact, the same. *Pillars of Society* is made up of a complex of sub-actions: the speculation on the land for the railway, the intrigue of the "stolen" money, Bernich's guilt in respect of Dina's mother, his crime against Johann, and so on. These events in the past are described more briefly, for the style and emotional world of Krleža are quite different from Ibsen's but they do have a part in the development of the action. They are already present and at the same time they are the action which is taking place.

> In view of the fact that the pre-history plays such an important role and that at the same time it can mean the action of the drama, the space in the drama given over to the introduction in older plays is too narrow and insufficient for it. Here it is not limited to the first act of the play, as was the case with the introduction previously, and closed up into a compressed and compact form with the help of messengers' reports, communications or prologues, but rather, divided into droplets, drips into the play throughout the whole of its course, serving there as explanation of those taking part, the resolution and development of the drama or as a means of drawing particular attention to a dramatic character. The pre-history and contemporary action constantly intermingle and it is a source of extraordinary tensions for the public to extract for themselves from the dialogue everything in the pre-history which is important to an understanding of the action and characters.

This is an extract from a study[8] which, when dealing with Ibsen, most often adduces a play with an apparently very narrow but in reality extremely intense action—*Ghosts*—and it holds true, it would appear, for both *Gospoda Glembajevi* and *U agonji.* If we condense the meaning of the drama thus composed and experienced into the function of the main character, that is, see the drama as a system which serves to elucidate the meaning of the central character, then we shall see that this character becomes crystallised as he places himself in relation to the false situation which is the whole context of the drama and his entire life. This situation is finally broken up melodramatically and the character transcends it through madness, death or cognition: whatever the case, a radical transformation at the very end (*Ghosts, Rosmerholm, The Lady from the Sea,* etc.). Ibsen and Krleža are in this respect part of the dramatic tradition running from Sophocles to Shakespeare and ending in their epoch of the European theatre. There is, however, something which sets them apart from their predecessors and brings them near to each other rather than to any other contemporaries. This is the psychological fullness of the dialogues in which the past has filled the present to the very moment before the melodramatic denouement. Without more comprehensive speculative analyses it would be difficult to prove that this structure is characteristic of Ibsen and Krleža because both are critics of bourgeois society, but there is little doubt that Leone's behaviour, for example, is much more complex and manifoldly significant than the aggressive or philosophically Utopian standpoints contained in the expressionist, more abstractly universal, symbols in Krleža's earlier plays. This manifold significance prevails at the moral level: is Leone really socially humane in the logic of his conduct towards Canjegova or are the Glembays right to condemn him (to use their "method" for a moment: they view his behaviour as being isolated from social logic, even though they themselves are to apply a logic similar to his—legal and formally humane—regardless of the emotional potential of the situation)?

Perhaps the abstract truthfulness of Gregers Wehrle in *The Wild Duck* is the same as Leone's—a weapon intended for the struggle against hypocrisy and illusory harmony—but its consequences do not destroy his own environment and are not of merely episodic effect. Affecting the family, outside which he himself stands, they provide the drama with yet another centre: in addition to Wehrle himself, we also have here the symbol of the wounded duck in the attic (an image for every member of the Ekdal family). Because of this structural difference it is not easy to discern the number of correspondences between this play and *Gospoda Glembajevi,* correspondences which show that Ibsen perhaps meant most to Krleža creatively where his subject matter was most complex. Gregers returns home after a long absence and the first act opens with a scene of the celebration which his father, the wealthy Wehrle, has given in his honour. The old man, a respectable merchant and factory-owner, has built his entire life on deceit. Old Ekdal went off to hard labour instead of him, he palms off a former mistress on young Ekdal for his wife and he has invited his son home to free himself of his business affairs and gain formal social recognition for his ties with the woman who keeps house for him. Gregers's condemnation of his father has none of the fury and passion of act two in *Gospoda Glembajevi* but it also culminates in accusations over conduct towards a sick woman, Gregers's mother. Wherle does not talk about "alien, maternal blood" in his son's veins like old Glembay, but he does say to him: "You are looking at me with your mother's eyes (. . .) Every word, just as though I'm listening to your mother," and he gives him an attribute which, in the German translation, is *überspannt*!

But this Gregers, a purist who lives in moral absolutes, feels the mission to "open other people's eyes" and lay bare the lies in the lives of these mere

Ivan Generalić *Raking Leaves*

mortals, who are happy in their illusions and whose lives have been made bearable by these lies. The suicide of little Hedviga, Hjalmar's departure for abroad—these are the final events in this unusual work in which Ibsen's standard theme of a rebellious anti-bourgeois love of truth suffered its implicit criticism; Leone also deceives himself thinking that through destruction he will make happiness possible for others. This self-critical aspect of the rebel is the expression of a more mature understanding of an attitude which is fundamental to both Ibsen's and Krleža's work and shapes their ideas on society. Is there also perhaps an echo of Ibsen in Krleža's later heroes, such as Dr. Nielsen in *Banket u Blitvi (Banquet in Blitva)* who "turns from a sentimental bungler into a man who 'knows what he wants' " and "on this journey of his like a burning fuse becomes the fatal destroyer of human lives?"[9]

However, Strindberg, another Nordic demolisher, means something different for Krleža. "Strindberg wrote many good scenes packed with lightning and sharply opposed, of the kind with which everything flashes in acts one and two of *The Father* (...) With the exception of Jacobsen, no one among the Nordic writers has torn into me so deeply and intensively—Jacobsen like lyrical calm and Strindberg like thunder on the open sea."[10] Nevertheless, it is precisely in the moments of peace in the scenes of self-revelation and confessions to loves and hatreds and unrestrainable urges, which at surface level give rise to perverse oscillations of mood, that Strindberg—the early Strindberg of *The Father* and *Miss Julie,* to whom the later Krleža is nearer—influences Krleža with his theme of family conflicts and the lasting hatred which children bear in themselves because of the parents' bitter struggle. This is profound inspiration, just as Ibsen's was in respect of technique and idea. Strindberg's obsession with the male-female antithesis is not essential to Krleža. From his works he derives the broader theme of the secret of heredity and orientation in childhood: the relationships between parents and children are equally important to him in *The Father* and *Miss Julie* ("Strindberg's two best things"[11]) and it was this kind of relationship around which Ibsen created his drama nearest to those of Strindberg, *Ghosts,* whose symbolic title speaks of the more effective illusion which casts its shadow over every family history.

The genealogical theme is clearly defined in *Gospoda Glembajevi* and in the prose *O Glembajevima (On the Glembays),* but in the other dramas and fragments on the members of this family it cannot be perceived without the context of the whole cycle. The cycle then, and not the individual play, is that whole in which Krleža should be compared with the genealogical works of other authors, even if these works are only perhaps one novel, for the single novel encompasses an entire totality or world, which the drama perhaps implies but does not express in the precipitate combustion of its characters' interhuman relationships.

THEORY

There are no cycles like those of Krleža based on drama (Eugene O'Neill reportedly wrote one in his youth but destroyed it!), and with which novelist should we begin? Balzac? "I consider the family and not the individual to be the essential social component,"[12] it says in the Introduction to *La comédie humaine,* but in the context of his political conceptions, not those concerning the writing of novels. *Le père Goriot* is the *King Lear* of a more modern capitalist society in the relationship between the father and his daughters, but it does not examine the family as an essential organic unit in social or natural continuity. *The Karamazov Brothers*? There does, of course, exist a profound and fully developed link between the heterogeneous sons of old Fyodr Pavlovich, and the insidious evil of lascivious "karamazovshchina" is latent in everything that is not holy in them. Dostoievsky links up his elements into a metaphysical whole which aims to present a picture of Russia and the world. His intention is spatial and not the principle of continuity which links the family in time. Nor in Butler's *The Way of All Flesh* do we find a truly genealogical theme. It is true that this sharp-witted eccentric concerned himself with the problems of evolution and heredity and eloquently defended Lamarck and the role of will in this process, but we find the traces of these ideas of his in the plays of Bernard Shaw (who was not, however, interested in the family from this point of view) and not in his own novel: the assertion by Zucker, who takes him as the initiator of the genealogical novel, is not correct. Even if he does trace the origins of Ernest Pontifex through three generations on his father's side and two on his mother's, this is only in order to set out before the reader his conception of the climate of ideas in which a bourgeois child of the Victorian era was born.

A young man's revolt against his family environment and its values and his desire to take up his own position in relation to the world—this is the subject of this novel in which Walter Allen[13] correctly sees the precursor of such modern autobiographical novels as Lawrence's *Sons and Lovers* or Joyce's *Portrait of the Artist as a Young Man,* works, then, which belong to the category of the *Bildungsroman* such as have existed since Goethe but which relate to modern times in their moral and aesthetic problems. However, these are all novels about an individual in which conflicts in the families are merely a phase or an admittedly important episode. Not even novels about the relations and conflicts between two generations, such as *Fathers and Sons* by Turgenev, present the typological context of Krleža's cycle. At issue in them is controversy over world views, ideological antithesis at one point in time, and not dialectic continuity in historic time.

"Genealogical novels (. . .) should be differentiated from the simpler family novels such as *Clarissa Harlowe* and *The Newcomes.* In the latter the fate of the individual hero or heroine is visibly influenced by his or hers belonging to some family group which thereby acquires a more active role than a mere background would have. In the genealogical novel, however, the family itself is the hero and its fate is followed through several generations. This plan is usually governed by an interest going beyond the features and problems of history; by a more scientific concern with the principles of the environment and heredity which can only be discerned through observations carried out within one cycle of individual lives. Its interest rests to a great extent on biological and sociological concepts which is why it developed only quite recently."

This excellent definition is to be found in an article on *Buddenbrooks*.[14] There are clues in this text which lead one to conclude that the idea of the genealogical novel itself was borrowed from the previously mentioned Zucker. However, it is much better developed in the above sentences, though the writer takes the theory no further. But this is sufficient for us to recall Zola. There really is no point looking for a genealogical novel before him. The question is merely whether the most general characteristics of the genealogical novels by other writers can be boiled down to Zola's conception, or: how much others were to be independent of Zola and how many correspondences there were to be in the mode of writing, structural characteristics and genealogical principles which link up the life of the generations in the family under study by the writer.

The very idea of following the history of a family as a whole which bears its own vital principle demands a certain rational organization and objective consistency which is characteristic of the scientific approach. Zola, living at a time when the natural-science methods received constant reaffirmation with new results and ingenious constructed systems, profoundly believed in their systematic application in the study of the human phenomenon under clearly defined circumstances and he adopted them as the methodology of his work. In 1868, while planning his cycle, he wrote *General Remarks on the Movement of a Work* in which he applies the biological factor of heredity to a family in social change (the goal of which is physical and intellectual pleasure) in the epoch of the Second Empire. In the foreword to the first novel about the Rougon-Macquarts he says:

> The group or family which I am about to study has as a characteristic excessive desires, a trait of our time, which pursues pleasures. Physiologically, they are a gradual sequence of nervous and sanguine events which appear in a race after the first organic injury and which, according to the environment, determine in every individual of this race feelings, desires, passions, all human manifestations, natural and instinctive, whose fruits have the adopted names of virtue and vice. Historically they come from the people, penetrate into the whole of modern society and climb to all positions with that essentially modern elan which the lower classes acquire in their passage through society;

thus they tell the history of the Second Empire by means of their individual dramas, starting with the coup d'état and going up to the betrayal at Sedan.[15]

A pre-supposition for such a programme is certainly determinism, but as Zola says in the notes for his general plan (1868), it would be ridiculous to talk about fatality for ten volumes. Zola therefore satisfied himself with the uncompromised expression of "force."[16] This expression is sufficiently vague to correspond to the resultant of the three factors which, according to Hippolyte Taine, govern human history: race, environment and moment. The nature of the mutual relationship of these factors is not explained in Taine, but in respect of the work of art it means the apparent abolition of metaphysical aesthetics and brings artistic creativity nearer to experimentation.[17] Under the influence of *Introduction to Experimental Medicine* by Claude Bernard, which he did not study in detail, Zola himself introduced the experimental method into the writing of novels, though this method—like Bacon's, from which scientific study proceeded in the New Age—is merely logical, deductive and not inductive-empirical.

Zola's liking for informing himself on the details of a particular environment which he intended describing in a book is not important to the conception of the whole. The fact that this documentation is superficial does not in itself make the novels worse, just as better verified and more complete observations would not necessarily make them better. What is important is the intention of the whole: that *all areas* of society must be embraced, for they are the environment, the milieu, in which the members of his family exist. His aim is not, he says explicitly, to show, like Balzac, society or the history of customs. The historical framework is indeed merely a historical framework. He is not interested in masses, in Balzac's three thousand characters. He does not want to analyse them for their own sake but rather a smaller number of them as members of a family. He even conceives of the composition of a particular work in the form of a limited series of large blocks which are to achieve their effect as a solid construction of mass.[12] Conceived of as a series of ten books on the modern history of the Second Empire, the execution gradually modified and expanded this whole, but not to the extent of exceeding or radically breaking the predetermined framework. The genealogical tree drawn before he even began writing the first book became somewhat more ramified and the traits given a character sometimes altered the bearer (Etienne Lantier, the hero of *Germinal,* remains a worker-revolutionary and does not become a criminal; this characteristic is acquired by a new character, the hero of *La bête humaine*), but in essence Zola was able, after 23 years and 20 novels, to say quite justifiably that he had completely realized his intention—an intention so broad and complicated that it hardly has an equal in the history of literature. If Zola is boring for the modern reader this is not because he fell short of the standard of which he himself was aware but rather because that standard does not satisfy us: *description* in the era of the cinema and television is neither literature nor testimony. The last volume of the series, *Le docteur Pascal*, explicates the principles connecting the entire family, all its members, and illustrates with strong idealization Zola's vision of life. This novel is a reflection not of Zola's literary doctrine but the thought which shaped and permeated the entire cycle. This book is undeservedly unfamiliar and ignored. It is one of the precursors of the modern novel of ideas and a key work in studying a unique phenomenon in modern literature: the tandem of science and fiction—the application in fiction of science and of the scientific shaping of a non-actual reality and subject created in the imagination.[19] *Le docteur Pascal* means something to the readers of Huxley and science fiction, not as an anticipation of this genre but as its first legitimate member. As with this book, the numerous less read works, in which the family links and key episodes in the history of the Rougon-Macquarts are shown, are more informative in respect of Zola's conception as a whole. They usually embrace a large number of characters from the family—sometimes from several generations—than the relatively autonomous units on individual isolated branches of these families which are as a rule more popular and better vindicated artistically: *Germinal, L'assommoir, Nana, La débâcle* . . . Zola's place in world literature, however, is not so much due to his individual better novels as to the impressiveness and consistent execution of an integral design. As a style, movement and school, naturalism has many teachers; *Les Rougon-Macquart* is not a collection of 20 books in the literary consciousness but more than this (and this "more" relies on the popularity of merely a few of them). Even if this world is not fully accounted for, it is complete like some scientific system and in this scientificness more influential than the open and imaginatively richer world of *La comédie humaine.* Balzac arrived at the idea of his cycle after he had written several novels which then became part of the cycle, while Zola drew up his project under the influence of Balzac's fresco—and as a conscious polemic with it. Together, however, they initiated a tradition which in the 20th century continued as the *roman-fleuvre* and which, particularly in France, comprised long series of novels of the most diverse artistic modes, from Romain Rolland *(Jean Christophe)* through Proust to the 25 volumes of *Les hommes de bonne volonté* by Jules Romains. What the *romans-fleuves* have in common is that their subject is not history or the background to one person but a certain reality which goes beyond the individual and that they have no central action but a complex or parallel flow of several actions. Time, as an unending procession, becomes a problem and it is the task of the writer to fix it as a moment of intuitive cognition of the world and himself, as the internal thread of meaning in history, as the discernible process of the rise and fall of a community. Understanding it as a totality of segments which is at the same time a contrapuntal composition, writers most often constituted the *roman-fleuve* as a cycle,[19] carrying on the custom of Zola and Balzac but with greater concentration on the central problems.

CYCLES

At the same time certain writers contented themselves with one volume, pronouncing on the same things as other writers wrote several times on. *The Golovlev Family* by Saltykov-Shchedrin is in the tradition of the satirically coloured realism of Gogol and is a profoundly Russian work in its every character and the dominant mentality of the family. Saltykov-Shchedrin did not write a cycle of novels but the reverse: the idea of a novel arose from a cycle of shorter pieces. In the midst of a series of satirical sketches and short stories there appeared *Family Court* (1875) which then became the first chapter of *The Golovlev Family*. Saltykov-Shchedrin probably began developing it into a novel as a result of praise from Turgenev and Goncharov.[20] It is necessary to mention this in order to understand another, in respect of structure, more important fact: the character of Yudushka is merely indicated on the margins of this first chapter but his presence as the centre of the family later provides the book with greater unity than a chronicle would have. Is it possible that awareness of Zola's idea of a cyclical whole could not have influenced these conceptions of the writer, who had written only one (satirical) novel and been very successful as a writer of sketches and satirical feuilletons? When he had already written *Family Court* Saltykov-Shchedrin personally met Zola and Flaubert in Paris at Turgenev's. An opponent of naturalism, he nevertheless printed some novels by the Goncourt brothers in "The Notes of the Fatherland" while he was working on *The Golovlev Family*. Thus in the history of the development of his compositional technique it was to be irrelevant that he was never very fond of Zola and that in 1880, at a time when he had finished his novel, he even attacked *Nana* and the world view in that book.[21]

The unspoken presence of Zola is merely one aspect of *The Golovlev Family*; it does nothing to diminish the autonomous value of the novel but it is important in its connection with the family of genealogical literary works. In the next generation the family about which Maksim Gorkiy wanted to write was so different from the Golovlevs that this dictated a different approach to the internal structure. The entirety of the relations between the father and three sons is to a certain extent analogous to the pattern in *The Brothers Karamazov*, but the idea for the novel, inspired by Russian problems, was developed in the European intellectual climate. In his memoirs on L. N. Tolstoy Gorkiy mentions how (in winter 1901-2 in the Crimea) they arrived at the subject of degeneration whilst talking about a novel by the Goncourt brothers. Tolstoy initially maintained that this phenomenon did not exist and that it was imaginary, but then Gorkiy related the history of three generations of a merchant family which he knew and in which "the law of degeneration operated in a particularly cruel fashion." Tolstoy became excited: "That is—true. I know, in Tula there are two families like that. That should be written about. Written about briefly in an important novel, understand? Definitely!" In the ensuing conversation Tolstoy's enthusiasm was aroused for the character of a monk, a member of this family, clearly the prototype for Nikita Artomonov, and for a second character "who is bored, amasses money and builds." Tolstoy also thought him to be realistic: "And he drinks, is an animal, a libertine, and likes everything and then suddenly he kills—ah, that is good!"[22]

A Soviet analysis of *Decadence* shows profound links between this novel and *Buddenbrooks,* correctly contrasting the tone and ideological atmosphere in the two works: in Mann there prevails a gloomy, lyrical, elegiac sullenness; in Gorkiy a sharp and severe moroseness. In Mann there prevail semi-tones; in Gorkiy bright, clear colours. Without adducing Lukacs, it reiterates his assessment according to which there is more internal drama and tension in Gorkiy, more expression of irreconcilable social contradictions, while in Mann the action proceeds gently, uniformly and peacefully.[23]

Buddenbrooks is quite consciously permeated by moods of decadence; the psychological sensitivity finds its counterpart in the physical degeneration of the later Buddenbrooks. It is hardly surprising, therefore, that Felix Bertaux, for example, says that the work would have been impossible if it had not been preceded by Zola's fesco of the Rougon-Macquarts.[24] Mann himself denies this: prior to *Buddenbrooks* he had never read Zola and the direct stimulus to transfer from short psychological stories to a larger composition came from the social novel *Renée Mauperin* by the Goncourt brothers.[25] The literary atmosphere came from the Nordic family novels of Kieland and Lie, for *Buddenbrooks* is conceived as a book about the bourgeoisie of his native Lübeck, a northern Hanseatic town.[26] Even without a knowledge of Zola's method, Mann threw himself into note-taking, the compilation of chronological schemes and family trees, a search for psychological points of interest and material and the questioning of experts and acquaintances.[27] Instead of a local document appearing from this material,

> under my hands the novel about Hanseatic bourgeois life started to acquire an epic character, an epic spirit, epic dimensions; diverse and heterogeneous experiences which contributed to its formation. French naturalism and impressionism, the gigantic moralism of Tolstoy, the music of motifs from Wagner's *The Lay of the Nibelungs,* Lower German and English humour, Schopenhauer's philosophy of the study of suffering, and the dramatic scepticism and symbolism of Henrik Ibsen all flowed together into the novel during the two years' work and what appeared was the spiritual history of the German bourgeoisie in which

not only it itself but also the European bourgeoisie in general could feel that it was being talked about.[28]

This internationally determined literary character[29] of Mann, this Europeanism of his, made him to a certain extent a central personality in the literature of the 20th century, not in his means of expression or literary technique but in the depth of the problems, in which respect his work concurs with that of Joyce, Proust, Faulkner or Lawrence. This could be summarised, with simplification, in the idea of various levels, cycles, the renewal and modified repetition of constant anthropological motifs at various levels oc culture and consciousness: in this sense *The Magic Mountain* follows on from *Buddenbrooks* and, in turn, *The Legend of Joseph* follows on from this. This is also the mutual relationship between Joyce's four books from *The Dubliners* to *Finnegans Wake*; this is the implication of Faulkner's confrontation of history, genealogy and stream of consciousness, in which each of his more important books can be understood as a centre about which the other, equally relevant books are arranged (*The Sound and the Fury, The Bear, Requiem for a Nun, Light in August*); this is also the meaning of Lawrence's *Rainbow*.[30] And so Mann, having read *Les Rougon-Macquart*, prized above all the very concept of the cycle and compared Zola's work with Wagner's *The Ring*,[31] while in Ibsen's oeuvre he found an essential analogy with Zola's and Wagner's art.

Buddenbrooks is also in the general direction of Mann's art; it is an essentially cyclical work, though in the characters and genealogical relations the novella *Tonio Kröger* is the only thing linked to it. An interesting contrast with him is presented by John Galsworthy, whose *The Forsyte Saga*, among Western European works, is most frequently mentioned as analogous to *Buddenbrooks*. However, Galsworthy is a classic example of the unplanned but gradual, indeed rhythmic formation of a cycle without so much as a trace of the impressive intellectual consciousness of the cycle which Mann had. His composition is the product of the experience of a calm, pragmatic British observer, though the genealogical problems essentially correspond to those in kindred works by other writers.

The hero of one of his early novellas is called Swithin Forsyte. Even though the environment in which the novella is set is completely uncharacteristic, the very title (*The Salvation of a Forsyte*) betrays that Forsyte is not merely a chance name for the writer but the name of a potential category. The story is printed together with the novel *Villa Rubein*, in which one of the themes is the conflict between a philistine and rebellious artist, and one of the characters from this novel was to acquire a marginal role in *The Man of Property*, in which Swithin Forsyte from the above-mentioned novella becomes one of the pillars of the family group.

The Man of Property, then, crystallizes the earlier thematic tendencies of Galsworthy's narratives into a symbolic socio-familial complex which is representative of an entire national civilization. The relationship between this work and those which follow on from it is similar to the position of *Gospoda Glembajevi* in Krleža's cycle: all the features of the whole are already contained in it; only the historical process of the generations is not felt in temporal evolution. *The Man of Property* is complete and at the same time pregnant with possibilities for literary development, for non-mechanical multiplication from the germ. Galsworthy's feeling, then, twelve years and several different books later, that he had to return to the Forsytes was quite understandable. The additional two novels with two short narrative episodes (interludes) between the individual books were, taken together with *The Man of Property,* correctly recognized as a harmonious and logical trilogy. Then Galsworthy went a stage further in terms of composition and in the artistic sense behaved mechanically—and erred. He continued his historical fresco in another similarly constructed trilogy *(A Modern Comedy)* and then revived this in a third one *(End of the Chapter)* whose connection with the Forsytes is quite fortuitous but which has the same social milieu and cultural horizons as the later Forsytes. The three ramified trilogies thus comprise a cycle of cycles, especially if we add to them the small and subsequently conceived episodes (collected in the book *On Forsyte Change*) which in terms of the chronology within the work return to the earliest Forsytes. Galsworthy's imagination, however, grew weaker from *The Man of Property* onwards the more he spent his energy on quantitative prolongation. From a vision of a social reality and its implicit criticism his work was turning into benign and sentimental entertainment, the writer all the while apparently not trying a different key or new artistic possibilities for rejuvenating and refreshing his vision.

Roger Martin du Gard is taken to task by some critics for doing precisely this: for executing within a cylical whole a technical break of importance to the content, with the result that, despite the continuity of time and personalities in the latter half, one feels as though one is reading a different work. He had conceived a cycle of 13 or 14 volumes covering about 40 years and created a chronological documentation for every character. However, having arrived in book seven within sight of World War he felt he had to do something new. He burned the manuscript for this book, which was to continue dealing with the civilian lives of its heroes, and only six years later did the disproportionately long volume of *L'été 1914* appear,[32] presenting the events of 44 days in 880 pages. The civilian life to which the Thibaults belonged, with their temperaments ranging from conservative to revolutionary, leads us up to the European catastrophe. Subsequent events can, therefore, only be developed in this way if the conversations and ideas of the heroes in the days of crisis leading up to the catastrophe contain the entire economic, diplomatic and class-political complex of circumstances and reasons, as they would certainly have been reflected at that time among the most aware and intellectually active people. Just before World War II Martin du Gard added a long epilogue—book eight in the cycle—which covers the last six-and-a-half months of the war in 1918 and gathers together the threads from the preceding book, returning in respect of method—and as far as the material allows—to earlier parts of the cycle.

In dealing, then, with the genealogical theme we see that six writers from four different national literatures shaped their conceptions in the form of a cycle and that the following of a direct model in this connection was of quite secondary importance or none at all. Even when a family history is completed in one book, this book is either constructed in independent chapters, which are novella sketches in their literary origin (Saltykov-Shchedrin), or it treats the chain of generations as a complete process (Gorkiy)[33] or as the exhaustion of a vital sphere which the author continues in later works at a symbolically higher level (Mann). When in 1917 the young Krleža wrote that "one should (...) work in cycles in a planned manner like Zola, or even better like Michelangelo," this was only partially an expression of a vigorous energy which wanted to make up for the fact that "since 1908 no one has uttered one single word about any important and, for Croatia, perhaps fateful question in that (I shall not say what kind of) coffee-house literature."[34] In part this is also certainly an affinity for exhausting, returning and redelving into the depths of a subject. After the "Michelangelo" series of expressionistically realized titanic heavenward lunges there followed the *Hrvatski bog Mars (The Croatian God Mars)* cycle—novellas and the drama *Galicija*—which kept him down on the black and bloody soil of Croatian historic reality—both traditional and topical. After this he also developed the subject of death in a series of novellas about this same Croatian life, but now in peace-time and among the petty-bourgeoisie. Just as *Hrvatska rapsodija* is the link between the first and second series, so among the later civilian novellas *U agoniji* (1924)—its present-day title is *Na samrti*[35]—stands out as a metaphysically inclined fixation of the central situation in the drama *U agoniji* (1928), including an important episode which entered the final act of *Gospoda Glembajevi*. In *Na samrti (On the Deathbed)* the characters have no names, nor do they have the attributes which belong to their bourgeois public life, but in the next cycle they acquire the determinants of the social set of the Glembays in an accurately drawn historic period. For this reason it is probably not by chance that the first prose piece, which was later to become part of the Glembay cycle, is the main body of what is today *Ivan Križovec* and that the central Glembay characters are arrived at via Križovec and following the bizarre picture of Faber, who became a Soviet general, having divorced himself from Zagreb bourgeois society.

More precisely, two different texts bear, in their first published versions, the title *U magli (In the Mist)*. The first (1926) is the present-day fragment *Ivan Križovec* (omitting the last section which begins with the words "Posljednji put sastao je doktor Križovec barunicu Lembachovu na ratištu u Galiciji"). The second (1928)[37] consists of two unconnected parts of which the first is that impression of Laura Lenbachova which now forms the end of *Ivan Križovec* (but in this first version it is narrated in the first person) with a note at the end: *Iz uspomena dr. Paula Altmanna (From the Memoirs of Dr. Paul Altmann)*. The second is the present-day *U magli*, but the name of the hero is Marcel Ivanović Faber (whereas, if it is the familiar character from the Glembay family tree, it should be, as in later versions in the book, Marcel Rikardović Faber). We shall talk about the significance in terms of content of these changes for the cycle as a whole at a later juncture. The next text printed was *Barunica Castelli—Glembajeva*[38] (today part of *O Glembajevima*), 1928; in the next three years the body of the entire present cycle was published in journals, with three exceptions. The third and fourth acts of *Leda* and the prose piece *Barunica Lenbachova* were written for the first time in book form (Minerva edition, *Glembajevi*, 1932) and *Pod maskom (Beneath the Mask)* was also first published in a book (*Novele*, 1937, in the Biblioteka hrvatskih pisaca edition). Also published in this book, and not in the *Glembajevi* volume, were fragments which were published previously in journals, but their link with the Glembay themes is indirect, though there is mention in them of personalities from the Glembay set. They are *Dobrotvori (The Benefactors), Kako je doktor Gregor prvi put u životu susreo Nečastivoga (How Dr. Gregor Met the Evil One for the First Time in his Life), U magli* and *Klanfar na Varadijevu (Mr. Klanfar at Varadijevo)*. Let us mention here that in respect of the subject the play *U logoru (In the Camp)* also belongs in the Glembay sphere (not *Galicija*, but its later version first published under the title *U logòru* in 1934) as one of its heroes is Dr. Gregor; we shall deal later with the less formal aspects of this.

With the prose piece *Glembajevi* ("Srpski književni glasnik," 1928) there is a note to the effect that this is "a fragment of a larger work about a Zagreb lower-town patrician family" but today we cannot say how Krleža conceived of the whole of this work. Was he thinking about a novel or precisely the kind of cycle we now have, in which the same people appear in prose pieces and directly—or reportedly—in various places? It is probable that *O Glembajevima* as printed in book form was put together later and that its individual parts first appeared individually—as they were published in the reviews. The original *Glembajevi* prose pieces which corresponded to pages 7-17, 25-27, 41-46 and 58-60 in the Zora edition of 1950, had added to them in the book edition (1932 and later editions) the texts on Urban (17-25), the baroness Castelli (27-41) and the general's wife, Warronigg-Glembay (46-58).[40]

Apart from the previously mentioned redistribution of the two different *U magli* prose pieces into the present-day texts of *Ivan Križovec* and *U magli*, and the joining of two separately printed halves[41] of the present-day *Ljubav Marcela Faber-Fabriczyja za gospodicu Lauru Warroniggovu (Marcel*

Faber-Fabriczy's Love for Miss Laura Warronigg) into a single whole, to which we should also return later, this is the only other major surgical operation on the body of the cycle as it gradually first appeared in print.

Perhaps the following hypothesis could be posited: in 1928 Krleža conceived the prose text of *Glembajevi* as a major introduction into a much larger number of texts on the Glembays than was written in the next four years (up to the Minerva edition). In order to lend this programmatically important text a certain amplitude of more comprehensively developed individual characters, he incorporated the above-mentioned fragments on three life careers. A whole series of Glembays, about which there is not a word in the other plays and prose fragments but which are mentioned in the introductory prose, thereby remained merely a plastic backdrop for those lives which are developed in the prose pieces and plays. *O Glembajevima* remains, therefore, an introduction, but at the same time a kind of autonomous, if not harmoniously composed, whole, worthy of standing at the head of a cycle realised fragmentarily. In 1932 Krleža's interests were completely elsewhere: *The Return of Philip Latinovicz* was written, the theme of Leone and, going even further back, of young Kavran from *Devil's Island* and Dr. Wagner from *In extremis,* thus acquiring another variation, this time completed in a great novel. He was already planning *Banket u Blitvi,* writing major literary critical essays and producing new poems. The Glembay cycle became part of a broader cycle of his artistic settling-of-accounts with the historic fate of his country.

In this impatience and hurry, in which he slipped from one thematic sphere into another, embracing within the space of a year an entire sphere of spheres, Krleža was different from all the previously mentioned novelists. Regardless of whether, like Zola, they proceeded systematically according to a prearranged plan, expanded the work with geometric progression from one phase to the next like Galsworthy, changed the structural proportions in the midst of the gradual, arithmetic build-up of previously envisaged parts like Martin du Gard, or confined their family's course to one book like Gorkiy, Mann and Saltykov-Shchedrin, all these writers rounded off their conceptions in complete compositions with the tracker's certainty and creative routine which belong to writers of the great narrative traditions. If we look for an analogy with the open and incomplete nature of the Glembay cycle and its potential link with other focal points of Krleža's vision we shall only find it in the work of William Faulkner, in which (though this is merely a coincidence) 1928 is also a key date (except that *Gospoda Glembajevi* and the works accompanying it already mean the height of crystallization, while *The Sound and the Fury* and *Sartoris* are two initial successes which in later books are complemented by equal achievements).

One can only talk in the same breath about Krleža's and Faulkner's narrative works if one intentionally ignores the differences in dimensions. The events in those 15 or so novels by Faulkner and his 60 or more long tales are devoted to one world, his homeland, which he situated in the imaginary but recognizable region with the Indian name of Yoknapatawpha in Northern Mississippi. The main body of Faulkner's works deal with the historical reality of this homeland, but brought to life in the viewpoint of a personal, mythical interpretation; with the defeated, socially backward, exhausted and impoverished American South, ridden with prejudice, hatred and abstract ideas. Concentrated in the town of Jefferson and its environs, the action of all these works, presented in the form of direct events, reportedly through the voice of an imaginary narrator, or brought to life in the notes of chroniclers, depicts a geographically and temporally determined, unified and relatively homogeneous world. The bearers of the action are various families through the course of the generations. As regards Krleža, writing about Zagreb and Northern Croatia, he also seems every time to have taken a family for his pivot: in some works the Glembays, in others, changing the sociological focus, the Klanfars, elsewhere, concentrating on the intensive search for roots, Philip Latinovicz, or, moving to the extensive Austro-Pannonian world, the Emeričkis....

In Faulkner one novel is devoted to the origins and ruin of the home of Sutpen, a second to the disintegration of the Compson family, a third, in fact a trilogy, to the rise and fall of the parvenu Snopes. The minor characters from one of these books became the central heros in another, the action of some short story appears as an anecdote in a novel, or the further development of events started in one work is recounted or mentioned in passing in another, many years later. Time in the novels themselves exists in two forms: the stages of the external, measurable, objective course of events are clearly marked by objective phenomena and relationships, but in the minds and assessments of the heroes themselves time often does not exist. The world is experienced as an immutable constant which was formed at the moment of defeat in the Civil War with the impoverishment, abolition of slavery and onslaught of unscrupulous profiteers from the North which this brought. For this reason the Irish critic Sean O'Faolain does not agree that Faulkner's families should be viewed as variants of the Thibaults, Buddenbrooks or Rougon-Macquarts.[42] They are not chronicles from middle-class history but aspects of a complex extra-temporal situation which the writer dissects and develops in an intuitive, undisciplined and chaotic fashion, every time through a different prism of narrative organization and on the most unexpected principles of composition. Or precisely through the inadequacy of every principle: *Go Down, Moses* was first printed with the sub-title "and other stories" and later the author himself called it a novel. This is indeed a book about the members of the MacCaslin family in various generations, together with their slaves and legitimate and illegitimate branches, both white and half-cast. The largest part (chapter, story?) of the book, *The Bear*, appears here in its third version, which differs from the previous two, published independently in journals, mostly in the inserted fourth part, which is written in the hallucinatory technique characteristic of the key moments of Faulkner's vision of the world and which reveals his essential genealogical principle and the meaning of this family complex in his literary work as a whole. This fourth part of *The Bear,* as he once warned his confused readers,[43] is not part of the novella *The Bear* itself but it is part of the novel *Go Down, Moses* of which *The Bear* is a part.

In the unorthodoxy of Faulkner's technique we see, in fact, an exuberant variant of Krleža's expression of anti-traditional, non-classical, modernistic sensibility. Faulkner's cycle of genealogical novels and novellas is what the Glembay cycle would have been if each of the 11 prose fragments had been developed into a novel, certain novellas had been brought into narrative connection with the Glembay cycle and the connection between the Glembays and other works by Krleža had been stressed more strongly than is suggested by the mere name of, for example, Titus Andronikus Fabriczy in *Zastave (Flags),* Bobočka in *The Return of Philip Latinovicz* and *Leda* and Križovec and Urbanov in *The Return of Philip Latinovicz.*

To underline the analogy between Faulkner and Krleža in the context of the genealogical narrative works of the major writers of a long period in literature does not mean to identify their position within civilization or the literature of their own country; nor does it mean to draw a parallel between their ideological orientations towards events in history. It does not even mean to identify their creative temperaments (Faulkner the hermit and Krleža *engagé* in the battles of the moment) but rather to observe a literary phenomenon.

Participation in a cycle in some of the works by these two authors is a more radical and essential aspect of the overall literary meaning than in other writers, as their individual works are more strongly dependent on mutual illumination; they interlock more than in the case of Zola and do not present a mere continuity in a single temporal dimension as in the other writers under discussion. Organic unity in an unintegrated form is the result of resistance towards all classicism and towards any sacrificing of spontaneous expression for the sake of harmonic completeness of the aesthetic core. Arnold Hauser found an interesting theoretical-historical framework for this phenomenon, though he did not, of course, mention either Krleža or Faulkner.

While classical works are immanent within their own aesthetic sphere, he says,

> any naturalism, that is, all art obviously dependent on real models, breaks through the immanence of this sphere and every cyclical form which unites in itself various artistic expressions removes the independence of an individual work of art. The majority of works of medieval art appeared in this cumulative method which embraces several independent wholes. The chivalrous epics and adventure novels

with their long, interminable stories and their somewhat repeated characters also belong to this category, as do the cycle of medieval painting and the innumerable episodes of the mysteries. When Balzac discovered his system and arrived at the idea of *La comédie humaine* as to a certain extent to this medieval compositional method and accepted a form for which the self-sufficiency and crystal clarity of classical works of art had lost their meaning and value (. . .) Zola, Wagner and Proust mark the further stages of this development and attach growing importance to the cyclical, encyclopaedic world-wide style, contrary to the principle of unity and selection.[44]

Krleža's and Faulkner's open vision, always capable of expanding its range to new possibilities and, without changing the totality, of multiplying the forms in which it is manifested, is based, therefore, on Balzac. Balzac is the common denominator and precursor to both Krleža's and Faulkner's cyclical expression of the world they experienced. After all, Croatian literature does have its own kind of Walter Scott in the form of Šenoa but it does not have its Balzac until Krleža. American literature has its psychological Balzac in Henry James, but the world which fires Faulkner's imagination is quite different, essentially different, from James's in the way in which the worlds of Stendhal, Balzac, Flaubert (in *Madame Bovary* and *Une éducation sentimentale*) and Zola are mutually not so. Hauser's observation regarding the unity of Balzac's work at the level of the characters which people it also holds true in its general sense for Faulkner and Krleža:

"Of the two thousand characters in *La comédie humaine* 460 characters appear in several novels. Henri de Marsay, for example, appears in 25 different works and in the novel *Splendeurs et misères des courtisanes* alone there appear 150 personalities which play more or less important roles in other parts of the cycle. All these characters are broader and more substantive than the individual works and we always have the feeling that Balzac is not telling us everything he knows and that he could tell us about them."[45]

This "dove-tailing of stories into each other" suggests, says the French critic, Claude-Edmonde Magny, "the idea of a total world which can barely be felt in advance and which it is certainly impossible to understand when only one or two of its parts are known." She recalls that, for Malcolm Cowley who edited the selection *The Portable Faulkner,* all the works which relate to the imaginary geographical unit, which we might call *Terra Faulkneriana,* present parts of the same vivid reality and this reality constitutes Faulkner's true literary work[46] more than the volumes which he printed and which contained only one part of it.

GENEALOGICAL PRINCIPLES

This Balzacian totality of a created reality is an external, superficial (but very substantive), aspect of Faulkner's narrative work. However, the links between the members of his families (that constant which unites them in time and justifies the repetition of names), the returning to key situations which are important to both the grandfathers and great-grandchildren of a single family line—this idea, then of an internal, genealogical principle, if we want to call it this, comes, as we know, not from Balzac but Zola. Pondering *La comédie humaine* as a whole which was to unite his works written in recent years with those which he still wanted to write about France in the 19th century, Balzac wrote that only society was to be the historian and he, the writer, its secretary. His work, "in order to be complete, also had to have its conclusion. Thus deprived, society would also have to bear in itself the cause of its motion."[47] About this *causa efficiens* (his idea probably corresponds to this concept of Aristotle's) we find nothing in the foreword, provided it is not the ideological principles of the Church and Monarchy (the degree to which these institutions are unimportant to the overall picture of his society, developed and tied up in a firm money chain, has long been familiar). Zola criticised the internal determinant behind Balzac's motley and overly rich stage and constructed his own standpoint in opposition to Balzac:

> My work will be not so much social as scientific. With the help of three thousand characters Balzac wants to create a history of customs: he bases this history on faith and the monarchy. His entire science consists in saying that lawyers, loafers, etc., exist just as dogs, wolves, etc. exist. In a word, his work aspires to be a mirror of modern society.
>
> My work will be something quite different. Its framework will be narrower. I do not want to paint a picture of modern society but just one family, showing the chance game of race modified by environment.
>
> *If I accept a historical framework, then this is only in order to have an environment which reacts*; trade and domicile are also environments. My great aim is to be purely naturalistic, purely physiological. Instead of having principles (royalty, catholicism) I shall have laws (heredity, inherence). I do not want, like Balzac, to decide the affairs of people, be political, a philosopher or moralist. I shall content myself with being a scholar, with saying what is, seeking its innermost reasons. No conclusions, whatever the case. The simple presentation of the facts about a family, showing the internal mechanism which drives it. I even accept the exception to this.
>
> My characters no longer have the need to return in individual novels.
>
> Balzac says he wants to depict people, men, women and things. I treat men and women the same, recognising, however, the natural differences, and I subject men and women to things.[48]

On the basis of Letourneau's *La physiologie des passions* and Lucas's five principles of heredity in *Traité de l'hérédité naturelle,* Zola constructed a system with which he connected dozens of Rougons and Macquarts. The scheme is interesting but quite contrived and arbitrary and in no way more scientific than the connections which other writers, following his idea of the cycle, constructed without scientific pretensions. Thus in Faulkner's case biological heredity is of immense importance and "rape, robbery, incest, murder, suicide, fratricide, drug-taking, alcoholism, idiotism, madness, the desecration of graves, the sexual mingling of whites and blacks, necrophilia, infidelity, debauchery, prostitution, lynching, betrayal, selfishness, ingratitude, terror, gallantry, courage"[49] provide the fundamental picture of his Sutpens, Compsons, MacCaslins and their neighbours. In these phenomena, however, is manifested a more profound metaphysical fate which follows from the moral vision which Faulkner has of his world: slavery has also enslaved the slave-owners (let us recall here, in a different connection from Faulkner, Hegel's profound thought in *The Phenomenology of the Spirit* on the dialectic between the master and the slave) and both the whites and the blacks, inseparably linked even through the blood of white violence over black women and the incestuous links of white fathers with black daughters, are suffering for the common sin of their soil, the soil taken from the original Indian owners, and only in the common recognition of this inseparability in suffering will their mutual freedom be realizable. This eschatological element, vague and conceptually undeveloped, is rarely set out explicitly in Faulkner's narrative works. These programmatic pages are very frail in their apodictic certainty and the abstract ardour of their tone *(Intruder in the Dust).* The cause of this lies in Faulkner's rather unfortunate attitudes in practical crisis situations of racial terror. The American Civil War is a moment of tribulation for this tragic historic bond which has become metaphysical fate; a moment of moral pathos and futile heroism after which there follows existence in decadence and nostalgia for the past, be this the purposeful, lost brandish of the builders and creators or the mere desire for the immaculateness and fullness of childhood.

When in the history of the genealogical novel we return to the time closest to Zola, we see that Saltykov-Shchedrin on Russian soil was observing the family, for which 1861, the year of the emancipation of the serfs, means economically what the 1861-65 Civil War over slavery means for their American counterparts, in a similar way: social reality is not merely the framework but also the occasion for writing and a cause of the genealogical process which is described, and the phenomena, the internal logic of that process itself, follow paths which French naturalism perceives and which are indeed—it is sufficient to observe without constructing any rigid biological schemes—inspired by the natural "way of all flesh."

But this social reality does not motivate the very evolution of the family as a single human being, as the hero of the novel: in spite of his resistance to Zola, Saltykov-Shchedrin's conception is much closer to Zola's than Balzac's. He does not write about the Golovlevs as a broader social phenomenon and only mentions economic and social relations as the concrete circumstances in which the Golovlevs exist, vegetate and die. This process of dying in the Golovlevs (on average more than one dies per chapter!) is the writer's subject and they bear the principle of this dying *in* themselves. The characters are, indeed, realized in a realistic manner. The psychological motivation of everyone's behavior is clear, for it is generalised and relates to perceivable phenomena in society. The writer's analysis of the hypocrisy in contemporary France and its literature has the nature of a polemic which adopts and applies the message against which it is arguing. Yudushka, however, "was not so much a hypocrite as a good-for-nothing, liar and blabbermouth,"[50] for in Russia this kind of behaviour was not so marked as in France. The character of Yudushka is the only one in the book which lasts from the beginning to the end of the action and is omnipresent at Golovlevo with the result that it bears the essential characteristics of the family as such: in the isolation of free solitude and the endless variations of each motivation, like the force of heredity in Zola's family, the spontaneous and uncontrolled complex of Yudushka's characteristics is not measured according to some external determinant like those incorporated in the plot in the realistic novel. With time "these characteristics were completely transferred onto an abstract, fantastic basis, where there could no longer be resistance or defence, where there were no strong or weak, where there were no police or arbitration courts (or, more correctly, there were, but only to defend his, Yudushka's interests), where the whole world could be easily entwined with a web of intrigues, tyranny and transgressions." The chronicle of this entire family unfolds in this kind of isolation and there are no indications that it is a typical case. The Golovlevs are not an instance in a series of prominent landowning families but distinctly alone (the other gentlemen land-owners are rarely mentioned and never appear). This vacuum is not merely around them but also between all the members of the family and in themselves. The atmosphere is stifling; obtuseness and mindless repetition prevail, "picking mushrooms" is considered the height of summertime pleasure, and not a single book is to be found at Golovlevo. The novel is unpleasant in its strength: there is not a single person to act as an antithesis to this Golovlev totality. Arina Petrovna and Yudushka are the only ones to be active in the imposition of their selfishness, in the severity of bigoted pedantry, and to lack the spirit which is manifested in others (though in them too) in general irresponsibility and chaotic behaviour and crystallized in the naturalistic phenomena of drunkenness, suicide, moral atrophy and sexual lability (so that even in Yudushka's attitude towards Anushka there is a suggestion of an inclination towards incest). The naturalistic information acquires symbolic meaning as in Zola's strongest passages. It has already been noted in criticism that "the landscape (. . .) underlines the dying in the Golovlevs (. . .) even the Golovlevo springs fail to (. . .) bring life, and they are 'rotten' and sick."[51] Moreover, the Golovlev's behaviour and speech are expressed in metaphors of unabated tumefaction: "And indeed, a kind of putrefaction oozed through Yudushka's tittle-tattle. This was not simple tittle-tattle, but an abscess from which pus ran constantly."

Near the end of the book the writer felt the need to generalize the depicted phenomenon: "There are families on which an inexorable fate seems to press." Saltykov-Shchedrin distinguishes between fortunate and unfortunate families, their fates describing a constant developmental curve. "For several generations three important features have run through the history of this family: idleness, the inability to do any kind of work, and drunkenness. The first two brought with them idle talk, frivolous thoughts and an empty life; drunkenness was the conclusion in the general disorder of life, as it had to be." However, we do not learn the way in which these fortunate and unfortunate families are determined, for Saltykov-Shchedrin contents himself with hinting at the deterministic framework into which he was to squeeze the cylical chronicle. He does not, however, want Zola's "scientific" scheme to enslave it.

In this respect he is characteristic of all subsequent writers of the genealogical cycle. Having abandoned the realistic diversity of the social scene, they restrict themselves to material which could provide a copious scientific definition but do not wish to give it. Gorkiy, writing after the October Revolution, concludes his original conception of physical and moral degeneration with the historical logic of proletarian revolution. Thomas Mann sees decadence as a relentless part of the same process of the bourgeois family, as they do, but he appraises it differently. He is at pains to "reveal the psychological roots of decadence in the alienation of the individual from his social class."[52] This process, which Mann calls *Entbürgerlichung* (the losing of bourgeois characteristics), means the loss of biological strength through differentiation, through the prevalence of the artist's sensibility. In fact, art is the re-realization of an inherited and blood-transferred form of existence at a different level. Man does not thereby cease being what his fathers were but rather continues being this in another, freer, more spiritual, symbolic form.[53] According to Nietzsche, the goal of mankind lies in its highest specimens, in a heroic, Dionysian aestheticism which makes Nietzsche the greatest critic and psychologist of morality whom spiritual history has known. Mann accepts Nietzsche's notion but holds that the intellect and consciousness, as opposed to instinct and will, are not a danger to culture, to the "nobility of life," and that it is not morality but precisely beauty which is connected with death.[54] Little Hanno Buddenbrook is playing a short harmonic piece he has written on the piano on his eighth birthday, accompanied by his mother on the violin:

> A very strange impression was made by the contrast between the primitively childish musical means and the heavy, passionate, almost refined manner in which these means were emphasized and employed (...) He did not want to 'resolve' his composition; he denied himself and those listening this satisfaction. How was he to resolve it, what sort of resolution would it be when he sank, ecstatic and liberated, into H major? This sinking would be indescribable joy, the sweetest satisfaction, assuagement, bliss and paradise.... But no, not yet! Put it off for just a moment more, draw out the resolution, the tension will become unbearable, and it will be all the sweeter and more wonderful when relief comes.... Once more, just once more to sip this desire which was inexorably transporting and pushing him forwards; to taste once again the desire which filled his entire being; to strain all his powers once again with a final, convulsive stretching of the will so as to postpone the moment when all this would be fulfilled, the moment of redemption, knowing full well that happiness is only a moment.... Hanno's body gradually stretched upwards, his eyes became huge, his compressed lips quivered, he shook from head to toe as now and then he drew in short breaths through his nostrils.... And then he could hold it back no longer, delight overtook him. His muscles relaxed. Weak, tired and subdued, he lowered his head which slumped onto his shoulder; his eyes closed and a sullen painful smile of inexpressible bliss played about his lips, while with the aid of the pedals his *tremolo* dully boomed, rumbled and whispered, splashed by rippling passages from the violin which were joined by other passages in the bass. And thus he went imperceptibly into H major, rose suddenly to *fortissimo,* swelled into resonance, stopped and fell silent. It was as though something had been broken off.[55]

This could be a classic paragraph as regards the link between art and decadence; the will as a flame which flares up and dies out in artistic sensibility and which, in the act of creation and the perpetuation of the created, is permeated by the rhythms of a vital and even lustful desire for fulfilment and relief, after which there follows the satiety of a complete life, but also death. His father, a businessman, is upset over his son's development: "Did the child really only take after his mother? The heir, who was awaited so long in vain and who in countenance and stature greatly brings to mind his father's family? He hoped his son would carry on his life's calling more happily and freely. Is this son really to remain in soul and nature foreign to the whole environment in which he is called upon to live and work, and even to be alien to his father and become estranged from him (...)"[56] However, Thomas himself at a later date, while reading Schopenhauer, the philosopher of the Will as something inevitably leading to suffering, was to think: "Death is happiness, such profound happiness that man can measure it only in moments of grace such as this. It is the return from inutterably arduous wandering, the correction of a great mistake, liberation from the most repulsive fetters and confines—it puts right a lamentable misfortune."[57]

In an article written half a century after *Buddenbrooks* Mann acknowledged that while he was starting the book the character and experience of little Hanno was what he had most at heart and that the book's most profound concern was the psychology of the exhausting spiritual refinements and aesthetic transformations which accompany biological descent. However, the epic instinct in him was what drove him also to write an entire family pre-history. The Buddenbrooks' awareness of historic events is also embraced here (the revolution, economic upheavals, the Franco-Prussian war) for this was not meant to be an epic work in the Homeric on Tolstoyan sense but, to take Mann's definition, "a social novel disguised as a family saga." The external circumstances are absorbed into the Buddenbrook horizons, whose later characteristic is precisely subjectivity. In this lies the strength, value and greatness of the bourgeoisie's transformation in decline: "Without less extrovert and more sensitive types (. . .) without decadents, without little Hannos, mankind and society would not have progressed one step from diluvial times. Unfitness for life is what advances life, for this unfitness is linked to the spirit (. . .) We, the Buddenbrooks," Mann concludes, "have reached further into the world and given life more after our bourgeois decomposition than was ever permitted our dry ancestors and their walls."[58]

In writers who do not accept decadence as a positive principle—Galsworthy and, at a different level of artistic integrity, Krleža—we shall nevertheless discover this same element, this artistic sensitivity as the main phenomenon in the internal decomposition of bourgeois families and as the spiritual correlate of socio-economic transformation and biological extinction. In Gorkiy, Martin du Gard and Faulkner the accent is on different spiritual features and the categories of moral order (in Galsworthy and Krleža the moral standpoint is implicit in the artistic reaction). They are not, however, any more closely linked to Nietzsche's thoughts on decadence than Krleža. It is impossible and unnecessary to try and establish a scale or progression of single values in the spectrum of standpoints occupied by these highly individual writers. Nevertheless, it is characteristic that not one of them accepts Zola's natural-science scheme or the methodological hypotheses of the experimental novel.

The later Galsworthy did, however, flirt with some of Zola's ideas, perhaps because, working empirically, he found himself in the midst of his genealogical work with its broad cyclical dimensions without ever having thought about any theoretical principle.

Even though only the descendants of two of the ten children of the old, provincial Forsytes are at the center of the plot, Galsworthy does not let many other branches out of sight either. Even if he does not write separate books about them, as Zola would do (after all, he is not so interested in the individual mutation of the specimen as in the Forsyte constant), he endeavours to form certain synthetic conclusions and thus "lists" the descendants of the third generation and sees that the number of Forsytes is declining.[59] This is a quite unnecessary reference to the natural-science approach to the genealogical subject, as are the frequent allusions to the decline of the Forsyte type in the fourth generation. However, it is not a case hero of a genetic conception but rather a moral evaluation which in the later books increasingly replaces the initial, social-satire impulse. The Forsytes, as realized in the first, self-contained part, *The Man of Property,* are defined by their instinct for possessing, which is spent equally between their consumption of beef, marriage, dealing in pictures and their professional activities of lawyer, financier and publisher. They are not builders but middlemen; they do not operate through their imagination but with the logic of investment; they do not create but acquire. The Forsytes do not build factories, railways or mines but those who do must turn to them. Their virtues are average and they are symbolic precisely in this averageness.[60]

In the Forsytes Galsworthy sees the embodiment of something which forms part of the national character of the English, or even the national character itself, in as much as their so-called upper middle class contains the English history of the acquisition of material wealth. And when it is said of old Timothy's globe that he never even looked at it since he never really believed that there was anything real other than England, this is an unusually appropriate symbol. Galsworthy's trouble is that when he develops, in the midst of the Forsytes, the drama between the rigid principle itself and that antithesis which is a part of the Forsytes themselves, he fails to be convincing. The antithesis, which is a sign of the inevitable corrosion of the Forsyte condition, does not follow either psychologically or existentially from the condition itself, as is the case with Alyosha's Karamazovshtina, Leone's Glembay dimension or, in particular, the Buddenbrook elements in Hanno and Thomas himself. The idea is there but executed at the level of mere assertion, so that if we are to understand the Forsyte saga at a level above that of casual, realistic, amusing narrative, as *The Man of Property* really does suggest, then this is a score on which Galsworthy falls down. From book to book this novel increasingly becomes a historical chronicle in its external framework and the allusions to events from the Boer War to the general strike in 1926, and the main heroes are Forsytes who have *lost* the basic Forsytian characteristics. As a result of the writer's enthusiasm for his ideally conceived characters of young Jon and Fleur, whom fate had earmarked to atone for the former drama between Soames, Jolyon and Irena, even their relationship remains an idyll devoid of any more profound meaning. Soames himself in this context and in his later relationship with Fleur (who becomes a typical "unconventional" female character of convential literature) turns into the bearer of the writer's sympathy with the inevitable disintegration of the Forsyte phase in English history. This sentimentalization, particularly of Jon and Soames, dissolves the very conception of the Saga, which was so successfully executed at the start, particularly in *The Man of Property*, written without Galsworthy's having even thought about the range of the entire Saga. He quite rightly called the second trilogy *A Modern Comedy*, not stretching the title of the Saga to this extension of his account of Fleur and her family.

The word *Saga* was borrowed from Galsworthy by those who wrote, for instance, about Faulkner's families or the Glembays, and even Thomas Mann himself, as we have seen, used the word for his novel about the Buddenbrooks. In the book by Wilhelm Rabius on the internal structural similarity between *The Forsyte Saga* and the old Icelandic sagas a series of analogies are set out between kinship as depicted in the sagas and among the Forsytes. This is something primeval and in itself understandable and it is manifested in solidarity, in familial relations, including betrothal, marriage, and matrimony, in the attitude towards material goods, fate, death, emotions and in social institutions. "Succession, blood, kinship, marriage, the family and the awareness of these forces—here lie the traditional powers behind the strength of the Nordic action,"[61] says Rabius in his comparison. He also analysed the personality's attitude towards the material being (the body, possessions) and towards spiritual values (friendship, love, fear, honour, the nation-state and fate-death-afterlife) and found an analogy between these two completely different family civilizations. Galsworthy denies that he was influenced by the sagas and states that he was only superficially acquainted with them but that in his saga, as in them, the motive forces are the family, the tribal instinct and respect for the home and property.[62] It is impossible to accept Rabius's racist interpretation of this parallel as the northern Germanic spirit. He even discounts the Buddenbrooks and fails to see the social (extra-ethnic) meaning of the Forsyte connection, thus neither taking into account Galsworthy's underlying tone in the best parts of his Saga nor his irony and criticism, which is satirical in some chapters. This aspect of Galsworthy's Saga is neither fortuitous nor formal but rather lends the work a historic-critical value; and in those aspects in which it corresponds to the old national epics the Saga is much more than an ordinary entertaining novel. The definition given by Andre Jolles of the character of the Icelandic saga also extends to it: "They (i.e. the sagas) do not in essence provide the history of one family but rather show that history exists merely as family events; that the family makes history."[63] Perhaps it is precisely this that should be the fundamental question in the meaning of literary works which have pretensions to a genealogical structure: how does the family make history?

If this is so, then an important place in this family of works falls to the cycle by Roger Martin du Gard. It is precisely in the final parts (where Galsworthy did not live up to expectations and fell out of the category) that *Les Thibault* vindicates its place. When he was preparing the plan for this work in 1920 the writer noted the following in his diary: "All of a sudden I was fired with enthusiasm for the idea of presenting two brothers: two beings with different and opposing temperaments and which are nevertheless deep down marked by the concealed similarities which a very powerful common atavism creates between blood brothers. This subject afforded me the possibility of fertile multiplication: in it I saw the opportunity to express at the same time the two opposing tendencies in my own nature: the instinct for independence, flight, revolt and the rejection of all conformism, and the instinct for order, measure and the rejection of extremes, qualities which I inherited."[64]

Les Thibault is, therefore, conceived as a family novel based on the polarization of features in one and the same character, while *L'été 1914* brings the cycle to the level of Tolstoyan comprehensiveness—through Jacques's socialist contacts, discussions and journeys—without a differentiating perspective. "*L'été 1914* is a powerful work but its power is oppressive: with its sights set on every cruel detail, it makes us want a sovereign view, the divine view of the author (who is God to his work) which would allow us to put everything in its place and see the whole in a supreme moment,[65] writes Jean Prevost. Henri Clouard complains however, that the final volumes of *Les Thibault* "allow first conversations, then commentaries to grow, rise, penetrate, which is no longer appropriate for the psychology or the vision (. . .)"[66]

In form it starts becoming a novel of ideas, nearer to Huxley or *The Magic Mountain,* if the ideas had been individual and if they had not depended on interesting but already familiar and borrowed historical analyses. The framework, however, remains the two brothers, an intelligent, objective middle-class person and an impatient revolutionary. Both are Thibaults and the epilogue returns to the internal link between generations.

Les Thibault is the only example of an attempt to extract the question of "how the family makes history" from the middle-class context. The internal link is less frequently analysed but the structure remains essentially the same as in more characteristic genealogical works.

As distinct from the other writers which comprise his context here, Krleža arrived at the family through history, through a cycle of expressionist incompleteness and through realistic satire with toned-down elements of grotesque. He found himself faced with the problems which are generally worked out in large compositions—and he temperamentally wanted to go further: for this reason the genealogical aspect is perhaps even more explicitly stressed than in the large compositions in which the relations between individuals in the generations, and reciprocally between the generations, are more gradually revealed in time. This notion of familiar determinism is completely postulated in *Gospoda Glembajevi* and the prose work *O Glembajevima.* Krleža conceives of the unity of this family as progression and in this process the individual Glembays constitute *series* or a *procession.* At the very beginning of *O Glembajevima* he wonders where and why the Glembays are going. The purpose of this motion is in them themselves: "The Glembays, taken synthetically, mean the progress of persistent, fortunate and talented existences breaking out of the mud, crime, illiteracy, smoke and lies to light, profit, taste, good education, a gentleman's life (in a word, movement from the darkness to light), but at the same time it seems in retrospect that this motion, like everything else, is subject to certain constant, invisible and unwritten laws."

Are these laws a certain external, universal force and the Glembays determined "like everything else"? Or, just as "everything" has its own laws, does the Glembay progression have its own inherent regularity which provides it as a whole with a single tendency, recognizable over several generations? The bursting from the darkness into light is the movement of generations in time, but in no way is it simple in its meaning: the darkness is reality and the light, illusion which deceives with a glare in the eyes. In the last three or four decades the Glembays and those "Sziretscheks, Urbans, Szlougans and Szepkas, Novlyans and Szeveretz de Szeveretzes of ours, who used to play bridge in the Vienna Herrenklub, they all know full well that everything about them is in fact a mask." The Glembays, therefore, are not the only family of lower-town patricians "which has become bourgeois on blood and tears"; they too, "like our entire wealthy nobility, went from poverty to riches through crime and deceit, arriving at their high trading and business standing and the morality of their trading titles and banks." But at the peak of their success the Glembays, through their persistence, represented "the 700-year old Barboczys, the barons Zygmuntowicz-Remetski and the Corfu multi-million concern of Basilides-Danielli and the illustrious, wealthy upper-class family of Agramer-Bukovečki, which in its original line was directly connected to the Habžinić-Murakeözys, descendants of ban Nikola Zrinski-Čakovečki." Typical, and at the same time unique!

They appear typical to the reader in the symbolic, poetic imagery at the level of style—and not on the basis of some preformulated conception. "Laws" are mentioned as a possibility and a reference to the more doctrinaire writers and determinism, whose historical importance Krleža respected as an integral part of Zola's ideas[67] but which always remained alien to him personally. Instead of theory we have here, above all, that symbolic portrait gallery, in act one of *Gospoda Glembajevi,* which is followed up by the legend of old Barboczy's exclamation and then the sonorous catalogues of names and careers in the prose fragment. The meaning of the Glembay family as a whole is constantly defined by the numerous references to the dead outside the Glembay drawingroom: "Alice drowned in the Kupa at Goranjsko at the Zygmuntowicz's place! In the boat they found (. . .) her parasol, which means Alice jumped into the water with her clothes on (. . .) Alice drowned herself because of the evidence!" Only in this context does the conflict between old Glembay and Leone take on its true dramatic value: "We are two different races"—the Glembays and their ill-starred connections with the Greco-Venetian blood of the Daniellis, to which old Glembay ascribes Leone's revolt! However, Leone, who rejects the Glembay values and their talent in exploiting rates of interest, feels the Glembay in himself and fights against it, wanting to rid himself of it, for the Glembay qualities spell crime. "Since the very first day that I began to think I have done nothing else but fight against the Glembay in me! This is the most terrifying thing in my own fate: I am a pure, unadulterated, one-hundred-per-cent Glembay! All my hatred for the Glembays is nothing other than hatred for myself. I see myself in the Glembays as in a mirror!"

From armed robbery to shady business deals on a national scale—this is the historic range of the Glembays' rise and a measure of the modernization with which they develop their environment. Suicide, madness and adulterous relations in the family—these are the private, secret, circumstances accompanying their public expansion. This is not mere physical degeneration in the Faulknerian or Mannian sense but the loss of any moral pivot. The Glembays appeared when Max Nordau and his theory of degeneration as a cultural phenomenon of the *fin de siècle* had not yet been forgotten and his book devoted to Lombroso had not yet been replaced by the ubiquitous writings of Freud and Spengler. Krleža's tableaux are inspired by the general literary context which the epoch created for his highly topical historical subjects but in interpretation he went no further—or lower—than Marx's model of historic development and Nietzsche's poetic annihilation of the existing social topography! In his review of the first edition of *Gospoda Glembajevi* Marko Ristić pointed to the genealogy, which was "just as pathetic and fundamental as that of the Rougon-Macquarts," in Ignjat he saw "an old Balzac- or Daumier-type banker" and called the Glembay curse "class in character and Oedipan,"[68] thus establishing in this exceptionally perceptive passage the main literary and idea framework in which the genealogical aspects of this drama, and even the entire cycle which was only just developing at the time, should be placed.

In common with the other seven cycles, present in Krleža's there is also the notion of genealogical totality. The family is not merely a convention or superficial pretext to paint a society or epoch. Its evolution, rise, fall and disintegration are the very substance of the epoch, the very content of historic change. Zola finds a scientific explanation for this process (more exactly, he constructs the process according to his natural-science theory), Mann perceives the physiological foundation but does not stop here and goes on to work out its spiritual correlate, while for Faulkner the psycho-physiological reality is a symbol for the historic meaning of natural and moral behaviour, and it is a similar case with Saltykov-Shchedrin and Gorkiy. Martin du Gard, Galsworthy and Gorkiy subordinate themselves to the objective circumstances of historic fact. In Martin du Gard history absorbs the genealogical problem as lesser and less important, finally returning its independence and weighing it down with speculation. In Krleža's cycle the lines of epic continuity remain marked out merely as a possibility so that the cycle's prospects cannot be embraced by a single stroke. In *O Glembajevima* the author's voice mentions heredity as a distinct factor in the socio-historic order, the internal logic of which remains a secret, and the characters in the play make unambiguous and emotive allusions to inherited blood as the carrier, of the evil characteristics which will destroy the very heredity it contains. The principle underlying the whole, then, is more a metaphor of moods and experiences than a category which epic persistence succeeds in defining in narrative works.

However, as in the seven other cycles we are examining here with Krleža's, the question of internal unity can be defined in terms of the depiction of history and society (the tradition of Balzac's realism in European literature) and by the biological and naturalistic undertones first set out explicitly by Zola and later retained by other writers as symbols for the hidden causes, or the mysterious lack of a common cause, of the moral and aesthetic order. These two tendencies define the essence of the genealogical work and provide in their interaction, regardless of whether the result is nearer one or the other, the literary historical framework for all these cyclical works from Zola to Faulkner.

FRAMEWORKS

To determine these more precisely we must also compare the scope of the action in the works, examine whether the structure of the family principle in time is also essentially uniform throughout the genealogical works and establish whether the cylical features, an inherent aspect of the subject itself, are so analogous that these works can be reduced to a common denominator and whether the specific values of one of these works can be appraised in a more complete and integral manner in their mutual context.

First of all it is necessary to establish the extent and position of the families in each cycle. In Zola, Galsworthy, Krleža and Faulkner they are broken up and ramified while in Saltykov-Shchedrin, Mann, Gorkiy and Martin du Gard we find a small number of individuals in each generation, one line with unimportant and easily surveyed off-shoots. With the exception of *Les Thibault*, these works are unified novel-chronicles in form and only cycles in a more profound sense of composition and theme. In Galsworthy and Krleža we also find one main line of generations but the brothers and cousins in the same family tree are important not merely as thematic parallels and contrasts but also as essential participants in the development of the plot. In many books in Zola's cycle the family is not present as a group. Rather, the hero of the story is an individual member of the family, connected to the main Rougon-Macquart line in other works and on the plan of their family tree. Zola drew up this family tree before he wrote a single line about the family itself and published it ten years and ten books later without barely having had to change anything on it. Later, however, he constantly modified and expanded this plan as the conception changed during the realization of a particular novel. This family tree was exceptionally important to Zola and he treated it like an authentic document. It was, in fact, a summary of the entire cycle in which the more prominent individuals were fitted in, together with those who served merely as links or the bearers of personal traits. For every individual Zola gave the exact year of birth and described his marriage, descendants and the circumstances of death. He also noted physical similarity with ancestors and always indicated their physical and moral inheritance (which might skip an entire generation) and the way in which these inherited traits were fused[69] and composed. He also sometimes provided the professions of his characters.

It is possible that Galsworthy and Krleža based their family trees on Zola's model but this is not necessarily so. Their plans have no scientific pretensions but rather serve to orientate the reader (Zola's plan was not printed with each book for, with the exception of two or three novels, it is only of relevance to the cycle as a whole). With his names Galsworthy gives only the profession, address (very indicative in London society!), nickname, year of birth and, on occasion, death. Krleža rarely provides years; more frequently the profession and an observation on the individual's fate in the process of the Glembays' degeneration. As distinct from Galsworthy, his plan is not merely an objective scheme but also arouses the imagination to new possibilities and serves to indicate the future dimensions of that imaginative breadth which he never realized in the works, having only dwelt on the fates of certain figures in those plays and fragments he did complete. Krleža's plan must also have appeared at the start of his work on the cycle and it is not quite consistent with the text or complete. Four errors were rectified only in a later postwar edition and certain names in the text are still not to be found in the table. There are also inconsistencies in the text itself. The Baroness married Glembay at the age of 36, she is 45 and has a seventeen-year old son—from her marriage with Glembay! Such inconsistencies are naturally quite unimportant not only to the general picture of the Glembay world but even to the story. In the works of William Faulkner there are many more. In recent years certain literary critics have turned into biographical researchers in an attempt to reconcile the ambiguous allusions and contradictory dates in various works by Faulkner.

The family relations in his literary world are extremely complicated—and there are at least half a dozen families. However, typically Faulkner did not bother to work out the family trees himself but rather created these families of his, not in chronological order or in generations, but in the order in which the individuals appeared in his imagination, intuitively. These families sometimes grow from story to novel, from novel to later story, though usually the time of the action retreats into the past so that the extra-temporal meaning of the present acquires more weight. Some Faulkner critics constructed these diagrams subsequently through an inductive process. The family connections concur in their findings, though Cleanth Brooks and Edmund Volpe,[70] for instance, drew up apparently quite different models for tracing one family succession. In addition, Volpe distinguishes between legitimate and illegitimate connections and specifies blacks and half-breeds (even noting the proportions in which their blood is mixed), which is important to Faulkner. Brooks discreetly passes over this for the sake of political delicacy, a delicacy befitting a genteel American Southerner.

The genealogical plans in the case of four of the eight writers concerning us here do not, then, have any formal significance but rather express certain essential notions of each of them. Thus a comparison of certain other factual aspects of these cycles may serve as an indication of the meaning of the genealogical cycle in general and of the particular content of each of them.

There are five generations of Rougons and Macquarts in Zola's twenty novels and each of them is present in the final novel. Five generations are also mentioned in Mann and Galsworthy, and even six in Krleža's case, while with some of Faulkner's families (the Compsons, MacCaslins) the known histories are even longer and more detailed. However, in all the cycles after Zola's, three main generations take part in the immediate drama, if we ignore the family traditions. These are the three stages in the evolution and exhaustion of the genealogical substance. Sometimes in Faulkner these three stages last through several generations, but then each generation does not have independent significance in the process. In Martin du Gard we have before us the father and his two sons but in the epilogue the summing-up of the ideological consequences is completely directed towards the future consciousness of the newly-born member of the third generation, little Jean-Paul. Three generation elements or three focal points in time appear, then, as the recurring structural constant.

However, "generation" is a completely abstract definition and may mean one person or a number of parallel branches in the same generation which complement each other or clash in their characters and attitudes, or both, and thereby show the multifacetedness of their moment in time and the family history. A second question is the relationship between the family (its members) and the environment. Is the family somehow set apart from the social context or is it integrated into this context? Are there parallel phenomena to this family in the social context? In some cycles the answers to these questions are already contained in them to a certain extent but it is worthwhile indicating the logical sequence and range of possibilities which apreads out and ramifies from Zola to Faulkner, though admittedly not in any strict chronological order.

Zola was not concerned with the generation as a stage or characteristic moment in development. Important to him were psycho-physical features embodied in the character of the individual as a member of a group linked up by the hereditary principle. These individuals rarely communicate with each other and never appear as members of one distinct generation. In the case of Saltykov-Shchedrin the three generations are quite unambiguously delineated. The structure is exceptionally clear, for the work deals with a small and quite distinct family whose distant relations do not, in fact, even exist right up until the last words of the novel. This is not merely an arbitrarily taken focus of "artistic treatments." The Golovlevs are Russian landowners, spatially isolated from all the others with whom they could mix socially. With the Artamonovs, whose fate is taken much further (to World War I and the Revolution), it is a similar situation. The builders and owners of a factory far away from the industrial centres and the uncontested main figures in their small provincial settlement, they are exclusively the object of Gorkiy's observation and their contacts are only with the odd worker, subordinated keepers, policemen and courtesans. The branch of the family which went off to the city disappears or we are only aware of it when it is in contact with the Artamonov centre. However, as distinct from Saltykov-Shchedrin, in this instance it is more a case of artistic selection, as with Martin du Gard, whose Thibaults live in Paris. Their links with the surrounding world are very intensive at all class levels but they do not mix with families at the same level as themselves on the social scale, with the exception of the Fontanins who serve more as a thematic contrast (women as opposed to men; Protestants as opposed to Catholics) than a class context. The family as a characteristic social unit, which is not only a representative of a social stratum but also lives in it and has its own individual timbre as a part of the stratum, is depicted for the first time by Thomas Mann. The Buddenbrooks are merchant patricians and consuls like other families in their Hanseatic town but they are nevertheless different from them (the Hagenströms, for instance) and in their contacts with other merchant families of different traditions and moral principles their individuality is even further underlined. The Forsytes, rich and influential in the business world, belong to the London scene and can, therefore, only be an element in the much more involved and enormous complex of the later Victorian business world. Galsworthy was not writing—no matter how much superficial critics might assert the contrary—a socially realistic novel in which the social scene was to provide the subject with the Forsytes playing their roles at the socio-economic level as in Balzac. The Saga is not only a family novel in its form but also the writer's interest is directed towards the events and, to use a modern sociological term, disintegrational processes in the family. Writing about a representative example of a society with very clear traditions (the Forsyte name becomes a class symbol but only because its content is so concretely defined by one family), Galsworthy had to compose his subject matter around conflicting generation profiles. It is true that in the work Soames, for example, has an important role in all three volumes, but in the first one this is because he embodies the inherited norms of a former generation, in the second because he is in conflict with his contemporaries and in the third because he is the bearer of tradition in the face of the young people who are to transform and dilute the Forsytes' moral-psychological complex.

In the place they occupy in the social context the Glembays are probably nearest to the Buddenbrooks, and in their ramifications and social profiles (and not in individual characteristics), nearest to the Forsytes. However, proceeding from the same realistic link with historic reality, Krleža made from the Glembays something much larger, more powerful, more metaphysical and richer to the point of fantasy than the other two writers. Krleža is primarily a poet not only in technique but also the conception of the whole. The Glembays are not a symbol for the innermost issues in the writer's moral and aesthetic personality, as in Mann's case, nor do they represent the national character. They are a newly-formed myth which eclipses all realistic attempts by other Croatian writers to depict the domestic capitalists. The Glembay cycle depicts capitalism at a completely different level of artistic creation. This is not merely a matter of relative success but of a different quality of imaginative presentation.

The way in which Krleža places the Glembays on the social scene means that their position is much more important than the positions of the other families in the other cycles. The underdevelopment, subordination and poverty of Croatia meant there was no room for a lot of "Glembays." If the Glembays were to be a European type of rich man, then Krleža, grappling with this Croatian question which, as distinct from that in the *Hrvatski bog Mars* cycle, is European in form, was not going to content himself with dimensions less than European. And however much journalistic criticism might have stressed the depiction of social reality in Krleža's work, the Glembays are, in fact, a picture in which the bounds of reality are stretched to the extreme limit which the imagination will allow; a source of new social imagination and, for us, a notion of mythical dimensions.

This mythical tendency is present in Faulkner, though perhaps more consciously developed. He did not only follow in the wake of European styles but also of the world of the forest hunter's pre-civilization which in romantic narration, ranging from the idyllic to the blasphemous-metaphysical, had been laid down in American literature from Cooper and Melville to Twain and Hemingway. The splendour of the past and the anxiety of the Southerners' decline are hypertrophied to the point of myth, which also has a prehistoric dimension. Just as the creation and composition of the cycles link Krleža more to Faulkner than to his European precursors, so does the position of the family about which he is writing. But if the Glembays branch out, intermix and become universal in the course of the generations, in Faulkner they meet and together form the milieu of mythical reality and all its families. The cycle is only completed with the entire body of his works.

With the exception of Zola, who was interested in the family in a way different from the writers who followed him, the authors of the most important and most ramified families all employ personal names as marks of continuity in the generations. Ilya Artamonov is the name of the grandfather and—in contrast to him—the equally lively grandson; of the five bearers of generation in the Buddenbrooks four are called Johann; in the Forsytes we at first follow the Jolyons, of which there is at least one in each generation; two main Glembays are Ignjats and two Leones; in Faulkner's Compsons the constructive or central representatives are Jasons (four) and Quentins (four, the last one being a girl!) and in a later appendix to the text even Faulkner himself denotes them with Roman numerals as though they were a dynasty; among the Sartorises there are three Bayards and three Johns. The writer's narrative mode, which does not break down the Sartoris complex into an objective progression of people and events, heightens the impression that individuals are not important but only family principles, even if the reader does fail to grasp the drama in its evolution and only in its total meaning.

FOCAL POINTS IN THE STRUCTURE: THE THREE GENERATIONS

Where does a genealogical cycle begin? Is not every beginning, strictly speaking, purely arbitrary? The family stretches from time immemorial. The socio-historic moment of beginning is dictated by the writer's choice and this choice implies the formation of an entire family model. As the setting for his family succession Zola chose the contemporary period—the Second Empire, starting in 1848—and to it attached the activities of aunt Dide's three children and their descendants, following individuals among them from book to book in the provinces, the city, high society, a den of poverty and vice, the army and the countryside. The initial impulse was the factor of social change: on the whole, ascent and the flow from the provinces to the capital. This is also the case to a certain extent in some other cycles. Galsworthy and Krleža do not start with this factor but do look back to it and take the origins of their oldest heroes back to the member of the family who in the provinces first set foot on the ladder of social success and transition to a new urban class. Krleža cites the peasant-like persistence of Glembay and Galsworthy's Jolyon who says of his uncle Swithin that there is something primitive in him. "The town and urban life have not yet digested him. All those centuries of rural work and brute force are deposited in him and have remained there in spite of his standing."[71] Gorkiy is the only one to show directly and at length the rise of his first family member—the first historically free subject in his family. At the same time the family line in Gorkiy's work is very short for it lasts from the beginning to the end of the epoch of capitalist enterprise in Russia. In Faulkner's work the pioneer beginnings are lost in the earlier phases of the American settlers. Only

Absalom, Absalom! traces the rise and fall of a house—in the literal sense: Thomas Sutpen, whose pre-history we also get to know, but in the retrospective recounting of other characters, builds a house which is the material and spiritual centre of family identity and unity. The way in which he builds it, the coercion exercised upon the architect and a certain amoral friendship towards the black slaves define the unconventionality and impetuosity of his later actions towards his descendants.

Saltykov-Shchedrin, Mann and Martin du Gard do not seek beginnings but rather start at the top with the generation in whose hands the family estate, reputation and power are all at a peak, and if we abstract the historical surveys of the other four writers from this circle after Zola, then the first generation which is directly present in the drama is analagous in every case: these are the generations of Johann Buddenbrook; old Jolyon, James and Swithin Forsyte and their brothers; the generation of Ignjat Glembay and old Fabriczy; the generation of Oscar Thibault and that of Ilya Artamonov. Faulkner is the only case where these personalities only exist in the construction of the great plantations, which were to last for ever, or in the past at the historic moment of the Civil War. It is difficult to state briefly all their character traits and moral convictions: old Thibault, the embodiment of the bourgeois institutions of Catholic France and the former muzhik Ilya Artamonov are clearly not the same. The Glembays are social climbers and frauds while the Buddenbrooks are the embodiment of the honesty and solidity of a class which is a pillar of the North European type of civilization. Jolyon stands out from his more shortsighted brothers, who reason in a narrow, materialist way, while he is capable of devoting himself to "non-personal reflections so uncharacteristic of a Forsyte and in which partly lay the secret of his superiority over them."[72] Perhaps, however, the writer is sentimentalizing him while the others are the blatant object of satire, and their duality is a condition for being able to write about them at all. But he is one of them: Jolyon is not a speculative Thomas Buddenbrook just as Galsworthy himself is not a Mannian Tonio Kröger, the artist who belongs to the Buddenbrooks but has separated from them. At very best Galsworthy is young Jolyon. Whatever the case, the Forsytes can be crude, merciless, clan-conscious people who, if necessary, will cruelly pursue their interests, though always legally and hardly ever violently.

The range, therefore, of the people in this generation is very broad. To analyse it would mean to enter into the stylistic totality and world view of each writer individually. Nevertheless, they all have one thing in common: within the genealogical whole to which they belong each of them is the vigorous and more or less autocratic bearer of the constructive or at least strictly conservative principle of persistence, work, acquisition and preservation. Only thanks to them is the family what it is. They unite their discordant and incongruous descendants. These are energetic figures even when they do not fall within the framework of the prevalent norms of the bourgeois world: old Fongue (aunt Dide) and other earlier Rougons, for instance, or the full-blooded, sensuous Ilya Artamanov and Sutpen, or the upstart Flem Snopes in the later Faulkner trilogy, or the indefatigable landowning Arian Petrovna, who will not allow the estate to be ruined.

These firm pivots of the first generation—the generation leading the way to decline—are also the social centre around which are woven the offshoots and branches in direct and indirect lines. In several cycles (*Buddenbrooks, The Man of Property* and *Gospoda Glembajevi*) their homes are the place where at the very start of the work a family gathering is held (*Family Court* is the title of the sketch which became the first chapter of the first cycle after Zola's, *The Golovlev Family*!). L. M. Yuryeva has observed, when comparing *Buddenbrooks* and *Decadence*, that family celebrations in the two works have an important role.[73] They are the highest point of the families' prosperity but are spoilt by unpleasant events which have adverse consequences for the companies, and we might add, for the firmness of the family unity. This is precisely what happens in the lower-town house of the Glembays "one night in late summer a year before the 1914—18 war" and in the house of old Jolyon Forstye at a family gathering for the engagement of his granddaughter, June, and the architect, Bossiney.

At these gatherings[74] a family crisis starts which sometimes merely anticipates the following disintegration (chapter one of *Buddenbrooks*) or sometimes provides the occasion for the polarization itself (Porfiriy Vladimirovich Golovlev against Stepan and Pavel, the spendthrifts and drunkards). This split usually takes place horizontally, between members of different generations. Krleža's Leone is the only genealogical hero (this *ad hoc* used term has some dramatic justification) openly to stand up against the elders, against the father himself. The only one, that is, except for Jacques Thibault who does so undesignedly, as a lad running away from home with his friend, Daniel, later manifesting in the search for his own orientation the same pride, stubborness and violence as his father, in fact his brother, Antoine, notices. This, however, is far removed from the "instinctively animal" Glembay *argumentum ad hominem* ("that was the Glembay blood in us fretting"!).

On the whole this separation occurs along a line dividing the old norms and accepted life style from the new, rebellious, anarchoid or positivist, and even decadent life style which does not respect the inherited moral values. Soames, who embodies the principle of ownership and is literally, according to the title of the first book, "a man of property," is set against the more easy-going, likable but not particularly deserving, younger Jolyon.[75] The legitimistic formalism of Puba Fabriczy is set against the artistic lack of responsibility in Leone. Yudushka is set against his brothers. In the majority of instances, however, it is a case of a subtle modification of the father's values. Antoine is in no way old Thibault: he is more rational, willing and able to understand his brother. What worries Pyotr Artamonov, if we read the novel carefully, is not so much the "business" itself as the disobedience of the son and the emptiness of the family relations. Aleksey has also inherited his father's practical mind and both, after all, respect the hunchbacked Nikita and are hurt by his withdrawal to the monastery. Thomas Buddenbrook combines the business acumen of the older Buddenbrooks with the sensitivity of little Hanno. If he opposes his brother, Christian, with a vehemence and violent fury otherwise not present in him it is because he sees Christian's softness, love for the theatre and surrendering to his wife as a danger to himself, something which could break to the surface in himself. Herein lies the core of the genealogical question as a subject concerning history and processes; the writer's artistic sensibility meets its most stringent test here. During the course of the action Yudushka disintegrates and degenerates worse than was ever the case with his brothers, while Jolyon is a rebel only according to the scheme. Galsworthy fails to realize a fundamental negation of the Forsytes within them themselves. In the composition of Krleža's drama Leone rounds on his father because he has no partner in his own generation; and the subjective problems of the Glembays, who following the stereotype channels end up in their "decay and false condition," are more fully expressed in the prose pieces on Olga Warroniggova and Laura Lembach. The mother and daughter would belong to two generations, were the biological and not historical principle to be crucial, but in view of the fact that "generation" is a concept for a historic and psychological focal point in the family process, both women[76] must be seen at Leone's level. His cousin, Oliver Urban, on the other hand, is a part of the complex dealt with in *Leda* and by virtue of this more important conceptual criterion belongs to the third stage of the family decomposition. Among the second generation are Ivan, the suicide, and Angelica, who is ordained and then somewhere outside the pages that Krleža wrote unites her life with Leone's after his future recovery. With the exception of Faulkner, the range of antitheses in the family circle as early as this generation is broadest in Krleža.[77]

Any analysis of the genealogical relations in Faulkner is very complicated for several reasons. Firstly, his books contain at least six family cycles (it is not important here that they meet and come into contact and even intertwine); secondly, the original focal point of the genealogical problem is usually situated several more neutral generations ahead of the second focal point and the second generation. These are always people who feel themselves the inheritors of the former family code of honour but who are now in new circumstances with the family economically ruined and squeezed off the social scene or respected by old people and negroes alone. In *Sartoris,* which takes place after World War I, John has died as a pilot and Bayard, a restless "rebel without a cause," dies in a car like some premature James Dean but in fact as a typical member of the lost generation of Hemingway and Fitzgerald heroes. There is a characteristic relationship in the most concentrated of Faulkner's genealogical "cycles," the novel *Absalom, Absalom!*

in which the action is narrated by means of a special technique which could attach another new meaning to the word "cyclic."[78] Thomas Sutpen, already mentioned several times here, has several children: Charles from his first marriage (about which we learn very late in the novel), Henry and Judith from the generally known and recognized second marriage and a daughter by a negro slave Clythie. Accompanied by persistent, tyrannical and frantic interventions by Sutpen, there develops between them a complicated, melodramatic story of love and jealousy, war comradeship and incestuous inclinations, all coloured by racial prejudices which destroy the most profound interhuman propensities. The fundamental picture of Faulkner's underlying myth here acquires its fiercest expression, stronger than the similar tale narrated breathlessly in *The Bear*. As distinct from the divisions in the European cycles, it is much less a case here, therefore, of different evaluations or conscious departures from tradition than of a fate carried in the blood as inherited convictions, which suits the barbaric drama to which the unpredictable course of events inexorably leads.

In the other novels, however, the path from creation to destruction corresponds to the stages with which Faulkner in one of his works marks the development of man the individual: first of all, elemental existing, after which come work, reflection and finally remembrance. The period of the pioneers' struggle on the edge of a wilderness corresponds to mere existence; the second phase to the generation of the builders, and the third to the reflection by their descendants—moralists like Ike MacCaslin in *Go Down, Moses,* lawyers like Horace Benbow *(Sanctuary),* Jason's father (who is mentioned but does not appear in *The Sound and the Fury*), Gavin Stevens *(Intruder in the Dust),* the people who theorize and generalize the dramas of the moment.

The final phase belongs to the characters who are young but represent the old age of their families. As Olga Vickery says, instead of having new experiences, they live the lives of their forebears and lay down and preserve for posterity the legends of the past which they never say themselves. Quentin Compson, the intellectual centre of *The Sound and the Fury*, is a typical example. Olga Vickery[79] also mentions the young Gail Hightower from *Light in August* and Bayard Sartoris (whom we have already mentioned).

Confining ourselves to these characters, each of them introduces a problem into our structural scheme. If Hightower, of whose forbears the reader is not aware, serves as an example of the third generation, this is because we are perceiving Faulkner's entire *oeuvre* on the American South as a single cycle and accepting the real world of generations only conditionally. The three developmental stages or three phases in the drama of decadence will be essential to us. Bayard Sartoris, whom we have just taken as a representative of the second phase, can also serve as a representative of the third. His grandfather Bayard then stands as a representative of the second; we did not give him a special phase earlier as we first of all perceived him as a bearer of mere existence and the embodied memory of the supreme legendary character of colonel Sartoris, a hero of the Civil War. By the same token, in *The Sound and the Fury* we could leave out Jason Compson III, who does not appear personally in the narrative present but only in the characters' reminiscences. Instead of him we may take his four children as the second generation, thus adjusting this work too to our conditional structural schema. In both *The Sound and the Fury* and *Sartoris* another generation, the youngest, is also mentioned: the child with whom the disintegration of the family is possibly halted. It all depends how we want to take it, then: the middle and third phases are elements in the developmental process whose culmination we may see in an earlier or later physical generation, but the general tendency is not thereby changed: it remains completely analogous to such far removed and structurally simpler works as *The Golovlev Family* and *Buddenbrooks.*

The generation of Jason Compson IV, his sister Candace, and the brothers Quentin and Benjy in *The Sound and the Fury,* is an excellent example of the horizontal rupture of the family unity and the degeneration of the family principle. The constructive enterprise of the early Compsons is replaced in Jason by the petty, perfidious and rapacious pedantry of the dishonest small-time trader; Candace, a prankish girl full of maternal feelings, leaves the family home because of the consequences of her promiscuous lust; Quentin, sensitive to a degree which completely paralyses any consistent reflection and makes him the victim of hallucinations and complexes regarding family purity, which in respect of Candace oscillate between the desire for incest and the desire for joint suicide; and finally Benjy, the 33-year-old idiot with the mind of a three-year-old child. This is the horizontal span of the Compsons in decadence and at the same time it reveals the elements which, to lesser extent, are present in the syndrome of family degeneration in the other writers. Candace's daughter (to whom is given the uncle's male name of Quentin) follows in her mother's footsteps and thereby concludes and underlines the ultimate fall of the Compsons. They have no descendants and she is lost forever from their horizons, but this does not add any new elements to their downfall or change the general structural model of three generations. In *Absalom, Absalom!,* on the other hand, after the bloody melodrama involving incest and race, the only (and illegitimate) Sutpen grandson, with the pathetically grotesque name of Charles Etienne de Saint Velery Bon which is meant to indicate his connection with the New Orleans French "aristocracy" through his mother (who is one eighth black), marries a stammering black woman and the last Sutpen offspring turns out to be the black, gibbering and barbaric Jim Bond. "I think," says one character in the novel, "that in time Jim Bond will take over the western hemisphere. That will not, of course, happen in our time and naturally, when they spread out towards the poles they will turn pale again as happens to rabbits and birds, and they won't stand out so sharply against the snow. But this will still be Jim Bond; and so, in a few thousand years' time I who am looking at you will also appear from the loins of African kings."[80]

Under the influence of this extreme and dense symbolism it is difficult to discern the basic forms of the essentially similar development we find even in a genealogical work with quite a different moral tone. The last offspring of the Thibaults is the three-year-old Jean-Paul, conceived in the single night of love between Jacques and the long loved Jenny de Fontain. Large parts of the epilogue in Martin du Gard's cycle are made up of daily notes dedicated to the child by his uncle Antoine and written as he lies slowly dying during the last months of the war, his lungs destroyed by poisonous gas. But even in this condition he reflects on the possibilities of life. There is no reason why the Thibaults should die out. "The energies of the Thibaults,"[81] he thinks with satisfaction, "my father's authority, taste for governing . . . Jacques' unruliness and rebellion . . . my persistence . . . and now, this power the little one has in his blood, what form will it take on?" Antoine's appraisal of Jacques as a rebel is neither a negative one nor the uncritical affirmation of feelings of restlessness. "(. . .) Your father, like all who are impetuous, created the impression that on the majority of questions he had diverse and often contradictory views, which he himself would not manage to reconcile. He failed even to draw from them any firm, precise or lasting certainty or clearly oriented directives. His personality was also composed of diverse elements, opposed and equally strong—this was his richness— but between which he found it difficult to choose and from which he never made a harmonious whole. Hence his eternal unrest and the passionate uneasiness in which he lived."

This acceptance of contradiction is perhaps the main message of this mature book: "Do not feel displeased about these contradictions. They are uncomfortable but healthy. Always at moments when my spirit saw that it was the prisoner of contradictions from which it could not extricate itself I have felt at the same time nearer to that Truth with a capital letter which is constantly revealed." Life will not be the poorer for his dying, Antoine realizes: in his reflection he discovers that in his past there was nothing the consequences of which would remain in his spirit alone and to which there would be no witnesses to outlive him. The last word of the Thibaults—in Antoine's diary as his pain is becoming intolerable in the final days of his life and the war—is simply the name of the child, the very possibility of a future: "Jean-Paul."

In comparison with the optimism of Martin du Gard, Galsworthy's hovers above the reality of the present world, despite the fact that the final part of the epilogue in *Les Thibault* is all in reflection while the third part of the *Forsyte Saga* is a dramatic conflict. The main subject of this volume is the endeavours of the young generation to be free from the burden of the elders' past. Thus, if the son of Irena and Jolyon declines marriage with Soames's daughter because of the gloomy memories of the previous unhappy marriage between Irena and Soames, this is admittedly recognition of the Forstye legacy but also an act of free will, a sign of a certain maturity and the result of a free decision and not prejudice. If the reader fails to accept this, this is again because Galsworthy, no matter how much he might need positive, free characters in order to affirm his belief in broad, selfless humaneness, does not know how to create such characters. The elegiac mood of Soames, who feels that the young generation is far away from him, that in his own house he has never replaced the emptiness with a new, lively, relationship and that dust is gathering on the objects he has preserved and which symbolize the permanence of the Forsytes while the original inhabitants of their homes have become grotesque fossils—this mood, then, is infinitely more authentic than the idyllic goodness and spontaneous tactfulness between Jolyon, Irena and little Jon which is full of a certain cloying feeling of an attained absolute happiness. If Galsworthy has a place in literature this is only thanks to Soames, her and the children suited only to a light novel with a socio-psychological orientation. It is true that contemporaries uncritically saw Soames's artistic ambitions. In the second trilogy the genealogical process continues merely mechanically, with Fleur growing older, and the relations between Soames, her and the children suited only to a novel with a socio-psychological orientation. It is true that contemporaries uncritically saw Soames's daughter as the "embodiment of the disharmony of the present days." To them she was a "symbol of the chaotic, cynically superficial, restless and yet blasé, craving for sensations, eternally dissatisfied, fascinating, egoistic and disturbingly aimless in this time of transition."[82] This, of course, means reading Galsworthy within the confines of a bourgeois outlook and is what the conscientious citizen and real artist, Thomas Mann, transcended in the non-rebellious Thomas and in the previously illustrated talent of Hanno. Behind the decadence of the Buddenbrooks there stands a well thought-through and correctly observed theory; behind the transformations of the Forsytes merely good intention.

Saltykov-Shchedrin's characters lack the spiritual breadth of Mann's heroes and do not move about the space of the novel's action as self-assuredly and swaggeringly as Galsworthy's. Yudushka has condensed in himself all the potential freedom of the other characters and—at the expense of his mother, brothers, sons and nieces—become one of the greatest characters in Russian literature. He is present in the degeneration of the third generation of the Golovlev downfall, is quickly bereft of his sons Volodya and Pechenka, and the decline of Anyushka and Lyubinka takes place while their grandmother is still alive. Nevertheless, we are conscious that this dying is taking place at the same time throughout several generation strata. It is the youth, clumsiness and naivety of these young actresses, whom no one can stop and save, which are touching in a book against which perhaps the only black mark is that not one single character, not even in the third generation, is likable.

In the third generation of the Artamonovs Pyotr's sons, Ilya and Yakov, are the only interesting characters while the rest, even the young liberal entrepreneur, Miron, form the backdrop for these two. Ilya is an intellectual, thinks independently and has opposed his father since childhood. Near the end of the book he is a revolutionary but we only hear about this, as it happens, outside the course of the novel. Yakov remains in his father's business but we know him only as an observer of character, a lover and someone who vacillates in political events demanding decision. As Lukács correctly points out, Gorkiy "interprets the downfall of the merchant family as the process of disintegration in the camp of the class enemy." Thomas Mann, he goes on to say, "sees in the decline of the old merchant class the disintegration of the class with which he is connected, the extinction of an ideal and the appearance of a new social type which is alien to him and which he rejects."[83]

However, social struggles are no more directly present in Gorkiy than in Mann and even though events at the end of the book indicate that the October Revolution has arrived, Pyotr, the central personality among the Artamonovs, has the floor: "I will not. Get lost!" He, and not the children, moves along with the current of history; he, like his father before him, has made history; in the writer's presentation he remains the protector of the younger characters, who are never completely realized. It is precisely what he did not achieve in his intentions that contributed to Gorkiy's realizing or exhausting the family cycle in the same sense in which other-non-proletarian writers did so. To set him apart from or opposite them means to introduce false considerations into literary assessment because of extraliterary facts which are not discernible in the work.

Who are the representatives of the third generation in Krleža? If we see *Gospoda Glembajevi* as the first stage of decline, *U agoniji* as the second, then *Leda,* after a fashion, becomes the third—death after the agony. In the social atmosphere on the very eve of the war *(Gospoda Glembajevi)* " 'masked card-sharps, cheats and murders' dominated the splendour of capitalism," and immediately after the war *(U agoniji)*—" 'speculators and smugglers' together with the Križovec Philistine Pharisees, and now upstarts of and intellectual cast in addition to the brutal Klanfars."[84] In *Leda* the Glembay is Oliver Urban but in fact the play has two major themes. One, in a more sociological manner, examines the conflict between the parvenu Klanfar, who has risen from the countryside to the world of big business, and his wife, the daughter of a wealthy Zagreb citizen. The two prose fragments in the cycle also deal with Klanfar. The second theme, the one in which Urban is included, is the life of superficial comfort, fashionable taste, uncertain talent and unlawful sexual play, to which the women hysterically attach greater importance than the rules would allow, but quickly calm down. The momentary serious tension and trepidation over possible death is quickly dispelled, the dramatic knot is unravelled without any main point being made and the "carnival night" is carnival not only in that the madness and partner-swapping last a short time but also because this is a life in which a mask of feelings, passions and inspiration is donned and important crises played out. Krleža later announces that Laura has only been hurt, as has baroness Castelli, and this anti-tragic tendency reaches its peak here. Scandal does not replace tragic catastrophe (the latter is situated at the beginning and the action, now deplete of impact, henceforth drags on to the end of Act III when Aurel notices that Klara has disappeared). The denouement is catastrophically ironic and no one suffers any consequences. These people have always merely marked time, or even better, masked life.[85]

Leda is game at many levels. The aesthetic discussions, for example, are completely irrelevant. They conceal the personality and do not reveal it as is the case with Leone. When Urban talks about death this is also in stark contrast to Leone's contemplation: "To tell the truth, I look at my last chip on the green baize—the nickel on a Browning is pretty cold—I feel the way it often makes me shiver through my pocket lining." The very theme of *Leda* is affection. In 'Plamen' Krleža was forming a new literary programme, demolishing the decorative and false aesthetic paraphernalia: "What do we want with those terraces and those Ledas and swans and homosexual princes? What do we want with those Nordic marriages, palms and crinolines, vases and cyclamens, marquesses and purple curtains? Does the ardour of a Balkan race, a young race thirsty for undiscovered intensity, boil in us, or are we merely some riff-raff in powder form which has spent all its strength on Viennese, Berlin and Budapest spiritual prostitutions?"[86] Leda is used here so as to compromise her, though she herself does not appear anywhere. The structural characteristic of this play is the series of dialogues about absent people.[87] In his very thorough analysis of this play Ljubomir Marković perceives many of its characteristics but demands of it what there should not be in it:

> And for this reason everything dissolves into the hopeless pessimism of bitterness, the cause of which is not any profound *taedium vitae* resulting from the cognition of life's truth but rather a surfeit of cynicism about life which has exceeded here all bounds of satirical justification, which is why it does not create an impression of life but rather a dramatized *feuilleton*. Likewise, the author has gone too far here in the paradoxical reasoning, which creates the impression in places of an unnecessary flaunting of the most diverse knowledge. The matter of whether we shall be convinced of the intellectual nature of a character or not lies in the organic construction of the character itself. Unending tirades are not necessary. One gesture by Leone Glembay says more than half an hour's monologue in dialogue by Urban.[88]

True, but this is the whole point. *Leda* is not a drama about private score-settling but a rationally constructed and intentionally schematized entertainment.[89] The Glembay complex of problems dies with Urban and he quite rightly disappears for ever somewhere between Quebec and Montreal; the most familiar and favourite quotation from *Leda* is the street-walker's exclamation: "Oh, if only I could travel off somewhere, even in a hearse, just to travel off somewhere!"

Urban, however, is not the only consequence of the Glembay decline. It has already been indicated that on the family tree he belongs to the generation of Olga and Leone. He is, therefore, older than Laura! If old Glembay and his brothers represent the first generation, which is directly dramatized in the Krleža cycle, and the first in the process of the Glembay extinction, then in addition to Laura we know another three members of the third generation (which is the sixth if we count from the mid eighteenth century miller, Ignac, with the scales in his hand): they are Leone the younger, the son of Leone and Beatrice after her departure from the mental asylum (following the "criminal scandal" with baroness Castelli), Dr. Kamilo Gregor and Marcel Faber-Fabriczy. The first is only mentioned on the genealogical plan and remains an interesting and bizarre possibility—food for speculation. The second, with his "strange talent for internal contemplation and quite a sensitive conscience, which after years of crises and delusion broke through to perceptive clarity and crystal-clear logic," is the only wise, honest and good Glembay. We have a suitable but insufficient fragment on him—*Kako je doktor Gregor prvi put u životu susreo Nečastivoga*. The greatest amount of material on him is afforded by the play *U logoru* where Gregor is the formal link between this play and the Glembay cycle. If connection to the family were the criterion for what belongs or does not belong to the cycle, the place of this play would be equally justified among the various things on the Glembays as that of *Leda* (this is worth returning to later). We have a certain image of Gregor, a positive hero, but it lacks the fullness which brings certain other Glembay characters so much to life. The third is Marcel Faber, who is most completely realized in the fragments *Ljubav Marcela Faber-Fabriczyja za gospođicu Lauru Warroniggovu* and *U magli*. However, to understand Krleža's intentions in respect of this character we must first of all return to the texts on him as they were first published in reviews.

In 1926 a prose piece was published in 'Književna republika' under the title *U magli* (the present-day prose fragment entitled *Ivan Križovec,* with the exception of the last section, which this review version lacks). However, as we have already indicated, in 1928 Krleža published (in 'Savremenik') another prose piece under the title *U magli* (this time with the sub-title *Odlomci novele—Extracts from a Novella*).[90] This piece consists of the section which today concludes *Ivan Križovec,* with the exception of the first sentence—"Doctor Križovec last met Baroness Lenbach on the battlefield in Galicia"—and certain other minor differences, the main one being that the section is written in the first person and that at the end it says: "(Iz uspomena dr. Paula Altmanna)"—"(From the memoirs of Dr. Paul Atlmann)." The second part of this prose piece in 'Savremenik' comprises the present-day fragment *U magli*.

Why did Krleža recompose these fragments? The review version of the present-day *Ivan Križovec* did not mention Laura anywhere while the addition of the section from the other text establishes, through the mention of Laura, a direct link with the Glembay cycle. It is more important, however, that the writer's original intention was clearly to link Laura and Marcel, at least thematically, in a more profound way, regardless of the story. Thus, Laura's experience on the Galician front appeared as a counterpoint to the account of Marcel as a Soviet official in Russia.

Ljubav Marcela Faber-Fabriczyja . . . deals more directly with the relationship between Marcel and Laura. This fragment, with minor variations in the title, was also published in part in 1928 in 'Savremenik' and in part the following year in 'Pantheon.' This prose piece differs from the later text in that in the book it is introduced by a short passage which mentions Križovec's acquaintance with Marcel "from those distant Zagreb days" when they were both young and Marcel was in love with Laura, the granddaughter of Ambroz Glembay. This addition brings Marcel into relationship with Križovec, as though implying that his case is important in the context of Križovec's presence in the Glembay cycle.

Why? Probably because Križovec, as a social type and as a character directly present in the crucial crisis of Laura, a direct Glembay offspring, is more important in his function in the internal links of the Glembay cycle. If the writer planned to give the character and fate of Marcel a more complete and definite synthesis, he never realized this.

Marcel should represent two poles of the negation of the Glembays: first of all, sensitivity and secondly, an unusually acute moral sensibility, which is manifested in his attitude towards Croatian national feeling and his wound from a Hungarian sword. Thus, the ideal fidelity in his spiritual cognition of Woman leads to complete erotic suffering over Laura. This timorous experiencing of Laura, who is indifferent or does not know of Marcel's feelings is extremely reminiscent of the way in which Krleža, in his essay *O Marcelu Proustu* (On Marcel Proust) from 1926, saw Swann's relationship with Odette. An atmosphere is achieved in these passages which has no equal in any of the other descriptions of the Glembay drawing rooms. Marcel's pining is accompanied by a refined sense of the decorative; the milieu is an irremovable part of the feeling itself. The way this same Marcel then becomes a famous revolutionary cavalry general was never, unfortunately, dealt with properly. It seems that only in *Zastave* did Krleža leave himself the room to carry out such a narrative synthesis. Marcel joined the revolution because "to his mind the greatest joys were certain explosive ideas, certain verticals full of dynamism, certain straight lines of zeal for which he had longed since his earliest days in the gymnasium." However, after rushing around "in armoured trains in nights full of danger, in the dark," Marcel finds himself in Soviet Kitaygorod in a situation of bureaucratic stagnation. Krleža's trip to Russia produced very profound perceptions which, scattered around his literary *oeuvre* in various references, are at least as valuable as *Izlet u Rusiju (Outing to Russia)* itself: "He is drowning in petty-bourgeois trivia, he has become a kind of higher bank official and he is gradually coming to feel that he himself is disappearing in the most odious condition of helplessness, monotony and boredom; that he is sinking in the mud, in the heavy leaden substance of helplessness." The last we know about Marcel is that he met Laura—"like two castaways in life"—when, "having returned home from Russia, he wandered about our mist for a while, compass-less." We never find out what happened to him later.

Nowhere in the genealogical cycles, which are linked to the bourgeois era and follow historical reality, regardless of the picture arising from the subjective interpretation of an individual author,—nowhere, then, is a social revolutionary realized. Gorkiy avoided depicting Ilya Artamonov the younger and Jacques Thibault (who seems to anticipate Malraux, the vigorous poet of anti-fascist Spain, and the night flights of the humanist fighter, Saint-Exupery) is a revolutionary in his enthusiasm (let us recall Marcel's explosive verticals!) but remains with his entire being within the complex of Thibault contradictions. The letter from Martin du Gard to Marcel Lallemand about Jacques is exceptionally illuminating when applied to the problem of such a character in a work dealing with the family circle in the bourgeois world: "There is a 'hole' in the intelligence of Jacques, (. . .) His nature is 'in revolt,' but complicated and 'uncertain' (because of the many tendencies, inherited traits and contradictory elements in him). He is capable of 'enthusiasm' but on no account 'belief'." He wrote to the same friend nine years later, after France's liberation from the Germans, in connection with the people who wrote to him in a "puerile" fashion full of admiration for the character of Jacques: "Jacques, with all his heart, nobility, intelligence and, above all, his personal charm, is, at the intellectual and social level, a 'false spirit,' incorrigibly false; as to constancy, he lacks it. He is too given to reasoning and too accustomed to seeing the for and against in everything."[91] This also holds true to a large extent for Marcel and Gregor, as well as the positive desires of the young idealists in various novellas by Krleža.

What, then, is the real conclusion to the Glembay cycle? *Leda* is lost in triviality, in drunken sleep after the carnival excitement; Marcel remains in the mist; all we know about Gregor is that he fails to recover from his meeting with the Evil One; we have never even seen Leone the younger; Laura, also part of their generation, has got out of her existential impasse through suicide . . . Krleža carried on with this set of problems outside the Glembay cycle, but this does not solve the question of the artistic form of expression. Is this cycle also analogous to the other genealogical cycles in its final phase?

It seems it is: in this connection it is not important that this crumbling away at the end, this absence of conclusions to the various fates involved reminds us of the open-endedness of various life paths in the Rougons and Marcquarts. In the cycles from Saltykov-Shchedrin to Faulkner the third and final generation is made up of children not actually present (*Les Thibault,* Faulkner); young people who have rejected the values of their family yet at the same time continue to feel part of this family (Galsworthy); people who have developed a sensibility, the foundations for which have come from the family but the manifestation of which means the transcendence of the family principle (Mann), or sometimes people who, denied the opportunity for genuine creativity or lacking the strength or adequate talent, remain frivolous, with tragic or burlesque consequences (the Golovlevs, *Leda*); sensitive intelligent revolutionaries who fail in the reader's eyes to develop their full potential; tolerant successors to their elders, without the imagination or strength to maintain the continuity (Yakov Artamonov, Jason Compson); gibbering, inferior bearers of a biological stigma (*Absalom, Absalom!*) and madmen. Whoever they are, their function within the structure itself is essentially the same.[92]

DECOMPOSITION

If the genealogical cycle in all the works here is the same in its basic structure, we may pose the following question: are the forces which corrode and break down these families, so diversely determined by history, also the same? If we also find constants here, are they going to be historically determined as an element of extra-literary reality or are they part of the literary treatment? In the latter case, where is this a convention and where the apt and artistically appropriate manifestation of a similar imagination?

The decadence of all the families here means above all a decline and loss of vitality and the exhaustion of those powers which gave the family their vigour, wealth and standing. This decadence is a historical process but all the writers from Zola to Faulkner observe this historical dimension from the inside, in the individuals and the relations between them. Zola admittedly shows Rougons and Macquarts in public life and in key moments in the epoch but these are merely the external medium. As Rougon-Macquarts he sees them as manifestations of an inherent hereditary force.

This is why the social aspect remains outside the essential genealogical subject in these works. The scandal *à la* Ibsen or Balzac in *Gospoda Glembajevi* intensifies the action and indicates the social significance of the entire Glembay "procession" at the culminatory moment of its external splendour. The real drama, however, the one which affords meaning to these social dimensions (and we, the public, accept the interpretation of Leone, who in a dramatized form sets out the facts presented impersonally in the fragment *O Glembajevima*), lies in the relations between the members of the family. In *Decadence* matters are interrupted by the revolution but the drama is not in the conflict between the Artamonovs and the revolution but in the grumbling dissatisfaction, the internal decomposition of their talents and the loss of their joy in creating and working. In *Les Thibault* the family is lost as a result of the fatal blows dealt the brothers by the war, but before little Jean-Paul there lies a future. This genealogical novel is, therefore, the only one to remain open outwards and upwards and towards what is to come after the catastrophe. Perhaps, in the strictest sense, *Les Thibault* is not even a genealogical novel, for in the major part of the work we are preoccupied with history. However, in this history the characters are treated not as a group of individuals but as Thibaults, linked by common characteristics manifested in very diverse ways. In *Buddenbrooks,* which appeared before the great social upheavals, biological exhaustion precedes economic decline and brings it about, and not the converse as happens in the realistic novel, to whose composition and structure the early Mann was so near. In the speculation with the green wheat we are even shown how, by compromising his principles of business honesty, Thomas stands on the threshold of moral decline.

In Faulkner, too, the changes which were to take place in the economic positions of his families have already occurred. In *The Sound and the Fury* Benjy's meadow has been sold to enable brother Quentin to go to the university. This is one of the leitmotifs of the novel and has symbolic meaning within the family relationships. As a statement on their circumstances it is merely a sign, an external shell whose content the writer does not develop. The Golovlev's situation does not change as a result of the emancipation of the serfs but because of the parasitic relationships between themselves. This parasitism has, we realize, brought the previous class relations to absurdity but the subject of the novel is not the criticism of these relations. Finally, *The Forsyte Saga:* the Forsyte principle comes in for criticism and is profoundly transformed from inside to the point of being unrecognizable, but the wealth and family name live on.

Thus, if the objective co-ordinates of time and place do not add up to an external crisis, we may say that, with the possible exception of the Glembays, the family as a genealogical unit does not perish from social causes.

There are two internal factors which produce the genealogical cycle's drama and determine its place in literary history, and any serious criticism of this kind of work as a whole must perceive in what way they are present. They are sensibility and illness, two characteristics which easily pass from one to the other, for physical inadequacy or weakness demoralizes or intensifies the spirit and concentrates its efforts in one direction while sensitivity in isolation becomes morbid and, creative in its own sphere, prevents healthy growth elsewhere.

Nietzsche saw the cause of European decadence in ethical awareness. Thomas Mann disputes this understanding and considers ethics to be a constructive feature in every civilization. In aesthetic sensitivity, on the other hand, he saw the cause of decline in the organism's general tone; the Buddenbrooks, he himself says, are built on this idea. Hanno's feverish art, perhaps introduced into the family at some stage or inherited from his mother, closes his mind to practical affairs, material interests and functionality. He would not take over the firm even if there was no other consideration (typhus) preventing him from doing so. Hanno takes the name of Buddenbrook into another sphere. For Mann and Nietzsche this is the higher sphere of culture, but this does nothing to alter the fate of the Buddenbrooks.

An artist introduces unrest at the very beginning of *The Forsyte Saga*: at the gathering for June's engagement the appearance of the foppish, nonchalant, swaggering Bosinney, an architect, sets off alarm signals. His freedom in architectural undertakings does not tolerate any such realistic considerations as cost. At dinner at Swithin Forsyte's he says, with English subduedness but directness, approximately the same about the sculpture which introduces "culture" into the sober Victorian dining-room as Leone says, more loudly and coarsely, to the offended Fabriczy about the picture of Ferenczy.

Through his unhappy engagement to June and amorous connection with Soames's wife, Bosinney breaks the solid family ties between the Forsytes. He disappears from the scene but there remains young Jolyon who, already lacking contact with the family and tacitly at odds with his father, acts like a rebel on the Forsytes. But he is no more a rebel than he is an artist. He paints watercolours but does not believe in them himself, calling himself an amateur and not a creator. Nor does he have any illusions that disagreement with the other Forsytes would be very radical. It is sufficient for him not to live a Forsyte, even though he lives on the Forsyte money.

Other Forsytes also flirt with art. June takes care of poor artists, opens galleries for them and helps their families. Soames is a collector of infallible instinct. Aunt Juley says of him that he has wonderful taste and always knows in advance what will be a success—a commercial success, of course, the only kind she as a Forsyte is aware of.

A real counterweight to the Forsyte spirit is to be found in Irene, whose beauty brings so much suffering to herself, Soames and others. Because of her Galsworthy calls his work "a personal incarnation of the unrest which Beauty introduces into people's lives." Irene is not an autonomous, realistic character. She is only present, the author himself warns, "through the senses of the other characters" as the "concretization of a disturbing beauty"[93] affecting the world of the rich. Beauty, as a force which disarms the Forsytes, people of entirely materialist values, becomes in Galsworthy a substitute for more serious reflection on the forces which transcend the mere state of ownership. This attractive but contestable idea induced Isidora Sekulić to devote an entire essay to the "problem of beauty in the work of John Galsworthy." In an admittedly rather nebulous context she underscores a thought very relevant to *The Forsyte Saga:* that beauty is "never anyone's property." In beauty she sees a bearer of social progress and a guarantee for the transformation of the Forsytes: "In the Forsytes beauty appeared and prevailed, firstly through Irene then gradually through an artistic sensitivity; through a feeling of the beauty of self-denial; through the desire to acquire an art gallery for the common good; through joining up with the volunteers and the giving of one's life for a beauty in which not only the Forsytes but the world believed; and finally, through the generation which 'no longer knew how to make money.' Galsworthy's irony gave the final parts of the trilogy the inscription *To let,* Melancholy, Galsworthy's heroic and refined melancholy, had in mind here: if only all could have what has hitherto belonged to a few."[94]

Here, of course, lies Galsworthy's weakness. He was honest enough to depict the psychology of the Forsytes; a sufficiently realistic satirist. But in creating the principle of opposition and the internal transformation of values he grew weaker. We simply do not believe his frequently anthologized story *Indian Summer of a Forsyte* about the friendship between old "uncle Jolyon," fascinated by beauty, and Irena, valuing the goodness of dignified old age. D. H. Lawrence's bitter words about the anti-Forsyte pose of Jolyon the younger and Irene, who have "all the wickedness of the Forsytes without their energy,"[95] and the mechanical, vulgar, feeling of wealth in the younger generation, cannot be understood at the level of light reading with moral pretensions but must be seen from the point of view of an uncompromising art which rejected the bourgeois ethos. It is worthwhile recalling what Frank Swinnerton, having noticed certain Turgenevian elements in Galsworthy, wrote: that the difference between these two was that Turgenev was basically a poet while Galsworthy was in his heart of hearts a gentleman.[96]

It was necessary to dwell on this in order to emphasize the difference between the aesthetic sensibility present in Galsworthy and that in Mann or Krleža. For art as a theme has in essence the same corrosive effect on the Buddenbrooks, Forsytes and Glembays, and between *The Forsyte Saga* and Krleža's dramatic trilogy (separating the dramatic works from the rest of the cycle, as is sometimes done in criticism) there are even broad structural analogies.

As distinct from all the Forsytes, Leone is a genuine artist who in the very first words of his part (and *Gospoda Glembajevi* in general) mentions the fundamental issues of aesthetic sensitivity, the same ones which Filip Latinovicz was later to develop in his meditations on whether it is possible to paint, how to translate sensory impressions into another medium, and how to realize graphically his intellectual notion of a rural Christ. It is only as an artist that Leone opposes the Glembays; as a painter who bears in himself Glembay heritage which, in its material form, has allowed him to go off abroad, thence to come and stay in his father's house like a stranger, attend the celebrations and—travel off again. This is a more extreme separation than Jolyon's and yet at the same time that essential, natural link in temperament with the Glembays is acknowledged. Jolyon's separation from the Forsyte complex is primarily a matter of ideas. Leone revolts in himself against the Glembays and Glembay by virtue of his artistic sensibility (Krleža is nearer Turgenev's than Galsworthy's category—restricting ourselves to Swinnerton's distinction for now!). His perception of Beatrice-Angelika, the only completely non-Glembay presence near him, is that of a painter and at the same time it has erotic and moral dimensions. It anticipates the later connection which the writer was only to note down on the genealogical tree. Leone reacts with antipathy to all the other characters, with the exception of the doctor, Paul Altmann. This antipathy is manifested in the fact that he subjects every assertion, every intention and every expression of emotion to analysis. The picture is shown to be *kitsch*; the plan concerning Rupert-Canjegova, a legitimistic trick; the precondition for the success of the Glembay business (explosives, refuse), death or usury; the family ties, debauchery; the family misfortunes, a reaction to the false mask of bourgeois probity and to licentious deceit. Leone is not a moralist; he dwells on the phenomena from which he has removed the veil of words. Edward Goy's observation that the problem of perception constitutes the motive force of the plot in *Gospoda Glembajevi* is interesting:

"The problem of perception runs parallel with the symbols of degenerate limbs, suicides and madness. It is the motive force of the plot and constitutes a symbolic representation of history perceived from a Marxist standpoint. The degeneration of moral and artistic perception, the fact that truth has become an instrument of animal self-preservation and that logic is not sufficient to preserve truth if the inner 'laws' are lost—all this is to be found at the heart of the drama and provides the central themes with its true dramatic motif; all this comprises the internal symptom of the Glembay family's degeneration. The Rupert and Canjegova incidents and the entire intrigue in the play form merely the external structure in which the problem is developed."[97]

In examining *Leda* we may return to this observation by Goy. The problem of perception now lies in the artists themselves, including here Urban, the connoisseur. The triviality of the details which are discussed, the insignificance of the associations (for in the play vital decisions are only talked about, used as threats but never carried out), the absurd self-satisfied phrase-mongering, the blasé acceptance of phrases and the cheap irony—here too art is a motif in the degeneration of the Glembay social complex but this time it is in the very representatives of this, the third Glembay phase. The irony here is not directed against them but rather, belonging to them themselves, it creates the moral wasteland which this irony in itself denotes.

The pitiful provincial dilettantism of the Golovlev grandsons in Saltykov-Shchedrin's novel has the same role. Here the tone is different from the exhibitionist variations of Krleža's snobs. They are unhappy beings; the stifling Golovlev atmosphere has forced them into this path and now through their own lives they are finally liquidating that Orthodox manorial hypocrisy. In none of the other genealogical cycles does the dialectic of the internal exhaustion of a closed world appear in such a complete form.

In the more expansive cycles of Martin du Gard and Faulkner the sensibility is not aesthetic but moral, though Jacques' activism, the more rational objectivity of Antoine Thibault[98] and the convulsions of the mind inspired by childhood and an exaggerated belief in historical timelessness in Faulkner's heroes set these characters apart from the mechanical routine of class convictions. On occasions enthusiasm or protestation will be expressed in images of beauty or ugliness but the main link with artistic spirit is that these offsprings in the younger generations of their environments have broken away towards their own subjective reappraisal of heritage. The fact that this sensitivity can be intense to the point of illness is most clearly shown by Faulkner, most often precisely in the characters who see themselves as the protectors of their forebears' ideals and principles. There is much self-deception in this moral purity. It sets people apart from their environments, brings isolation and gives rise to eccentricity, sexual aberrations or improbable forms of asceticism. Such characters are to be found in many works *(Light in August, A Rose for Emilie)* but Quentin in *The Sound and the Fury* is the most distinct example, and he is created within the context of a complex family situation. In Faulkner's works illness is sometimes manifested in pathological behaviour resulting from physical defects, excesses or violations of human nature. With all due respect for the originality of Faulkner's inspiration, we cannot help but recall Zola. We almost always come across this naturalistic symbolism wherever a family line is shown in his work. After all, exhaustion and deformation also appear as a subject here—when they are not what is happening to the subject itself.

In two letters separated by almost two years Gorkiy compares the case of Leonid Andreyev's sister with that of the boy in Zola's *Le docteur Pascal:* "In people with bad inheritance—in so-called degenerates—as a result of their inheritance in moment of excitement the blood vessels open up anywhere: on the neck, leg, the blood gushes out and they die."[99] (In Zola Charles, the greatgrandson, is sitting at the table with his mad aunt Dide. All of a sudden "A red drop moved along the edge of the boy's left nostril. It fell, another formed and went after it. This was blood, a bloody dew dripping, this time without injury, without a blow; coming out and flowing away by itself, weakened by the exhaustion of degeneration.")[100]

Illness suggesting degeneration also hounds the Artamonovs. Nikita is a hunch-back, fond of flowers and sensitive about Nataliya. In despair over his position, he attempts to hang himself. Aleksey's children die very weak.

Why? Gorkiy had great respect for Zola's depiction of society[101] (just as he respected Galsworthy's)[102] and he clearly found a pattern in his conception of the physical correlate of psychological and social functioning. In any case, illness as a symbolic expression of disintegration and the loss of social strength was not new in Russian literature. It appears throughout the entire course of *The Golovlev Family*. It also appears later in the genealogical themes of Faulkner. We also find it in Krleža's cycle (the fate of the five daughters of the incapable and passive Marijan Glembay and their 20 unfortunate descendants) where an entire page is taken up with example after example of suicide, paralysis, criminality and tuberculosis: "The mists of death and madness even today envelop these legitimate and illegitimate, direct and indirect Glembays with a heavy and fateful depression."

This impressive line-up is also a "theory of inheritance," with a hypothesis somewhere between Zola and Lombroso. It is not important to the thematic development of the Glembays and is only insignificantly echoed in the other Glembay prose pieces. However, as an idea it links the Glembays to the other genealogical works, incorporates them more fully into the family of families and brings to mind a determinism which, as a world view, suggests some general order in the series of family fates, even though it does not necessarily have any more profound meaning. The neurosis of a character like Leone is quite a different matter. Even though we do not see him as a genuine painter in action (not the case with Filip Latinovicz), we feel, as we have already endeavoured to demonstrate, that this neurosis comes into play as a result of his reaching to the things around him as an artist. Here we have left Zola and drawn nearer to Freud, whose part in an interpretation of Mann's artists, and also little Hanno, is much better suited to their intellectual realization. In *Buddenbrooks* dying is also treated systematically and, although this is no longer such a novelty as it was when Mann was writing his work, the cold style and clinical, detailed observation are still startling. Naturalistic, scientific, detached pedantry? Be that as it may, despite the numerous descriptions of death in each of the genealogical cycles, *Les Thibault* is the only other work to contain this clinical precision. Medicine is one of the principal themes in this cycle, though it is difficult to say whether it is a case of a particularly individual inclination on the part of the writer or of a deeper link with the questions of family heredity. Medicine, however, is also present outside the family action and relations: the passages dealing with Antoine's practice as a doctor and his professional reactions are an irreplaceable part of the construction of his character. As elements in the natural course of the generations the desperate tenacity of old Thibault on his death-bed and of Thomas Buddenbrook's mother perhaps evoke mutual associations, but there is nothing of the like in any of the other cycles.

It is interesting that precisely *Les Thibault* and *Buddenbrooks* are the only two cycles where sex does not enter the sphere of illness, dying and hypersensitivity. No matter how strong the presence of sexuality might be, or crucial in the formation of Antoine's character and as an illumination of it, or crucial, for instance, in Thomas's psyche in the later phases of his moral debility, it does not have any consequences for the development of the family as a whole. Similarly, Galsworthy never allows the reader *to feel* Irena's attractiveness and that persistent, implacable and fatal craving Soames has for her and about which the writer only *talks.* In accordance with the writer's scope, which is not inconsiderable at the level of the realistic penetration of the social situation but does not even venture into the inexplicable, in *The Forsyte Saga* Irena's adultery is merely the first link to be wrenched from the chain of Forsyte certitude and self-confidence. This event, however, includes non-Forsytes and does not characterize the family alone, does not destroy characters and does not turn out to be representative of what happens to the Forsytes in subsequent generations. Likewise, the Forsytes' dying and illnesses merely mean departure from the social scene, a part of the normal natural process of which we are aware in the genealogical theme but which is not raised to the level of a central problem.

In Faulkner and the Russians we are, of course, dealing with quite a different world: the lust is real and present. Personalities become warped because of it, pride is lost and masters sleep with servants, slaves and workers and by this very fact become the captives of their serfs. It is in *Decadence,* however, that we feel most strongly the full torment of lustful craving, which sends the constructive energy in one generation up in flames and paralyses it, dissipating it in the second and third. This is on no account a social evil or the pathological result of a combination of inherited characteristics. Zola's degenerates and perverts belong within quite a different framework of ideas. In the Artamonovs physical desire is a force free of all extraneous causality, a sensuous passion at odds with the social norms. These norms, however, are not so strong or firmly implanted by tradition as ever to thwart this passion. Old Ilya Artamonov contentedly and only half secretly lives with the mother of his daughter-in-law, and Nataliya, the daughter-in-law, despite the abyss which separates her from the character of her Pyotr, cuddles up by his side every night. Pyotr, like Yakov and Aleksey, is promiscuous, takes part in orgies and while in the embraces of one mistress thinks of another. These mistresses constantly influence the actions and take part in their decline as part of the natural disintegration within the incurable contentment which Gorkiy never clearly substantiates. *Decadence* is a strange work, imperfect but suggestive beyond all the canons usually used to assess it: placing the emphasis on social-class analysis means seeing it in a distorting mirror and establishing non-existent arbitrary proportions between its parts. It is at least as much a fairy story as it is a social novel: a murder at the beginning, when the father and three sons knock the brains out of the assailants with a club; the evil wanton murder of the lad, Pavel, in the middle; the unhappy mood brought into the Artamanovs' lives by Nikita's attempted suicide; and the permanent presence of Tikhon Vyalov, who in the closing pages acts as a kind of avenger in history, but in the name of the extra-historical reality of Russian national suffering. All this brings us into the realm of legendary curses, of which there is none explicitly in the genealogical cycles up until old Barboczy's exclamation about the Glembays being murderers and cheats. Her *"Falschspieler"* relates to cheating in games and indeed the entire success of the Glembays is the result of luck and cruelty in the game of life. The Glembay exploits also begin with a murder on the road, in a forest, in fact. It is also mentioned in the prose piece *O Glembajevima* as a part of the family tradition and legend and the author returns to it later as a definite fact. Also, sex, more so than in any other cycle, appears as the fatal cause of numerous deaths and broken human relationships. Sex is Castelli's game, her stake in a multi-million gamble. Because of her people die and lives are built on lies. Her "erotic intelligence" is a living force. If old Glembay sounds pathetic when he talks about her it is because he has no other kind of sincerity. Leone's mental oscillations, already extreme as a result of the madness just beneath the surface, also give way to quite lucid memories which not even the baroness disputes.

As it is a part of the Glembay game, sex largely takes the form of scandal, or at least piquant intrigue. Olga Warronigg, wounded by her empty and pitiful marriage, takes to nightly walks by the Danube canal, then surrenders herself to flirts with garrison soldiers, who, as in the case of Baroness Castelli, suffer by imprudently taking these erotic ecstacies seriously. In *Leda* are mentioned the tragic consequences which can result from wounded female feelings, but the game here has already closed into a frivolous circle in which adultery not only no longer raises moral questions or creates deep emotional reverberations but has also exhausted the possibilities of intimate feelings. With the exception of Laura's relationship towards Križovec, in the whole cycle there is not one mature love relationship in which the entire personality is involved. Her ecstacies and sufferings are the only pure human component in Glembay sexuality. The latter, though constantly present, is much more a symptom and accompanying feature of the decomposition of familial cohesion and much less a genuine, fatal force.

If we bring together the various factors involved in the decadence of these families we see that these general phenomena are to be found in their greatest concentration in the Glembays: artistic hypersensitivity and excessively disturbed moral imagination, illness, murder, suicide, business reputation based on deceit, madness and the disintegration of erotic restraint—all this is present in the decline of the Glembays (even if only potentially in some instances) as part of the general picture in which only certain components of the disintegration are revealed in action. In the Russians and Faulkner the very characteristic artistic temperament—accepting Mann's interpretation—is lacking, while in *Buddenbrooks* there are no scandals, murders, sexual excesses or foul dealings. The world of the Zagreb patricians is more vulgar than the world of the Hanseatic merchants. *The*

Forsyte Saga and *Les Thibault* are nearest to social realism. Here, however, the themes of illness, rebellion and sexuality are not as fascinating as when they are part of the inner motive of disintegration, and the criticism of the bourgeois principles in these works does not indicate that these principles are necessarily criminal or that their champions are lying about themselves. The Glembay cycle has, then, the most extreme and searing effect. Ibsen's plays with their sudden dramatic turns, pregnant with motives from an unsavoury and buried past, are more of a parallel to it than any novel. Nevertheless, in respect of the completeness of the genealogical evolution shown in the Glembay cycle, it must also be measured against the novel cycles which we have been analysing.

CONTOURS

Is it at all possible to consider the Glembay cycle an integral structure or a complete work which can be compared with the rounded-off novels or series of novels? In our discussion so far we have examined the continuity of generations in each of the eight writers and established that the genealogical cycle is formed around three key generations, or more exactly, three phases in the history of the family. The external form need not always clearly underline these three phases and the composition of some of the cycles even conceals them. The mammoth seventh volume of *Les Thibault (L'été 1914)* is the best example of this, but in it the genealogical theme passes into a broader narrative space, in which it presents just one dimension, and then returns to itself in the epilogue.

With the exception of Martin du Gard, after Zola's scientific ambition of arranging "his" family about locations characteristic of an entire epoch, all the other writers purposely lent their cycles a particular *timbre* which sometimes—as in Mann or the prose pieces of Krleža—turns into a subjective perspective, or at least the metaphorical expression of certain characters' inner experience.

The general arrangement is nevertheless most often objective. Thus *The Golovlev Family* unfolds homogeneously, each chapter presenting a stage of a common dying process and in each the reader saying good-bye to at least one victim. In *Buddenbrooks,* too, the action is not formed of dramatic intrigue but a series of independent episodes which only acquire their full meaning when taken together in the movement forwards, continuity, thematic repetition and development. Each chapter has its message which is also often death (though presented with a more easily understood sequence of generations than in Saltykov-Shchedrin) or at least some realization or final abandonment of previous possibilities. There is also, however, the subjective arrangement of the objective course of time, as in *Decadence* (of which Gorkiy himself was aware).[103]

Faulkner was, of course, much more radical in the subjective fragmentation of his material. His genealogical histories acquire their full significance in the fractured narration, the contrasting and counterpointing of narrators and in narration at different levels, where one narrator explains a story which he has heard from another, and sometimes the original anecdote has gone as far as three or four spectators. Alternatively, the same situation might have light shed on it from different angles in time. In the totality of its parallel layers and detached elements this polyphony is an expression of the quite subjective key to the interpretation and emotional evaluation of both the narrow personal story and the very history of Faulkner's country. This kind of narration can skirt round certain central events, embrace their consequences and develop their psychological meaning both forwards and backwards, return to the vicinity of this focal point in the action and then resolve it only at the very end. This circular movement, probably born with Conrad's *Lord Jim,* makes *Absalom, Absalom!* a particular *tour de force* and lends the family history in this novel an additional, circular, "cyclical" dimension, a horizontal one at the level of the narrative.

Faulkner was the only one to bring the tradition and essential structure of the genealogical cycle into a literature which is realized through a modern psychological technique. Perhaps this is an indication of the vitality of the genealogical theme and of a continuity running from the traditionally omnipresent narrator to the narrow horizons of a myopic, neurotic and even sub-normal person.

Although the composition of Krleža's cycle contains the seeds of a modernistic perspective, in the totality of its main parts it is nearer the contours of *The Forsyte Saga,* no matter how distant and often antithetic Galsworthy's world, his taste and his characters as individuals and representatives of social values might be to Krleža. The only point we are endeavouring to make here is that Krleža's three plays, as three focal points in the Glembay history, correspond to the three volumes of *The Forsyte Saga* and within the whole of each trilogy the individual parts have analogous scopes and functions. It has already been mentioned that *The Man of Property* and *Gospoda Glembajevi* open with a family gathering and that here is born the crisis which, within the dimensions of each work, leads to disintegration within the heart of the family. In *The Man of Property* this is the real beginning on which the writer develops with narrative effortlessness in his epic space. In Krleža's drama everything is already present; the several conflicts lying accumulated just beneath the surface break through the veneer of the happy jubilee in the technique of an Ibsen drama. This technique is, in fact, a condensed and at the same time universal expression of the idea of accumulated (and conditionally, "genealogical") inheritance being brought into the present, an idea which in the narrative structure replaces progression in time. In both works the authors, each with his own means, present a broad array of characters from the family gallery, both alive and dead, and then, in the second book of the Saga and the second play in the trilogy, close in on the heroes of the second generation and shape them into a concentrated and well-constructed dramatic conflict involving the disintegration of a doomed marriage and the female protagonists's approaching new amorous partnerships. In the third part the structure is not so pure or simple. It is based on a comparison of values and experiences in life styles: the more easy-going, unencumbered and, to put it that way, spiritually fresher (and in Krleža's case, more frivolous) remain in the battle. *To Let* and *Leda* in themselves do not offer any obvious mutual parallel; there is merely a very general one between the first parts and second parts. It is important, however, that within the entirety of the Saga and the Glembay cycle each part has an analogous function. The parallel between Krleža's play and Galsworthy's novel probably stands out because the three-part composition, which suits the internal, more substantial structure, has been employed precisely in these two cycles. This treatment would appear to suit some inherent law in literary works dealing with heredity (even when this does not relate to genealogy but merely culture or history: Ivo Vojnovic's trilogy, *Allons enfants, Suton (Twilight)*, and *Na taraci (On the Terrace)* deal with the fate of the ethical principle as summed up in the concept of "Dubrovnik," and the overall dimensions of the internal drama correspond exactly to the cycles which we have analysed here.

If it were not for the danger of this being understood as the creation of an abstract model, one might even say that both *Na taraci* and *To Let* present two kinds of young generation: serious Jon, who takes on the responsibility of his position, and the more frivolous and selfish Fleur in one work; in the other, Vuko and the young people around baroness Lidija, who are not part of the same plot but rather a kind of contrast, though both are thematic counterweights to Lukša (as both Jon and Fleur are to Soames). Again we would stress that the purpose of this observation is not to create some abstract model but rather that it should be a contribution to the question of structural openendedness or the simultaneous existence of several conclusions to the genealogical history.

It is an important fact that in the last generation of all the cycles there appear a number of attitudes which are mutually opposing and that in the emotional alignments of the writers themselves we find the source of the ideological meaning which they attach to the entire subject of genealogy. This certainly is not the same in each cycle. In Zola, even if Dr. Pascal, in whom the author wanted to depict himself, a scholar in advanced years, is dying, life is creating and going on: "One must live, live completely with one's entire life, and suffering, suffering itself is better than the renunciation, the death of all that is living and human in man himself (. . .) I believe in a life which constantly rejects harmful bodies, which rejuvenates the tissue to heal the wounds and which through impurity and death is nevertheless going towards health and continuous renewal."

This is too declarative to elicit a genuine response in literature; it is more an expression of a conceptual endeavour, and even perhaps the relevant cultural climate, but whatever the case, it is there and provides the colour for the conclusion of the cycle. In spite of all the unhappiness and ugliness in various books and the insensitivity, brutality and inhumanity in the conduct and circumstances of certain Rougon-Macquarts, Zola believes in man for he believes that science, which has already systematized the relationships of heredity, leads the way to the future. He believes this so fervently that it takes on the form of a mystical optimism: "As one must always learn, reconciling oneself to the fact that all things will never be learnt, does the acceptance of the mysterious, eternal doubt and eternal hope not mean the desire for movement, for life itself?"[104] A few pages later comes the last word in the cycle, *Life,* just as in *Les Thibault* this was to be the name of the surviving descendant, *Jean-Paul.*

Social criticism, criticism of the family as a unit in a historic class system is more specific where there is none of Zola's optimism, and particularly in the case of Saltykov-Shchedrin and Gorkiy. In presenting the Glembay fate, Krleža, a confirmed socialist like Gorkiy, does not go beyond the bounds of the conduct, habits and moral potential of the old, class world but in his attitude towards the Glembay illusion of civilization there is nothing sentimental. His feelings always lie with the victims in this world: in his *oeuvre* there is no Thomas Buddenbrook, rent asunder by his inclinations, or Soames, for whom Galsworthy was unable to create tragic dimensions. Leaving aside Faulkner, of whose writing he was not aware, Krleža is the only one of these writers of genealogical cycles whose prose transcended naturalistic description or realistic factual narration and created the atmosphere through style itself. In an essay on Marcel Proust Krleža complains that "Thomas Mann (...) writes in a dry and boring manner like Galsworthy. The writers from that dry and boring period of bourgeois prosperity are boring, just as boring as all the rights acquired by that society, which won through its members the greatest civil rights in the history of social development."[105] When Krleža considers Mann and Galsworthy boring, this is criticism of their mundane expression and also probably anger at the sentimental yielding to their profound attachment to the bourgeois way of life from which they themselves originate. Faulkner was, indeed, the only one to go further than Krleža in creating an idiosyncratic style in which rhetoric determines an orientation contrary to the way of life and thoughts of his heroes. If this all-embracing attitude towards character indications is also potentially Krleža's, the latter's social and (not too narrowly understood) political alignment is, as opposed to Faulkner's, quite unambiguous. Krleža is the only one whose style is rich and trans-realistic and who in his sympathies is removed from the world he is describing towards a positive negation of the present lying beyond our ken.

As such a broad range of concepts and expression marks the genealogical cycles, how do they, conceived over a period of more than 60 years, constitute a unified phenomenon in the literary historical sense? Can we really talk about an integral category and how would we define it?

The answer to this question is, in fact, a summary of everything that has here preceded it. The genealogical cycle appeared in the literature of the 19th century, with Zola, as the thematic concentration of Balzac's social, realistic cyclical novel conceived as a series of imaginative documents on the contemporary history of France. The social novel is, of course, much older than Balzac—we find it in England in the 18th century—but it differs from Balzac in that it lacks the historical awareness of the concrete conditioning underlying the depicted circumstances and their change in time. Balzac inherited this awareness from Scott. Zola retains this historical awareness but his interest is narrower: through the method of scientific study, which in his view is the only way to establish laws, he follows the individuals comprising the family in their inner mutual links. The society in which they live and manifest their personal talents and inclinations serves as a medium and framework (and is no longer the subject of the novels themselves, as in the case of Balzac).

After Zola, a number of writers conceived of family histories whose unity lies in the internal evolution linking the generations and manifested in very diverse individual characters and temperaments. As opposed to Zola, these writers have no documentary pretensions and do not claim a scientific accuracy, established outside the work itself, in the genealogical relations. In their conceptions the family members are not scattered in their activities about all the areas of their nation's life (as in Zola) but more connected to a common domicile (individuals, of course, leave the family home, physically or spiritually, and return to it and oppose it, actively or passively, from within). They witness the life of the social community and its historical changes within their own horizons, which are not all-embracing and often very restricted. In these post-Zola cycles the accent is very often on subjective experience, be it present in the very atmosphere with which the omniscient and omnipresent author, in the 19th century tradition, colours his picture of the people, environment and action, be it manifested in the narration of family events from the point of view of individual selected characters (Pyotr Artamonov, Thomas Buddenbrook). This stress on subjectivity corresponds to the evolution of European narrative prose from Naturalism towards the symbolic depiction of a spiritual profile and the break-down of these profiles into the subjective impressions of their bearers. In this process from documentary description to the stream of consciousness an increasingly crucial role in the action was to lie with characters of more pronounced sensibility, often with distinctly artistic, creative potential; whatever they might be, they are people who because of their sensitivity have different attitudes towards the material family inheritance and mutual obligations from those who carry on the tradition. In most cases these differences lead to conflict and always to splits and the decomposition of the unity. Together with physical degeneration (a motif inherited from Zola and currently the concern of interest, as a subject outside the historic epic context, in the literature of the Art Nouveau period, returns to Naturalism and individual forms of Modernism, there also appeared situations of blood intrigue involving crime, suicide, blatant or covert extortion and erotic fixations, which most frequently took the form of incest and even led to madness.

In its conception the genealogical cycle is historical, though the history which it depicts is the inner one of the family itself. In all the cycles, stress is laid on three elements which usually correspond to three generations: the generation of founders or builders or those who reached the culmination of wealth and constructiveness; the generation of their successors in which division and the polarization of values sets in; and finally the generation in which illness, frivolity, artistic isolation or a revolutionary orientation which negates the entire family inheritance smother the principles of the ancestors with the result that the family ceases to exist as a coherent, organic whole.

After Zola Thomas Mann alone had clear and new theoretical conceptions on the genealogical theme, in which he shifted priority from the naturalistic and physical to the spiritual and symbolic, guided in this by Nietzsche's criticism of bourgeois civilization. The others most often retained certain forms, statements and images which Zola left in the European literary atmosphere, though in their own negation of the social system and its economic and moral consequences they were inspired by Nietzschean or similar individualistic ideas and manifested to a greater or lesser degree an awareness of Marxist criticism (Gorkiy, Krleža). If in their inclinations they were much nearer the socio-historic level, in their work the naturalistic-symbolist line is lost and forms of the English socio-realistic novel return, perhaps with even educative features (Galsworthy), or Tolstoyan epic combines with the more modern discursive or essayist prose of the novel of ideas (Martin du Gard). The means and searches of modern European prose found more fertile and varied reflection in Faulkner than in any European novelist. Thus, in American history and the motifs of the American cultural heritage they were able to produce in Balzacian proportions a work imbued by a purely individual mythical and moral interpretation of them. The genealogical theme here has the dimensions of a specific problem: the blacks and the whites and the content of their society—slavery and the Civil War with its consequences.

Eight cycles, starting with Zola's, display a number of common features. It is clearly a case, then, of a broad trend in the literature of the European cultural sphere after the realism of the 19th century. Our analysis could most probably also be extended to include a series of cycles in individual national literatures too, these works, like Krleža's, deserving an equal place in the circle of internationally accepted and famous ones. At the same time they should be differentiated from the numerous family novels in several volumes whose subject is not material and spiritual inheritance from generation to generation but merely the changing of attitudes towards society. This includes a broad array of works. They may bear the character of humanist information on an exotic environment (as in Pearl Buck's *The House of Earth*) or, within the scope of one novel and with the economic technique of subjective construction, realize a range of orientations towards a sociopolitical complex (Heinrich Böll's *Billiards at Half Past Nine*).

The problem lies, therefore, in the theoretical location of literary works with a genealogical subject. Their subject does not denote such a broad general area as "society in the concrete past, which might be the subject of such a clear and ramified sub-group of novels as the historical novel. Even less is the genealogical novel, in spite of its quite characteristic structure, parallel to the main line of the new novel, the so-called *Bildungsroman* which shows the maturation and, particularly in more recent literature, the self-cognition of a young hero (in the principal representatives of this tradition, Stendhal, Balzac, Dickens, Flaubert and James this is, more precisely, "a young man from the provinces").[106]

On the contrary, the structure of the genealogical cycle is much more definite than that of the *Bildungsroman*, while the historical novel does not have a structure which, in its most general features, sets it apart from other novels of the same period. As a literary phenomenon the genealogical cycle is theoretically delimited by the category of subject and the category of sub-group, simply reducing the cycle to a novel or a series of firmly or loosely connected novels. It is impossible to call it a sub-group as it was clearly not such a lasting phenomenon as to cut across the borders of a large number of stylistic formations. It belongs entirely to the epoch when the realistic picture of the world was broken down, with the result that not even the firm naturalistic structure following the phase of Saltykov-Shchedrin and *Buddenbrook* could bear the burden of this subject and the genealogical novel underwent its formal decomposition. This decomposition meant at the same time the possibility of constituting new, original entities with an inner genealogical theme. But these works are entities only in a qualified sense (*Les Thibault*, Faulkner's novels), which does not, of course, alter the historical place of the genealogical cycle.

Here we arrive at yet another theoretical aspect of this classification problem, which is exacerbated by the existence of Krleža's *Glembajevi*, which do not constitute a narrative whole. The genealogical cycle can under no circumstances be a sub-group of the epic, novel or narrative literature in general; it transcends the traditional, accepted and generally useful divisions into genres. Perhaps it should be put as follows: we are dealing here with a hybrid sub-group linked to one particular historically concrete theme, which also imposes a constant basic outline on the work's structure.

The "cycles," as we have already seen in the previously quoted observation by Arnold Hauser, upsets the classicist immanence of closed form in a work, and one cycle may contain works belonging to different genres. Mann spoke about Wagner, Zola and Ibsen as a unified phenomenon, probably feeling that Ibsen's plays about people from contemporary bourgeois families comprised a single series. They all drag along their pasts in the present, regardless of whether we are talking about a bearer of success and power *(Pillars of Society)*, a degenerate scapegoat for parental sins *(Ghosts)* or marriage partners responsible for their subconscious actions *(Little Eyolf)*. Even though Ibsen's plays rarely show two generations and never more than this, the theme of heredity is present in the dramatic method itself. In these works the past is identical with the present and the character's self-cognition is realized in this circular simultaneity. It is worth stressing this here, as the cycle appears to be the natural form in which the genealogical theme comes to the authors' minds, regardless of whether it is developed over a period of several generations or condensed into one eventful evening in a naturalistically presented bourgeois salon or on a suggestive gravel beach by a stormy northern sea. The cycle means continuity in time and a transformed repetition in the vertical. In this sense Ibsen's technique brings into the present the simultaneous myths in Mann's anthropological motifs and the renewal of the family problem in new generations. At the same time, however, it unites the biological flow of time in a horizontal diversity. The imagination of a writer tackling the genealogical subject was naturally constituted in a cycle, regardless of whether an impersonal "objective" narrative form, Ibsen-like dramatic form or Faulknerian subjective organization of a fragmentary picture of the historical truth, together with a dramatization of the "stream of consciousness," might prevail.

THE OPEN-ENDED NATURE OF KRLEŽA'S CYCLE

As it is always possible to add to a cycle or reorganize the order in such a way as to shed new light on the existing parts, thus modifying it, the cycle means great artistic scope for new possibilities. Faulkner, in spirit the most modern writer of those examined here and at the same time epically constant, was supreme in the full application of the open-ended *modus* of the cycle. Next to him stands Krleža. Aware that the Glembay cycle is merely a small part of the main body of his works and not wishing to extend our conception of the cyclical to other works by him, we shall not gainsay the observation that this achievement has a special place among the other writer's cycles in its positive incompleteness, the open possibilities in human relationships which have merely been sketched and the strength of the associations linking situations which are only potentially to be realized.

This is a feature we only perceive when we read the three complete plays, which are the very pinnacle of modern Croatian dramaturgy, in the context of the prose fragments, for all these together make up the cycle. Among these writers this incompleteness is unique to Krleža's cycle, but not necessarily a virtue in itself. However, as a work of art *Glembajevi* lives in this textual openness and incompleteness and its artistic merits exist in this state. The aim of this study is to talk only about the value *Glembajevi* has as a cycle and not about everything in this work which shows what Krleža means to literature in general, i.e. not to return to his qualities as a writer and, therefore, merely to parts of *Glembajevi* as one of his foremost achievements.

In the examination of the cycle's topography or the way in which the three generations are present and linked in it, the totality was indicated of this vision and of its deeper meaning as an attitude towards history. In the case of this cycle we should replace the "bird's-eye view" with the "mouse's-eye view" and note how the reader, by wandering around and returning to certain pages, allusions, names and even sentences, or individual prose fragments, experiences this open-ended Glembay whole. The worlds of Yudushka or Thomas Buddenbrook—and in the view of this reader the works of Saltykov-Shchedrin and Mann are the most completely closed achievements in the genealogical novel—are all in the text. We do not seek either, trace them further or weave combinations around them in our imagination. In Krleža our relationship towards the characters in the cycle is to a certain extent like that which we have towards acquaintances outside works of literature. During periods when we do not see them they continue to live and we meet them in new circumstances which do not always display continuity with our last meeting. The difference is that in Krleža's work, even if we are tied to the indications in the text, the edges of these suggested possibilities, these gaps and omissions and improvised seams all *radiate* something. Not only do they have the quality of poetic expression but they also suggest new combinations which will complete the picture.

This modern feeling of the marginal and arbitrarily possible; this simultaneity of what is already fixed and what is potentially here; this dialectic, as it were, between the already present and that which is in itself dialectic or latent—this could perhaps be illustrated by the very structure of the fragment *Barunica Lenbachova (Baroness Lenbach)*. This prose piece finds its dramatic and factual background in the play *U agoniji* and the prose lends the play a lyrical dimension, which can also be read in the play in certain passages of Laura's but nowhere so completely, constantly or untinged by the effects of the immediate dramatic tension. *Barunica Lenbachova* is a pure phenomenological analysis (if only this did not sound so rational, as though it were a case of systematic analysis!) of a condition in which the external circumstances, denouement of the story and facts relating to the person and spirit being talked about are all put in parentheses. It deals with Laura's feeling that the intimate friendship which ties her to Križovec is at an end, but there is no definite information to this effect.

"Symptoms were appearing," that "their . . . affection . . . was gradually . . . fading"; "vague, thin shadows of darkness and mournful half-light" "grew unnoticeably but more and more fatally" "day by day." This undefined, pale presentiment of the truth," this "phosphorescing of the truth," this "constant movement apart" and the fact that "with every second the gap is growing" fills her with panic. "It is all still here and still going on," but "in his words can be felt a vague inner passivity"; "in his look a ray appears of some unpleasant, undefined suspicious perspicacity" as he "observes the still fresh but already ashen grey, downy colour of her flesh (. . .) under the rings under her eyes . . . (resulting from) long vigils and waiting." She feels that "in him there is appearing . . . the thought of that unknown girl's white throat, the girl who exists somewhere in the background and who is growing on the horizon like a sunny, white May cloud at midday." "In the desperate depths of nocturnal meditation" she has "thoughts like lightning" and feels "how necessary it is for her to determine her position in respect of this" and "for her to begin, unnoticed and with dignity, the elimination of this condition." In the "desperate process of this decline, in these voids of hers lasting an immeasurable fraction of a second" there appears the "salutary thought that nothing has happened yet and that it is all still going on unbroken." In contrast to these statements heaped up on four pages, which confirm that this "estrangement is after all natural and logical and that the picture of a ship going further away with every second is the only wise and appropriate thing in life," we find definitive words such as "crisis," "breaking," "touch of reality," "clear sight," "plastic and truly real," "intuition . . . which is poisonous and stings like acid," "analytical penetration": "Laura knows full well that something should be done, a letter written to Ivan, an energetic and definitive one"; "it already seems that it has all snapped."

And so, between these two *modi*—the potential, the continuing process on the very threshold of realization, and the final, inevitable and already accomplished—it remains for Ivan Križovec to "depart, to go further and further away from her with every day, with mathematical certainty, really, truly, irretrievably, gradually, like a ship moving further away from the quay," all this being couched in other opposing images, attributes from the two series which comprise this key idea to the entire fragment. Finally, here are two sentences which, apart from small details, are apparently the same but which arise from two different moods—the first probably from a presentiment of the reality, the second from the optimism of hope:

"Like the first violin in an orchestra, sweetly, in long and sensual waves of a cantilena, there began in her that tender humming of sorrow over the infinite interval of a collapse, and, as though above a void of death, despair and solitude, as though above the black infernal abyss of a misfortune, in

Laura there grew the motif of indefiniteness and of all possibilities being still open and full of light and joy and hope."

"Like the first violin in the orchestra, sweetly, in long sensual waves of some sad cantilena, certain bright dreams hummed above Laura at night in the rich instrumentation of the panic of love, quietly and woefully like ringing planets from immeasurable distances."

The way in which the unresolved nature of Laura's situation is expressed is a quality typical of a distinctly modern sensibility. The "Glembay" reality, realized in language, is extended through this quality to an area towards which the text is intentionally directed but which lies beyond the text.

More precisely, the numerous possibilities in the family histories which might develop along the lines of the Glembay principle and which are suggested in the existing texts—particularly in the prose pieces and the family tree—were never realized. For example, a specific naturalistic novel about the Croatian bourgeoisie, the like of which has not yet been written, could have grown up around Marijan Glembay and his unfortunate daughters. Dr. Paul Altmann, who according to one plan was obviously to be an intelligent, objective observer close to the Glembays but not one of them, remained merely Leone's interlocutor in a few calm lines. As a revolutionary, Marcel Faber remains something for the imagination to play with. Young Leone, the son of Leone and Beatrice, could have become the centre of a new, hypertrophied or fascinatingly degenerated consciousness which, unquestionably declassé, might have experienced the intellectual and artistic problems in the crises of the thirties and forties about which the author spoke only as an essayist.

Dr. Gregor appears in a later version of the pre-Glembay play *Galicija*, published as *U logoru* several years after the trilogy and fragments on the Glembays. If all the works in which some character from this family plays a role belong to this cycle (so that even *Pod maskom—Beneath the Mask—* with its mention of "Laura's millinery," belongs here, this name being the only link between this fragment and the other parts of the cycle) then *U logoru* should also be treated as part of the same whole. After all, Dr. Gregor's role in this play is hardly less important than Urban's role in *Leda*, and the character of Dr. Altmann reappears here after *Gospoda Glembajevi*, though admittedly still not developed in any depth. Thus, as regards content *U logoru* is part of the Glembay cycle, though in fact it does not expand the dramatic trilogy but remains outside it (no matter how much this trilogy might exist as such only conditionally). This is so because *U logoru* means the deepening or expansion of the Glembay presence to war, with the result that the dominant theme of the play is different from the general bourgeois subject matter of the peacetime Glembays.

When Krleža's evolution as playwright is under examination, *U logoru* is usually treated together with *Vučjak* and *Golgota*, though the original text, *Galicija,* the earliest play in this series, would be much better suited to such analysis. However, Marijan Matković,[107] and after him, Branko Hećimović,[108] are the only ones to describe the important dramaturgical difference between the two versions. Thematically this play certainly belongs to that cycle from which Krleža arrived at the Glembays, but in the dramaturgical sense *U logoru* represents in many respects a departure from *Galicija* and could be said to be nearer the Glembay trilogy of plays than its own source form.

With the post-war variant it is even possible to discern four phases: *Galicija, Gospoda Glembajevi* (in which the relationships between certain main characters are, in fact, echoes of *Galicija* or the source of situations in *U logoru*), *U logoru* (1934)[109] and the post-war version of the same play. As the author himself has pointed out, "this version (. . .) returns to the conception of *Galicija*": it contains a prologue in which cadet Horvat is in the company of the baroness so that the incident with the peasant-woman, whom he later hangs, takes place before him and baroness Maldegg-Cranensteg. This and the Macbethian scene with her ghost in the third act enhance the scenic effect of the play.

If we take Leone's situation in the family and his protest against stupid insensitivity, dishonest dealings and greed under the hollow guise of good bourgeois upbringing, and transfer all this to the location of the Galician army camp, *U logoru* is the result: the immediate action inaugurates the incident between the baroness and the old poor woman. Horvat-Leone does not want to sell his conscience to the erotic whims of the baroness, he is an accessory to the old woman's calamity and his revolt against authority leads to the melodramatic and bloody debauchery at the end.

Galicija is still near to general human revolt and develops as a series of tableaux; *U logoru,* on the other hand, even though it has the simpler line of the basic dramatic conflict which unfolds in *Gospoda Glembajevi,* presents in fact an Ibsen-like accumulation of previously developed tensions which are implicitly present from the very start of the play: this is a deeper, social conflict between the protagonist and the social environment. Horvat—and this is more a personal reference on the part of the author—mentions Ibsen's *The Lady from the Sea,* but his parallel in Ibsen is someone else: he is intransigent in his opposition to the system, whose representatives seem to have conspired against him, like Ibsen's Dr. Stockman, "the enemy of the people." It is in keeping with Ibsen's psychological realism, which in Krleža matures in the phase of the Glembay plays and contains resonances of a broad symbolic range, that in *U logoru* the historical theme, the picture of the *Croatian camp,* is more explicitly stated and developed in Horvat's poetic realization of his position: "That is the curse on us: that with our contradictions we have been standing for so long under the bloody gallows." This is because after *Galicija* the characters, in more extensive passages of dialogue, acquired a more profound individuality. In *Galicija* Orlović is stricken with remorse over the hanged woman in a way reminiscent of Russian literature and Janković kneels before the idea of Russia, but their attitudes are not so clearly differentiated as to develop in the dialogue into a dramatic confrontation of two opposite temperaments, as in the later version. "I am standing in the mud, but I am not muddy and cannot get muddy," Horvat, the idealist, thinks at the start. "I am completely free of all these idiotic gravitations around us (. . .) it does not matter what happens to me physically, but it is certain that the will exists in me to step out of this mud." On the other hand, Gregor, whom Horvat upbraids for reconciling himself to his "vague social-democratic Buddhism," is rational and consistent to near the end: "One must face up to things. One must reconcile oneself to the fact that we are up to the elbows in blood and we must find a way of washing away the stench." This, however, is nothing more than the polarization of Leone's constant dilemma, intoned at the very beginning of *Gospoda Glembajevi*—the dilemma of the senses and reason as the sources of cognition. The post-war version of *U logoru* repeats this beginning: in Horvat's meditation before the baroness we find: "Is music merely the play of vague emotions (. . .) or a deeply concealed Chopin-like thought—who could say whether this is so or merely so (. . .)." What painting is to *Gospoda Glembajevi* and *The Return of Philip Latinovicz*, music becomes in this play and the dramaturgical function of the artistic atmosphere is very similar. Horvat's playing to the baroness is analogous to Leone's experiencing Angelika as a painter.

However, the structural parallels between these two works are not always symmetrical. Horvat's relation, Puba Agramer (whose Christian name and surname belong to the Glembay circle but not in this combination) is, in the legal formalism with which he clouds theft and crime, admittedly identical to Puba Fabriczy. Moreover, Leone's beginning is similar to Horvat's, and the way in which he is wooed by baroness Castelli is also reminiscent of the first scene in *U logoru*. Also, Leone's attack on baroness Castelli at the end of the play is contained in the conclusion to the second play, in Gregor's show-down with the revolver. The baroness, however, is a Castelli in her debauched scheming, though at first she is also briefly Leone's Angelika in Horvat's imagination. As the baroness in *Gospoda Glembajevi,* she is the target of the old woman's insults, while Castelli's vulgar cursing in the last act (we saw it for the first time in the novella *Na samrti*) is given to the old woman herself in the second variant of the first act.

It is as though these motifs contained in the dramatic conflicts of *Gospoda Glembajevi* were of such immediate urgency to the writer that he had to establish, by returning to the earlier ground of his war scenes, a link with his more recent, central subject matter. The repetition and reworking of motifs provide one of the links between *U logoru* and the Glembay cycle. The characters provide another. When in the reworking of *Galicija* he felt that the characters demanded individuality, he clearly remembered

Dr. Gregor from the gallery of the Glembay descendants as a potential character capable of holding a dialogue with Horvat, of placing the situation in a logical context (his subject is always resistance to stupidity) with his precise and brief rejoinders, and of bringing down moral exaltation and compunction to the level of reality. Before suffering sudden madness like Leone, Gregor endeavours with his final words to assuage and explain. The madness which then breaks to the surface[110] is manifested without words in a mechanical homicidal mood which in its silence has a suggestion of bestiality; Leone's remarks about the Glembay in himself also seem to have applied to Gregor.

U logoru also contains a reference to the disappearance of Faber-Fabriczy, obviously the same one, Marcel, who in *U magli* emerges as a Soviet general. While this in itself is an insignificant detail, which adds nothing new by way of content, it is interesting that the passage which comprises the second instalment of the original review of *U magli* on Faber and which was later added as the ending to the fragment *Ivan Križovec,* places Laura in the situation of the baroness in *U logoru*—the same place, the same circle of officers and the same piano performance. Why? Not so that Laura might acquire the characteristics of the baroness (though let us recall that Horvat's feelings towards her are initially at least ambivalent: she has characteristics of Castelli and, as far as he is concerned, Angelika) but rather because the writer, remembering the situation in *Galicija,* all of a sudden wanted to develop new individual possibilities from Laura and even perhaps ennoble the Galician situation. At that time he probably still had in mind a large narrative work about the Glembays; whatever the case, at least different relationships between the characters—and between the parts of the cycle. The few pages of *U magli,* 1928, suggest a range of mutual relationships between Faber, Križovec, Laura and Altmann which is never realized in the cycle as we have it.

U logoru, however, shows that Krleža not only trimmed his original plans for the Glembays but also subsequently expanded the concluded cycle. That he returned to Laura and wanted to fix her values firmly in our minds is shown by the fact that the book contains the excerpt *Barunica Lenbachova,* which was not printed in periodicals, and that even *Pod maskom* mentions Laura, who was probably meant to become a focal point for subsequent depictions of female sensitivity too. It is sometimes difficult to explain the variants of the Glembay fragments. Some of the best pages on Križovec's personal provincial experiences are not to be found in the Minerva edition but were taken from the review version and published only later in the complete sets of the cycle. There are parts in *Sprovod u Teresienburgu (Funeral in Teresienburg),* mostly on Ramond's agony over Olga and some wickedly comic details during the funeral, which did not appear until the fifth edition (1961). The most important post-war addition by the author, however, again concerns Laura. This is the third act of *Agonija* which

Ivan Lacković Croata *Lamentation over a Dead Rooster*

criticism has largely interpreted as the concretization of the social context in which Laura must come to ruin. But at the same time this is a new dimension of Laura herself, the broadening of her emotional tribulations. And did not Krleža, by adding the third book of *Banket u Blitvi,* deepen the character of Karina Michelson, with the aid of minor changes to the first two books, and thus write some of his richest passages on a woman's experience of the world?[11] In the light of the "personal," most subjective pages in the second markedly political novel, *Zastave (Flags),* it becomes clear that in the genealogical cycle, too, the entirety of Krleža's artistic statement should be experienced primarily through those parts which objectivize the moods. Atmosphere is his subject and is placed above story and the social motif, which is perhaps why he did not decide to write a novel right until *The Return of Philip Latinovicz.*

Krleža the storyteller remains in his plays at a distance from the subject or character about which he is narrating, but he even wanders about history in order to contribute to the density of the atmosphere. Listing names and creating catalogues of titles, personalities, objects and institutions, he brings to life a historical reality in which the subjects perceive themselves in their naked essence. The genealogical theme, which connected Leone, Laura and Urban in an environment amply substantiated in the sociological sense and existing even in Krleža's lifetime, appeared in its entirety less important to the writer than the inner life. This life, in the markedly structured manifestation which Krleža shared with the most important European writers of his literary period, throbs like a pulse and also breaks the shell of any preconceived form, demanding new imaginative means of statement.

(Translated by Gregor McGregor)

NOTES

1. *Les Nourritures Terrestres,* (Plodovi; Novi plodovi, prev. I. Markovič, Sarajevo, 1958. Pp. 61, 62, 40, 27).
2. "Plamen," 1919, no. 15, p. 28.
3. *Miroslav Krleža,* Zagreb 1963, pp. 266-267.
4. Edward Goy, "Problemi i faktura u Krležinoj drami 'Gospoda Glembajevi'," 'Izraz,' Sarajevo, p. 3. Translation from the English by Živomir Mladenović.
5. The *P. M. L. A.* Journal, Vol. 43, 1928, pp. 551-560.
6. *University of Washington Abstracts of Theses,* Vol. 3, 1938, pp. 337-341.
7. "Pogovor," *Glembajevi,* Zagreb 1950. Unless otherwise stated, all quotations from the Glembay cycle are also from this edition.
8. Johanna Kröner: *Die Technik des realistischen Dramas bei Ibsen und Galsworthy,* Leipzig, 1935, p. 72.
9. *Banket u Blitvi,* post-war editions of book I.
10. Miroslav Krleža, *Eppur si muove,* Zagreb 1938, pp. 155, 152.
11. Miroslav Krleža, *Sabrana djela,* vol. 20, *Eseji,* book III, Zagreb 1963, p. 22.

12. "O realizmu," 'Kultura,' 1949, p. 40 (transl. by Dr. Dušan Milačić).
13. Walter Allen, *The English Novel*, Harmondsworth 1958, p. 300.
14. Robert Morse Lovett, *Buddenbrooks,* in the collection of papers *The Stature of Thomas Mann,* ed. Charles Neider, New York 1947, p. 113.
15. cf. Emile Zola: *Les Rougon-Macquart I,* Bibliothèque de la Pléiade, 1960, p. 3.
16. Henri Massis, *Comment Zola composait ses romans,* Paris 1906, p. 22.
17. Zucker, *op. cit.*
18. *Notes générales sur la nature de l'oeuvre,* in Massis, *op. cit.,* p. 21.
19. Claude-Edmonde Magny, *Histoire du roman français depuis 1918,* pp. 305-309.
20. K. N. Grigoryan, *Roman M. E. Saltykova-Shchedrina "Gospoda Golovlevy,"* Moscow-Leningrad 1962, pp. 20-21.
21. Kyra Sanine, *Saltykov-Shchedrin, Sa vie et ses oeuvres,* Paris 1955, pp. 209-213, 255.
22. Maksim Gorkiy, *Djela,* Book XXII, Belgrade-Zagreb 1948, pp. 103-104 (transl. by Rodoljub Čolakovič).
23. L. M. Yuryeva, *M. Gorkiy i predovyye nemetskiye pisateli XX veka,* Moscow 1961, pp. 63-64.
24. Martin Schlappner, *Thomas Mann und die französische Literatur,* Saarlonis 1950, p. 25.
25. Thomas Mann, *Gesammelte Werke in Zwölf Bänden,* S. Fischer Verlag (Copyright 1960), vol. XI, p. 379.
26. Mann, vol. XI, p. 550.
27. Mann, vol. XI, p. 380.
28. Mann, vol. XI, pp. 550-551.
29. Mann, vol. XI, p. 383.
30. The genealogical idea structuring this novel is quite different from that which we are examining in this discussion. Freed of naturalistic determinism, it does not relate to the process of landowner-patrician degeneration but rather forms a cycle in which the essential subject is the subjective relations between men and women.
31. Mann, vol. X, p. 930. cf. vol. XII, p. 82.
32. Pierre Daix, *Réflexions sur la méthode de Roger Martin du Gard,* Paris 1957, pp. 14-16; cf. Antun Polanščak, *Od povjerenja do sumnje,* Zagreb 1966, pp. 176, 188.
33. In a letter to N. K. Krupskaya from Sorrento, dated May 1930, Gorkiy mentions how on Capri he spoke to Lenin about his desire to write the history of a family from 1913 to the "present day," the members of peasant origin, being "officials, priests, factory-owners, Petrashevtsy and Nechayevtsy" etc. Lenin replied that the present times did not provide such a novel with an ending and that it would have to be written after the revolution. (A. M. Gorkiy, *Sobranyye sochinenya v tridtsati tomakh,* Moscow 1949-1955, vol. 30, p. 168.
34. *Davni dani,* p. 253.
35. *Sabrana djela Miroslava Krleže,* Vol. VIII, *Novele.*
36. "Književna republika," IV, book III, no. 4, pp. 230-238 and no. 5, pp. 241-274 (Zagreb, 1st September and 15th October 1926).
37. "Savremenik," XX, no. 1, pp. 4-7, Zagreb, January 1928.
38. "Književnik," I, no. 1, pp. 18-24, Zagreb, April 1928.
39. "Srpski književni glasnik," NS, book XXIV, no. 5, pp. 321-332, Belgrade, 1st July 1928.
40. The last page of the original text on the general's wife did not go into the book. Cf. "Srpski književni glasnik," NS, book XXIV, no. 6, pp. 407-415, Belgrade, 16th July 1928. The following year ("Savremenik," XXI, nos., 2-3, Zagreb, February-March 1929) the entire text up to this page was included in *Sprovod u Teresienburgu* and then in the

first (Minerva) edition of the book (1932) the text was separated from this novella and became an integral part of the *O Glembajevima* prose.

41. "Savremenik," XX, no. 11, pp. 460-469, Zagreb, November 1928: "Pantheon," I, no. 2, pp. 53-60, Zagreb, February 1929.

42. Sean O'Faolain, *The Vanishing Hero*, New York 1956, 1957, p. 81.

43. cf. Cleanth Brooks, *William Faulkner, The Yoknapatawpha Country*, New Haven and London 1963, p. 416.

44. A. Hauser, *Socijalna istorija umetnosti i književnosti*. II vol., Belgrade 1962, p. 264. Transl. by Veselin Kostić. The following place in György Lukács is interesting in respect of the pre-history of the theoretical assumptions relating to the genealogical cycle: "In the conversations between Lucien de Rubempré and D'Arthez (in *Les illusions perdues*) on Lucien's historical novel, Balzac dealt with the great problem of his own transitional period: the intention to show recent French history in one connected cycle of novels which would give poetic form to the historic need for the birth of a new France. It is in the inadequate cyclical links between Scott's novels that Balzac saw the inadequacy of his great precursor's system." György Lukács, *Istoriski roman*, Belgrade 1960, transl. by F. Filipović, pp. 72-73.

45. Hauser, *op. cit.*, p. 265.

46. Claude-Edmonde Magny, *L'age du roman américain*, Paris 1948, pp. 230-234.

47. *On realism*, pp. 38-39.

48. Massis, *op. cit.*, pp. 25-26.

49. Robert Coughlan, *"The Private World of William Faulkner," Prize Articles, 1954*, Ballantine Book, New York, p. 139.

50. All quotations from *The Golovlev Family* are taken from the translation into Serbo-Croat by Iso Velikanović, Belgrade-Zagreb 1950.

51. Aleksandar Flaker, *Ruski klasici XIX stoljeća*, Zagreb 1965, p. 117.

52. György Lukács, *Tomas Man*, Belgrade 1958, p. 126 (transl. into Serbo-Croat by Irma Lisičar and Vera Stojić).

53. Mann, vol. XI, p. 384, 385, 386.

54. Mann, vol. IX, p. 690, 695, 685, 696.

55. Thomas Mann, *Buddenbrookovi*, Zagreb 1950, transl. into Serbo-Croat by Iva Adum, p. 489.

56. *Ibid.*, p. 490.

57. *Ibid.*, pp. 625-626.

58. Mann, vol. XI, p. 554, 556.

59. John Galsworthy, *In Chancery*, London 1924, p. 6.

60. Edouard Guyot, *John Galsworthy*, Paris 1935, p. 72, 59.

61. Wilhelm Rabius, *Die innere strukturelle Verwandschaft von Galsworthys "Forsyte Saga" und den isländischen Sagas*, Marburg 1935, p. 13.

62. *Ibid.*

63. Andre Jolles, *Einfache Formen*, Halle 1930, pp. 77-78.

64. Polanščak, *op. cit.*, p. 166.

65. Jean Prevost, "Roger Martin du Gard et le roman objectif" in *Problèmes du roman*, Brussels 1945, p. 88. Cf. André Gide, *Journal des faux-monnayeurs*, Paris (Gallimard, Soixante et unième edition), pp. 32-33.

66. Quoted in Thomas White Hall, "A Note on the So-called 'Change in Technique' in 'Les Thibault' by Robert Martin du Gard," 'French Studies,' December 1953, vol. 27, no. 2, p. 110.

67. "Danas." The index, register and explanation of names, books, events, phenomena and concepts mentioned in the first book (Jan-Feb-March 1934). p. 19.

68. Krležini Glembajevi," 'Politika' 11th Feb. 1929; cf. *Miroslav Krleža*, Zagreb 1963, p. 99. For Ristić the concept of "glembajevština" is "just as real as Dostoyevski's 'Karamazovshchina'." For Oedipus aspects of the work cf. Hugo Klain, "Gospoda Glembajevi u svetlu dubinske psihologije," 'Forum,' year VII, book XV, no. 1, Jan. 1968, pp. 103-135.

69. Massis, *op. cit.*, also contains Zola's notes and summaries of *Physiologie des passions* (Letourneau) and *Traite de l'hérédité naturelle* (Dr. Lucas).

70. Brooks, *op. cit.*, and Edmund Volpe, *A Reader's Guide to William Faulkner*, New York 1964.

71. *The Forsyte Saga I*, Leipzig 1926, p. 241.

72. *Ibid.*, p. 44.

73. Yuryeva, *op. cit.*, p. 56.

74. The dispersal of Zola's heroes, who do not possess much subjective family feeling, provides only rare occasions for such meetings. In *Les Thibault* there are only three; too few, then, for this kind of scene to have the function it has in other cycles. In Faulkner the generations are too far apart in time, usually separated by death or violence, or the group has already disintegrated with the result that there are no large gatherings here, either.

75. Jolyon says of himself that he is a "sorry specimen who merely represents the end of the century, unearned income, amateurishness and individual freedom" (In *Chancery*, p. 132); cf. *Glembajevi*, p. 327.

76. In the article "Glembajevski čvor ili nadeno vreme," 'Putevi,' IX, May-June 1963, no. 3, pp. 268-284, Milivoje Marković puts forward the idea that "Olga Glembaj is in a certain sense the central personality of the Glembay complex for all the other numerous personalities are either distant shadows of her dark visions or the continuations of her endless dramas. In relation to other Krleža characters, she is merely a sketch but her motivation is profoundly one of ideas and contains those most important psychological communications which connect all the personalities of the Glembay family tree. In fact, her problems are the problems of everyone." (pp. 277-278).

77. Perhaps Krleža was first associated with Faulkner in this country in the title of a review by Tomislav Ladan on the occasion of the translation into Croatian of *The Sound and the Fury* ("Faulknerovi Glembajevi,'. 'Izraz,' year III, Feb. 1959, no. 2).

78. See later.

79. *The Novels of William Faulkner*, Baton Rouge 1964, pp. 261-262.

80. cf. *Absalom, Absalom!*, New York 1951, p. 378.

81. All quotations trans. from *Les Thibault*, vol. V. Gallimard 1955.

82. Leon Schalit, *John Galsworthy, Der Mensch und sein Werk*, Berlin, Vienna and Leipzig 1928, p. 137.

83. Lukács, *op. cit.*, p. 120.

84. Ljubomir Maraković, " 'Leda' g. Miroslava Krleže, 'Hrvatska prosvjeta,' XVII/1920, 4, p. 93.

85. *Ibid.*, p. 94. Ervin Šinko talks about this as the simulation of human lives and art. Cf. *Miroslav Krleža*, Zagreb 1963, p. 307.

86. "Hrvatska književna laž," 'Plamen,' I, 1, 1949, p. 35.

87. Branko Hećimović, "Fragmenti o Krležinoj dramaturgiji," 'Republika,' XIX/1963, 7-8, p. 322.

88. *Op. cit.*, p. 95.

89. "The rising action towards a culminatory moment turns into (. . .) a circular action, into a concentric dramatic composition which, as in Chekhov, reveals the powerlessness of the *dramatis persona*. The conclusion of Leda is a return to the point of departure, a return which is not the affirmation of the person but rather its negation." Mirjana Miocinović, "Krležin dramski krug," *Miroslav Krleža,* Prosveta, Belgarde, p. 247.

90. Perhaps the original intention of the writer was for Križovec, Marcel, Laura and Dr. Altmann to people the same prose work.

91. Jacques Bremer, *Martin du Gard,* Paris 1961, p. 83, 87.

92. Dinko Šimunović seems to have had this rich corrosive ecology of the late genealogical phase in mind in the novel *Porodica Vinčić (The Vinčić Family),* of which this is not the central subject: "Octavio (. . .) could see his family becoming different day by day: it was changing as a tree changes when ivy and moss start to envelop it and mistletoe shoots start to appear on the twigs." (transl. from the Belgrade 1926 edition, p. 29).

93. *The Forsyte Saga,* I. Leipzig 1926, pp. 9-10.

94. Trans. from Isidora Sekulić, *Iz stranih kniževnosti,* II, Novi Sad, pp. 152-153.

95. D. H. Lawrence, *Phoenix,* London 1961, p. 549.

96. Frank Swinnerton, *The Georgian Literary Scene,* London 1938, p. 147.

97. transl. from Goy, *op. cit.,* p. 18.

98. In very modest measure the function of aesthetic awareness is taken over by Jacques's friend, Daniel de Fontanin.

99. A. M. Gorkiy, *Sobraniye sochineniy v tridtsati tomakh,* Moscow 1956, vol. 29. p. 83; cf. vol. 28, p. 386.

100. Emile Zola, *Doktor Paskal,* Belgrade 1953, trans. by Emilija Anđelić, pp. 188-9.

101. Gorkiy, *op. cit.,* vol. 24, p. 487; vol. 25, 94; vol. 26, pp. 89, 92.

102. Gorkiy, *ibid.,* vol. 25, p. 163.

103. K. A. Fedin in a letter to Gorkiy, makes the criticism that the first half of the novel deals with only seven years while the business is being created and the second half with 47 years, in which the most important theme emerges: the business becomes the principal character and crushes those who made it. This shortcoming in the composition is responsible for the book's being more schematic and drier towards the end (Cf. Gorkiy, *op. cit.,* vol. 29, p. 650).

104. Zola, *op. cit.,* pp. 51, 87, 295.

105. *Eseji,* book I, Zagreb 1961, p. 55.

106. Lionel Trilling, *The Liberal Imagination,* New York 1954, p. 68.

107. "Marginalije uz Krležino dramsko stvaranje," *Miroslav Krleža,* Zagreb 1963, p. 256.

108. " 'Tri drame' u Krležinu dramskom djelu,". 'Kolo,' new series no. 7, year VI (CXXVI), Zagreb July 1968, p. 95.

109. It is not important in this connection whether this version precedes *Gsopoda Glembajevi* or *vice versa.*

110. The post-war variant contains a suggestion of this nervous state as early as act one.

111. cf. "Dvije razine 'Banketa u Blitvi'," *Krležin zbornik,* Zagreb 1965, pp. 257-259.

AMERICAN MOTIFS IN THE WORK OF BOHUMIL HRABAL

Josef Škvorecký
University of Toronto

A discussion of borrowed motifs and influences can be treacherous: unless the matter is exceedingly obvious, or unless the author himself confirms that he began by borrowing and imitating, we may be dealing with coincidental affinities. Therefore the phrase "American Motifs" in the title of this paper should be understood not in terms of linear causal links but rather in terms of complex intercorrespondences. Instead of looking for evidence of imitation we may seek an explanation in the mass media network of this century which, of course, includes the proliferation of cheap and accessible books. It is a network extending over the European mental landscape, and against it some of the recurrent motifs of American literature and arts are silhouetted, removed from the two dimensions of the printed word and the electronically projected image, and elevated into the three dimensions of reality.

Let me quote a passage from a remarkable writer:

Before the furnace a huddled black puppet was lying. It was charred all over and its right eye, molten and fallen out of the skull, was staring at me. When I walked down a few steps it burst open and began flowing out quietly on the floor.[1]

Who wrote this? Is it perhaps a putrescent vision from *The Case of Charles Dexter Ward*, that twentieth-century Gothic tale whose Rhode Island hero learns the diabolic arts from the unmentionable *Necronomicon*, translated in sixteenth-century Prague from Enochian by Dr. John Dee with the help of Edward Kelly, and preserved under lock and key in the vaults of Emperor Rudolf the Second's Hradčany castle? No—while the story from which I quote has a lot to do with Prague, it has nothing to do with the *Necronomicon*, and it has *not* sprung from the pen of that darling horrifyer of the secure, H. P. Lovecraft. Another passage:

... a religious man who craved for holiness so much that one night he lifted the lid of a crypt in the local church and, having entangled himself in the shrouds and in the petrified intestines of that holy woman, he shot himself through the head and at the same time closed the lid so that he was not found until years later. Until he looked almost like that saint.[2]

Perhaps the master of "The Strange Case of Mr. Valdemar" could have written something like that. But he is not the author of this passage. Both quotations come from "The Legend of Cain." What is not generally known, at least outside Czechoslovakia, is that "The Legend" is the original version, the Ur-Faust if you will, of a story later to become world-famous as a film by the same name, the Oscar-winning *Closely Watched Trains*; a tale contained in a book of contemporary novellas called *Macabrosa and Legends (Morytáty a legendy)* by Bohumil Hrabal, one of the most beloved writers in the Czech Socialist Republic, and one of the greatest nuisances to the Party's literary establishment in that same socialist republic.

If the name Edgar Allen Poe is synonymous with morbid imagery, than "The Legend of Cain" is truly Poesque. The cannibalistic horrors of the Antarctic sea, the image of the spectral *seagull, busily gorging itself with the horrible flesh, its bill and talons deep buried, and its white plummage spattered all over with blood*, the vision of the same bird when it drops its *horrid morsel. . . with a sudden splash immediately at the feet* of Arthur Gordon Pym,[3] is carved out of the same vein of imagery as that of the man who observes the eye of his friend, whom he led to a horrifying suicide, *burst open and begin flowing out quietly on the floor*.

But what is the link? Is there direct literary influence at work here, the general impact of massive doses of Poe who was by far the American author most frequently translated into Czech? Or is it the circumstances I mentioned earlier, namely the fact that the two-dimensional horrors, allegedly borrowed by Poe from Germany and claimed by him to have originated in his soul, have been made three-dimensional in the regions of Bergen-Belsen, Treblinka, Maidenek?

All three links are probable. Hrabal's generation—and my own, for that matter—have all read "The Premature Burial"; but we also saw, with our own eyes—SS-men tortured to death and still twitching as they were tossed into a mass grave right behind a Lovecraftian artificial nineteenth-century ruin of a twelfth-century Gothic church in the military cemetery near the lovely medieval castle in my native town of Náchod. SS-men who, undoubtedly had witnessed similar things done by men to men and very probably committed them, some months or years earlier, and in another country.

"The Raven," in its thirty-odd Czech translations, became part of big-city folklore in Czechoslovakia, so that not only the poem itself, but also elements of the related aesthetic theory from Poe's celebrated essay "The Philosophy of Composition" have found their way into the palavering of beer-hall Don Juans. In Hrabal's story "The Death of Mr. Baltisberger," the playboyish Uncle Pepin has the following conversation with one of those macabre girls who frequently appear in Hrabal's humorous-horrifying tales, apparently having stepped out of the skin of Lenore or Berenice:

"Why don't you come and have dinner with us?" [says the girl].
But I didn't say anything, because her brother had syphilis. So then

she said to me, "I can't seem to catch my breath! Oh, how I wish I were dead and buried!" And I agreed with her and consoled her with the thought that poets say the most beautiful thing in the world is a dead beauty.[4]

Writers, literature, reality—this trinity, I think, explains the affinity of motifs, and not just in Hrabal's case. Poe, together with Whitman, Longfellow, Bret Harte and Ambrose Bierce—and, of course, with the morbidly humorous amalgams of that most adult of children's authors, Samuel Langhorne Clemens—are parts of the imagination of every Czech reader who, in his lifetime, has witnessed the cruelties of Injun Joe happening in the land of Schweik, the black horrors of *The Parenticide Club* with its staggeringly prescient vision of men converted into soap, of "Hop-Frog," all come to life.

But out of the cruel, yet hilarious narratives of Bierce, Twain, Harte and other superb entertainers of the harsh world of the American West, another artistic genre was born which flooded the world after World War I to become a permanent part of the subliminal mental landscape of European readers and writers: the silent film comedy, the celebrated two-reeler, and its absolutely unique art. Hrabal's story "A Dull Afternoon" opens like this:

Just after noon a young man—no, he was more of a kid—walked into our neighborhood bar. Nobody knew who he was or where he'd come from. Anyway, he sat down at the table under the compressor and ordered three packs of cigarettes and a beer. Then he opened up this book he had with him, and from then on all he did was read, drink, and smoke. His fingers were all yellow, probably from smoking each cigarette down to where it burned him. Now and then he'd feel around on the tablecloth for a cigarette, light it off the old butt, and puff away. But never for a second did he lift his eyes from his book.[5]

Apart from the cluster of images characteristic of the American Western —a mysterious stranger, the saloonlike setting, the mystery surrounding the unknown *hombre*—the opening, in its accent on the visuals, is truly cinematographic, and it would not be difficult to write an essay in imitation of Eisenstein[6] demonstrating that a similar technical principle is at work in Hrabal as that which so surprisingly worked in Dickens, half a century before the birth of the cinema. But I have something else in mind. The youngster, absorbed in his book whose title is never revealed, becomes the leitmotif of the long short story. The action shifts, various persons appear and disappear, the bartender strikes up a conversation with a man absurdly carrying everywhere he moves a pot of sauerkraut. Patrons alternately discuss soccer and the outrageous passivity of the reading kid. As the story unfolds, our attention is focused again and again on the voracious reader, and each time he returns, it marks an increase in the sense of absurdity.

> The bartender purposely dropped a cracked stein from as high as he could reach, and even though it hit the floor like a cannon ball, that guy just kept on reading. There was even a smile on his face. The bartender waved his hands in front of the kid's eyes but they never left the book.[7]

That is the second appearance of the kid in the story. After some exchange of opinion on the famous centerforward Bican, the writer's camera pans to the kid again:

> The bartender squatted on his heels and looked the boy in the face from below. When he'd had his fill, he stood up and said, "I'll be damned if that guy isn't actually crying!" And he pointed to the tears that had begun to fall all over the page — drip, drip, drip — like beer from the tap.[8]

Another discussion follows about the respective merits of the English crackerjack player Jimmy Ottaway and the German ace Kannhäuser, and then:

> ... in a burst of high spirits [the kid] banged his fist on the table — and so hard that everything took a leap. The bartender was just bringing him another beer... the young guy — he was still reading and chuckling away — felt his way up to the glass of beer, took it out of the bartender's hand, and managed to take a deep drink without moving his eyes off the page. "Beer number six, cigarette number twenty-one," said the bartender in disgust.[9]

By now those of you who have been reared on the insane world of American silent film comedy will, I assume, have recognized the technical device used here. In that beautiful but, alas, forgotten art, it used to be called the "extended gag." Remember that two-reeler featuring Chaplin? (Or was it Keaton? or perhaps Lupino Lane? Or Harry Langdon? In this most democratic of all arts, personal achievement often dissolves in the ferocious beauty of the anonymous genre.) Anyway: Chaplin (or Lloyd or Ben Turpin) starts about his important silly business, but suddenly — soon after the beginning of the film — a fat lady appears pushing a perambulator at top speed, in accelerated motion. The perambulator crashes into a distinguished-looking, ancient and appropriately bearded gentleman who performs an acrobatic somersault, only to leap up like a Jack-in-the-box, waving an angry fist at the disappearing lady. Then the action shifts back to the funny business of Chaplin (or Lloyd or Larry Semon), only to return, a while later, to the pram-pushing lady, still single-mindedly pursuing her mysterious goal. This time the baby carriage crashes into a cart loaded with eggs. Again the action cuts back to Chaplin, then back to the speeding lady whose perambulator now hits a cop in the behind with the explosiveness of a gun shell going off.

By now, I believe, you see what I have in mind: in both the film and in Hrabal's story we follow the highly unusual, single-minded and eccentric behavior of a person, who is oblivious to the surrounding world, presented in installments of increasing craziness. In Hrabal's next installment the reading boy obeys the call of nature:

> He pushed back his chair like a count and then stood stock still in the middle of the room. There must have been some magic in what he was reading. Then he made his way over to the door at the other end of the room with *Rest Rooms This Way* painted on it, opened the door as if he'd done it a thousand times before, and disappeared . . . the bartender had just enough time to say, "What a nut," and point to the closing door, when suddenly we heard a loud crash of bottles followed by a soft tinkling of glass. He threw open the door for all to see, and what they saw was that young punk stumbling his way through an ocean of empty bottles, and—get this—his book still planted firmly in front of his face. Finally he got to the next door. He felt around for the doorknob, turned it, and went into the men's room.[10]

Here you have it all: the heedless single-mindedness of the eccentric clown, leading to the crushed eggs and the broken bottles. In the meantime our fat lady, after having bumped into several other increasingly absurd obstacles and zigzagged her dangerous way among speeding cars (the masters of the extended gag called this string of installments "the routine"), is finally approaching what the same masters used to call "the topper": exceeding—with the help of the favorite trick of the undercranked camera—the speed of a top race horse, she eventually reaches a dock from which a paddlewheeler is just leaving. The gap between the dock and the steamboat is widening. The fat lady manages to shove her perambulator aboard, but she herself plunges involuntarily into the river. The topper of the gag, extended throughout the mad comedy, has been achieved.

In Hrabal?

> The bartender tiptoed to the door, opened it a crack and peeked in. Then he closed it again, crossed through the club room, came back into the main room, and said mournfully, "What an awful sight. Picture his—standing there pissing away, and with the other hand he's holding the book—and reading. . . I've been serving beer for thirty years now, and never have I seen the likes of it. . ." He shook his head. . . "This generation will be the death of us."[11]

Not as strong a topper, perhaps, as the unfortunate lady parted from her pram, but the principle is the same. Now: the old masters sometimes managed to combine several extended gag routines, and climax them all in a single topper. Hrabal does not quite manage to pull that off; nevertheless, when he abandons the reading boy, he develops another extended gag involving the man with the sauerkraut. He is still sitting in the bar, exchanging opinions with the bartender, when suddenly a gorgeous woman appears outside the pub's plateglass window, enters, and then leaves again. Carrying the pot of sauerkraut in his outstretched hands, he follows the sexy apparition out of the pub and into the street. The focus is transferred to a group of dejected soccer fans, there is some funny business with the leader of this angry crowd which has obviously just witnessed a disastrous defeat of their team, the action shifts from person to person, but from time to time we again get the glimpse of the second leitmotif figure of the story, the moonstruck man following the swinging fanny of the gorgeous woman, the pot of sauerkraut held in his outstretched hands like an absurd monstrance. At the very end of the story, the bartender looks out the glass door, and:

> He didn't even notice that the beautiful woman, the one with the twirling handbag, had turned back onto our street, and that the outside right with the pot of sauerkraut was still sleepwalking ten feet behind her. She went into the movie theater, and there he was, right behind her.[12]

Certainly nothing can be proven. But I doubt that, without Chaplin rollerskating blindfolded on a railingless balcony to impress Paulette Goddard, without Keaton standing in a hurricane-devastated street, unaware of the front of the collapsing house which has just fallen on him, fortunately with a strategically placed open window coming down exactly on the spot where Keaton is standing, without all these mad inventions by the silent film geniuses, such a sequence of highly stylized exaggeration could ever have been written.

In another story, "The World Cafeteria" — a quintessential example of a cocktail of horror and merriment by the way — the tapwoman finds the corpse of a young girl who just has hanged herself in the ladies' room. She cuts her down, carries her to the taproom and puts her on a table close to the cafeteria's plateglass window. Then she looks up: ". . . there was a man standing out in the rain on the other side of the cafeteria's plateglass front, staring in at the table."[13] As in the previous story, the observer beyond the window becomes a recurring motif and a morbid extended gag. The tapwoman calls the police, but before they come, various odd characters enter the cafeteria, the tapwoman has odd conversations with them — but time and again she, and the reader, turn to the window. On the other side of it, the morbidity climaxes:

> By now a group of curious onlookers had gathered in front of the window. They were leaning their hands up against the glass, and their palms looked white and unnaturally large. Just above the hands shone a row of inquisitive eyes.[14]

And two pages later:

> "Why, that's awful," said the tapwoman. "Just look at them. Why, that bunch of no-goods has even brought along their own stools." . . . She drew herself a small beer and walked over to the large plate-glass window. Dozens of onlookers—some replete with stools—had gathered out front in the pouring rain. They were whispering to one another and pressing their hands up against the glass as if it could keep them warm. They looked like monsters.[15]

There is further action in the tap room: a morbid painter enters, sits at the bar, from which the corpse on the table cannot be seen, and starts talking about his vanished fiancée who, he says, has survived several suicide attempts. It becomes clear—though not to the painter—that the girl on the table is the fiancée. Then the tapwoman has another look out the window:

> A group of onlookers was now perched on the slippery, resiliant boughs of a linden tree, hanging onto the branches above like passengers on a tram. They had a bird's-eye view of the entire cafeteria, including the chintz curtain, now slightly open, behind which the corpse lay on the dirty-dish table.[16]

Finally, the police arrive to inspect the dead girl:

> "In here," said the tapwoman, drawing the curtain. The glass front of the cafeteria was covered with white hands, and the people in the second row were trying to push away the people up front. Several of the onlookers looked as if they were hanging from street lights, and one old man stood in the crown of the tree like a baboon, and the wind whipped up the rain like a set of draperies.[17]

Is all this just observation of real life? Observation it certainly is, exaggerated for the purpose of making a philosophical statement on human nature. But I wonder: Have you seen Keaton's *The Cops* with its exaggerated proliferation of policemen?

Or take "The Palaverers," a story about an eccentric father, who:

> poured a bucket of carbide into the outhouse and emptied his pipe into it a few minutes later. I happened to be leaving the house at the time, and what should I see? An explosion like a cannon shot, a quarter of a ton of flying feces, and Father, twenty feet off the ground, somersaulting his way through the middle of it all! He was lucky though: the manure broke his fall.[18]

Isn't this incredible aviator a brother of all the rubbery silent clowns who, though they suffered the worst kind of punishment at the hands of other human beings or from the natural elements, always survived unharmed? Remember the mechanic in *Modern Times* who, swallowed up by the forbidding machinery of a huge and purposeless mechanism, his head protruding from among the cogwheels, is being served his lunchtime coffee by Charlie Chaplin through the hollow corpse of a baked chicken? Read this:

> [Father] spent some time fixing the drainpipe. He would walk all around the edge of the roof laughing, and never thought to strap himself down to anything. Mother stood watch on the cement walk so if he fell she could run for the ambulance. On the fourteenth day Father finally strapped himself down, and fell off the roof. There he was, hanging by one leg upside down. I passed him things to drink through the window while Mother spread out all our quilts on the cement walk.[19]

Reading Hrabal, one is often reminded of Faulkner's novel *The Hamlet*, in many places also baptized not by Shakespeare but by the obscure Hollywood gagmen, Faulkner's one-time colleagues:

> They saw the horse the Texan had given them whirl and dash back and rush through the gate into Mrs. Littlejohn's yard and run up the front steps and crash once on the wooden veranda and vanish through the front door. Eck and the boy ran up onto the veranda. A lamp sat on a table just inside the door. In its mellow light they saw the horse fill the long hallway like a pinwheel, gaudy, furious and thunderous. A little further down the hall there was a varnished yellow melodeon. The horse crashed into it; it produced a single note, almost a chord, in bass, resonant and grave, of deep and sober astonishment; the horse with its monstrous and antic shadow whirled again and vanished through another door. It was a bedroom; Ratcliff, in his underclothes and one sock and with the other sock in his hand and his back to the door, was leaning out the open window facing the lane, the lot. He looked back over his shoulder. For an instant he and the horse glared at one another. Then he sprang through the window as the horse backed out of the room and into the hall again and whirled and saw Eck and the little boy just entering the front door. . . It whirled again and rushed down the hall and onto the back porch just as Mrs. Littlejohn, carrying an armful of clothes from the line and the washboard, mounted the steps.[20]

This wild chase, with its many gaggy details, even has a topper. The horse rushes out of the hamlet and down a country road, where he runs into a wagon drawn by two mules and occupied by Mr. Tull's family, just as the wagon is crossing a bridge. The mules, frightened by the horse, jerk the wagon, *flinging Tull. . . backward into the wagon bed among the overturned chairs and exposed stockings and undergarments of his women,* finally snatching him bodily out of the wagon, whereupon he falls onto the bridge on his face.[21]

Can there be anything more filmic? Anything more vintage silent comedy? But let us stay with Faulkner awhile. Of course, in the late fifties and early sixties everybody in Prague read him in translation. *A Rose for Emily*, a selection of his best short stories, *Mink*, the last part of the Snopes saga, *A Fable*, with its virtuoso yarn about the three-legged race horse, *As I Lay Dying*, that absurd tour-de-force of black humor, *Intruder in the Dust*, Faulkner's homage to the debased genre of the detective story. Faulkner, like Poe, and like the silent film comedy, has entered the subconscious mind of the Czechs. He is among the few American authors Hrabal mentions explicitly — in reference to Mink Snopes, a character, by the way, who would feel at home in the Hrabalian world. A direct tribute to the Southerner's linguistic mastery is Hrabal's novella *Dancing Lessons for the Advanced and Elderly (Taneční hodiny pro starší a pokročilé)*, written all in one endless "Faulknerian" sentence. Here, however, the similarity is superficial: whereas the true Faulknerian sentence, with its numerous parenthetical sentences and labyrinthine dependent clauses, is among the most complex syntactical constructions in the English language, Hrabal's book-length supersentence is just a string of relatively simple units connected by "ands." But there is much of the more subtle Faulkner in Hrabal's stories. At their very core lies Faulkner's admiration of the beautiful inconsistencies in folksy narrative, his spellbound abandonment to the raconteurism of the talkative semiliterate, that primordial figure standing at the hazy beginnings of fiction, which, in spite of all experiments and refinements, is essentially storytelling. Naturally, there are other possible American godfathers. The central term in Hrabal's aesthetic canon — *pábení* — is nothing else but campfire palavering: a close relation to the American "tall tale," to the eccentric exaggerations of Davy Crockett, Paul Bunyan or Pecos Bill, who stand at the outset of a tradition which, by the process of refinement developed through the crudities of an Artemus Ward or a Petroleum V. Nasby to Bret Harte, to Ambrose Bierce, to Twain and so forth, to Ring Lardner, to Damon Runyon — all well known in Prague through recent translations.

Naturally this is not to say that Hrabal's inspiration is bookish. But even the richest real-life experience usually needs a key to unlock the door to literary art. There are two older Czech writers who have provided Hrabal with such keys: Jaroslav Hašek, the notorious creator of *The Good Soldier Švejk*, and Karel Poláček, whose Czech, poor man, was so lively, idiomatic, poetic, humorous and original that I fear he will forever remain unknown to the West for lack of an adequately ingenious translator and a publisher able to publish good books, not just good sellers. But there is far too much of the American imagination in Hrabal, of the "power of blackness," of the mixture of "high" and "low" which you will search for mostly in vain in Hašek or Poláček, but which you easily find, among other Americans, in

Faulkner. And there is also Faulkner's rustic gentleness, coupled with the unthinking cruelty of his simple folk. *Closely Watched Trains* contains a story about the transporting of animals by train to the slaughterhouse:

> If any of the beasts resisted the herdsmen broke their tails... There was a bull tied on behind; he had broken knees, and a torn nose from having ripped the ring out of his nostrils. Now he was tied by his horns to the cart, and dragged along like that... his bloody knees left behind him two red streaks.[22]

Typically, this vision of sadism is juxtaposed with an image of beauty. The bull with the torn nose was lured to the butcher's cart by a pretty girl and then cruelly tied to the vehicle:

> Maybe the bull had realized, too late, that the girl... was handing him over to the butchers by treachery, betraying him by the scent of her skirts to which the bull was accustomed, and after which he would have trampled along to the end of the world.[23]

I sense a distinct echo of the master of Yoknapatawpha County in this moving dirge. I may be mistaken. But I do not think I am.

Among the influences Hrabal talks about himself, most prominent are the painters: Matisse, Munch, the surrealists, Jackson Pollock, and many others. Hrabal even asserts that he has learned much more from the painters, from the technique of the collage, from the abstracting process of modern art, than from writers. That may be true, and anyway, he would not be alone in this respect. The influence of painters on Hemingway's descriptions of landscape has been demonstrated by Emily Watts,[24] Picasso's cubism obviously has something to do with the reduction to all kinds of "bottom natures" in the work of Gertrude Stein, Dos Passos' dazzling visual images, and his striking collages would not exist without the galleries of Paris, and so on. But there was also an American writer, very well-known to the post-Stalinist Prague of the fifties when most of Hrabal's stories were written or took their final shape, who also, quite manifestly, learned a lot from nineteenth-century impressionists. He is the man who created that famous image, quoted in many essays on visual imagery: *The red sun was pasted in the sky like a wafer.*[25] Yes, Stephen Crane, also one of the first accomplished users of big-city slang in *Maggie: A Girl of the Streets*, another combine of cruelty and loveliness, in *The Bride Comes to Yellow Sky*, and in many other yarns. Just listen to this:

> In the eastern sky there was a yellow patch like a rug laid for the feet of the coming sun, and against it, black and pattern-like, loomed the gigantic figure of the colonel on a gigantic horse.[26]

Or:

When another night came the columns, changed to purple streaks, filed across two pontoon bridges. A glaring fire wine-tinted the waters of the river. Its rays, shining upon the moving masses of the troops, brought forth here and there sudden gleams of silver or gold.[27]

And now listen to this:

And then I slipped back down into the water, into the brass-colored water, and swam and swam, round and round in the reflection of the moon, pushing away the metallic paint with my hands. Each time I raised my hand, it came out bronze.[28]

The same principle can easily be recognized here. This is no longer description. This is impressionistic painting. Or perhaps expressionistic painting, but painting anyway. It may have been Hrabal's favorite Munch, or van Gogh, but, My God, it is so close to Crane! Consider the way Crane constantly uses unmixed, undiluted colors in *Maggie*:

Over the island a worm of yellow convicts came from the shadow of a gray ominous building[29]... The rough yellow of her face and neck turned suddenly crimson[30]... Her yellow brows shaded eyelids that had grown blue[31]... the blue policeman turned red[32]... in a room sat twenty girls of various shades of yellow discontent[33]... An orchestra of yellow silk women and bald-headed men, on an elevated stage near the centre of a great green-hued hall[34]...

And now listen to the following passage from a story by Hrabal called "A Prague Nativity":

... the black propman's green skull emerged from the black velvet backdrop... then, as black velvet drapes were slipped open by the green skull suddenly as it had appeared, it slipped back into the deep purple darkness.[35]

And finally, my favorite Cranian image from Hrabal's "Romance," where a gypsy girl:

carried the hemisphere of the half-load of bread beside that black hair of hers and the white crust sketched her path in the darkness.[36]

Very well, then — but does all this constitute a genuine use of American motives. A linear influence? A dependence on the transatlantic masters? Certainly not. It is just another, supremely aesthetic proof that the best literature of the small nation, now under Russian rule, has nothing to do with the literary traditions of the real East, whose writers' *mentality and emotionalism*, to quote Joseph Conrad, have *always been repugnant* to us, *hereditarily and individually.* An indication that the deepest roots of our Czech literary tradition are firmly rooted in the life-giving soil of Western art. That, at least to me, is the ultimate, political if you wish, message of the work of that remarkable Western literary artist, Bohumil Hrabal.

NOTES

[1] Bohumil Hrabal, *Moritáty a legendy* (Prague: Československý spisovatel, 1968), p. 18.
[2] Ibid., p. 18.
[3] Edgar Allan Poe, *The Narrative of Arthur Gordon Pym*, in E. H. Davidson, ed., *Selected Writings of Edgar Allan Poe* (Boston: Houghton Mifflin, 1956), p. 320.
[4] Bohumil Hrabal, *The Death of Mr. Baltisberger* (New York: Doubleday, 1975), p. 160.
[5] Ibid., p. 49.
[6] Sergei Eisenstein, "Dickens, Griffith and the Film Today," in *Film Sense* (New York: Harcourt, Brace & World, 1949), pp. 195-256.
[7] *Death of Mr. Baltisberger*, p. 50.
[8] Ibid., p. 51.
[9] Ibid., pp. 52-53.
[10] Ibid., p. 54.
[11] Ibid., p. 54.
[12] Ibid., p. 60.
[13] Ibid., p. 175.
[14] Ibid., p. 176.
[15] Ibid., p. 178.
[16] Ibid., p. 179.
[17] Ibid., p. 183.
[18] Ibid., p. 26.
[19] Ibid., p. 27.
[20] William Faulkner, *The Hamlet* (New York: Vintage Books, 1964), pp. 302-303.
[21] Ibid., p. 304.
[22] Bohumil Hrabal, *Closely Watched Trains* (New York: Grove Press, 1968), pp. 48-49.
[23] Ibid., p. 49.
[24] Emily Watts, *Ernest Hemingway and the Arts* (Urbana: Univ. of Illinois Press, 1971).
[25] Stephen Crane, *The Red Badge of Courage* in *Great Short Works of Stephen Crane* (New York: Harper and Row, 1965), p. 56.
[26] Ibid., p. 14.
[27] Ibid., p. 20.
[28] *Death of Mr. Baltisberger*, p. 83.
[29] Stephen Crane, *Maggie: A Girl of the Streets*, in *Great Short Works*, p. 128.
[30] Ibid., p. 132.
[31] Ibid., p. 136.
[32] Ibid., p. 140.
[33] Ibid., p. 142.
[34] Ibid., p. 147.
[35] *Death of Mr. Baltisberger*, p. 139.
[36] Ibid., p. 1.

SLOVAK SURREALISM AS A PARABLE OF MODERN UPROOTEDNESS

Petro Petro
University of British Columbia

There may be no Shakespeare, no Montaigne, no Goethe in Eastern European literatures, yet this is not how these literatures are seen from *inside* their respective nations. Invariably, literature is treasured, it is a priori great; for the crux of the matter is, as Milan Kundera but recently reminded us, that in Eastern Europe (more precisely *Central* Europe under Communist domination) literature defines nation, and even creates it. Individual works are often treasured more than individual authors. And as for the authors themselves—we have heard them groan under the weight of an obligation that disallows them patrician hauteur, splendid isolation, bemused estrangement and forces upon them prophetic mode, political participation, and even martyrdom. But what happens if a spontaneous literary movement attempts to break with this tradition in order to try, for once, to lead an existence normally reserved for the colleagues of the older West? The story of Slovak surrealism supplies an instructive answer: a closer look at this phenomenon might take us very far indeed; it might even throw some light on the Western malaise of spiritual uprootedness, a malaise no longer exclusively Western, as we shall see.

Slovakia, the eastern part of today's Czechoslovakia, is often compared to the smaller, but much better known Switzerland with which it shares the mountainous geography and a great potential for tourism successfully exploited in Switzerland, but far from developed in Slovakia. For the Hungarians, Slovakia was the wild North of impenetrable forests and stubborn mountain folk. For the Czechs, it was the poor, but exotic East whence itinerant peddlars, wandering craftsmen, and starry-eyed youths with an immense thirst for knowledge appeared in an uninterrupted stream of peculiar personalities. It was also the vacation land, and a fabulous country to be discovered by writers, painters, and photographers. To its stronger neighbours Slovakia appeared powerless and thus inspired suspicion. On the other hand, Slovaks were tired of playing the role of a subject, of being under suspicion, of being the eternal students and wanderers always at the ready with a profession of gratitude addressed to the world at large. But perhaps the dual natural isolations of geography and poverty have not been such an unmitigated evil. Certain traditional virtues and essential qualities were preserved in Slovakia until this century, though elsewhere they have been extinct since the Reformation. Traditional life, as we are beginning to realize, had much commendable about it. Despite its many shortcomings—chief among them being the generally low standard of living—traditional life was the *natural* life. Thus it embraced the people in the protective shield of security, well-being, and even happiness, such as are generally unavailable to them in our modern, bewildering world.

Yes, there was something to be painted, photographed, written about in these villages right up to the fifties, when *kolkhoz* entered the villages on tractors, tearing into shreds the fine web of traditional society, drawing the young to the cities and turning neighbours first into enemies and then to shrewd, small-time businessmen intent upon enriching themselves by selling farm produce privately to the cityfolk. It is impossible to make heads or tails of Slovak literature without an understanding of the relationship of the village to the city. For the two greatest accomplishments of modern Slovak literature—(and is there anything else but *modern* Slovak literature, if we use the word in a wide sense, including the Romantic period?)—must be the development of *lyrical prose* and the appearance in the mid thirties of Slovak *surrealism*.

As for lyrical prose, confused even today by some critics with expressionism, we are dealing with literature that at worst is a cozy idealization of the village life with artificial folkishness, and at best a relative of the much admired Latin American phenomenon of "magical realism," illustrated by works such as Garcia Marquez's *Hundred Years of Solitude*. The genius of this school was J. C. Hronský (1896-1961) who died in exile. Milo Urban (1904-) also an accomplished practitioner of this genre, was allowed to publish after 1948, but he produced works in the proper socialist realist convention. Fortunately, in the sixties, a new voice appeared, mindful of Hronský and Urban, and what is more with a voice of his own: Vincent Šikula (1936-). Thus, the genre of lyrical prose is alive, developing and gaining adherents and practitioners. As far as Slovak literature is concerned, it is still unknown in the West, and if good translations were available, the Slovak lyrical prose would astonish the western reader with its magic, as was the case with the Latin American phenomenon. Slovak lyrical prose is a rediscovery of the paradise of experiences open to children from which we are, as we grow up, gradually being pushed out with the attendant ruthlessness that, in turn, engenders mighty bouts of nostalgia. It is to this nostalgia that both lyrical prose and magical realism address themselves. We can add to these basic characteristics of the genre also the inventiveness of the practitioners, inasmuch as the accomplishments of the imagination tend to be accompanied by the no less impressive inventiveness of composition or form. But Slovak lyrical prose is still with us; it survived, it is popular with its readers, and enjoys a modicum of official support, despite the constant criticism that naturally charges it with escapism, lack of class approach, and vaguely inimical ideology.

Such is not the case with Slovak surrealism, for it was not allowed to survive. Slovak surrealism was killed, in 1951, during an *"aktív"* (a meeting of activists) of writers and party hacks; but even before this date, ever since 1945, the surrealists themselves were prudently modest about surrealism, learning how to write patriotic verses about the resistance, about the Red Army, the radiant future, villages teeming with tractors and combine harvesters that, as in the Soviet Union, would bring about an era of prosperity, happiness, and peace. And so, even if we are to be generous, the era of Slovak surrealism did not last more than some fifteen years (1935-1950), but those years produced a fascinating harvest that has scarcely been noted by the world at large. The reason for the neglect—at home and abroad—is obvious, if we note that the best work of this movement was produced *during the war,* when three of the four almanacs that contained the best Slovak surrealism produced were published: *Yes and No (Áno a nie,* 1938), *Dream and Reality (Sen a Skutočnosť,* 1940), *In the Daytime and at Night (Vo dne a v noci,* 1941), and *Greeting (Pozdrav,* 1942).

To acknowledge that a successful literary movement was alive and well during the existence of the Slovak Republic (1939-1945) used to be tantamount to treason. Finally, a way has been found out of this impasse, as the erstwhile surrealists gained importance and found courage after the worst ravages of Stalinism, that is, after they became pillars of the new regime, having identified themselves totally with it. The closed chapter of Slovak surrealism was reopened, in the sixties, and the surrealists themselves refurbished as brave partisans, fighting the nonprogressive, parochial Slovak Republic then at war with both the Soviet Union and United States. There is some truth to this. Michal Považan, a theoretician of the movement, declared already in 1944 that "At the time of the most widespread political cretinism we furthered the cause of personal and artistic freedom on this stupid island of Slovakia." But what is Považan's point of reference? The pre-war Czechoslovak Republic. That the post-war Communist regime would allow even less "personal and artistic freedom" was something unimaginable. But it is the prerogative of the unimaginable to happen again and again.

We must address then another issue: why should Slovak surrealism claim special attention? In what ways does it differ from French, or for that matter Czech surrealism? The general outlook of Slovak surrealists is present in a programmatic statement, or manifesto, by Vladimir Reisel (1919) entitled "Poster" (1939):

> The time when we cried over a sunset is gone
> Impressionist nights rainy swallows of evenings
> Stars are counting our steps
> Stars are putting horseshoes on our poems and these emit drugs

> A long time ago a poet sat on a rock and cried
> The moon used to sit on Mácha's lips
> Rimbaud was the first to discover the art of being free
> He travelled round the world
> He visited all the countries he did not look for death
>   he lived for his freedom
> He knew how to take a stand against the whole army
>   of rhetoricians and spit on them
> Baudelaire glorified Satan
> Lautréamont writes poems which fascinate us like
>   our mistresses
> And until in the darkness of poetry turned profane there
>   appeared Guillaume Apollinaire
> Who set about changing the world
> The night reigned

And so on. In other words, a confession of Francophilia, of wholesale acquisition of a foreign sensibility; an aesthetics that is opposed to the sacharine romanticism, or pseudo-romanticism, and even more so to the realism and even symbolism of such poets as P. O. Hviezdoslav and Ivan Krasko, admittedly the greatest poets of the pre-surrealist period and arguably the greatest Slovak poets of any period. And is there not something pathetic about the following verses from the same poem by Reisel?

> We invented the way of putting people to sleep using
>   a dose of hashish
> To lead them to places which cause movement of all
>   the senses
> We invented the way of changing the worlds
> We see the stars through the eyes of lunatics
> We watch the seas hovering above the cities
> We see the cities transformed into sepias

And yet the surrealists include some of the most talented poets, artists, and critics born, roughly, between 1914 and 1920. Thus, it was not a movement exclusively of poets. The only competition seemed to be the Catholic *moderna* movement, but even Rudolf Dilong (1905), an outstanding Catholic poet, was drawn to surrealism and never abandoned the surrealist imagery, taming it masterfully into service of God. Thus, in distinction to Czech surrealism, which also attracted artists and critics, there was, in Slovakia, virtually the entire generation involved in a movement clearly limited in time, flourishing under conditions that at first sight might seem particularly inclement. Czech poetry was never exclusively surrealist and then, Czech surrealism had a distinctly leftist orientation which was by no means a majority sentiment in pre-war Prague and elsewhere. Thus, it is difficult to ignore this movement in Slovakia: by the dint of attracting real talent, it had to produce something worthwhile. The orientation was decidedly Francophile, that much is clear. The critics, or theoreticians of Slovak surrealism—M. Bakoš, M. Považan, K. Šimončič, and I. Hrušovský—looked elsewhere as well. They were influenced by Russian formalism represented by B. Eichenbaum, R. Jakobson, and Yu. Tynianov. but also the Czech structuralism of J. Mukařovský. But the poets and painters mention Rimbaud, Verlaine, Corbière, Nerval, Baudelaire, Lautréamont, Villon, Breton, Eluard, Crevel, Apollinaire, Tzara, Jarry, Ribemont-Dessaignes, Gauguin, Delacroix, van Gogh, Rembrandt, and Poe.

There is then an almost naive earnestness in the Slovak surrealists' attempt to appropriate for themselves the representatives of the emerging modern sensibility and aesthetics; it seems that they had to be engulfed by this foreign tide with the result that might follow a hungry urchin's feast in a pastry shop after he had been overlooked and left to his devices overnight. But on the way to a finished poem something happens: inevitably, because there was no hashish, they were not lunatics, had no sea in a landlocked country, and so they had to invest the foreign husk of surrealism with some sort of realism, that is, with some realia all their own. It is nowhere as visible as in Rudolf Fábry's poem "To the Poet of the Caligrammes":

> You are waiting for us dear Guillaume
> greetings from Bakoš, Šimončič, and myself
> this *I* of my cruelties
> is the candle which sets this letter on fire for you

*　　*　　*

> So we got as far as here
> Where the beautiful woman sleeps
> Where the old land lies
> Where we let the poet speak:
> Here is our land
> Where the road from concepts to images
> Reaches up to the thin threads
> They are hair, hair I embrace
> Beyond the high mountain
> Under the jug of air rock and water
> By the river and three rivers
> Female legs rock the boat Martha
> Here stood the water mill
> And lower by a roebuck's leap
> The Old Post Office
> Then the wide road

> A constantly dead street
> An old woman's fingers blossomed three
> Days before death
> They watch
> Bridesmaids behind the rushing train
> The constantly dead street with glazier's eyes
> Will not return during an eclipse
> Ah, on the road from love to images
> Against the breasts of an adder
> In the life beyond

And lo and behold! After all is said and done, the Slovak surrealist Fábry resides on *terra firma* of Slovakia. No, the mountains, rivers (or rather mountain brooks, as implied), the dead street, and even "constantly dead street" are not the usual urban habitat of either the French, or Czech surrealists. But they are properly the habitat, the preferred topography of Slovak surrealist and Slovak patriotic poets, such as Andrej Žarnov (1903). There is, of course, nothing strange about this. The big city, as a theme, is virtually non-existent in Slovak literature. Only recent prose attempts, not very successfully, to zero in on this theme in the general spirit of catching up with the world; we shall have to wait for a genuine urban, "big city" author until the emergence of a genuine big city. Bratislava was for the surrealists, as it still is for the contemporary author, a big city *in statu nascendi* only. As the surrealists realized, the only metropolis was Prague, and Fábry admitted as much in his poem to Prague: "The Heart of Europe":

> Why wouldn't you compare this city
> to Olympia by Manet
> this city
> with seven hills
> throttled by lilac in spring
> a beauty walks on its bridge
> (the bridges were built of egg yolks here)

and

> there are all kinds of things here
> ghetto City Hall and an old cemetery
> which Apollinaire liked to visit
> there are all kinds of things here
> which we like
> when we drink the stout of *Weltschmerz*
> there are all kinds of things here
> even Claudel likes them
> the Infant Jesus of Prague is here

Well, Bratislava certainly did not have "all kinds of things": no bridges made of egg yolk, no Chinese prostitutes that Fábry mentions in another verse. It was no metropolis. But Bratislava (also known as Pressburg and Pozsony) has been a fascinating city nevertheless. It was certainly, though only embryonically, a great city. It had an international atmosphere that Prague could not match with its German component. For in addition to its Germans, Bratislava had a large Hungarian population, and a sizeable Czech minority as well. This Slovak capital was, paradoxically, so cosmopolitan, that in 1937 students organized a demonstration with the slogan *"Na Slovensku po Slovensky!"* (In Slovakia, Use Slovak!) The city also boasted of an important port on the Danube, the river that separates Slovakia from Austria and Hungary. Finally, there was a regular electric tram connection with Vienna, which further increased the contact among the various elements of population of both cities. A true "Pressburger" would be trilingual, which for some at least meant *not* having a good command of any of the three languages alive in the city. All nationalities had their schools, but only Slovaks had a university, named after Comenius, and originally staffed by excellent Czech professors who commuted from Prague. And Slovaks, as befits a capital of Slovakia, had their National Theatre, their opera, operetta, symphony, and so on. In the late thirties when the surrealists gathered in this city, it had, with its population of 250,000, more theatres and movie theatres than my new home, Vancouver, British Columbia, where more than a million people live.

But herein lies the key that might help us to understand the phenomenon of Slovak surrealism. By large, the youthful Slovaks who enthusiastically joined the movement were newcomers in their capital. It bewildered them. Some probably felt more at home in Prague. Certainly, Prague must have seemed more "Slavic." This is rarely recognized. Of course, this state of affairs changed dramatically during the establishment of the Slovak Republic (1939-1945), when Bratislava, willy-nilly, took upon herself the mantle of a varitable capital city, where Slovaks, for better or worse, were this time *de facto* in power. Thus, they could not have been simply overlooked, or ignored, as if they did not matter—as was often the case before. Now they mattered. And this new-found importance coincided with the flourishing of the surrealist movement. But we should not therefore think that these surrealists identified with the regime. It has to be admitted that the surrealists had contempt for much of what went on: some of them were leftists, others fashioned themselves after *les poetes maudits* (and thus were at odds with any establishment); others still, like the above-cited Považan, arrogantly saw themselves as an elite whose tragic lot it was to have been born in such an uncivilized country that they could actually speak of the "stupid island of Slovakia." Such attitudes were hardly going to endear them to the public.

But they were Slovaks. And living in Slovakia at that most turbulent time in the history of the world. Except that . . . Slovakia at that time also happened to be *an island of peace.* Heaps of scorn were directed at this observation from all possible sides, friendly and not so friendly. But until 1944, this was a fact. And, one has to admit, an uncomfortable fact at that. For what solace can the Slovaks get, contemplating this "island of peace," knowing what went on in their immediate neighborhood? But all the same, it is an amazing fact. The German soldiers returning from the eastern front through Bratislava could not believe their eyes: sides of bacon and ham in butcher shops, when Germany was on *ersatz* supply!

These are the facts of the period, there is no escaping them, and without some knowledge of them it is very hard indeed to make sense of anything that went on in Bratislava. Certainly, they make the appearance of surrealist alamancs in the middle of the war seem less outrageous. But important as all this no doubt is, we have hardly touched upon the key fact: that the surrealist movement, as it existed in Slovakia in those years was a movement of uprooted people; its history is actually an instructive parable of modern uprootedness. And a multiple uprootedness at that.

First of all, most of the surrealists came from the country, rather than the city. And the country meant at best a little town, but more often than not, a village. And even those from small towns would have intimate knowledge of the village life, since some of their relatives would live in a village. And the Slovak village was at that time still a repository of traditional life. The modernity had penetrated it in one way only: with schools. Even a small town would have a *gymnasium,* or a high school, whose entire program was calculated to strip one of the least remnant of the traditional life. It was vehemently anti-religious and cultivated in the student a love for the supranational, in the general attempt of "catching up with Europe." So, when the surrealists came to towns, and then big cities, they left more than the village mud behind. But more consequential still was their uprootedness from their native culture.

Needless to say, in a predominantly Catholic Slovakia, surrealists with their monstrous imagery and dabbling in sex and satanism were certainly not in harmony with the traditional Slovak poetry—whether of the nineteenth century, or even with such geniuses as Hviezdoslav and Krasko. That it was possible to develop further the native poetic traditions was more than abundantly proven by E. B. Lukáč, Ján Smrek, Valentín Beniak and the Catholic *moderna,* or Modern Catholic movement, which incidentally, also kept a steady eye on the modern French Catholic intellectuals and poets (such as Maritain), and some not so modern, such as the tortured prophet Leon Bloy.

But the surrealists, being after all poets, could not exist in a vacuum, nor could they draw inspiration from it. Their foreign models could offer them little besides the general framework—their aesthetics, mainly. Thus they found Janko Kráľ (1822-76), a Slovak poet whose romantic poetry seemed to fit the surrealist aesthetics—inasmuch as Kráľ's work with its idea of regeneration, the importance of dreams, as well as his rather exotic imagery neatly fit the requirements of surrealism, while, very opportunely, Kráľ was also a genuine hero and a poet with a safe place in the national Pantheon.

From their native environment the surrealists also accepted the folklore, or at least the folk tales: the miraculous, the magic that is an integral part of the world of folklore. To be fair, the new seeing did transform reality—the often dull mundane objects of everyday life—into shimmeringly brilliant and translucent objects of the surreal universe:

"Without Sword Without Guilt"

(Ján Rak, 1942)

What is it I see through the coloured glasses of huts days marching by
Through smoking inlets of childhood
Army of tropical ants
Or this strange castle turning around on a chicken's leg
Of overly massive glass
Like a breast like an endless river
Full of spring water
Full of rainbow-like bandages of laughter
Full of the lilac of stars
What makes me think about you
My first girl
So fragile
It is because the antique vase was broken
On the hard pavement
From broken splinters
A violet smoke
Rises into billiard balls
While a butterfly
Turns into a lamp
I found an extinguished volcano
Quite similar to a full moon
And a pair of decomposed eyes
On a gilt string
This way we frequently return
All of us
To our childhood
Through a magic glass

Finally, the chief agent of uprootedness, as is universally recognized, is the war that, "island" or no "island," even Slovakia could not escape. Some surrealists were drafted and saw action in the war in, for Slovaks, very exotic places. Štefan Žáry, for example, thus discovered his lifelong love: Italy. But even before 1939, Europe was far from tranquil; thus, Reisel focuses his sight on the war in Spain:

"Woman Whose Lover Fell at Madrid"

Paler than a rain-wet mermaid
Paler than a poisonous flower
Dead hand sleeping on the barricades
Dead hand which will not sing nights anymore
Dead hand devoted to other worldly rivers
Dead hand near the stars
In the land of harps and dark castanets
In the land attacked by magnetic storms like cosmos
Over the cemeteries of cities he sleeps his icy sleep
In the mirror of olives
A swan's song of love rules the waves of nonsensical rapids
A swan's song on warm breasts covered by a face only yesterday

* * *

Here the usual necrophiliac surrealist preoccupation with dead bodies, their decomposition, is turned upside down. The death is no longer as desirable, or as beautiful, as in Reisel's "Poster," where he wrote:

How beautiful smells the foreign flora on the breast of a dead woman
Is it not the polyp?
Is it not the only eye which you adore?
Is it not the look of a woman who rocks you into the most beautiful
    delirium?

Overturning the order of the world, war negates the values on which the fine fabric of society rests. But what happens when this negation visits surrealists, themselves negators? Should they not welcome war? After all, does it not create the surrealist kind of beauty? The bombs, fragmentation shells, flame throwers, and even ordinary hand granades, right down to the humble bullet, are all instruments that actually recreate surrealist poetry in reality. Could the surrealists really have been against the war that was doing then much to turn the world into one big surrealist poem? Perhaps it is indecent to ask, considering that a corollary of the surrealist aesthetics ("ugly is beautiful") is still with us. It is indeed the cornerstone of modern art, as anyone with eyes to see cannot really help noticing. No, it is hardly a coincidence that synchronises the flourishing of the Slovak surrealism with the climax of the war. Reisel said: "We invented the way of putting people to sleep using a dose of hashish." Well, that is very fine, but how lucky that there really was no hashish, that it is a Baudelairesque hashish that he is speaking of in his manifesto, that is, a purely literary conceit: what on earth would they do with sleeping Slovaks? What good would they be doped with hashish for the resistance movement in 1944! Besides, hashish is not really a sleep-inducing drug. But perhaps one should not take this surrealist poetry too literally. . . .

This multiple uprootedness is, of course, nothing new in the world at large. Most of the present crises are one way or other linked to uprootedness, physical or spiritual. And Europe, as its literature abundantly testifies, has been struck with this ailment at least since the Reformation. But that means that despite the occasionally vehement violence, it has been a *lengthy,* though no less painful process. Not so with Slovak surrealists who, with their "catching up with Europe," as Žáry and Považan put it, had to digest the experience of centuries in a very short time. Not surprisingly, this too was reflected in their work. And, sometimes even positively. Slovaks were not as radical in their surrealism as the French. The Frenchman Robert Desnos could say, for example, that "for me it is less a matter of making people admit the reality of things taken for illusory than of placing dream and reality on the same plane. I care little after all, whether everything is false or everything is true. . . ." Now this is sophistication betraying a degree of refinement inaccessible to the culturally "younger" Slovaks. Vlado Reisel, in his article "New Poetry and the Public" (1940), defended the surrealist movement (notice how modest he is about surrealism, calling it, quite simply, "new poetry"), laying much stress on—*reality*:

> We also belong to those who are trying to see reality.
> We were not afraid of it and we are not afraid of it now.
> We did not escape to other worlds as our critics say. But
> our seeing of reality is different from the one found in
> poetry until now. We wanted to see the whole universe,
> the whole life in its diversity, condensed in a single
> verse. We left it to the journalists to paint the "Pictures
> of Life," but we put into poetry the whole man, a man
> who feels, sees, and is blinded by what he sees; we offered
> this to the eyes which wanted to *see* the man. Those who
> were afraid to see the man turned away from us and cursed us.

This clever stratagem did not work. From the point of view of the public acceptance, movement was a failure. A more conservative, more traditional aesthetics prevailed, sentencing surrealists to the unenviable role of an aberration; at first through non-comprehension (they were, as an elite and vanguard, after all, too *recherché*), and later, after the war and Communist takeover, by an administrative fiat. But they forfeited their existence or its justification the moment they took sides in the war, in the resistance. The feverish imagery replete with putrid corpses was conveniently actualized and failed to attract them. After seeing the real thing, the *sur*-real paled into insignificance. After all, nothing is as real as humble reality; and the humbler it is the better.

Yet, one has to admit that Reisel was right in that the poetry produced by the Slovak surrealists did not go as far as the French; some respect for realism was preserved, however tenuously. And their poetry, at the same time, often breathes the mountain air of the village; which is why their application of "the ugly is beautiful" type of aesthetics seems so patently false side by side with real gems gleaned from the precious trunk of the folk tales. And in the poems of the best of them, Štefan Žáry (1918), the entire process of uprootedness, sketched here ever so briefly, appears in a nostalgic light, as if the poet, through some mysterious process, understood all the hazards of the breaking away from the tradition, giving us, as it were, a poetic description of the painful process:

> I will
> I will leave on a black train of thoughts
> To the cities
> Which flash by like the yarn spun in winter
> A man will walk up to me in midnight waiting room
> He is an employee
> Get up sir your love is leaving
> Don't you hear the whistle of birds
> Maybe I will open an eyelid slightly
> The station will be lit by a woman with an auburn walk
> The sleep of death will overcome me
> Some child will put my paralyzed legs on a bench
> It is awfully cold
> The unheated room will foster me
> It is the awful cold of hate
> My train is coming
> It has a fierce stormy boiler
> It is already calling to me
> And I will not go so that I will not have to return
> It will howl like a faithful dog
> For heaven's sake do not force me to gamble
> Everything will happen quickly
> Sad fathers and widows will fill the spaces near the windows
> They will weigh the hair over the mask of the platform
> Fertilized mothers will spread themselves around like soil
> To make a comfortable space for their yet unborn children

Who are sleeping in their wombs
As I sleep over a manuscript
And dream
That
I will leave
Please do not look for me
Do not look for me in the tubes of streets of ill repute
Do not look for me in the colonnade of women
My train crosses over a thumb
It is a ship without primogeniture
It purchases the distances for a bowl of lentils
I am turning off the light in the smoke-filled compartment
Ignoring a woman who is putting her hands under my head
And admiring my features
Ravished
Ravished
Crystallized by Death
    (From "Station Death," 1944)

In this poem, written at the fateful juncture of old and new, at the time, also, when the war had caught up with Slovakia, when carnage and chaos were everywhere, Žáry fixed in brilliant imagery the reality of modern uprootedness. The "yarn spun in winter," the "whistle of birds," the humble "bowl of lentils" evoke the pastoral security of millenia untouched by change until the coming of the train with its "fierce stormy boiler." The transition to the cities is swift and horrible: "It is the awful cold of hate," but above all, sad, the "sad fathers and widows." The stormy train of modernity has arrived, and it will take one away for ever into the world that resembles nothing better than a waiting room of a station: *Station Death*. Could there be a better symbol for modern uprootedness than a crowded, dirty, noisy, and tired waiting room?

    The Slovak surrealist movement is a closed chapter in the history of modern Slovak literature, and that allows us to view it with some detachment and perhaps even sympathy. One would want to commend the effort of Mikuláš Bakoš, the critic who participated in the movement himself, and then in the sixties reminded us of its existence. It was an altogether pleasant surprise to rediscover surrealism. Of course, by that time, the modern sensibility has totally penetrated the literary milieu: surrealism seemed so *contemporary*. . . . And yet. Side by side with the rediscovered surrealism, lyrical prose was making a modest return, after its impressive showing between the wars, due to the genius of J. C. Hronský. And with the return of lyrical prose, brought back by Vincent Šikula, traditional Slovakia returned as well. Only time will tell whether lyrical prose will find enough strength to engineer a complete return to traditional themes, thus ending a literary search that has led to uprootedness. Or will lyrical prose serve only as a veneer covering an empty husk—once filled with the brilliant gems (however foreign-inspired), of Slovak surrealism—the empty shell of the modern world, as reflected by the crowded, comfortless hell of a railway waiting room, as yet another parable of modern uprootedness.

CONTEMPORARY POETRY IN POLAND, HUNGARY, AND CZECHOSLOVAKIA*

Emery George
University of Michigan

Eastern Europe is one-half of Europe. It is a vast and vital realm of society and culture which, for all the attention lavished on it since World War II, remains for too many Americans either that sinister expanse "behind the Iron Curtain" or, at best, "the old country," where tales of Dracula, ethnic grandmothers, and good recipes come from. That the region, which embraces ten countries and at least fifteen languages, should be every bit as human and civilized as ours and should also be a source for much of the best in contemporary poetry, may come as a pleasant surprise even to those who are better informed on life and letters in "the Soviet bloc" than is the average citizen. The present selection aims to contribute to this state of informedness, by way of a fresh glimpse at that genre in East European literatures of which their own reading public has reason to be the proudest — the poetry...

The translation process is, we might say, the picture window framing the great landscape of which it offers a view, and to readers it is this latter that will prove the more exciting of the two. A seemingly strange land appears, in which we all recognize features of our own terrain. It is almost a truism by now that East European countries, at least those north of the Balkans, found their way into the full light of modern literary history by turning toward the West. Poles were always intensely French-oriented; Czechs and Hungarians were, willy-nilly, German-oriented during the Empire, and in the period between the two world wars turned toward France, England, and America on their own. The Hungarian literary biweekly Nyugat *(West) (1908-1941) is an excellent example for this militant self-commitment to things Occidental, although it is instructive to note that in 1935 another journal under the title* Kelet népe *(People of the East) was inaugurated, as it were in answer to* Nyugat. *Indeed the flight of writers from the question of eastern origins, during those heady days of secession and modernism, meant that East European writing pretty much followed developments in France and elsewhere in Western Europe. Symbolism around the turn of the century, along with all the other isms of the modernist phenomenon (cubism, futurism, surrealism, and all the rest) was certainly in full swing in Hungary by World War I, and in Czechoslovakia and Poland as well. Whether we are talking about the various avant-garde groups contemporaneous with Skamander in Warsaw, poetism in Prague, or expressionism and dada in Budapest (and in part also in Vienna), we are observing a shared desire on the part of artists of northeastern Europe of the interbellum generation to be identified as thoroughly westernized — European...* [From the Introduction by Emery George]

---

*Selections from the Anthology of East European Poetry, edited by Emery George, to be published by ARDIS in 1982.

Czeslaw Milosz

SCREENS WILL BE SET THERE

Screens will be set there
And our life will be seen from beginning to end
With everything we managed to forget, it seemed for good,
And with the costumes of the time that would be only ridiculous
    and pitiful
If it was not we who wore them, not knowing any others.
Armageddon of men and women. It is futile to shout I loved them,
Each one seemed a greedy child longing for caresses.
I liked beaches, pools and clinics,
There they were bone of my bone, flesh of my flesh.
I pitied them, and myself, but this is no defense.
Every word, every thought is gone: moving a glass,
Turning the head, fingers unbuttoning a dress, clowning,
A cheating gesture, contemplation of clouds,
Killing for convenience. Only this.
What if they depart with the jingling of bells
Around their ankles, if slowly they enter the flames
That took away both them and me? Bite your fingers, if you
    have them,
And look again at what once was — from the beginning
    to the end.

(Berkeley, 1964)
Trans. John Carpenter

Zbigniew Herbert

ELEGY OF FORTINBRAS

for C. M.

Now that we're alone we can talk prince man to man
though you lie on the stairs and see no more than a dead ant
nothing but black sun with broken rays
I could never think of your hands without smiling
and now that they lie on the stone like fallen nests
they are as defenseless as before The end is exactly this
The hands lie apart The sword lies apart The head apart
and the knight's feet in soft slippers

You will have a soldier's funeral without having been a soldier
the only ritual I am acquainted with a little
There will be no candles no singing only cannon-fuses and
    bursts
crepe dragged on the pavement helmets boots artillery horses
    drums drums I know nothing exquisite
those will be my manoeuvres before I start to rule
one has to take the city by the neck and shake it a bit

Anyhow you had to perish Hamlet you were not for life
you believed in crystal notions not in human clay
always twitching as if asleep you hunted chimeras
wolfishly you crunched the air only to vomit
you knew no human thing you did not know even how to
    breathe

Now you have peace Hamlet you accomplished what you
    had to
and you have peace The rest is not silence but belongs to me
you chose the easier part an elegant thrust
but what is heroic death compared with eternal watching
with a cold apple in one's hand on a narrow chair
with a view of the ant-hill and the clock's dial

Adieu prince I have tasks a sewer project
and a decree on prostitutes and beggars
I must also elaborate a better system of prisons
since as you justly said Denmark is a prison
I go to my affairs This night is born
a star named Hamlet We shall never meet
what I shall leave will not be worth a tragedy

It is not for us to greet each other or bid farewell we live on
    archipelagos
and that water these words what can they do what can they
    do prince

Trans. Czeslaw Milosz

S. Baranczak

DEFECTS, SECONDS, SUBSTITUTES

So this is it always like this, always instead of
stars of first magnitude, cod second freshness,
and always the earth with artificial honey and watered
milk will be flowing, and the Book of Destiny
will be printed on paper of the fifth class and always
somewhere in the middle a section will be missing?

So this is it always, like this, always. Instead of
the ultimate brightness and absolute freshness
we'll have continually before our eyes warped doors
with loose handles, not the gates of paradise.
Stuffing yourself hastily at a rickety table
with half-price stew, how can you whisper:

"So this is it." Always like this. Always instead of
crying out: "I want to live like a man," searching for
a fault in the stars, handed to you—you will live like a man,

in other words: pretending to close your eyes, to look the other way.
The stars will still shine, if you keep living like this.
And your rusty crown will not fall off.

So this is it forever? Like this, forever. Instead of
remnents, rejects and third category
will not be the wishful world, wondrous, and well-made.
Besides who knows if elsewhere in the world is any
brighter, if no one is responsible
for the hidden shortcomings. And no one answers the cry.

Trans. Valeria Wasilewski

Gyula Illyés

SPACIOUS WINTER

Our respective views did better, finding each other
in that spaciously echoing and excessively lit
colonnade which that winter morning made.
Sunlight, with the sensitive touch of a doctor, walked
on the fragile, small branches of glasslike trees:
immediately they reacted by shaking down frost.
Everything around us was more finely shaded, more capable
of detailed rendition—and inside us—brought on, too, by the fact
that from under your sole and from under mine, the snow
crunched—conjured up that squeaking of childhood-new
shoes, and with it, the Eden-age of guilelessness.
With the courage of moving into a
new apartment, refreshed by the smell
of still-drying whitewash, we walked
illumining-clarifying all: how we should
refurbish with miniature furniture
—for it *is* possible!—our lives.

Trans. Emery George

Ágnes Nemes Nagy

PINETREE

Large, yellow sky. A mountain ridge
weighs on the level field.
On the magnet-earth motionless
dark iron-filings of grass.

A stray pinetree.
Something humming. Cold.
Something humming: in the bark-shredded,
scaly-rooted pinepost's
immense trunk now travels
a paleolithic telegram.

Above a bird, a nameless
bird in the sky—knitted
eyebrows, faceless—
behind it now the light fades,
falling eyelids, blind window—
only humming, only the night buzzing
invisible, from black foliage,
charred wrinkled treetops
whose black heart crackles to a purr.

Trans. Bruce Berlind

Ágnes Gergely

AUDEN IN OLD AGE

At last the critic Toynbee wrote with ease
of all that flowed from you: the vodka, booze;
replied your friend, the angry Stephen Spender:
to hurt a corpse this great just isn't tender.

You, with your handsome horse's head, chauffeur,
unsightly in the Spanish Civil War,
expert at rhythms killingly collapsing,
at worm-infested loves, at lullaby-lapsing;

walking the razor edge: cliché and terror,
caught in the end in your own verbal tether,
no, not of whisky, not of metaphysic
would it attack: the youthfully ecstatic;

old name, witness to great times you've become,
and no one would now say you'll start it again;
on the banks of the Thames no single oak
walked with you — only anxiety's tavern-smoke.

Rhyming even without, you ancient lion,
losing your good name, lonely over wine,
where even Eliot was no competition,
not the childless, not those with old-age pensions;

guilty or blameless? only you would know;
but while in the corner of an attic window
a candleworth of poem lights that dormer,
there's always one who, seeing it, grows warmer.

Translated from the Hungarian
by Emery George

Vladimír Holan

THE CAVE OF WORDS

Not with impunity does the youth enter, light in hand,
the cave of words . . . Bold, he hardly suspects
where it is he finds himself . . . Young, though suffering,
he does not know what pain is . . . A master before his time,
he will escape without having entered,
and he will blame a century not yet of age . . .

The cave of words! . . .
Only a real poet and at his own risk
will ruin his wings in madness there and lose the knowledge
of how to return them to the earth's gravity
yet not to hurt her, who attracts the earth.

Cave of words! Only a real poet returns from its silence,
so that, already old, he may find a crying child,
abandoned by the world at its threshold . . .

Trans. Bronislava Volek and Andrew Durkin

František Hrubín

THE CITY IN THE FULL MOON
for Bedřich Fučík

When the great wind blew the streetlights out
pedestrians were thrust into their shadows,
cobweb faces sat within the houses
oddly filling the old familiar seats,

and only half the ancient city rested,
others groped as if they felt for bottles
in cellars, while the wind was only settled
gradually after many days and nights,

great fields of snow encircled everywhere
the city, country-places were exposed
unready, much old paper set ablaze,

and the booming wind, unleashed and sheer,
drove down the nights and mornings with its snow
in all the streets where my lost face might go.

       Trans. Don Mager

S. *Daniel Simko*

THE JEWISH CEMETERY IN PRAGUE

It gets harder to walk
out of those crates which stop
light from entering.
The sky, bending over a body
touches the pale skin of grass
like the fevered head of a child.

You've left behind the town.
Trees long to life you
gently from the splintered bed
into the wind. There is none.
It has stepped out of your bodies.

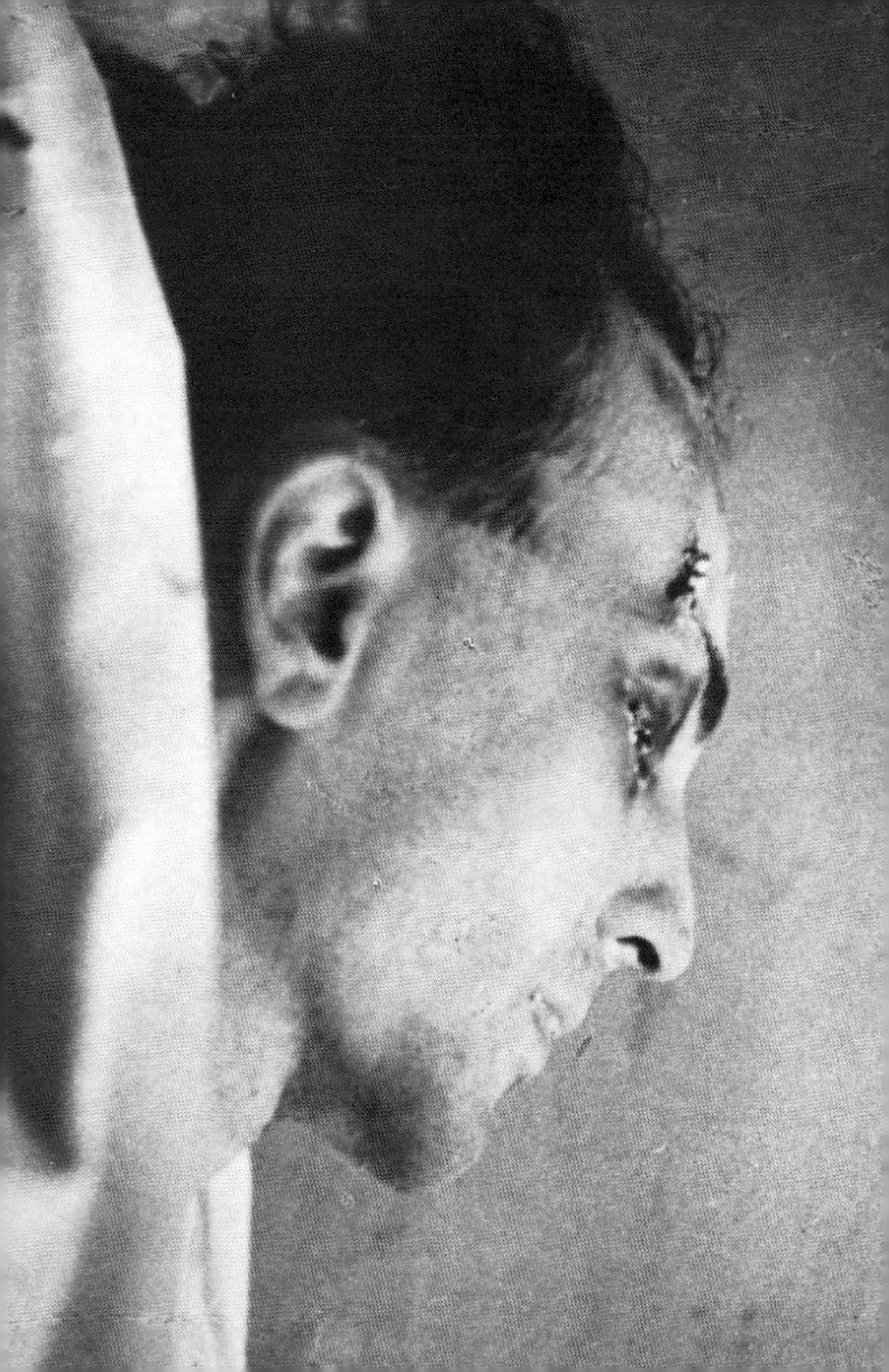

JIŘÍ ORTEN'S ELEGIES

George Gibian
Cornell University

Czech literature has been astonishingly rich in lyrical poets in the twentieth century. Most Czechs themselves are hardly aware of how remarkable it is that every generation of their nation seems to produce not just one great poet, but a whole group. Readers in other countries, of course, have no way to know of the existence of such verbal treasures, in such profusion, in an obscure language, in the heart of Europe.

Coming after the achievements of the Czech poets of the 20's and 30's (Nezval, Seifert, Biebl, Halas, Hora, Zahradníček, Závada, and others), Jiří Orten was one of the younger generation which developed Czech verse in a more subjective, inward direction. He is closest of all to Halas, and in turn, Halas liked him best of the younger poets.

Orten was born in 1919, in a Czech Jewish family, in an ancient small town, near Prague—in Kutná Hora, famous for its unfinished Gothic cathedral, its old town square with arcades, and for its history of medieval wealth derived from silver mines. Orten moved to Prague as a teenager and joined circles of young poets. He stayed in Prague after Munich and after the German occupation. Only four books of his poems were published during his life; because of his being Jewish, in post-Munich Czechoslovakia, his poems were published under pseudonyms. He died at the age of 22, in a bizarre, pathetic accident. Wishing to buy cigarettes, and called over by the cigarette kiosk clerk, he turned, tried to cross a Prague street, and was hit and dragged along by a speeding German car in the summer of 1941. A hospital refused to admit him because he was Jewish. He died a few days later in another hospital.

He was much read and published in the first years after World War II; post-1948 Communist Czechoslovakia, gyroscopically seeking socialistic realism, again buried his works and his memory; he was briefly resurrected during the Prague Spring years in the late 1960's; and he has one more time descended into official disfavor since the Soviet occupation of 1968.

Orten's poems go in utterly unpredictable directions. He is one of the finest, purest vocies of European lyrical poetry of the middle of this century. Geographically as well as aesthetically, he is half way betweeen Lorca and Pasternak.

Excerpts from Jiří Orten's *Elegie—Elegies*, a bilingual collection of poems, translated by Lyn Coffin (SRU Press, New York, 1981).

Orten, like most Czech lyrical poets, exercises to an extreme degree the freedom to combine images unexpectedly. This may be due to the permeating Surrealist influence in Czech poetry, or to Czech everyday and folk language, which is rich in wild, sweeping, freely associating metaphors. As with other modern Czech poets, surrealist and folklore influences are hardly distinguishable. His similarity to Dylan Thomas also impresses us: unabashed emotionality, elastic freedom of movement from image to image, one area of life to another, as though with a switch sending the poem along one direction or another, along several tracks, with the weld or joint consisting of the slimmest, slightest emotional connections. The logic of feeling, which provides the coherence, can often be sensed only most tenuously and tentatively; the logic of reason is absent altogether.

Orten writes with utter simplicity and directness: for example, in "The Start of Spring," "Lies are for April girls to hear and see," or in the poem "A Last Request": "An aching dream, which he hides at the back of the shelf. . . . And everything little retreats beyond the range/Of the poet's final bed." Sometimes he reminds us of E. E. Cummings, or of the Pasternak of the simpler poems. There is never anything *recherché*, esoteric, forced in Orten; he is always direct, perhaps naive, even unselfconscious. The reader must respond by letting himself go as freely as Orten, along his emotionally delicate, pure lines, and not seek erudite, intellectual matter.

Lyn Coffin, the translator of the poems, catches the lyrical directness of Orten, and she tries, valiantly, often with astonishing success, to recapture or reproduce his rhymes. The quality which is the hardest to transmit is of course the play on long and short, pure vowels—which the Czech language offers to poets as possible material, and which Orten uses abundantly. Other patterns, also not susceptible to metrical scanning, are established by vowel and consonantal phonological patterning. The reader of translations can savor Orten's other qualities, but not these.

Orten's images can be appreciated by the reader of the English texts. He addressed everything surrounding him as living, to-be-talked-to, metamorphosing beings. Orten's sequences are amazingly free, his poems are intimate, unrhetorical, touching. One of his several recurring emotional focal points is compassion. The poems do not make intellectual sense, but purely personal. They are unified by surprising, thin but firm threads:

> My lips are extremely dry today, and yet
> It's the blinding dark that sponsors my regret.
> ("Regrets")

The poems which do have some plot lines are those which are the most susceptible to being captured by a translator.

The outstanding Czech scholar and critic, Václav Černý, wrote about Orten: "He has absolute immediacy, directness. There is utter lack of mediation, absence of cunning, calculation, consciousness, deliberateness." Orten has a pointed understanding, an immediate perception of the objects of the world around him. And his approach to them is clear and delicate, even tender. He is the antithesis of Kierkegaard's bugaboo, the modern man of excessive reflection. Orten names, sees, and feels directly, unflinchingly and unreflectedly, unmediatedly. His universe is unified through his perception and feeling towards it. "Death is a frequent guest, almost a female landlord, lady, ruler, of his world," and not only in the elegies. Fear, anxiety, are not absent: a foreboding of disaster is frequent in his poems.

Besides the Czech Richard Weiner, Orten's favorite writers were Pasternak and Rilke, and in the last year of his life, he read above all the Bible and Shakespeare. Although, as one critic wrote about him, he was concerned with death and a Kafka-like anxiety, yet he felt man was born to be happy and he liked to link death with its opposites, light, joy, song. "I was born into this land for no other purpose than to bear witness," he wrote in his diary after the German occupation of Prague in March 1939, and later, in March 1941: "As one who had no friend, wife, or anything; and all that he had was in the distance; as one into whose doubts people tried to pour poison; as one who grew watered with pain; as one whose yearning was stretched on a rack—as such imagine me, such as that, when you have time for me, oh people, oh God."

The poet František Halas wrote after Orten's death,

> Indebted to nobody
> He spat out what was lukewarm
> Terribly thirsty for spirit
> He grew into the Psalms.

He has been called "the poet of exiles, the interpreter of anxiety, the prophet of destruction." Yet he is also a great lover of ephemeral, gentle things of this world—a tender admirer, close to the world of appearances.

He also continually affirmed his stubborn faith in life, despite all limitations and reverses:

> There are not many roads, there isn't just any road, there is only one sole road. Shall I say something about it? Shall I say what I want, what I really want? I'll try. If—right off the start I want to be done with concessions—if they let me. I want to live. Who is smiling? I know nothing else, I learned nothing else. If I believe in God, if I believe only in myself, if I believe in the crowds, if I believe in death, if I believe in justice, if I believe in poetry, if I do not believe in anything, still I am living. That is life. That is life—if I walk into aloneness, or if I become an apostle, that is life, if I commit suicide, if I give up everything, everything, faith, hope, love, that is life, if I help or let myself be helped, that is life, if I suffer or if I am happy, that is life, if I am cold or warm, or well off or badly off, if I have a friend or if I suffer from the yearning to have one, if I work or am idle, if I die or if I am born, all that is life.

In one poem, Orten symbolized human existence as "empty, cold fog." As Černý put it, Orten felt the impingement of existential *Angst* directly, "through my body—my pretense," as in the lines:

> A remote town. Fear. It carries something evil.
> My body, my pretense, suggest it through rhythms
> Which remove the fall further.
> You will try to listen
> And will hear nothing. Only a suggestion. Anxiety. Dusk.

Orten tried to escape anxiety, Černý said, through "the poets' ancient ruses—flight into dreams, flight into aloneness. Through the help sought in love, with which he liked to furnish his aloneness, the aloneness he shared with a beloved woman, or often, and I feel, preferably, only in memories and thoughts of her."

Poets often die young—in Russia, in England, as in Czechoslovakia. Orten's life was one of the shortest, even in the company of those of his fellow artists whose work was cut short by illness, accident, suicide, or a murderous government. Yet he left behind him a full life's literary legacy: many poems, diaries, even a draft of a novel.

JOB'S CLOSING WORDS
Job 31-41

For the pain of hands which couldn't touch
to caress, give me faithful belief
your escape into the night is much
too abrupt, leave slowly, not like a thief.

for the pain of a soul, completely destroyed by
the love that left, let me sleep all right
burn down my creations, let them die and lie
don't allow even one to survive the night,

for the pain of the throat which sang so long,
sang one pain higher, let him expire
let him finish, die out with his song,
which is burning solemnly in the fire!

> *Because thy rage is against me, and thy tumult is come up unto mine ears, therefore will I put my hook in thy nose, and my bridle in thy lips, and I will turn thee back by the way which thou camest.*
> Isaiah 37, 29.

JEREMIAH'S LAMENT

Oh, severe Lord of mine, volatile God of the terrible face,
the song addressed to you made time disperse,
the time toward which I was walking at my painful pace,
and I skirmished for ages and did battle with the universe.

Maybe time isn't bottomless, maybe it's a kind
of submersion by which one can touch ungrieving woman who
awoke from grief somehow and spend death like a stormy night
and find one can face the brutality of madness now.

Because foxes have walked the holy mountain for ages,
because she's left alone as only a tree can be,
I read the prophecy inscribed on those beloved pages,
which gives so much light and offers peace and serenity.

You covered yourself with clouds and hid behind a stream,
so you wouldn't hear what I yelled to the sky at all
and you covered me too, you gave me night, in which I dream
that I'm not allowed to sleep, since you may call.

I keep listening—you're as quiet as if you were mute.
I listen through tears, I listen, I can't hear a sound.
I listen with kisses, distances, with every tree-lined avenue
with fear and excitement, objects and silence, everything around.

I'm the country of Darkness who bore your angry ways,
that, covered with craziness, couldn't see a thing.
I'm the country of Darkness dying under the whip you raise
who couldn't provide milk for children in the spring.

I'm that country of Darkness to whom you gave little rocks,
to whom you gave a bare hillside and death in the wild,
you gave her the lidless eye of day that locks
so she can't make it dark for herself. And mothers were great with child.

Mothers great with child went in sweetly burdened fashion
to gather fruit, to harvest it with the fall-slow ways
they went, touching the ground which is driven by passion
toward the eternal beginning, the light of my youthful days.

And there was no light. Lord, that light went out, you know why.
And the sun burned with frost, that all-powerful lightswitch.
And all of your numbing cold and their bodies were shaken by
weeping, a great inner cry, you know which.

The face you turned away, the shine you chose
to avert was laughing at them and avenging the sorrow
of robbers to whom you gave pleasure and the names of those
lost little sons cut down by time and tomorrow.

But I'm that country of Darkness, the naked spine of my rod,
mother of everything luminous and I believe in my light
and you took it away from me to give to one orchard or another.
Yes. For a flowering cemetery, that's right!

But I'm that country of Darkness, your lover, your daughter,
you plundered my lap, my garden, my evergreen wood,
my fiery wine you poured into the lake water
with shining angels who wanted to go to heaven if they could

and they grew weary on the way, you kept them from seeing
you, oh, Lord, their flight was vain indeed,
they were angels, each a celestial being
and I am the country of Darkness and I have to bleed

and I bleed and cry quietly, cry sinfully, and I
blaspheme, oh, I know, and a pain splashes
in my head, what's left of your charity is used up by
the scourge. Night approached, they covered me with its lashes.

All those walks, all that wandering! Pain is measured
by how much shame is expressed in a cry. The chill
ocean of bad melting, by a flake of treasured
freedom. I'm the country of Darkness, yours, I believe in you still.

I pray until nightfall, I pray to the past, I pray
by means of sparks which will grow to be
fires one day when the fear is over, oh, one day
when madness will be spent on a symphony

when your wrath collapses, Lord God, your vengeful laugh,
when you are kind and recognize anew
that I don't suffer on any other king's behalf.
it's for you, up there in heaven, I'm dying for you.

The bugle of winter sounds. It summons a nation
of sparks who lost their way on windows, plains, in the snow,
the sparks of heavy words in the unfinished creation,
that hover now over the chasm of the story we know.

The bugle of spring sounds a trembling note,
the song of the horn dies out before it's sung,
it's been made fragile, sunk in a snowdrift up to its throat,
like every time which is too young.

The bugle of summer sings out, the uncertain summer, I mean,
which flies with women and falls behind the forest shelf,
which dreams as trees do and can't alight in the dream
and which waits a long time and finally accustoms itself.

Whom does she summon — the bugle of fall?
Oh, it's me, I already knew, by day and night I'm learning
that her song seduces my former fear of after death, of the small
wheel that spins inside when worms have ceased their fruited turning.

What names can I give them, how to make you be on my side,
you who aren't mine, by my tears and poverty?
From out of the bitter-cold snowstorm I call to you, with the wide
voice of prairies, I call: sleep, wait, spend the winter with me!

The storm of nothing comes from the most truthful things said.
The earth, an open hand and peace. Was life meant to extend
that to me? Behold, the coach set in motion by betrayal gallops ahead
and will do so forever until maybe it reaches faith in the end.

Oh, severe Lord of mine, volatile God of the terrible face.
the song addressed to you made time disperse,
the time toward which I was walking at my painful pace,
and I skirmished for ages and did battle with the universe.

I am that country of Darkness, I am dark, I am the dark land,
I'm waiting for you to bloom into love, to break severity's spell.
I'm waiting, I'm trembling, as if there were light in me, and
as if there were light in pain, and in you, in you as well!

ELEGY NUMBER TWO

Come back, things, which helped to carry
the cross of day, suspended between the breasts of queenly
blue-blooded night, bloodthirsty night.
My paperweights, come back to me again.
It's hard not having you firm and steady,
it's hard to call you without hurting one's throat.

Where are you escaping to, river, when did your banks
suddenly part to greet the ocean? Do you still
hold hands with the estuary which tempted you
to die in its wideness? Do your currents speak
their native tongue in that awful foreignness,
do they say "brother" to the cold stream
which chills more deeply than mountain hollows?
Oh, come back, river, my dear horizon,
under me, the ground cries, because it lost you,
your spring ran dry, your riverbed ran dry,
you're just emptying out, dying away, aren't you, river!

Why do you believe the fog, cliff, my faith?
The fog is taking off your clothes, don't think it will cover you!
Many nests have already been plundered,
many thieves have crept up to the top
and raised a flag splattered with death;
dry branches whip your sweet hips,
I can already see the geyser, which springs up in vain,
killing hands crawl after you
and strangle you and will have you strangled soon.
Crying people stand at your feet
and don't believe the disaster is real. I believe it, cliff!

My paperweights, come back to me again.
Come back, tree, come back, my yard,
come back, animals, suffering and quiet,
friend, come back, don't follow
that path which blindly leads
trusting and unaware children to an imaginary sky,
and those rebellious ones who only listened
to their heart, only listened to their mother,
it bricks in with a wall and stabs with grief,
come back, brother, look, blood bitterly
flows from vein into vein, for you, it looks for you,

it wants to flow through you like a mother's milk,
come back, father, a just man,
come back into my dreams, you who live only in dreams.
My paperweights, come back to me again.
I am so light now, having lost you,
the smallest wind plucks me from the ground,
one breath is enough to diffuse me
into unearthly, unheavenly music,
only one gesture somewhere behind the mirror is enough
and I cease to exist, I fall, I dissolve completely.

So God, who rules over everything,
except for his God, is probably dying without sorrow,
under the pressure of dimensions which grew away from him,
pain, come back, he says, come back, love,
and then his weeping starts
and we have spring here, for a little while.
Eternal is the moment and we are made of moments.
Eternal is God and we are lost objects
from his pockets, come back, he says,
he looks under the table, where did it roll,
he asks himself sadly, that key from a girl's heart?
Since God is longing for that, let's celebrate his passion,
he walks into the orphaned bedroom,
and lies down and puts his face in the pillows,
but he doesn't have any tears. And we have to cry.
Not only the stars are his lovers.
Even you are his lover, oh earth,
I am ashamed, I don't know how to name you.
I say Beautiful, Deep and Steady,
but it's much too little. I'd like to read the verses
which an angel once wrote in the dusk
about your youthfulness: you, where curves come together.
Did he sing well? Come back, come back, earth!
Ah, here you are, called in from all sides,
just let me touch, let me breathe once
and you'll cease to exist. Thank you, things,
even for this much. I owe you thanks. You have my gratitude.

And you, who have no more weight than receding dimensions,
you won't appear? You aren't made of the same material as we are?
Who created you? Who created you if not me?
Ah, I know—God did. But He didn't love you
like I do.

Why fret about it? Let's be silent now.
Let the phrase of love, broken in half,
be like a forest which was cut down overnight,
and animals, in the morning, when they came to the well,
burned in the light which was too abundant,
let the phrase of love have at least one branch
in exchange for all the clearings —
one, just one, one single branch,
and let that branch bloom one more time.

THE LAST POEM

Darkness stares from everywhere and no one's here.
Now all is as it was. — Suddenly
when I look crookedly around again, it's clear
my burning heart has turned to freezing me.

I hold my head in my hand. I keep weeping. Just
the same, no screams escape my throat but, at most, a kind
of shade — the shadow of a past voice like a meadow with a crust
of frost, the shade I was made to unwind.

—Over the hill, the river, the acrid heather, day after day
at first he persevered. Now he's untricked, forced to understand
in what kind of catacombs his future's been bricked away.
He longs for a peach like a child with a peach in his hand,

God, do you know how longing is? how the soul can long
for endless tenderness which all of a sudden burns low
and he is guilty!
                             —I am guilty for the nice aroma, the wrong
fragrance, for the vain longing for my father, I know,
for verses, yes, for love that's lost to me,
for shame, for silence and a land full of those who yearn
to be without pain, for heaven, for God who shortened my days
and gave me a dead paradise in return —

and still! Do you believe me? In places I won't try to mention,
deep in my wounds, I keep finding a country, a small nation
of little songs to which only winter pays attention,
I ask and ask these songs for information!

A SMALL ELEGY

My friends have left. Far away, my darling is asleep.
Outside, it's as dark as pitch.
I'm saying words to myself, words that are white
in the lamplight and when I'm half-asleep I begin
to think about my mother. Autumnal recollection.
Really, under the cover of winter, it's as if I know
everything—even what my mother is doing now.
She's at home, in the kitchen. She has a small child's stove
toward which the wooden rocking horse can trot,
she has a small child's stove, the sort nobody uses today, but
she basks in its heat. Mother. My diminutive mom.
She sits quietly, hands folded, and thinks about
my father, who died years ago.
And then she is skinning fruit for me. I am in
the room. Sitting right next to her. You've got to see us,
God, you bully, who took so much. How
dark it is outside! What was I going to say?
Oh, yes, now I remember. Because
of all those hours I slept soundly, through calm
nights, because of all the loved ones who are deep
in dreams—now, when everything's running short,
I can't stand being here by myself. The lamplight's too strong.
I am sowing grain on the headland.
I will not live long.

אין זה כי אם בית אלהים וזה שער השמים

RILKE'S EARLY CONTACTS WITH CZECH AND JEWISH PRAGUE

Daria A. Rothe
University of Michigan

Although the Rilke literature abounds with publication by or about Rilke's many acquaintances and friends, his relationship with Valerie von David-Rhonfeld has been largely ignored. Carl Sieber's biography of the young Rilke makes hostile and inaccurate remarks about Valerie and finally dismisses the whole relationship as a silly romantic involvement.[1] Peter Demetz in his book *Rilkes Prager Jahre* sees Valerie as a "mother substitute" for Rilke and echoes Sieber by saying that for her, Rilke only "provided an amusing flirtation."[2] Finally, Angelloz challenged Sieber's evaluation of the relationship and expressed the fact that Sieber minimized its significance.[3] It is, however, the opinion of Carl Sieber, who was Rilke's son-in-law as well as director of the Rilke archive, which has prevailed.

Valerie von David-Rhonfeld was far more than a romantic involvement; she played an important role in the life of the young poet. Her family's house provided a refuge for Rilke from his "exile," as he called his room at his aunt's, Gabriele von Kutschera. Valerie was also the benefactor who financed the publication of Rilke's first book of poems, *Leben und Lieder*. It was through her that Rilke became introduced to the Prague of the Czechs and the Jews mirrored in *Larenopfer*. Since Valerie was the niece of Julius Zeyer, a Czech poet with great admiration for Russia, Rilke also became exposed to a peculiar view of Russia held by the Pan-Slavs and shared by Julius Zeyer. This view strongly influenced Rilke's perception of Russia and is very much in evidence in his first major poetic achievement *Das Stunden-Buch*.

The letters from Rilke to Valerie von David-Rhonfeld are valuable documents which illustrate many interesting aspects of the young poet, some already known from other sources, others not previously looked at. The history of this correspondence is a fascinating story in itself.[4] The 130 letters span a three year period from January 4, 1893 to December 1895 (excluding a note written in June 1896). They contain 85 poems, or more accurately, rhymed verses of various lengths. Some are no more than four lines long, others as long as two pages. They do not comprise the complete correspondence since by her own admission to Carl Hirschfeld, Valerie destroyed many of the letters. In 1927, the year she sold the correspondence, Leppin published Rilke's letter to Valerie written on the eve of his nineteenth birthday as well as a poem sent to her at another time.[5] Excerpts from Valerie's letters to the purchaser of the Rilke correspondence were published by C. Hirschfeld in 1929.[6] Neither Leppin nor Hirschfeld dealt with the larger ramifications of the relationship.

Rilke was seventeen when he met Valerie who was a year older than he. His letters to her are love letters and as such are often repetitive and tedious to an outsider. Many were dashed off by Rilke during free moments while waiting for his tutors to arrive. Some are reflections on the day's activities. Others are notes which set a date for a meeting with Valerie and contain extravagant assurances of his eternal love for her. Quite often they are letters of apology in which he blames his "nerves" for his bad behavior. He frequently broods about death and at times threatens suicide. Generally, Rilke's letters to Valerie show him to be a highly undisciplined, emotionally unstable, difficult, young man.[7] His letters also indicate that Rilke's daily schedule was very demanding. He studied, wrote poems, dramas and short stories, corresponded with various publishers to get it all into print, dashed notes and letters off to Valerie, carefully arranging his time so that he could visit her in the early evening.

His letters to her support Rilke's claim that his life was indeed very difficult. His parents had separated by the time Rilke returned to Prague from Linz and neither of them appeared to show much interest in their son. Although his father was living in Prague, René lived with his father's sister, Gabriele. The Rhonfeld house offered Rilke a kind of refuge from his own bleak existence and provided a substitute family life. He was often a guest there and celebrated holidays as well as the completion of examinations at Valerie's. At the end of one term he wrote: "I have not yet told the outcome of my examination to the noble lady Phia. She will surely have no time to think of such trifles." He makes sarcastic remarks about his mother, the "gifted, clever lady in black," who was living in Karlsbad at the time, intent on impressing the local society.

In another letter Rilke writes that since the examinations are over he can devote more time to Valerie. Referring to himself in the third person he says: "But, the whole victory came about only through you. If you were not his Vally he would have given up these studies long before the examination—but now he gives you his word to work just as hard for the next two short years...."

Valerie's parents seemed to be precisely what his parents were not. David von Rhonfeld was a successful officer in the Austrian army while the army career of Rilke's father ended in humiliating failure. From what we gather from his letters to Valerie as well as a poem dedicated to her on her names day, Julia Rhonfeld was considered by Rilke to be an ideal wife and mother. He expresses his admiration for Valerie's mother in various eloquent terms and calls her "the most beautiful image of the noble German woman." This stands in violent contrast to the expressions used in describing his own mother for whom he felt great resentment, even hate.[8]

Vally was also the favorite niece of Julius Zeyer, a Czech poet through whom Rilke became introduced to a Slavic world he had not previously known. Until then Rilke had taken no notice of the Czechs. In his experience they comprised the lower classes of society. The Rhonfelds exemplified a situation which Rilke's keen sense of class consciousness could not ignore. They were a highly respectable officer's family who spoke German at home, but had a family member who chose to write in Czech only. Furthermore the mother of Julius Zeyer, that exotic individual who travelled all over the world bringing souvenirs from wherever he went, was buried in the Old Jewish Cemetery at Zižkow. Eleonore Zeyer's laces, which Valerie had inherited from her grandmother, helped cover the publication costs of *Leben und Lieder*.[9] Although she died in 1881 and Rilke could not have known her, her memory exerted great influence on Valerie and Rilke.[10] Rilke's letters to Valerie make repeated references to that effect. He wrote a poetic tribute to Eleonore Zeyer, and referred to her as "our talisman." Since she was chosen by René and Valerie as a spiritual guardian of their love, they often visited her grave. There are several references to the cemetery in the correspondence. In one instance it provides the setting for a love poem. The poem carries the postscript: "in the old Jewish Cemetery. Zizkov. Easter 1893." A subsequent letter in which Rilke speaks of his love for Valerie refers to the cemetery. He writes: "My every heartbeat belongs to you. The first moment of my happiness—indeed my life—begins there in the Jewish Cemetery." Shortly before Valerie left Prague for the summer holiday in Kamnitz and just before Rilke was to take his final examinations for the "Matura," he wrote: "Well, today we have taken our farewell greetings to you—good grandmother. May she let me successfully overcome this last hurdle." The evening after the examinations he sent a telegram followed by the note: "It is late at night. Only a couple of words. Thanks! Thanks! Everything went well, very well, with distinction, it's over. Thanks to you, your dear grandmother, the talisman. Thanks! The telegram will arrive before this. More tomorrow by letter. Millions of kisses, your totally devoted Hidi."

Valerie's world was far more exotic and cosmopolitan than Rilke's, and he must have been quite impressed by it. The remarks in his letter about his own relatives indicate that he thought them to be petty and narrow-minded. For example, he describes with great sarcasm his aunt's reaction to a Czech demonstration. While he and his aunt were sitting at dinner one evening a mob of people, singing anti-German songs rushed by the house on the way to Charles Square. "You can imagine my aunt," he writes to Valerie. "Good heavens, I hope they don't smash any of my windows. One pane costs 3.80 Fl. The fright and excitement forced her to retire to her bed where she could have sweet dreams about smashed window panes and empty wallets."

During the latter part of 1893 Czech words begin to be used by Rilke in his correspondence with Valerie. He calls her his "panička," his "Valička," and makes references to Czech as "the native, beautiful language" as well as "the tones of the great nation." Although Rilke used Czech words incorrectly, as L. Matejka points out, the fact that he used them at all illustrates

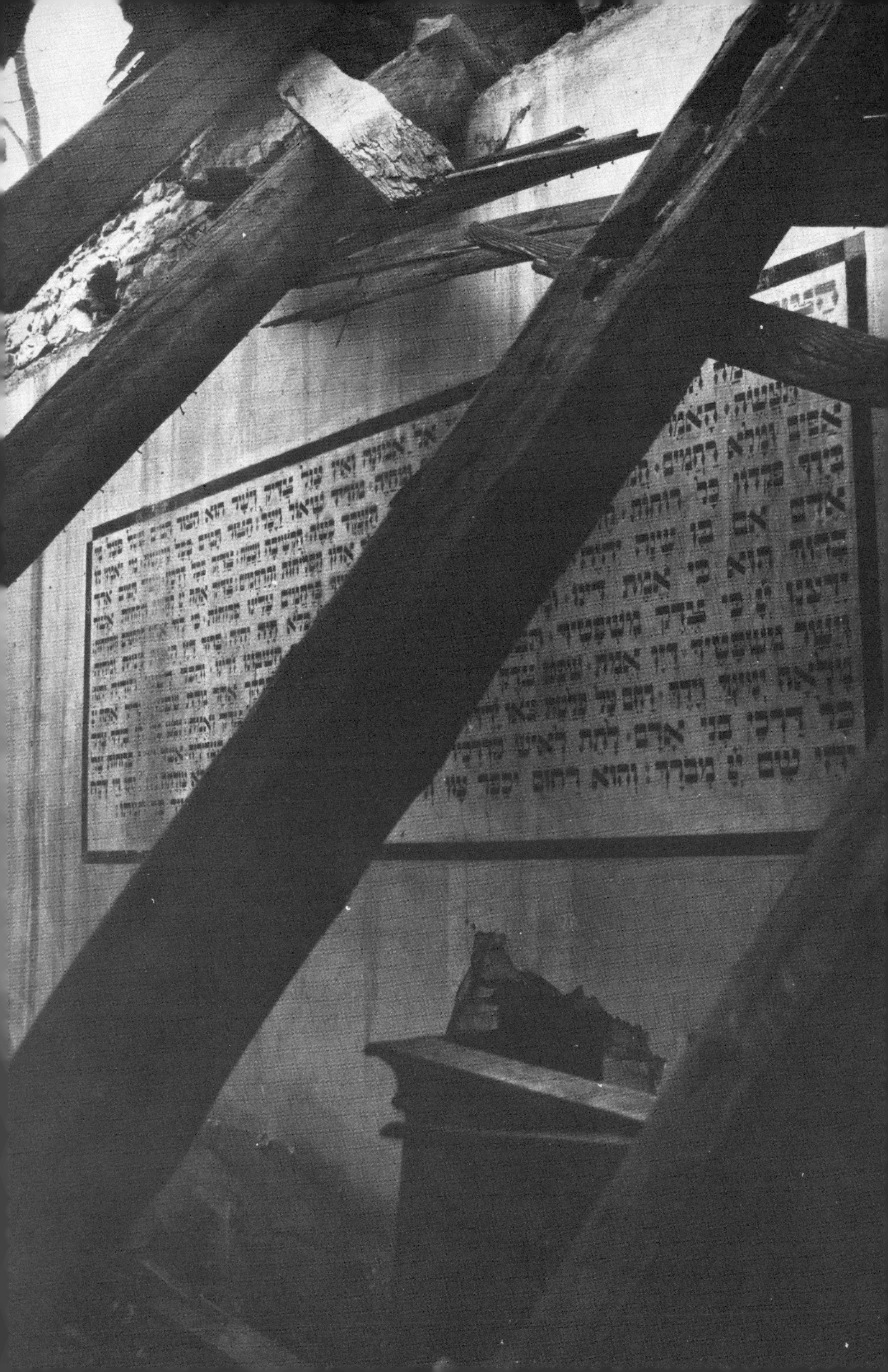

his desire to become an even more intimate part of Valerie's world.[11] Once Rilke's relationship with Valerie began to show signs of estrangement, he no longer used Czech. The interest in Czechs and the Czech language is directly reflected in *Larenopfer*. It is interesting to note that the poems comprising *Leben und Lieder*, written before Rilke know Valerie, are quite simple in syntax and do not contain any Czech words or other "foreign" and exotic elements found in *Larenopfer*, Rilke's second volume of poems. The cover of *Larenopfer* was designed by Valerie and the poems were published at Christmas 1895. Rilke used Czech in his *Larenopfer* to achieve an exotic effect, for his readers were, after all, German, not Czech. And as L. Matejka points out, "The Czech language which Rilke uses has... an especial peculiarity, it recommends itself not so much to a reader who knows Czech as to one who does not."[12] The exotic effect that Rilke was trying to achieve was recognized as such by critics.[13] While the critics may have been right, it was precisely their peculiarity which set Rilke's poems apart. Without it they would have attracted less attention than they did.

It is difficult to read *Larenopfer* without thinking of them as a poetic Baedeker of Prague and being reminded of Platen's "Sonette aus Venedig." This is no coincidence, for Platen happened to be Rilke's literary hero of the moment.[14] While Platen's sonnets are considerably more complex than Rilke's verses in *Larenopfer*, they are similar in mood and tone. Platen's poems present the glory that once was Venice. Similarly Rilke's Prague is also a city of ancient greatness. In *Larenopfer* Rilke saw an opportunity to immortalize his native city. He also attempted to present Prague not only as a German city but tried to include its Czech and Jewish components. He versified an anecdote about the legendary Rabbi Loew.[15] He also included poetic tributes to Jaroslav Vrchlický, Julius Zeyer and Kajetan Tyl.[16] Rilke's poem on Tyl contains the title words from the song written by him "Kde domov muj." These words are repeated in "Das Heimatlied," the last poem in *Larenopfer*.[17] The phrase "Kde domov muj" appears as a statement in both poems mentioned, for Kajetan Tyl as well as the Czech girl in "Das Heimatlied" knew where their homeland was. For Rilke, however, the statement becomes a question, "Where is my home?" It is a question which raised a rather complex problem. Rilke was a German poet living in a city that was not only German, but Czech and Jewish as well. The problem of where he belonged was a vital factor in his poetic development as well as in his personal life. It was also a problem keenly felt by two other German poets of Prague, Frank Kafka and Franz Werfel.

Through Valerie, Rilke tried to come closer to both Czech and Jewish aspects of Prague. While the Czech words and phrases Rilke used in *Larenopfer* give it an aura of familiarity with the Slavic component of the city, one detects a self consciousness and patronizing attitude on Rilke's part which ultimately flawed the attempt. This is vividly illustrated by "Das Heimatlied." In this poem a Czech girl, asked to sing her native song, sings "Kde domov muj." This particular song already had a special significance

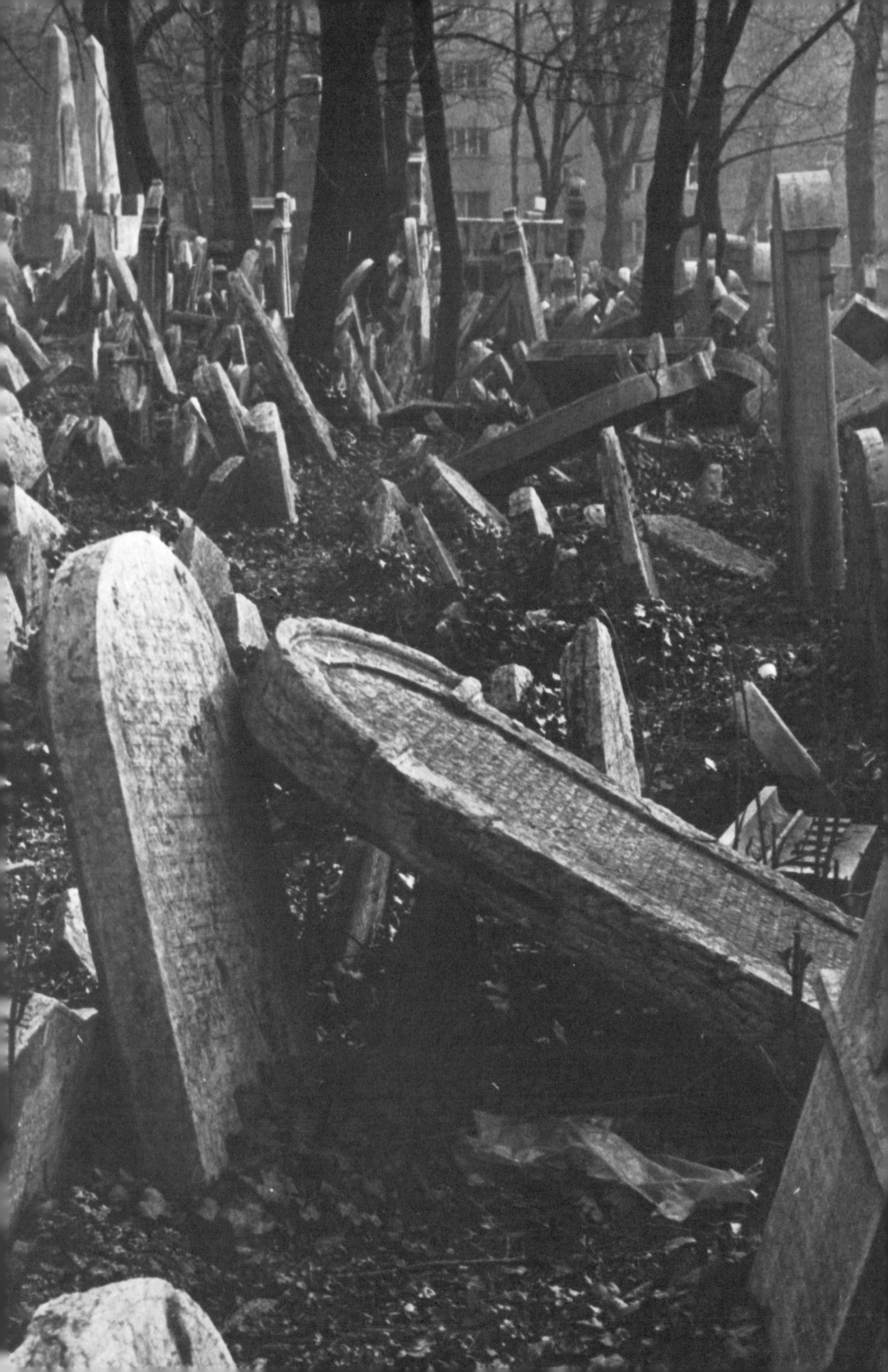

for the Czechs. Later it became the Czech national anthem. The Tyl exhibition, opened in 1895, was boycotted by most Prague Germans. While on the one hand Rilke went to the exhibition as his statement beneath the title of the poem dedicated to Tyl indicates, on the other hand he showed appalling insensitivity to the meaning of Tyl's song. In the poem "Das Heimatlied," Rilke's listener gives the Czech girl a copper coin when she finishes her song. The girl, with tears in her eyes, kisses his hand in gratitude.

Thus Rilke's attempt to come closer to the Czechs is reduced to a patronizing, theatrical gesture. The song is nothing more than a sentimental folk song. Its effect is similar to "Volksweise," another poem in *Larenopfer*.[18] There, the song "steals into the heart" of the poet moving him to sadness.[19] The melancholy mood that pervades *Larenopfer* reflects Rilke's feelings about Prague. He wrote to Valerie from the Baltic Sea resort Misdroy on August 31, 1985: ". . . the forest and sea have cast their magic nets about me and it is very difficult for me to tear myself away. I am afraid of Prague and her coal-blackened, dusty streets. . . ." The dread of Prague is also characteristic of Kafka's and Werfel's attitude toward their city, as Heinz Politzer points out.

Politzer writes that the German Prague was a community which many of its members feared and loathed and that precisely the most sensitive and creative of her offspring saw their city as being condemned to death.[20] He refers to the German Prague, isolated and surrounded by a non-German speaking population, an oppressive place that Rilke had to leave. But curiously enough this image of Prague was very similar to Zeyer's vision of the city. The Czech Prague as seen by Julius Zeyer was not a happy place. Zeyer saw Prague as a humiliated, grieving, tragic beauty. In the few words written by him in German, he exclaims: "Poor Prague. . . you pale, dethroned queen with your torn purple and your broken diadem."[21] It was a city ruled by Vienna and for that reason Zeyer as well as many other Czech writers of his time turned to Russia for inspiration. In doing so they were following a tradition begun by the Czech Romantics, who saw Russia "surrounded by an ideological halo."[22]

Svatopluk Čech as well as Julius Zeyer had travelled to Russia and their literary works were influenced by that experience. Zeyer went to Russia four times. The first trip was in 1873, the last in 1899. During his first stay in St. Petersburg he was employed as a reader to Prime Golicyn; later he was a tutor to Count Valuev, a minister in the Czar's government. Zeyer translated "Slovo o Polku Igoreve" into Czech in 1882; Rilke was to translate the "Song of Igor" into German in 1904. Zeyer's most authentic writing about Russia, according to M. Součková, was "Alexěi clověk boží" (Alexei, man of God) written in 1899. At the beginning of the story Zeyer describes a voyage on the Dniepr and a group of crippled beggars called "kaleki perexožii."[23] He also wrote *Tri legendy o krucufixu* (Three legends about the crucifix) in 1895 and gave a copy of it to Rilke.[24] Rilke began writing his "Christus Visionen" in 1896. Zeyer's primarily autobiographical work *Dům u tonoucí hvězdy* (The house of the drowning star) set in Paris, was published in book form in 1897. Gabriela Ducháčková has shown some very interesting parallels between this work and Rilke's *Malte Laurids Brigge*. [25]

Rilke told Ottilie Malybrock-Stieler, Zeyer's German translator, that he met Zeyer at Valerie's house in October 1895. At that time Rilke read to him poems from the *Larenopfer* manuscript and felt very pleased at the reception his work received from Zeyer.[26] Although the actual meeting between Zeyer and Rilke did not take place until 1895, the presence of the man made itself felt much earlier. Already in 1894, Rilke wrote a rhymed account of the return of Valerie's exotic uncle from a trip to Japan with gifts for the whole family, including a Japanese picture book for "little Vally." The image of Julius Zeyer, poet, world traveller, and dandy no doubt had an impact on the impressionable young Rilke, who wanted so desperately to be noticed, both in and out of print. The strange sight of Rilke solemnly walking in the Graben in Prague, an iris in his hand, speaks for itself.[27] Yet it was not so much the eccentricity of the man, but rather Zeyer's view of Russia which proved vital in Rilke's poetic development.

At the end of 1895 there was a break in the relationship between Rilke and Valerie. Already after his return from Misdroy in August 1895, there is a change in the tone of the letters, the hyperbole is muted, the extravagance gone. In a letter which begins with a simple "My dear Vally," Rilke writes: "I believe—we should not get too used to one another—that is not good." Although the sentence is followed by the reassurance, "I do care for you so much" and is signed by "your old, old Rene," it is quite obvious that this was no longer true. The engagement was broken off and in a note to Valerie, Rilke thanks her for "the gift of freedom," telling her that she was a "bright comet in his dark life." Then, reminiscent of Lou Salome's "letzter Zuruf" letter to Rilke, he adds: "And if you ever need a friend, then call. No one can be more of a friend to you than René." Unlike Rilke, Valerie did not call. She lived in Prague to the end of her life, alone, forgotten and obviously bitter about her relationship with Rilke. [28]

In the fall of 1895 Rilke enrolled at the German University of Prague. [29] There, he came under the influence of August Sauer, who was Rilke's professor of German Literature and later became his friend and mentor. August Sauer was also the leading force in the "Gesellschaft zur Förderung deutsche Wissenschaft, Kunst und Literatur in Böhmen" founded in 1891. Ten years later the society began to publish a journal entitled *Deutsche Arbeit*. In the first issue of the journal three Rilke poems were published.[30] A later issue printed "Der Panther" as well as the original version of "Die Weise von Liebe und Tod des Cornets Otto Rilke."[31] Rilke also received financial support from the society, as the published minutes of one of its meetings indicate. [32] Rilke's book *Worpswede* is favorably reviewed in the journal. *Das Buch der Bilder* is given a glowing review by Wilhelm von Scholz who states that in his opinion Rilke is the finest, most sensitive, most musically lyrical living poet. [33]

The introductory statement by the editors of the journal states that the intent of the publication was not to engage in political discussions but to deal only with "neglected sociological, economic and literary matters." It did not work out that way in practice, however. In articles which could be categorized as "sociological or economic" the policies of the Austrian government are severely criticized. The tone that permeates these articles is characterized by frustration and indignation that the Germans in Bohemia have been sold out by the government in Vienna. The sentiments are decidedly pro-German in the admiration of the Reich and its chancellor while there is nothing but condemnation for the Austrian Prime Minister, Count Badeni. [34] The journal obviously reflected the opinion of the society that founded it. Rilke's exposure to that group may have played a decisive role in his decision to leave Prague not for Vienna, a flourishing literary center at the time, but for Munich and later Berlin.

In 1896 Rilke came to Munich. Although he left Prague and Valerie, the sentimental attachment for the Slavs remained, as did his Messianic image of Russia. Thus Russia was not a sudden revelation to Rilke brought about by his association with Lou Andreas-Salome and their travels together. Rather, his view of Russia formulated earlier in Prague very strongly influenced his perception of the country during his two trips to Russia. The enthusiasm and the fervor of the zealot, characteristic of Rilke's view of Russia, was not shared by his travelling companion. Although Lou Andreas-Salome was also carried away by the Russian experience, her view of Russia lacked the Messianic component which was so vital to Rilke and the Pan Slavs.

While Rilke's Russia contained many geographic as well as historical details it was primarily an imaginary country full of vagueness and symbolic implications which made it suitable to become Rilke's mythical "homeland." There was a breadth and energy about it that was the very antithesis of Prague. Russia had a Messianic dream which had long ago faded in the cynical and profane West. It was a country which corresponded to Rilke's spiritual and emotional needs. It unlocked something in his creative personality and mirrored his own "spiritual landscape." He wrote to Helene Woronin: "I feel that the Russian things provide the best images and names for my personal feelings and expressions." [35] Rilke went to Russia at a critical time in his poetic development, a time when his great poetic gift was yet a promise. The Russia he perceived was a land which believed in its future greatness. The faith in Russia's future became bound up with Rilke's faith in his own poetic future. Russia became his talisman. At one point during his stay in Worpswede he told Clara Rilke that he no longer needed Russia. However, time and again he was to come back to its memory during his less confident days in Worpswede (1901), in Paris (1903) and in Rome (1904). Although with time, the need for the talisman diminished, the sentimental link remained to the end of his life.[36] The exile from Prague had resolved the question which "Kde domov muj" raised. Rilke, the non-Czech, non-Austrian, non-German, found his mythical homeland.

NOTES

[1] Carl Sieber, *René Rilke: Die Jugend Rainer Maria Rilkes* (Leipzig: Insel Verlag, 1932), p. 123. "Vally David Rhonfeld, wesenlich älter als Rene, war eine Spielerin mit dem Feuer, mit der Liebe,. . . Sie hielt ihn wohl zur Arbeit an durch das Vesprechen in weiter Ferne winkender grösserer Gunstbezeigungen, aber was war das gegen die Hilfe zum Positiven, die sie ihm als liebende Frau hätte geben können." To imply that Valerie should have married the nineteen-year-old Rilke, a student preparing for his "Matura," whose studies as well as his entire existence was supported by the generosity of an uncle, shows Sieber's total bias in the situation. It is to Valerie's credit to have realized that Rilke needed to be free of Prague and free of her, as she states in a comment to the letters. Sieber also avoids mentioning any of the quite negative comments about his relatives, particularly his mother, which Rilke makes in the letters to Valerie.

[2] Peter Demetz, *René Rilkes Prager Jahre* (Düsseldorf: Eugen Diederichs Verlag, 1953), p. 45. "Dennoch war René für Valerie nur ein unterhaltsamer Flirt, eine Kulisse mehr für ihre provinzielle Nachahmung der Boheme. Sie spielte sich rasch in die Rolle der Muse. . . . Valerie bedeutet René mehr: sie erschien ihm als jene Wesen, das ihm das Dunkel und die ferne Wärme der Mutter wiedergab; die war die erste Frau, die er nach dem Ersatz der Vergangenheit suchend, zu seiner neuen Mutter erhob. . . ."

[3] J.-F. Angelloz, *Rainer Maria Rilke Leben und Werk*, trans. Alfred Kuoni (Zürich: Arche Verlag, 1955), p. 35. "Sieber verkleinert sie (Rilkes erste Liebe) zum Range einer blossen Liebelei, die den Dichter in keiner Weise gefordert und inspiriert habe; . . ."

[4] Prior to the sale of her Rilke letters, Valerie von David-Rhonfeld made copies of them which she presented to the city of Prague. The originals were in the Preussische Landesbibliothek in Berlin from which they later disappeared. The copies were kept in the City Archives of Prague, housed in the Prague City Hall. During the last days of World War II, the city hall was shelled by the retreating German Army. While the building survived, its contents were destroyed by the fire. However, before Valerie's handcopied letters were destroyed, they were in turn copied by a young woman named Dida Čepek-Pistorius. These copies were preserved, and are itoday in the possession of Prof. Ladislav Matejka. They correspond with all the available published excerpts of the originals and are quoted in this paper in English translation.

[5] Paul Leppin, "Der neunzehnjährige Rilke," *Die Literatur*, 29 Jg., 1926/27 pp. 630-34.

[6] Carl Hirschfeld, "Die Erinnerungen Valery von David-Rhonfelds," *Die Horen* 8 (Berlin 1928-29) pp. 714-20.

[7] Health considerations were the reason for Rilke's trip to Munich in 1894, as well as his stay at the sea resort Misdroy in 1895. He wrote to Valerie that his "poor nerves" needed rest and that his physician ordered the trips.

[8] In one of the less violent outbursts against his mother, he wrote that his ex-mother should be locked up in a lunatic asylum.

[9] The volume of poems was published at Christmas 1894. It had a gold fleur de lys on its cover and bore the inscription "Vally von R. . . . zu eigen."

[10] Peter Demetz writes about Eleonore Zeyer as if she were still living when Rilke came to know Valerie.

[11] Ladislav Matejka, "R. M. Rilke and the Czech Language," *The American Slavonic and East European Review* 13 (December 1954), pp. 589-96.

[12] Ibid. p. 593.

[13] Ibid. p. 592. Carl Credner wrote in *Gesellschaft*: "In the struggle to say something new and ingenious, Rilke frequently allows himself to be led astray for the sake of powerful images and rhymes which prejudice the enjoyment of the verses." Stauf von der March wrote in the same journal: "The numerous affectedly ingenious twists and the juggling with rhymes are quite inexcusable; even more discordant is the effect of the forced introduction of Czech words, indeed of whole phrases."

[14] Rilke was greatly impressed by Platen. On March 21, 1895 he dedicated a sonnet to Platen (Sämtliche Werke, Vol. III p. 501) and on the same day he also wrote a ghasel (Sämtliche Werke, Vol. III pp. 500-501).

[15] *Rainer Maria Rilke Sämtliche Werke*, Vol. I. Insel Verlag 1962. pp. 61-64.

[16] Ibid. p. 20, pp. 35-36, pp. 38-39.

[17] Ibid. pp. 68-69.

[18] Ibid. p. 39.

[19] Heinz Politzer, "Dieses Mütterchen hat Krallen," *Literatur und Kritik* 18 (February 1974): 21. Prof. Politzer comments on the first stanza of "Volksweise": "Aber selbst die Innigkeit dieser Strophe, die jenem Volkslied abgewonnen scheint, von dem sie singt, ist nicht ohne falschenZwischenton. Der deutsche Dichter *erlaubt* es der böhmischen Volksweise, sein Herz zu rühren."

[20] Ibid. p. 19.

[21] Robert B. Pynsent, *Julius Zeyer: The Path to Decadence* (The Hague: Mouton & Co., 1973), p. 50.

[22] Milada Součková, *A Literary Satellite: Czechoslovak-Russian Literary Relations* (Chicago: U. of Chicago Press, 1970), p. 10. Milada Souckova writes: "During the 19th century a trip to Russia often meant more than any other travel experience to a Czech... For him, Russia had been surrounded by an ideological halo since the time of the Czech literary renaissance...."

[23] Ibid. p. 15.

[24] Ingeborg Schnack, *Rainer Maria Rilke: Chronik seines Lebens und seines Werkes*, 2 vols. (Frankfurt: Insel Verlag, 1975), 1: 39.

[25] Gabriela Ducháčková, "Rilkes 'Aufzeichnungen des Malte Laurids Brigge' und Zeyers Prosa 'Dům U Tonoucí Hvézdy' " ("Das Haus Zum ertrinkenden Stern") in *Rilke Studien zu Werk und Wirkungsgeschichte* (Berlin: Aufbau Verlag, 1976), pp. 177-96.

[26] Schnack p. 39.

[27] Angelloz pp. 43-44. Angelloz quotes Hugo Steiner-Prag who recalled the following image of Rilke in 1896: "... Durch das Gewühl der Menschen auf dem Graben schreitet gelassen ein junger Mensch, gekleidet in einem schwarzen, altväterischen Gehrock, eine schwarze Binde umschlingt seinen unmodischen Kragen, er trägt einen breiten schwarzen Hut. In der Hand aber hält dieser Seltsame eine farbige Blüte, eine langstielige Iris."

[28] Hirschfeld, p. 720. Valerie told Carl Hirschfeld that her passion for Rilke cost her dearly: "Die Leidenschaft für Rene bezahlte ich mit meinem Lebensgluck,..."

[29] Since 1882 there were actually two universities in Prague, one German, the other Czech. The establishment of the Czech branch of the Charles University was not looked upon with favor by many Prague Germans.

[30] *Deutsche Arbeit: Monatschrift für das geistige Leben der Deutschen in Böhmen* I (1901 1902), p. 5, pp. 19-21. "Auf der Leinseite" (p. 5) is a poem previously published in *Larenopfer*. "Gedicht" (pp. 19-20) later becomes "Der Schauende" in *Das Buch der Bilder*. "Abend" (p. 21) undergoes minor changes and becomes "Der Lesende" in *Das Buch der Bilder*.

[31] "Der Panther" appeared in *Deutsche Arbeit* II (1902-1903), p. 985. "Cornet" was published in *Deutsche Arbeit* III, pp. 59-65.

[32] *Deutsche Arbeit* II (1902-1903), p. 835.

[33] Ibid. p. 247.

[34] Count Casimir Badeni was dismissed from his post in 1897. One of the main factors leading to his dismissal was his "pro-Czech" policy in Bohemia.

[35] V. Boutchik, E. L. Stahl and S. Mitchell, "Texts of R. M. Rilke's Letters to Helene," *Oxford Slavonic Papers*, 9 (1960): 146-164. Helene Woronin was a young Russia whom Rilke met in Viareggio in 1898. Rilke corresponded with her from 1898 until 1899 and visited her in St. Petersburg during his first trip to Russia. His letters

to her provide us with vital information about his trip and its effect on him. In 1925 while living in Paris, Rilke "found" Helene again. She and her husband were émigrés living in Paris. Rilke visited her and wrote three letters to her in 1925.

[36] This was particularly evident during his stay in Paris in 1925. He saw many of his old Russian friends and acquaintances who were émigrés living in Paris. He also made new contacts. Boris Pasternak wrote to Rilke about his friend Marina Cvetaeva, then living in Paris. While their meeting in Paris did not come about, Rilke corresponded with her from Switzerland. Rilke's secretary at Valmont was a young woman, Genia Černosvitova, an émigré from Russia.

René Maria Rilke

TO ELEONORE ZEYER

I've not known the one who grants you protection —
Whose ties to you, even *there*, are as they were
But before I could ascertain her power,
I felt a sacred veneration for her
And a very special kind of affection.

Now it's clear to me why I look to and thank
The image of that dear one under death's lease.
When sharp dangers to you began to increase,
She strongly bid dark calamity to cease
In a warning dream — woman of noblest rank!

It wasn't enough for her, all she had done
On earth to unfold her love, blessedly wide.
Her mighty spirit continues to guide
Your fate from there. So, with honor undenied,
Let us follow the path of the holy one.

I almost pray to her: look, with how whole
A heart I thank the being who gave me you.
By saving your life, she saved my life too.
So on that way she shows us, let's continue
To strive. Believe me, it leads to the goal.

Translated by Lyn Coffin

KAFKA'S MILENA AS REMEMBERED BY HER DAUGHTER JANA

Jana Černá

Not until the end of the war, a year after Milena's death, could I believe that she was really dead. I was informed about it by one of the Ravensbrück women who was with her almost to the end. She wrote me a long letter about Mama's stay in the camp. It was filled with descriptions of complex relationships which were quite incomprehensible to me, and of names which, even at that time meant nothing at all to me. A letter which, by itself, was scarcely enough to enable me to grasp the simple and, for me, difficult to comprehend, fact that Milena was gone.

But a few days later she came to visit me and brought me a present: one of Milena's teeth. Mama had given it to her when she was pulling her teeth out one after another as her gums deteriorated.

I saw Milena for the last time in an office of the Gestapo in Peček Palace. And later I also saw a picture of her—a drawing by a Polish woman from Ravensbrück. But Milena alive—never again.

Until now. Before me on the table lies a piece of her body, a fragment of her smile, a part of her mouth which used to speak to me.

The explanation which accompanied the tooth was very simple: "That is all that has remained of Milena. I wanted to do something nice for you so I brought it to you."

This former prisonmate of Milena's is one of the best people I know. But even the best people are given a certain portion of genuine cruelty. Or, to put it more precisely, even the best people are sometimes forced to express all the cruelty of reality. I think that, speaking of Milena, no one else ever managed to do it with such terrifying and laconic precision. In any case, that was the first evidence of Mama's death which I couldn't refute.

Perhaps it is possible to live with an urn containing the ashes of a person who was close to us, a body which has altered its substance and in no way resembles the living person it previously was. I don't know. But I do know that it is impossible to live with a fragment of a body which is irrevocably dead. To touch an existing piece of a non-existing creature.

I know it because I tried in vain to do it. I couldn't live with it and I couldn't tear myself away from it. I didn't have the nerve to throw out

---

Excerpts from the book *Addressee; Milena Jesenská* by Jana Černá. The book appeared in Prague in 1969, in an edition of 1000 copies, but it reached only a few readers. We are printing excerpts from it in memory of its gifted author, Milena's daughter Jana, who died in a traffic accident early in 1981.

that irreplaceable relic, nor could I decide to give it away to anyone. But because I don't have Milena's consciousness, which could not be fooled, my faulty memory finally, mercifully came to my assistance. I put the tooth away somewhere and couldn't find it any more.

So I think that the ability to forget is one of the inalienable rights of man, one of the freedoms which can not be limited or taken away, and which each of us possesses. If a child had to remember everything it experienced before it finally came to terms with the world around it, the child would very likely be seriously neurotic at the age of five, at twelve it would be ripe for insanity, and at fifteen — for suicide. After all, even the little bit that a person retains in his memory is on the very limits of tolerability.

Forgetting the intolerable is equivalent to losing consciousness during unbearable pain. It is one of those small defenses which a person has both against the external world and against himself. And sometimes he damn well needs defenses against them both.

As far as I know, Milena never exercised these obviously useful privileges. She preserved in her memory every minute of her life with such clarity that it seemed as if her memory not only refused the relief of forgetfulness, but even at times constructed an ever more precise and clear image of the past. I think that this is one of the keys to her life: both its course and its conclusion.

When, after her death, I began to observe her in my memory, in statements by her friends and enemies, in articles, and in those few insignificant items which survived her, I discovered over and over what a burden that clear consiousness was for her. And at the same time what strength was concealed in it.

After her death I spoke to a number of people about her. Almost every one of them is convinced that he knew her well, and that it is proper to provide information about her. And that is really why I have decided, twenty-three years after her death and fifteen years after the first publication of Kafka's *Letters to Milena*, to write what I know about her.

No human life surrenders its secrets without a struggle, and an ordinary life of an ordinary person is actually impossible to examine. It is difficult enough for someone to bear witness concerning himself, and even more difficult for those around him to do it. Because I understand this very well, it was a long time before I could make up my mind to write anything about Milena. And even now I do not begin with the certainty that I will be able to say everything about her. But only with the certainty that so far no one who has tried to do it has succeeded.

It is amazing how the twentieth century of the Christian Era, a century known as the age of wisdom, enlightenment and the devil knows what else, has so much difficulty in coping with the naked truth. How difficult for its rationally beating heart to bear the thought that the lover of a famous man bore no resemblance to an angel, that even during her lifetime she was known as a person full of strange and incomprehensible contradictions, who could be understood only with difficulty, and who was not easy to get along with. (As though it is ever simple to live with someone, and particularly as if it is simple to live with a simple person.)

For this reason the majority of those who mentioned her in connection with Kafka attempted, at least a little bit, to idealize her or, in any case, not to mention certain facts which would too blatantly contradict her image as the angelic lover of a genius. It somewhat suggests the naive pictures of the Virgin Mary, sweet and pretty, blossoming and maidenly, where the mother of God has rosy cheeks and a sky-blue garment covering radiantly gleaming blonde hair. Such an attempt is just as misleading as those illustrations of Mary—but, like them, it also contains a bit of peculiar truth.

That is on the one hand. On the other hand looms the assumption that once Milena had been the great love of Franz Kafka, she was obliged to be a disciplined member of the party, and to demonstrate a readiness to indulge in all the errors which necessarily occurred in a certain period. In this way one could acknowledge the fact in order to be able to speak and write about her—at least in connection with Kafka. But she wasn't like that, and she showed no inclination to be.

Thus Milena Jesenská is depicted alternately as a traitor undermining morale in a concentration camp by asserting that Stalin's politics deprived many people of their freedom for political reasons, and as an inspired Czech patriot marching down Příkop Street or Ferdinand Street in Prague in a white robe preaching love for her country.

Basically, I think that for my readers Milena is important in two periods of her life. First, at the time when her union with Kafka began, ran its course, and ended. Although it wasn't a very long period of time, for both of them it was certainly an immensely important period. Secondly—when Milena left the Communist Party and stopped believing that the Soviet Union was, as it had seemed, the sole and genuine salvation not only of the working class, but also of world peace and order.

Neither period arose accidentally, (Indeed, very few things in human life arise accidentally, particularly when they are important things.) Each was preceded by a complicated development in Milena's character, her individual make-up, and her entire personality. Only because of that development and of everything that preceded the time when she first met with Franz Kafka as a writer, was she able to appreciate his worth and to be the first person who translated his literary works.

Gustina Fučiková, in an article in *Kulturní Tvorba*, stated that Milena should not be considered only as Kafka's girlfriend, but also as the person who doubted the role of the Communist Party and the Soviet Union. And that Franz Kafka's girlfriend can not be separated from the journalist in the years preceding the second World War.

Perhaps I may be forgiven if, on this point, I agree with Fučiková. Actually, it would be impossible to make such a separation. The person who recognized Kafka's greatness and understood the source of his eternal anxiety was the same person who, during the Stalin trials, was incapable of overcoming the fear she felt concerning events both on the inimical German side and on the side which was then ruled by I. V. Stalin.

I have often heard it said that in this way Milena weakened the force of resistance before and during the war. That at that time it was impossible simultaneously and in one breath to be against Germany and against whatever was in disarray in one's own ranks. This is possible and perhaps even true. But Milena was not a tactician. Milena was choleric. To wait until the battle was over and only then to cleanse the victorious side of its flaws simply never entered her mind, because it couldn't. It was not part of her world. She could heedlessly sacrifice a great deal for something which aroused her. But she seems never to have been able to keep a clear head when a beloved thing or person let her down. As far as I know Milena was genuinely passionate about the Soviet Union when she entered the Party. And as far as is generally known, that Soviet Union, ruled by I. V. Stalin, bloodily and evilly disenchanted those who passionately supported it. If I am mistaken—and how happy I would be to be mistaken—then the years until the Twentieth Party Congress (I won't mention the following years since they have no connection with Milena) were only a dream, and the revelations which were made are only a nightmare. But if I am not mistaken, I can't imagine from which position one can be angry at a person who, in her disappointment did not control herself, and who openly showed her bitterness.

Milena was born at the turn of the century, on August 10, 1896, in Prague. Her father, Dr. Jan Jesenský, was a professor at Prague Medical School, and a genuinely self-made man. And evidently that was not just a personal attribute but, so to speak, almost a hereditary trait. He was one of eight children, not one of whom was a failure. Three of them in one way or another managed to find a place in an anthology or textbook in their fields. Perhaps it is not entirely without interest that of the eight Jesenský children I, thanks to the natural selection of my grandfather and Milena, knew just those three who were successful. I got to know the rest of them only at grandfather's death, in his apartment filled with clocks and antiques, when they assured me that they were "your dear aunt" or "your dear uncle" whom I would certainly recall and to whom I would certainly give (from grandfather's estate, *in memoriam* and for all time) at least a piece of gold filling from the dead man's mouth, or else that painting on the wall where we are standing... (I didn't remember them, but I managed without their help to liquidate the estate myself in record time, and to this day I am told that I am just like my mother—but that's another story.)

Speaking of Milena's father, he was an eccentric in the classic sense of the word. All his life he was unable to adjust smoothly to his surroundings and vice versa.

He completed his studies under the most difficult circumstances and supported himself during those studies as best he could. He had perfect pitch, learned to play the violin, and in the evenings he used to play for the ears of ladies and gentlemen. In addition he gave lessons and even, they say—just like Milena in Vienna—carried trunks for rich people at the Prague railroad stations. Even among the poor he was poor, and he endured it much worse than he let on. He consoled himself and quieted his injured pride with the fact that he was a descendant of Jan Jesenius, the first professor of medicine at Charles University, who was executed with great fanfare in Old Town Square together with twenty Czech noblemen on June 21, 1621. But although this fact soothed his pride, it didn't get rid of the gleam on his shiny trousers or the weight of the trunks at the train stations.

When he had finished his studies he married Milena Hejzlarová, the daughter of a district school inspector, and her dowry enabled him to set up a private practice. As far as I know from Milena, both the inspector and his wife asked their son-in-law for at least a little gratitude for their daughter's property—assuming, I suppose, that he owed it to them. Well, he calmly remained indebted to them and never forgave his wife either the assistance or her parents. Stubbornly and sincerely in his heart he hated all of them with all the proletarian fury which he had accumulated in bars and train stations during his university years.

From a poor student, he later became a Prague dandy. His dressers were stuffed with an enormous amount of tailor-made clothers, and it was difficult enough simply to count the pairs of shoes he owned, let alone maintain them in good condition, which he categorically insisted on.

There was a time when he gambled wildly at cards and lost unbelievable sums of money. There were times when he had a whole series of lovers and romantic intrigues, one of which even resulted in the last duel ever fought in Prague. Although no one was killed, some blood was romantically shed. At the same time he worked with almost unimaginable zeal and tried to give his daughter an extremely puritanical upbringing. He was thin-skinned, proud, short-tempered, sentimental, fiercely healthy and immune to illness. He died two years after Milena at the age of seventy-five and, even on his death-bed, he still managed to wed a lover with whom he had lived for many years without marrying her, probably because only with the certainty of approaching death could he reconcile himself to the loss of freedom and to being married.

Milena's mother, Milena Hejzlarová, was a pretty, fragile and incurably ill creature, and she died when Milena was sixteen. For many long years before her death she was unable to walk. Milena and her father wheeled her about in a wheelchair and took turns at her bedside during the long, exhausting hours of the night. Until she was imprisoned, Milena would wake up every night at one o'clock, because that was when the invalid took her medicine, and her daughter, a child then, dared not fall asleep at her bedside at that hour.

Milena was not the only child born to Jan Jesenský and Milena Hejzlarová. She was about four years old when Mrs. Jesenská, even then anemic and not in the best of health, gave birth to a boy who was greeted with great hopes and was christened with the family name of Jan. But his mother, exhausted by childbirth and illness, had no energy left and was unable to nurse her son. Doctor Jesenský, filled with revulsion at anything that wasn't as fiercely strong and indestructible as he was, refused to obtain a wet-nurse for the baby.

"If my wife can't nurse the baby she can't have it," he supposedly said at the time, and he allowed the child to struggle along for several weeks with a sugar-tit and the sympathy of the servants, dependent on the moments when someone managed to break away from a household chore and moisten the baby's lips with the corner of a handkerchief which they had dipped in sugar water, or give him a bit of gruel in a rag.

I don't know exactly how long little Jan survived the sugar-tit, the sympathy of the servants and the hatred of his father, but it was not very long. When he was a few weeks old he caught a cold and died of it shortly thereafter. Then he again began to exist for Dr. Jesenský. He was buried in the family crypt with all requisite formalities, and his name was put on the gravestone. Ever since then I think that Milena was the only person who dared to mention him.

How is it possible, in spite of everything, that Dr. Jesenský managed to arrange a number of pleasant times for his daughter; that he went on long walks with her (which she loved so much that she never quite got over the loss of them) even though she was lame in one leg; that sometimes she recalled him quite fondly? This is one of those things which most likely belongs to the area of mystery, and no one will ever be able to explain it completely. In any event Milena's attachment to her father was the most wonderful example of its kind that I have ever seen. Besides, that mixture of incomprehensible fear, love, aversion, hate and respect so much resembled Kafka's own relations with his father that it alone was enough to have linked them together. And maybe not the relationships in their final forms, but most importantly, whatever shaped them, must have been almost identical in their broad outlines.

Milena's maturation was abruptly completed by her acquaintance with Ernst Polak. She met him in the Arco coffee house. At that time it was the meeting place for people who wrote, wanted to write, or at least wanted to meet those who did write. This country has always abounded in such people, so it was not a strange thing to see. But in the Arco there met a totally strange group which had no parallel in our country or, as far as I know, anywhere else: a group of literary people of Jewish origin, Czech subjects, writing in German.

I think that at that time Milena still didn't know that some day she would want to write. Surely it hadn't yet occurred to her that the time would come when she, like them, would sit in a coffee house and put down her thoughts in lines on paper. Meanwhile she only sat with them at the same table and listened to them. At that time she read what they were discussing and thought about the same problems they were trying to solve. They were quite removed from local concerns not only in their outlook and intellect, but also quite simply due to their origins and social standing.

Ernst Polak was one of them. His word carried some weight with them. He himself didn't write. But in spite of that—or a little bit because of it—he was honored and respected. His judgment was sufficient for all of them. They eagerly subjected their own differing views to his opinion.

And Ernst fell for Milena. He had eyes only for her. As soon as she would turn up at the coffee house he would liven up, be pleasant, sociable and affable. He listened to her as seriously as he would to a person with organized, well thought-out views. He charmed her as best he could. And he was very good at it. Milena readily let herself be charmed. She was enchanted by everything together: his admiration for her and her own admiration for him, his flattering attention to her and the concentration with which he listened to her words, and her enthusiasm for the words which she heard from him. The result was love: a great, colossal love—at that time still a mutual love.

But at home there's Daddy, steeped to the marrow of his bones in chauvinism, antisemitic, for whom a German is an enemy, Jew is a curse word, and Ernst Polak involved with his daughter is a catastrophe...

The horror felt by Prague society and those colleagues who saw his daughter walking about the city hand-in-hand with a Jew. Milena's secret departures from home, day and night. Her attempted suicide in which, to top it off, she used morphine from his office. All these things he endured—albeit unhappily and with difficulty. But that a descendant of his own blood, which he had so ardently desired, would be half Jewish—that he could not endure. And while his daughter lived at home there was no guarantee that she wouldn't continue her activities.

So in June of 1917, using his authority as a doctor and a father, he sent her to a sanatorium for the mentally ill in Veleslavín.

There was nothing in his actions which disturbed his conscience. Not only was he convinced that it was in his daughter's interest to be saved from that crazy Jew who had nearly captured her forever with his lecherous love. He was even more firmly convinced that he had encountered the most bitter thing that it was possible to encounter: that his daughter was completely insane. Because he could find no other explanation for her behavior, no matter how hard he tried...

When Milena left Veleslavín in March, 1918, there wasn't very much that he could do. She became a legal adult that year and Daddy could prevent her marriage only by continuing to deprive her of her rights, and that he didn't want to do. I don't think that concern for his daughter prevented him from doing so. It seems much more likely to me that he didn't want to live with the compassion which surrounded him, that he didn't wish to deal with the continued "Poor Milenka, so she's crazy now!" and "There's nothing you can do about it, doctor, maybe it will get better after a while." He knew well enough that things wouldn't improve with time, and so he finally agreed to the engagement of Milena and Ernst. But he set his conditions, and he did it quite categorically. First of all, after the marriage the newlyweds would live in Vienna so they wouldn't cause him any further embarrassment in Prague. Moreover, until their marriage they would see each other only in the presence of his sister, they would not meet secretly, and he wasn't to know if they broke the rules. If he did hear anything of the kind, he would disinherit his daughter and there definitely would be no dowry.

After the wedding the newlyweds indeed went off to Vienna, just as Doctor Jesenský had wished. It was not a bad beginning. Milena brought with her a very decent dowry, and didn't travel empty-handed. But the nest-egg didn't last very long. Ernst had his needs, his friends had their needs, and Milena operated on a grand scale and gave things away lavishly. She also spent a great deal on household needs, and when she ran short of money she began to pawn her trousseau.

Ernst didn't pay much attention to domestic affairs. He spent most of his time in coffee houses, had no particular needs, and whatever Milena bestowed on him he considered as one of her caprices, not done out of necessity. What he did need were his Viennese friends. Franz Werfel, who had arrived in Vienna shortly before they did, and a number of others who either were already in Vienna or who arrived afterward and were part of his life.

So that is how the situation looked when Milena met Kafka. They didn't recall each other in much detail. In his first letter Kafka writes: "It occurs to me that I cannot recall any precise details of your face. But the way you walked away from the table in the coffee house, your figure, the way you were dressed—these things I can still see." Their association actually did not begin with that meeting, but with Milena's translation of his stories. It gave rise to the correspondence now known as *Letters to Milena*. A correspondence which, by the way, was made public after her death regardless of the fact that probably neither she nor Kafka would have permitted it to happen. Thus the claims of her editor Willi Haase are not true. Milena never gave him Kafka's letters to do with as he saw fit.

The first letters are mainly concerned with Milena's translations, and are more business letters than love letters, with only hints of admiration and friendship. But soon they ceased to deal only with business matters.

In the beginning these letters were immeasurably important to Milena. They acted as a balm on all the wounds which were continually being reopened by her marriage to Ernst, by jealousy, by humiliation over being poor, which she had not previously experienced, and by desolation which she felt most acutely of all.

For Kafka they probably had the same effect—although on a different level—an escape from the feeling of solitude. All of their love, with a few tiny exceptions, took place in the letters. They did not have to make their love confront reality. They could permit themselves one of the greatest luxuries that ever existed in a love: they could be totally frank with each other, they could thoroughly get to know one another. They did not risk what people do whose bodies lie together as well as their souls. They did not risk abuse. Instead of physical closeness they had a yearning for it. And so, in spite of the fact that they probably knew each other better than they would have if they lived together, each remained for the other what he wished the other to be. At least at the start. Milena knew from the beginning that Kafka was a writer—a great writer. She grasped that quickly, and so she also understood and translated his stories. Additionally she knew that he had within him something of human greatness, and this she also grasped almost at once although it was so different, so distant from her own nature that it made her slightly terrified. The meeting with the actual, living Franz Kafka was not a disappointment—it was simply a meeting with something which she had never counted on dealing with in reality.

But the initial fascination helped to carry her past all her difficulties. She later wrote about it to Dr. Max Brod and recalled the meetings in Vienna with Rank when Kafka's illness had passed and his eternal anxiety melted under her smiles. It seemed that everything would be fine...

But Milena's everyday life in Vienna was not fine. To be sure, Kafka provided some financial assistance, but it wasn't enough. Also, although Milena never mentioned it to me, I know her well enough to imagine what it meant to her—there necessarily arose a bizarre situation: Kafka is helping in many ways, psychically and materially, but actually and, above all, he is helping to smooth her married life with Ernst. A married life which he hoped would fail and break up so that Milena would leave Ernst and come to him.

But Milena so clung to Ernst that she was at the time still inseparable from him. The assistance from Kafka necessarily meant assistance to her marriage. Everything else was not assistance. And so the whole merry-go-round was set in motion.

From the beginning the letters beetweeen Vienna and Merano were very frequent. Kafka, thirteen years older than Milena, was in many respects calmer and more patient. But from the way her marriage to Ernst was described to him, it seemed that Milena was not being unfaithful.

He suggests living in the countryside. She could live somewhere in a lovely Czech landscape, she wouldn't have to depend on her husband because he, Kafka, would send her enough money to live on and gradually, leisurely restore both her health and her nerves which were clearly in a mess —to say the least—due to her stay in Vienna. In all his letters one could feel concern, care, an effort to help, and one can also sense that in her situation Milena needed respect and love most of all. Already in these letters, letters in which the word "thou" still hasn't appeared, one can discover the beginning of love.

Milena doesn't accept his offer, doesn't leave Ernst in order to recuperate, nor in order to leave him and solve her problems radically and abruptly. But the letters which heal her ailing self-confidence also heal her nerves. Under his growing concern Milena regains her beauty, reacquires her former self-awareness and self-confidence, and gradually her husband once again begins to take an interest in her.

Milena's psychological situation begins to take a turn for the better. Her articles in *Tribuna* are admired and discussed, Kafka's love—despite all the complications which it entails—is truly an escape from the solitude in which she had been living, and Ernst's attention gives her a slight hope for something which she had nearly given up on and hence had not wanted to acknowledge.

The first meeting with Frank turns out well. He is sensitive and he likes Milena. Her good disposition is contagious. Thus they can walk together over the hills and not get out of breath. Thus it is sufficient to look into his eyes and his anxiety, his primordial eternal anxiety disappears for a moment. He is too loving to be able to imagine how many complex and contradictory feelings had preceded these joys and this happiness.

But then there ensued—I don't know exactly in what sequence, only that there ensued—a slight disenchantment. You had to know Milena in order to understand everything behind her description of Kafka sending a telegram at the post office, a description which seems in a letter to Dr. Max Brod to be a simple statement. A simple description of Frank: first looking for a window which would please him, then filling out a long form, paying the sum which the girl at the window told him, and then, calculating that she had given him too much change, going back to the window and returning the overpayment. A description of him counting his money a second time and suddenly finding that it was he who had been wrong and now doesn't know what to do, because to go back again would mean to enter into a discussion at the window where a long line of people was now standing. So this apparently quite simple description does not contain Milena's face at the moment when the change is counted for the second time, her impatience at making such a scene over a few hellers, and over not breaking the rules which actually made very little sense to Milena, her aversion to what she considered to be a petty matter, nor her own inability to deal with hundreds of crowns—let alone hellers. Perhaps she really didn't suspect her Frank of stinginess—at least that is what she wrote in her letter to Dr. Max Brod—and maybe she believed that in the second case he was just concerned with the rules which made him behave as he did. Or take the time he wanted to give a beggar-woman one crown, but the smallest coin he had was a two-crown piece. So he asked the beggar for a crown in change, but she didn't have it. (I can see before me Milena and with me someone who knew her: blushing to her ears, filled with embarrassment, fury, and pity all at the same time, her blue eyes goggling at the scene being enacted before her—surely one had to know her perfectly well to understand what lay behind the simple description of Kafka's actions.)

It was Milena who finally suggested that they give the beggar-woman the entire two-crown piece. Frank at first had pondered how to get change for the coin, but since there was no place nearby, he adopted Milena's suggestion and the beggar was left with two crowns. "Frank was very displeased with me," Milena adds in the letter. Perhaps he was. But I don't believe Milena was satisfied with the whole thing either. I knew her too well for that...

When she writes that she knows he would give her even 20, 000 if she asked for it, and that it would only cause him difficulty to give her 20,001 if she had said 20,000—I am afraid that this is partly true. Milena really knew that he would give her whatever she asked for as long as it was in his power to do so. He even wrote that if she would accept his suggestion to leave her husband he wouldn't get involved in the matter at all, he would not see her at all, at least until she had her affairs in order. But she also knew that it would be difficult for him to acknowledge what she still didn't entirely admit to herself—that it was impossible to leave Ernst.

Nevertheless Milena later did even that. But then it was a completely different situation.

The agreement between them was actually quite fragile. But they were complementary only to a certain degree. Kafka, reared by his father whom he feared all his life—as Milena did her Daddy—also submitted to the agreement. Milena feared her father, to be sure, but apart from that she easily managed to forget him in all her life's decisions. To ignore both him and her fear of him.

Kafka was meticulously careful in dealing with things, with money, with everything entrusted to him. Milena was generously frivolous—she calmly and with no twinge of conscience dealt with money and with things as if she got them from a bottomless source. And she did so regardless of whether there was enough, for the time being, or whether it would be the last she had for a long time.

Kafka was cautious in love, perpetually haunted by feelings of responsibility, eternal anxiety and eternal fear.

He never made up his mind to get married, although all his life he wanted to have children and a family.

Milena was *de jure* married twice, and *de facto* three times. And if anything did *not* haunt her it was a feeling of responsibility or anxiety. She gave all she had—in love, too. Sometimes it wasn't enough, sometimes too much for the recipient to handle. But it was always all that she was capable of.

Kafka was scrupulously honest.

Milena was able to risk anything for whomever she loved—and not only for him but for everyone who needed something from her. And in the final analysis, particularly for her own self.

This was not the case with Kafka's writings, nor with Milena's articles which Kafka praised both in his letters and in conversations with Dr. Max Brod. Speaking of Kafka's stories which Milena translated, it is clear that she had very good taste. The value of those stories has long been beyond argument.

It is a bit of a problem to evaluate Milena's articles in that period. They are certainly not mature yet, they are the first articles of someone who will some day be a fine journalist. Possibly Kafka recognized that. Perhaps he also loved her very much. Or he was aware of their true value and knew that the person who correctly assessed that value would one day be capable of good work. In any case—as is evident from his letters to Milena, and from the words of Dr. Max Brod, he valued them quite highly.

The relationship, though, was developing oddly. More oddly than one would have supposed when it began.

Milena and Kafka met in Gmunden—the unhappiest encounter imaginable. Energetic, intense, passionate Milena and sickly, cautious and simply dispassionate Kafka.

The center of intellectual activity when Milena arrived in Prague from Vienna consisted of people who lived in the country of their birth, who wrote in its language, and whose bodies and souls were permanently attached to it.

In 1920 the group Devětsil was founded, and it gradually moved to the cultural forefront. First in Prague and later with a branch in Brno. There was nothing chauvinistic about its members. Just the contrary. They were interested in everything going on it the world. They didn't have to be chauvinistic. They were not in a bind which would have made that necessary. They belonged as self-evidently to their country as they did to their apartments. They simply were not and could not become—in Milena's sense of the word—"foreigners."

Having a homeland simplifies a great many things. It provides some certainty in life. It has a past and a bit of the future. To lack a homeland means to be restricted only to the present and then to eternity.

Even if Milena was not in touch with the people of Devětsil the moment she returned to Prague, they were necessarily close to her and she to them. She was as disgusted as they were by the chauvinism which arose due to the pressure of the Austro-Hungarian monarchy and the revivalist movement. She was as interested as they were in everything which the new fresh breath brought to the musty corners which still smelled of the Emperor.

The enormous energy and enthusiasm for her work which Milena brought to Prague soon bore their first fruits. In *Národní Listy* she ran a column "Woman and Home." She managed to gather collaborators for it partly from former schoolmates and partly from among friends she had had in Prague before she left. Her Viennese adventure and what preceded it had slightly damaged her reputation in Prague, but when she reappeared, in radiant full bloom and not at all shabby, the old gossip lost all its interest. Also, she was successful, her articles were popular, and for a while the public forgot about her past.

Besides her columns in *Národní Listy* she also did her translations and started a children's series *Dětská četba*. The first issue contained a translation of the English story "Peter Pan."

In 1937, when Milena began to write for *Přítomnost*, World War II was already threatening.

The sadly senseless resistance of the Ethiopian soldiers with their spears and arrows against Italy's modern weaponry had ended, the Abyssinian ruler was in exile, and in his place the king of Italy was named emperor.

In Spain the Civil War was raging, bravely and vainly reinforced by international brigades from every country, weakened in cowardly but effective fashion by a boycott of all the great powers.

Meanwhile more and more refugees arrived from Germany, empty-handed, with weary eyes and incurable fear. They spoke in whispers, and in closed rooms as well as on the streets they would glance around in terror and suddenly begin to walk faster for no apparent reason...

In such a situation private, personal problems became insignificant and lost all importance. Previously important concerns became trivial quibbles.

But nevertheless the regular income from Milena's work at *Přítomnost* made many things easier at home. The income was urgently needed—without it the household would have been very shaky.

But it was not only a matter of money. Milena now required the opportunity to write. And not only to write but to publish her articles. There were too many things that were so pressing that she could not and would not be silent about them.

From the very start her work at *Přítomnost* was fortunate. Probably because at *Přítomnost* Milena was no longer managing a women's column, nor was she publishing feuilletons as an amusing addition to a more or less amusing page. True, this was not the first time. In *Svět práce* and earlier her articles had long been something other than a woman's advice to female subscribers—but for the first time Milena was doing important journalistic work which was mature and not hampered by any *a priori* views or party restrictions.

She continued to make contacts with many new people, translated articles by Willi Schlamm for *Přítomnost*, found a number of additional contributors, and herself wrote about everything that bothered her and which she didn't want to be silent about.

The chief editor of *Přítomnost* was Ferdinand Peroutka who (even though he was never a Communist, which was certainly a great drawback in a newsman) was one of the best journalists that we have ever had. Milena got along well with him on the job, and he with her. Occasionally he would say that she was so clever that it was impossible to live under the same roof with her and for that reason he got along so well with her—he was probably close to the truth.

Perhaps some of Milena's best work ever was her reportage which she wrote after a trip abroad in 1938. It was for her a year filled with events—not just world-wide but also personal.

Peroutka sent her to the German border, albeit unwillingly, and as far as I know a bit reluctantly. It was dangerous country there and could be fatal for a healthy man, to say nothing of Milena. But in the end she simply went, and the material which she brought back would by itself have sufficed to make a book.

Her ability to deal with people once again showed itself. She easily learned things from them which they would otherwise have carefully concealed from any foreign, unknown person because they feared the possible consequences of every word which they let drop.

And so Milena was not only acquainted with all the current facts with which reportage of that type was written, but she also knew something more. She knew about women who were afraid of their own children because the children were taught, in Nazi organizations, that it was an honor to report an enemy of the Reich, even one's own mother. She spoke with a woman who dared not stop her son from playing at soldiers and military massacres, because she risked the vengeance of a horde of hooligans, made fanatical and insane by their leaders and capable, when commanded, of incendiarism and other such barbaric acts. And she knew a great deal more. She learned it from people who feared their own sons and daughters.

She wrote about it and told us about it at home. But there is a vast difference between seeing something and merely hearing an account of what someone has seen. And the things which Milena had seen with her own eyes could only partly be shared.

And then the last school vacation arrived—July and August of 1939.

I have no idea how or from whom Milena found out about Medlov. Nor do I have a very clear idea as to why it was precisely to Medlov that she decided to send me and where she followed me in August.

At that time Medlov was a girls' camp—a group of wooden cabins on a lake surrounded by woods on all sides. It was run by Leoš Stehlík and his wife Aglaja, and it was so beautiful that it is difficult to describe. I arrived there in the beginning of July, but at first I could not get used to being without Milena. I missed her and I wasn't very happy when I was with the other youngsters. So I don't recall that July very well. I only know that Milena wrote sad letters from Prague in which she complained that Prague was nearly depopulated, she had no idea where many of her friends had gone, and on the streets she encountered only the most alien faces.

That spring preceding our school vacation was one of continuous leave-taking, and whoever didn't leave had one foot in Pankrác prison and the other in the Protectorate.

The war hung by a thread—people simultaneously wanted it and feared it; no one knew whether he would sleep in his own bed by nightfall or whether his wife would make it home from her shopping. Acquaintances who hadn't seen each other for a week breathed a sigh of relief when they met on the street—alive and still not locked up.

And in that atmosphere in August, in that beautiful, magnificent summer, there came to Medlov, for a month, actors, painters, photographers, journalists and poets, students, musicians and I don't know who else—with the knowledge that it might be the last vacation for a long time, and it must be considered as a truly miraculous gift.

Each cottage slept four people, with two bedrooms and two cots in each room, and by the woods there was a community building with a dining room and a small bar, and with a fireplace where, in the evening, they built a fire using real oak logs.

We lived in the same cabin as Jaromir and Riva—they in one room and we in the other.

At first everyone tried to act as if nothing was happening and there was nothing to be afraid of. They tried to behave like people who were on vacation and thus only wanted to lie in the sun or stroll through the woods or swim in the big lake and splash among the reeds. But, only a few days before the war and amidst total uncertainty, it simply didn't work. We weren't summer guests. We were frightened, uncertain people who didn't know whether tomorrow we would see the sunrise or the end of the world.

Actually, I knew most of those feelings indirectly from Milena, and when she was with me I didn't feel lost at all.

But all of the adults felt that the ground was trembling under their feet. After a few days they began staying close to each other. They felt safer in a group than by themselves. They gathered on the cottage porches, clustered tightly together, literally supporting each other. The time devoted to lovemaking was limited to the daylight hours. In the afternoon sunlight couples made love in the glades and clearings of the nearby forest and returned, still embracing, to the camp before dark. They all knew about each others' intimate relations, nothing was kept secret, and no one tried to do so.

Someone got the idea to organize—before everyone left the camp—some sort of carnival with a masquerade procession and carnival shows with booths scattered about the meadow and with a series of all possible kinds of exhibitions. The theater group "Burian's Folk Suite" began rehearsals, and they made themselves costumes and prepared masks. About the meadow in bright sunlight people in make-up moved about dressed as carnival knights and royal princesses. Around the camp resounded the squeals of an improvised march tune, and the woods returned a deformed echo. Everyone was slightly hysterical and it seemed that they were constantly a little drunk.

Milena went through one mood after another. Or, more accurately, she had them all at once. She sparkled with witticisms and barbed remarks, was high-spirited and madly hilarious, and at the same time very sad, and at night she would go swimming in the lake, her rhythm deformed by her lame leg, and she floated on the water like a drowning victim. And when she returned to the shore she was greeted at the dock by an unsteady, reeling student who vainly tried to keep his balance and who quietly mumbled: "I'm the crazy one from Pamplona—I'm afraid of the pale moonlight.". . .

The news that the USSR had concluded a non-aggression pact with Germany was followed in a short time by the news that the German-Polish war had broken out.

We couldn't leave Medlov, we had to remain for several days in the wooden cabins in the forest and wait. Finally it was definite that it was the last vacation.

They took Milena to Peček Palace for interrogation and then to Pankrác Prison. She was there for a while and when the Gestapo finished questioning her it sent her to Dresden to stand trial. There, too she had to wait until her turn came. The weeks and months went by and Milena's health grew worse and worse. In Dresden, besides rheumatoid arthritis and serious periodontitis, she acquired some kind of infectious rash which ate away her skin and was extremely painful and persistent.

But finally her turn came to be tried. Because it was a German court, they meticulously observed all the formalities. Milena received in the proper and prescribed time period the indictment and was even offered *ex officio* a defense counsel, which she was entitled to because she wasn't a German and the trial was not being held in her own country. Milena refused. She had no difficulties with the German language and she didn't want to let her counsel do her in. She defended herself. She managed to prove that there was insufficient evidence for an indictment so she was released, and thus the Dresden courts lost any claim on her, and they returned her to Prague.

In Prague she was originally supposed to be set free, but the Prague Gestapo was unwilling to release anyone once they had caught them. The Gestapo official who had charge of her case ruled that it was not really so much a matter of what Milena had done as what she would do if she were freed. So he decided that she should be sent to the concentration camp in Ravensbrück to be re-educated as a loyal citizen of the Great German Reich —naturally for an unspecified length of time.

I saw her for the last time during a visit which they permitted her to have before her departure for Ravensbrück. I came to see her with my grandfather. We waited in a corridor of the Peček Palace for her to be led out. The old man scowled and I couldn't bring myself to say a word to him. We both looked in the same direction—to a bend in the corridor through which they were to bring her. And when she finally passed by us in an officer's custody I didn't even recognize her.

Thin, with long hair down to her shoulders, with protruding facial

Jan Lukas *Medlov* (September, 1939)

bones and enormous blue eyes—she looked a great deal more like the Milka whom her daddy knew than Milena, whom I remembered. But at first he, too, didn't realize that it was she. Only by the movement of her leg, stiff at the knee, did I recognize her.

The officer let us be alone for a while in an office. Milena's interrogation was all over and there was nothing for him to worry about—and so I quickly and enthusiastically told her how we sabotaged the German language in school, that we didn't learn it and we pretended that we couldn't grasp it. I thought that she would be enormously happy about that, but Milena only smiled and told me I was a foolish kid, and that German was one of the most beautiful languages in the world and couldn't be responsible for the people who spoke it. Granddad scowled slightly at that—he had a different opinion on the matter—but he didn't say a word.

It was not a very long visit. Or maybe it just seemed that way to me—but I had the impression that it was just a short while.

Milena never wanted me to say "I kiss your hand" or even to greet old ladies by kissing their hands. She always joked about it and called it monkey business, and I had no real idea what kissing one's hand even meant. But when I sat next to her at the table and held her hand with its swollen knuckles, emaciated, white and feverish, I was somehow driven to kiss the back of her hand. She gave me a questioning look. Perhaps at first she was afraid it was only some monkey business which I had been taught while she was in prison, but when she saw that it was altogether different and that granddad was looking at me with equal amazement, she smiled a horrifyingly quiet and loving smile—and down her face rolled two big tears.

When the visit ended I accompanied her out to the corridor and only then left her. I never saw her after that.

Only when Margareta Buber's book *Kafka's Friend Milena* came out did I learn that Milena recalled that visit in the same way I did, and that it was just as difficult for her as it was for me.

What I know about Milena's stay in Ravensbrück is some of the most ghastly evidence of what human hate, heedlessness, fanaticism and malice can create.

I have before me notes from the accounts of some of her fellow-prisoners, fragments of reminiscences, and tales and stories which remained in their memories. Some are interesting and some are even very typical of Milena. But even so I didn't have much desire to include them. They are only tales and that is not what matters now. The same thing emerges from them as from all of Milena's life: she was fearless and aggressive, she was able to win over people, and—despite all the venom, all the experiences and events which she retained so well in her memory—she had an innate and self-evident humanism which marked all her actions and all her undertakings. She had a strength which was unusual, to say the least, which apparently enabled her to bear even the unbearable.

She had many friends in Ravensbrück. After the war I personally spoke with several of her camp mates who had liked her and had tried their best to make her stay in Ravensbrück a bit easier.

But the most important thing about her stay in Ravensbrück I first learned from a letter from the Ravensbrück woman who later brought me Milena's tooth. She wrote the letter right after she returned, before we met each other, and in it she tried to describe all of Milena's stay in the camp as intelligibly as possible. But at the time I still didn't understand it very well. Only later did I manage gradually, piece by piece, to put together the drama which was enacted there and which later was either passed over in silence or deformed.

When Milena arrived at the camp all the Czech women received her kindly. Even the Communists who knew of her from Prague and knew her views—even they were friendly to her. Even though there was not a very strong bond between them, neither was there any obvious animosity.

Naturally Milena gladly accepted the situation. There was no sense in continuing old Prague quarrels, and in the present circumstances people needed to be good to each other rather than to argue.

That lasted for a time, and it didn't look as if the truce would be broken during their imprisonment.

Until Margareta Buber-Neumannová arrived at Ravensbrück. She got there in a rather complicated way. She was the wife of Heinz Neumann, the general secretary of the German Communist Party. When Neumann went to the USSR for a meeting of the Third International, Stalin kept him there as a delegate, and Greta decided to go to Moscow to be with him.

At that time some of the Communists were still convinced that the Communist parties of all countries could prevent fascism from coming to power. Heinz Neumann was also convinced of it and at the congress he delivered a speech in which he defended his conviction.

But Stalin was definitely against such a position and very decisively rejected and suppressed it. Neumann's appearance made him extremely angry. He had Neumann locked up, and a few days later had him executed.

Many years later Neumann was rehabilitated at the Twentieth Party Congress by Nikita Sergeevich Khrushchev, when the whole incident was examined in connection with all the disclosures of Stalin's policies during the so-called cult of the personality.

But in 1939, after the non-aggression pact between Germany and the USSR was signed, Stalin turned over to the Third Reich all the German Communists, and the Gestapo literally took them from the hands of the Soviet police at the border.

Greta Buberová Neumannová was among them. At first they took her to Dresden—perhaps for interrogation, I don't know—and from Dresden, just like Milena, the Gestapo put her in the Ravensbrück concentration camp.

It is understandable that Milena began to be interested in her case. But when the Czech Communists found out who Greta was, and when they heard talk of Soviet concentration camps and learned the details of her case, they shunned her.

(In the letter which Milena's friend wrote me right after the war it appears that when Greta arrived in the camp Ravensbrück was still a fairly tolerable concentration camp which the Germans even showed to the International Red Cross. When Greta had looked it over a little she announced in the presence of the Czech comrades that Ravensbrück, compared to Stalin's prisons, was a hotel, and that they should be glad to be there and not in Stalin's camps. Her speech, it seems, got their dander up and thereafter they avoided Greta like the plague.)

But Milena not only didn't join in the hatred of Greta, she made friends with her and had Greta tell her the whole story in great detail. She had no reason to disbelieve Greta. The information she provided was not news to Milena but confirmed what she, at least partly, already knew.

Indeed, even before *Přítomnost* was suspended, it published an article by Milena which clearly shows that Greta's news was not a suprise, and that most of the Communist women in Ravensbrück must have at least heard of it.

I have in mind the article in which Milena writes of the fate of the Soviet International Brigade after the civil war ended in Spain. Stalin refused to let them back into the Soviet Union because his regime didn't want to let into the land of the Soviets anyone who knew by personal experience about life outside its boundaries, and who could tell how the capitalist part of the world really looked.

I don't think that Milena was even surprised by the fact that the Soviet Union handed over the German Communists to the Gestapo. Which doesn't mean that she wasn't shocked by it. And what she learned from Greta about the fate of Heinz Neumann, about his execution and the details which brought it about could only strengthen her conviction which she voiced in the camp and for which she was later reproached: the conviction that Stalin's regime did not imply any kind of freedom, and that to go from the hands of the Nazis to the hands of Stalin was to go from the frying pan into the fire.

And so the animosity of the Ravensbrück Communists which originally was directed only at Greta gradually began to include Milena. At first some of them tried to talk her out of her position, to get her to stop being friends with Greta and to return to them. They were probably even willing to forgive and forget her mistakes.

But Milena stuck by her position. She didn't feel that she had done anything for which she might be forgiven. She was sorry about the dispute because in prison every dispute is bitter and is much harder to bear than when one is free, and even if she was directly endangered – because the Communists in many cases had the ability to influence both the welfare, and the opposite, of a certain prisoner – Milena couldn't compromise.

What followed is described clearly and unambiguously by her friend in the letter which she wrote me: They took away the marmelade jar, they removed her bread, and Milena was alone.

Sometimes the animosity slacked off and was diminished by everyday concerns, but only to the degree that it wasn't continually in the open and that certain individuals remained silent about it. Otherwise, it lasted a long time, even beyond Milena's death.

Still, they didn't succeed in shutting her up in air-tight solitude, although it wouldn't have taken much more. Fortunately a few women were there who were defiant and above all there was Greta, the person closest to Milena at that time, who was happy to do anything humanly possible for her. And there was also Milena's fellow-prisoner who wrote me after the war, and a number of others about whom I know little or nothing.

But I *do* know that when Milena felt worst of all she didn't call to any of them and she didn't call to any of us who remained at home. She called — she who was such a convinced atheist before she left — in her despair she called on God.

After the war her friends returned to Prague. Evžen returned and a number of others. Not one of them had a bad word to say about Milena in front of me, and I still couldn't imagine that there were so many people who were still cultivating their hatred regardless of Milena's death and regardless of everything else. Before February, 1948 her name was even mentioned a few times in the press, reminiscences about her appeared in a women's journal, and a few times her name was greeted favorably.

After February there was no mention of Milena. A long silence. Until the appearance of Kafka's *Letters to Milena*.

For a short time Kafka ceased to be forbidden literature here. Milena's name began to appear in connection with him in Czech journals and literary studies. Only in that connection, naturally. But even that caused ripples on the surface.

And so Gustina Fučíková attacked Milena on the pages of *Kulturní tvorba*. It was quite a harsh attack, and I mentioned it earlier. Among other things she asserted that Milena's position versus the USSR undermined the morale of the prisoners in Ravensbrück and spread depression among them. Who really depressed whom in the camp is another question. The article also stated that Milena had never been a party member, as well as a number of other errors or half-truths. In reality, Milena's application for party membership was submitted, and it was even signed by a comrade who was sought by the law and was hiding at her place — Klement Gottwald.

She *did* work for the party while she believed in it, and she did a great deal of work.

But at the same time it is true that she was concerned about that work and not about her application and that she paid her dues irregularly or not at all.

So I phoned Gustina Fučíková then and tried to explain at least her material mistakes. I didn't succeed. She stuck to her position. Then I asked her if she thought she might have made an error. Actually that had happened once before, during the Slansky trial, where she had testified against a person who was later rehabilitated—although not quite in time, because in the meantime he had been executed.

But she stuck by that testimony as well and assured me that the procedures against Slansky were in order, and so was she. So I quickly hung up the phone. What else could I have done...

And again for a long time there was nothing about Milena until Professor Eduard Goldstücker came to her defense in *Literární noviný*. He stirred up a hornet's nest... It resulted in an article by a Mr. Kolár entitled "Loves of a Renegade." It exuded rather more fury than is normally permitted in a journalistic polemic...

Much had been said and written about Milena abroad, but it hardly belongs here, and besides, I haven't been able to follow the foreign reports about her. I found out about them accidentally, so that I can't discuss them in any detail.

And now I only wish to add that if I don't give the names of a number of Milena's friends who had good things to say about her even after the war, or if I omit the names of people whom she recalled after they had gone abroad—or even after they had been imprisoned, it is above all because I don't know whether they would like me to. Because to this day it is not entirely clear whether a connection with Milena Jesenská might not be a fundamental political handicap.

Translated by Mark Suino

SPELLBOUND BY PRAGUE

Jindřich Chalupecký

Prague has had a peculiar fate. At times it is an insignificant city, one that scarcely anyone in the world could locate on a map with any certainty: is it in the middle of Europe or to the east? At other times, it has been one of the great centres, a city where the future of the world is decided. The periods of greatness have given Prague its shape and its face: the high Gothic of Charles IV, the late Mannerism of the court of Rudolf II, Counter-reformation Baroque. The intervals of poverty have preserved it. Prague is still considered one of the most beautiful cities in Europe. Not only does it have individual monuments to the past, but whole large areas of the city remain as they were, formed by the mature styles of the past. This cannot help but leave its mark on the artists who live there. Brought up in and educated by so complex an environment of art and architecture, they un-consciously measure their work by the same strict formal standards.

In the 19th century, Prague was a quiet provincial city in the Austro-Hungarian Empire. The few unusually talented artists who lived there could not grow in that milieu. It was not until the turn of the century that Czech artists managed to establish contacts with the world of modern art. The *art nouveau* of Mucha and the abstraction of Kupka came to maturity in the climate of Paris, but in Prague, in the meantime, and very early, there appeared that expressionism which the work of Franz Kafka introduced into literature and, in the fine arts, there was the equally original work of a whole group of artists, particulary the painter Kubišta and the sculptor Gutfreund. These men developed their expressionism into Cubism. Dadaism passed Prague by, but Surrealism gained a significant foothold there in the early 1930s and remained an important trend for some time. During the Second World War, one group of artists derived from the Surrealist interest in reality, another from the lyricism of Surrealist painting, thereby coming close to abstraction.

When Herbert Read visited some Prague studies in 1947, Prague seemed to him to be the most lively city of art at that moment in Europe. A new generation was already entering the scene. Since the beginning of the war, contact with the rest of the world had been lost in Bohemia and for a long time afterwards, throughout the entire 1950s, in fact, it was impossible for Czech artists to re-establish it again. No one travelled abroad, and no western magazines were available. In their isolation, Czech artists refused to give up. Deep in the middle of the war, Václav Boštík moved from landscapes to a very deliberate and consistent form of lyrical abstraction. Shortly after the war, Vladimír Boudník developed an abstract art of gesture and action—in his case, it was action graphics, in which he would discover surprisingly new techniques. In 1958, Václav Cigler sketched out his projects for a work of art to be created directly in the landscape—a prefiguration of future land art. In 1959, Jiří Balcar opened a show in which expressionistic figuration flowed into expressionist abstraction, naturally provoking cries of outrage and indignation in the press. At the same time, Mikuláš Medek carried his figurative Surrealism into a form of monumental abstraction. Between 1959 and 1963, Nepraš, Dlouhý and Vožniak turned their Surrealist inspiration back in the direction of Dada. In 1960 Boštík, Janoušek, Kučerová, Janoušková, John, Kolíbal, Šimotová and others formed *UB 12*, a group that shared an emphasis on free and individual expression. Their first exhibition two years later was very sharply attacked. In 1960 another group of artists, who this time were for the most part still students in the Academy, held two private exhibitions with the title *Confrontation* in the cellars they used as studiós. In this milieu, Beran, Sion, Veselý and a number of others discussed and debated art; their work was informed mainly by the spirit of abstract expressionism. In 1961 and 1962 Jiří Kolář and Ladislav Novák both pushed their literary work into new forms on the border between poetry and images. In 1964-65 Eva Kmentová shifted from abstract sculptures to the use of direct prints and casts of her own body. Balcar also evolved from abstraction towards the new figuration. During those same years, constructivist abstraction, a trend alien to Czech art until this point, began to make inroads: besides Kolíbal, its practitioners were Malich, Demartini and Sýkora; the latter began to make consistent use of computors in the creation of his pictures. As early as 1949 Boudník had carried out proto-happenings in the streets of Prague. In 1963, Milan Knížák, very like Kaprow, whom he did not know at the time, began to hold "demonstrations" and "manifestations," which were in fact happenings, and after him, in 1965—this time in Bratislava—Alex Mlynárčik, along with Stano Filko, prefigured conceptual art with their "happsocs." A number of younger individuals and small groups are continuing in this direction today.

Thus art in Bohemia—and in Slovakia as well—had developed both from its own inner impulses, and from the reception of general trends, and it did so with the same inner logic as it did elsewhere in the world. In Prague there is a tradition of extremely critical distaste for mere imitations of modernity. There are special reasons for this. Soon after the war, young artists were faced with having to make a precipitiously formulated choice. In a word, it was a choice between the ethical and the esthetic. It was not an easy decision to make. There were both external and internal difficulties. The external difficulties consisted in the fact that the monopoly artists' organization that governed most of the opportunites to exhibit or publish, permitted, under the banner of "socialist realism," only the most conventional kinds of art. At first the permitted style was a naturalistic academi-

Eva Kmentová *Hands* ➤

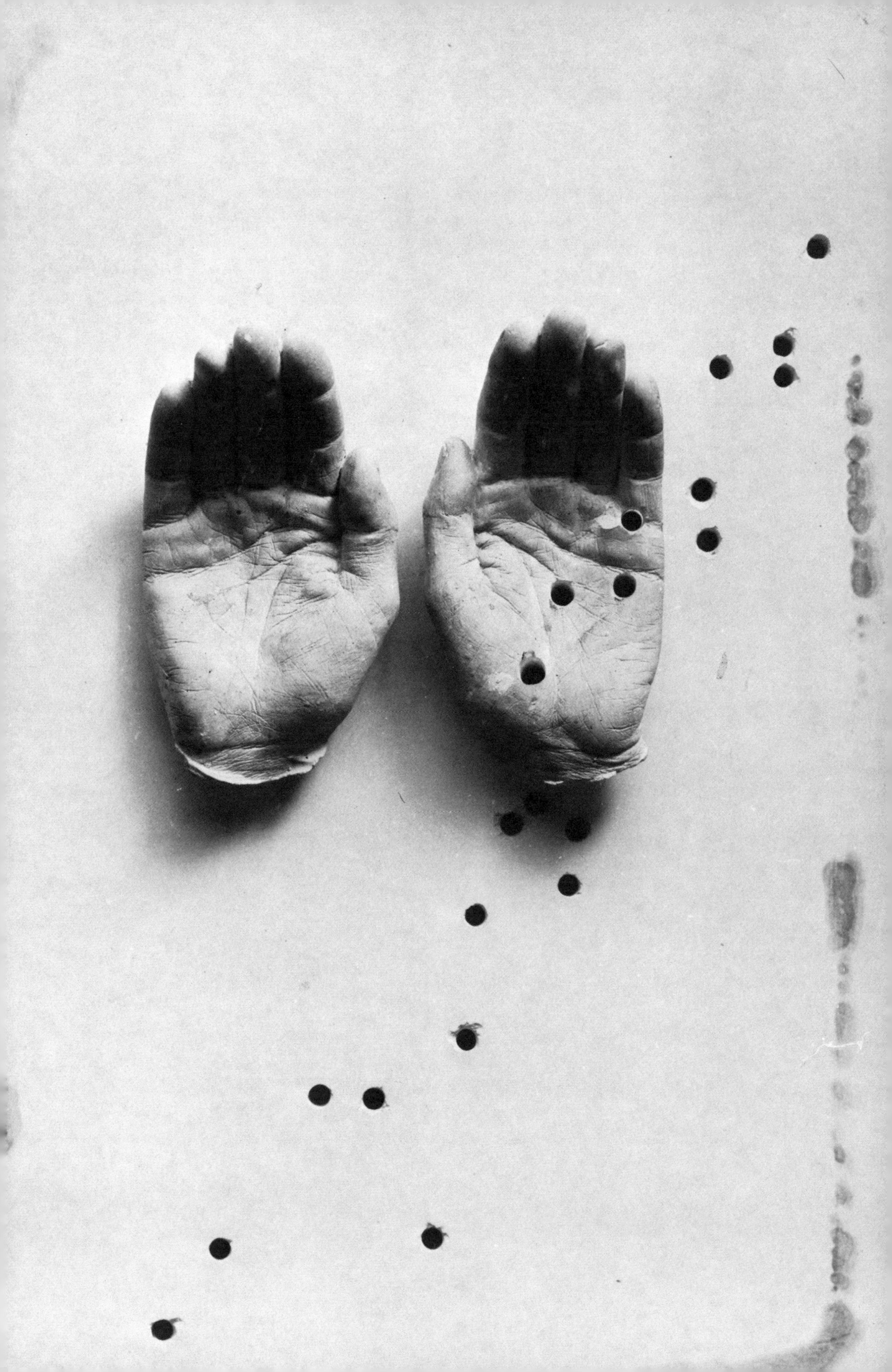

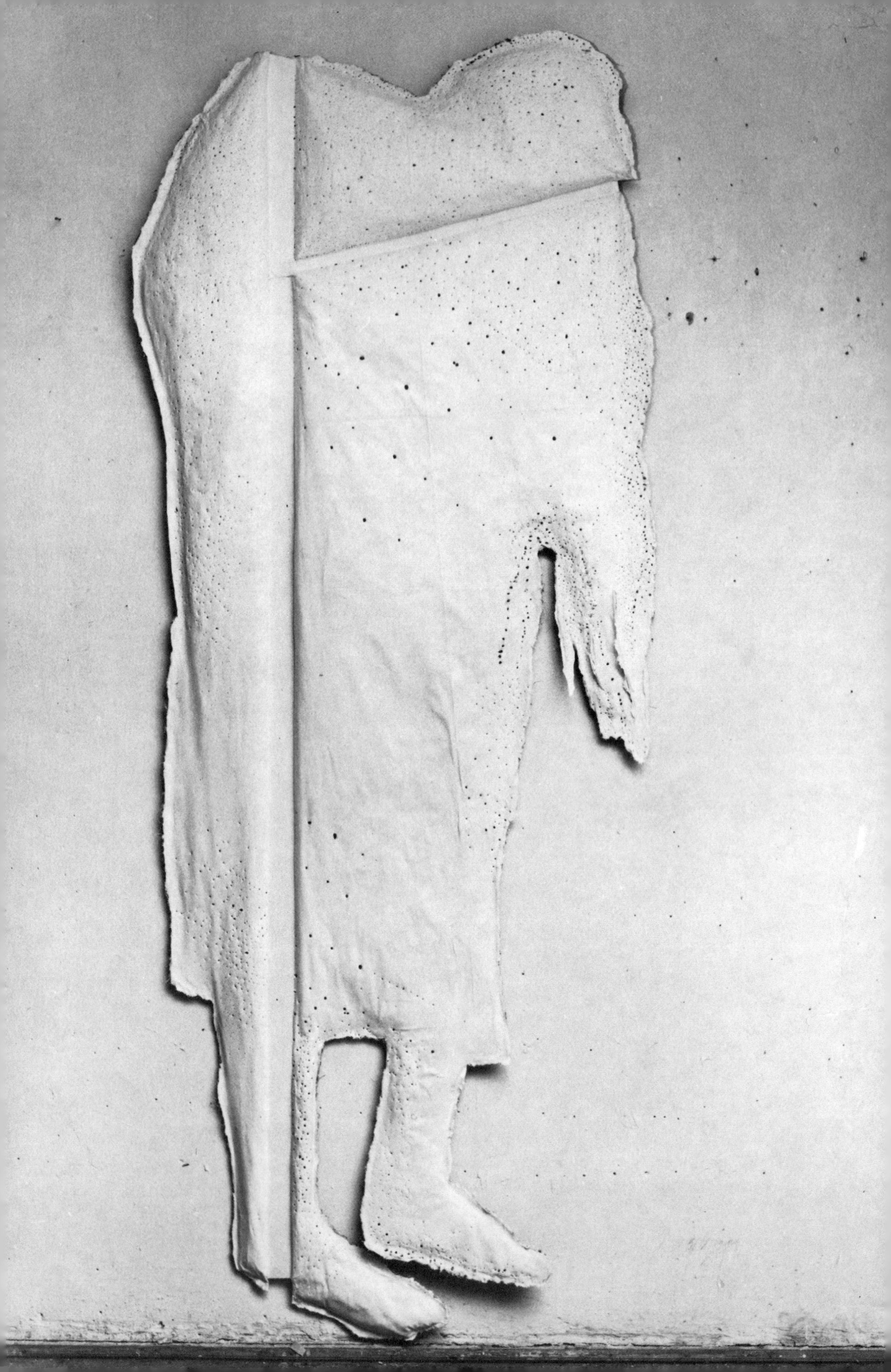

cism; then, as time went on, interpretations of visual reality along fauvistic or expressionistic lines were tolerated. Anyone who did not choose to fit into this pattern remained restricted to the resources of their own studios.

The inner difficulties were more serious. On the one hand stood a doctrine that required of the artists reliable service to the ideas of social progress. This meant returning to a conventional means of expression, but it gave the artist's life and work full social vindication. The other alternative was the adventurous and uncertain route mapped out by the discoveries of modern art: and who can say at all what the meaning of this modern art should be and what benefits it may bring? There was no third choice, no possible escape from the dilemma through compromise. In making their great decision, young artists at the time gave preference to art, even though they knew the risks involved. In this way, a new chapter in Czechoslovak art was begun.

There were no conditions here, however, for the birth of an epigonic, imitative modernism. Success could not be achieved through modern art, and anyone who decided in its favour could only have done so for themselves, from personal needs and necessities. This art could not be addressed to the public and therefore it produced neither schools nor trends, nor even theories and a body of criticism. Each artist worked alone on his own artistic destiny, in all its unpredictability. At the same time, the artist was not limited by any postulates or theoretical expectations. In particular, there was no market for modern art at home, and therefore that destructive transformation of modern art into a commodity could not take place. Paradoxical though it may sound, it is true that not knowing the terror of theory and the marketplace, untempted by success and uncowed by failure, the modern artist was able, in that very situation, to preserve his freedom more than he might have elsewhere.

The present-day face of Czech art is the outcome of a broad current of activity running from post-Surrealism through expressionistic and later constructivistic abstraction, to the widely varied forms of expression of the present. Though it is without a doubt authentic modern art, it will seem unusual here in America. It has developed out of the same impulses as anywhere else, but it did not continue to evolve in the same way. In the rest of the world, modern art became explicitly extrovert; it strives to make an impact and to find a legitimate place in the world. This art from Czechoslovakia is largely introverted; it is an art of monologue and meditation. Elsewhere, driven by the need to stand out, the artist has tried to carry his originality and experimentation to extremes. There is nothing like that in Czechoslovakia. The artist remains himself and his experimentation is only an adjunct to an enterprise whose origins and meaning lie elsewhere than in art alone. The subject of the work is human destiny itself, and the artist uses his art to clarify this destiny, to reveal new dimensions in it, to gain greater awareness. That, perhaps, is the main feature of this art. For the same reason it is also an extremely varied art, an art of individual experience. The work of each artist must be approached afresh, in a different way.

◀ Adriena Šimotová *A Large Obstacle*

This is also a reason why such remarkable art by women has appeared in Czechoslovakia. It is not feminine out of protest. Women artists had nothing to protest against, for they were equally as unsuccessful as their male counterparts. On the other hand, like the men, they were able to develop their own art in the refuge of their studios. And in fact in the most recent generation of artists, two of the most impressive personalities are Oriešková, a painter, and Jetelová, a sculptress.

Apollinaire, who spent a brief time in Prague at the beginning of this century, never forgot it. What he saw was still the provincial Prague:

"Terrified, you see yourself in the stones of St. Guy's
You were wretchedly sad the day you saw yourself there
You are like Lazarus, distraught by the day
In the Jewish quarter, the clock's hands go backwards
And you, too, retreat slowly through the city
Climbing up to Hradčany, and in the evening, listening
As they sing Czech songs in the taverns."

In one of Apollinaire's stories, an old gypsy woman says that she comes from Bohemia, "a fairy-tale land that one should pass through but not linger in, on pain of being enchanted, bewtitched and spellbound." Apollinaire was right. Prague is a city of destiny. Czech artists seldom emigrate, and when they do, it is difficult for them. They are also spellbound by Prague.

Their art, rarely exhibited, is not even very well known in their own country. For the rest of the world, it may seem too modest, too lacking in force, too self-enclosed. The specific atmosphere around it is created by several dozen artists, each of whom is very dissimilar, and who create that atmosphere by their very dissimilarity. Every selection of their work, therefore, distorts. These artists certainly feel that it is importatnt not to have their art remain a purely local affair. There is only one measure of art. Nevertheless, as they work, their minds are on more important things than their own careers and consequently they don't even concern themselves with the extent to which they differ from artists elsewhere. But it is quite possible that precisely in the dissimilarity of this art there is concealed the potential that the great art of the world has passed over. In today's crisis of modern art — if it is not already a catastrophe — this art may well remind us of something important.

Prague, August 10, 1980

Translated by Paul Wilson

BÉLA BARTÓK AS A COLLECTOR OF FOLK MUSIC

Albert B. Lord
Harvard University

In the Introduction to the edition of Béla Bartók's *Slovak Folksongs* published by the Academy of Sciences in Bratislava in 1959, Oskar Elschek indicated that Bartók had noted down 3700 Hungarian, 3500 Romanian, 3223 Slovak, 89 Turkish, 65 Arabic, and more than 200 Ruthenian, South Slavic, and Bulgarian folksongs.[1] Elschek added, "Bartók's work as a composer of art music and as a scholar are so organically linked that it is not possible to comprehend the one without the other." I might add, that one cannot properly judge his work in the analysis of folk music without an understanding of his views on and methods of collecting that music in the field.

Bartók's definition, to which he frequently referred in later writings, of what he called "peasant music," was given in full in the Introduction to his *Hungarian Folk Music* in 1931:[2] *"The term 'Peasant music,' connotes, broadly speaking, all the tunes which endure among the peasant class of any nation, in a more or less wide area and for a more or less long period, and constitute a spontaneous expression of the musical feeling of that class."*

"From the point of view of folk-lore, we may define the peasant class as follows: it is that part of the population engaged in producing prime requisites and materials, whose need for expression, physical and mental, is more or less satisfied either with forms of expression corresponding to its own tradition, or with forms which, although originating in a higher (urban) culture, have been instinctively altered so as to suit its own outlook and disposition."

It was characteristic of his thoroughness as a scholar collector that, shortly after beginning to collect and to analyse Hungarian peasant music, Bártok turned to collecting and studying the peasant music of Hungary's neighbors. Slovak songs were the first to receive his attention, and slightly later Rumanian. Between August 1906 and the year 1913 he had noted down 730 Slovak folk songs, although he must have known something like 3000 Slovak folk melodies, mainly from the published collection *Slowakische Gesänge*. Elschek writes (p. 22), *"Bartók devoted himself with such intensity to collecting that from the spring of 1915 to the spring of 1916 he noted down 1800 melodies in the Pohronie district."* The whole passage from Elschek (pp. 22-23) is worth quoting because it is typical of Bartók's temperament and extraordinary industry. *"He succeeded in this period of time to collect 507 melodies from the 40 year old singer Susanne Spišjak of Poniky and a hundred from several other women singers. This tempo of working made it possible for Bartók within a short time to put together a large, respectable collection of 3409 Slovak folk song melodies abd 4000 song texts and to make a beginning of a comprehensive work. This collection contains 3223 melodies of Bartók's own recording. Z. Kodaly sent Bartók 113 (in this collection we find Kodaly's very first folksong notations which he had noted down in 1900 as a Gymnazium student in Trnava), and A. Banik sent 73 Slovak folksong notations. All those notations came into being in the years 1900-1918."*

Bartók's introduction to the Slovak collection is itself noteworthy. After a detailed classification of the music itself he commented (p. 67, in German) on the writing down of the texts.

"Whenever possible I attempted to write down the texts in dialect." But there were difficulties—and Bartók tried to explain why he could not reach perfection. First, with some peasants who had a little schooling, reading and schooling influenced their dialectical expression of the text. Second, in some places his assistant was from the burgher class (a teacher or priest) who for the most part did not write down the texts in dialect. In spite of this, he wrote, certain dialect peculiarities came clearly to light, and he set them forth systematically (as always).

Then he set down some important and fascinatingly down-to-earth principles from the field. *"When collecting I intended to investigate the material of the village I was visiting as exactly as possible (it can never be exhausted, of course). I chose women as informants most especially, first, because according to my experience in general they have a much richer stock of songs than men, second, because they are less influenced from outisde in their performance—also in general—and have preserved the peasant style of performance much more intact."* (p. 69). *"My informants were of many different ages: the youngest was a five-year-old girl (from whom, to be sure more for curiosity's sake, I wrote down a melody and took down a phonograph recording), the oldest was an 82-year-old woman. The best age for women in this respect is around 40: at that age a peasant woman who takes pleasure in singing is continually learning new songs, without forgetting whose which she learned earlier and is thus to a certain degree a typical bearer of the songs of her region. If she is older, then she forgets ever more numbers from her repertory due to cares, sorrow, the gradual breaking of age."*

Later Bartók noted that the truly ancient ceremonial songs were known to people of all ages, but wedding songs were sung mainly by women.

Bartók's collecting technique developed over the years. In the Preface to his *Rumanian Folk Music*[3] he said *"I have to confess with regret that I did not heed all the requirements of folklore research in the first two years.*

At that time I attacked the problem purely as a musician, not paying much attention to extra-musical circumstances. In the beginning, for instance, I collected only the melody of the dances, not heeding their choreography or designation (that is, genre or function). I did not take down the names, age, and other circumstances of the performers either. Moreover, I did not examine folk music as a living phenomenon with a special view to its being a form of expression of life in a rural community. These deficiencies disappeared gradually so that the collecting work of the last years was quite adequate."

Because Bartók's definition of folk, or peasant, music, as given above included everything regularly sung in the peasant community, some of the melodies in his collections are not "pure folk." And he was very much aware of this fact. As he puts it in the Preface to his *Rumanian Folk Music*, Vol. I, p. 4-5, *"As to the material, the guiding principle in general was to include everything which I had reason to believe was part of the music of the village community. That is, a specimen brought by an individual from a distant area and known only by him was left out. However, everything else, whether rare or well-known, whether of urban or foreign origin, was included. No one should be surprised, therefore, at finding well-known, almost hackneyed, urban, and even foreign melodies in this publication, since the purpose of it is to give as complete a picture of the folk music—that is, all music which the village folk spontaneously use as expression of their musical instinct and feelings—of each area as possible."*

This principle is an admirable one, for an ethnographic report, especially if, like Bartók, the collector can differentiate between urban or foreign and indigenous, and labels it as such. Otherwise music which is urban or foreign may be erroneously labelled as indigenous, because the definition of peasant music given above is not based on musical but on geographic and sociological criteria. In lesser hands than his the material might be misunderstood.

Bartók described his Rumanian collection as follows (pp. 4-5): *"The subject being folk music, I made my collections exclusively from peasants and from people who either were an essential part of village community life or else fitted musically into this life by functions which gave them importance in it (e.g., gypsy violin players). . . . But even with the restriction of our choice to peasants and to village gypsies, some sort of selection [was] necessary. It is not only the mere form of the melodies we have to care about, but also whether the performance and the singing technique of the singers have been spoiled by urban influence. Oddly enough, the Rumanians are especially inclined to take over the habits of performance of urban people. This shows itself mostly in a certain high-flown, sentimental way of performance and unnatural tone-emission. In places where there were Rumanian public schools and mainly where the teacher or other highbrow personage of the village founded a singing chorus for the peasants, this influence proved almost destructive to the style of performance even though the autochthonous melodies were preserved. Fortunately, at the time of the collection whole areas were still almost completely illiterate. . . . There was no need of selection at all. Moreover, with some care and circumspection it was also comparatively easy to find 'unspoiled' singers elsewhere who, although having gone through school, were not affected by the destructive urban influence. It happened but rarely that because of some reason or another one of the peasants used by me proved to be spoiled. . . . As might be expected, women were much more reliable in maintaining the rural style of performance. Men were more subject to wandering; also, compulsory military service tore them away from their homes. This explains the often roisterous and ostentatious manner in the performance of such lads (this is the same with Hungarians and Slovaks as well)."*

Bartók had an unusual sense of order and almost an obsession for accuracy of detail and fulness of information. He wrote an extremely important article on the subject of collecting of folklore, "Why and How Does One Collect Folk Music." It was published in Hungarian in Budapest in 1936 and later translated into French and German, but alas is not available, to the best of my knowledge, in English.[4] It should be required reading for all folklorists, although it sets, indeed, an admittedly impossible goal for the collector of folk music. Bartók wrote, *"It is not enough to have perfect recording equipment, if it is not matched by an equally complete intellectual equipment. In fact, the ideal folklorist should possess a truly encyclopedic erudition. He must have a knowledge of philology and phonetics in order to grasp and appreciate the most subtle nuances of dialectal pronunciation; he must be a choreographer, to be able to define with precision the interrelationship between music and dance; only a broad general knowledge of folklore will permit him to determine in their smallest details the bonds which unite music with the customs [of a people]; without sociological preparation he will not be able to establish the influence exercised on the music by upheavals in the collective life of the village; any final conclusion will be made impossible if he does not have any notions of history, notably in regard to the migration and settlement of various peoples; if he wishes to undertake a comparison among the music(s) of several people, he will have to learn their languages; finally and above all, he must be a musician with a good ear and a good observer."* (p. 5). While he admitted that such a person would never be found, he nevertheless tried earnestly to become such a one himself, and succeeded, if not perfectly—to his own chagrin—more than many others.

[In the same article he continued] *"Once the exploration of a well defined whole, conducted according to the most modern methods has been completed, it will then be a question of confronting the repertoires of the different territories explored and to untangle those elements which are common and those which belong properly to each of them: descriptive musical folklore yields place then to comparative musical folklore. This comparative study, like its neighbor comparative linguistics, often brings to light surprising facts."* (p. 5).

He gave two striking examples from opposite corners of the cultural continuum from central Asia to north Africa. In 1912 he had discovered that the Rumanians in Maramures had a melodic type with an oriental coloring, abundantly ornamental and to some degree improvised. In 1913 in a Saharan village in Central Algeria he came upon a similar style. He was immediately struck by this but didn't dare to attribute it to anything other than coincidence. Only later, as his studies progressed, he began to find the melodic type in question in the Ukraine, in Iraq, in Persia, and in ancient Rumania—not of course, all from his own field trips, for as far as I know he never collected in Iraq or Persia (or in the Ukraine either). So he had to give up coincidence as a hypothesis to explain the similarities. This type he concluded, rightly or wrongly, was indisputably of Persian-Arabian origin, yet it had penetrated to the center of the Ukraine, following an itinerary which is still obscure; *"in fact,"* he wrote, *"we do not know whether a similar melody exists or ever existed among the Osmanli Turks or the Bulgars."* Bartók, a year or so later, was to make a brief investigation of the music of the Osmanli Turks.

"How can one explain these analogies? Thanks to what combination of circumstances can musically identical cultures maintain themselves for centuries among people separated from one another by thousands of miles?" (p. 6). *"The solutions to such problems represent the final goal of musical folklore. If our young discipline places itself conscientiously at the service of such a cause, the practical interest of which is evident, it will be worthy to take its place with its elders. At the same time it will continue to render the service which at the beginning was thought to be its only merit: to give artistic pleasure to all those who have preserved a taste for the beauty of the flowers of the field. Perhaps I do not need to add that it will succeed better by precise and accurate communication, in keeping with scientific standards, than by collections in which folk music is 'corrected' and 'pruned' according to 'the rules of art.'"* (p. 7).

Having outlined the goals of collecting, Bartók turned to a detailed discussion of methods. It was with these principles still clearly on his mind that in November 1936 Bartók went on what was to be his last collecting trip, this time into southern Anatolia at the invitation of the Turkish government and of his great admirer Dr. Adnan Saygün.[5] He spent ten days there and reaped about 90 melodies. Part of his goal, certainly one of the main purposes for the invitation, was to demonstrate to the Turkish scholars who accompanied him the proper methods of field collecting. He described the trip in an article published originally in Hungarian in Budapest in 1937. There are two English versions, one in the *Hungarian Quarterly*[6] and the other an abridged form in *Tempo*,[7] "On Collecting Folk Songs in

Turkey." In the town of Adana he spent two days and was fairly successful. Singers were sent to him from the surrounding villages. This method did not conform with his ideas of proper collecting, which required that the collector go to villages and live with the peasants. But Bartók had been ill and did not think it wise in his first days in the field to go out to the villages.

On the third day he went to a coastal town but found very little. He commented, however—and you do not read this kind of statement in his published collections, but it gives an insight into an aspect of Bartók that was not often seen by outsiders—*"Still there were some compensations: this was a sub-tropical country and then, at the end of November, the weather was warm and lovely; we walked under banana trees in full bloom and covered with fruit, amidst blooming pepper trees, sugar canes, and date trees around us and the temperature never falling to the point of frost."*

The next day he travelled 80 kilometres eastward to a large village called Osmaniye where some of the nomadic Yürüks had settled some 70 years earlier. It is best to let him tell in his own words what happened there:

"We arrived at Osmaniye at 2 pm. At 4 we entered the courtyard of a peasant house and I experienced deep joy because this was the real beginning of collecting peasant music as I had had it in my mind. The master of the house, Ali Bekir oglu Bekir, received us in a friendly way. When asked about his age he answered with some pride (through an interpreter) that in spite of his not having a tooth left he could still eat powerfully whatever he liked and that in spite of his 70 years he could run about in the mountains as quickly as a hare. We soon found out that he himself played an instrument, called 'kemenese,' which was a stringed instrument in the form of a 'rehab.' It is held in the old fashioned way as a violoncello, though an size it is nearer to the violin and it is also tuned as a violin, only the a string is tuned in d.

"There in the courtyard the old man started singing without much further ado. It was an old war-time epic he sang:

Kurt pasa cikli gozana
Akil yetmez 'bu düzene...

"I could hardly believe my ears. Good Lord, this seemed to be the variation of an old Hungarian melody. I was overjoyed and made two records of this song sung by the old Bekir man.

"Meanwhile the sun had set and we had to stop our work while our old friend and his people had their supper. This was Radmadan, a month of fast; for a whole month true believers were forbidden to eat during day time. In the words of the Koran: the daily fast is at its end only when you cannot tell a white piece of string from a black one. The entire population is

religious in this part of the world, even the black-coated officials of the villages are strict in keeping the fast. So the fast caused a little hitch in our plans.

"The second melody the old Bekir gave us was again the variation of a Hungarian melody. This was almost uncanny, I thought. This song was sung in the interior of the house, in a room which no woman was allowed to enter. Sons of the old man and other people gathered around us and gave us their songs, one after the other. The whole evening was spent in work according to my heart's desire."

His experiences in central and southeastern Europe, in essentially non-Moslem regions, had led him, as we saw earlier, to seek women singers, because he had found them the best informants. They preserved, he believed, the old ways of performance better than the men. But in vain did he seek women singers in Turkey. The day after the incident just related he went to another village, but had little luck until one of the men said he would send him "crowds of singers." *"He was as good as his word. He called together a big gathering at the school hall, invited two musicians from a neighbouring village, and the people began dancing. And what a dance this was! The music was strange, almost frightening. One of the musicians played an instrument, called 'zurna,' which was a kind of oboe of very sharp tones; the other had a big drum, called 'davul,' slung over his shoulder. He beat his drum, using a wooden stick, with a diabolical fierceness, so that I expected that either his drum or my ear drums would split any moment. Even the flame of our oil lamp, flickering so peacefully, leapt high at every beat! And the dance! Four men performed it, one as a 'solo dancer,' the other three linked together, accompanying him with a few scanty movements only. At intervals the musicians, too, entered the dance with accompanying steps and movements. All of a sudden the music came to an end, the dancing stopped and a song broke forth. One of the three accompanying men had started singing, sunk in himself with an expression of devotion that I cannot describe in words. He started the song on the highest note of his high tenor voice and moved slowly downwards, as the song neared its end, to more human spheres.*

"I really had reason to feel ashamed of the shabbiness and inadequacy of my recording apparatus. But the best apparatus would still have been less than good enough to do justice to this incomparable scene we had witnessed. It should have been filmed by a very clever artist. There was one factor only that acted as a damper on the fantastic beauty of the scene, and that was the complete absence of old national costumes. All the people wore ordinary shabby suits as worn by Western factory workers. I really could not tell how it was possible that these hideous suits have found their way to the nomadic tribes of the Yürüks and their descendants, whilst in Transylvania and on the Balkans we still could find the most picturesque national costumes."

On the next day they went in the rain to a tent village. The men of the village were away and the women wouldn't sing without permission from their husbands. So they went on to the next camp.

"*Our cart drove across rivers (big and small), the road grew stonier and ceased altogether, and our cart just went on and on rattling over rocky hillsides. This manner of travelling was not very pleasant. It might have been all right without the care of our instruments. But we had to keep the phonographs and the records firmly on our laps. At last we had enough of that business; we walked on, on foot, carrying our fragile treasures on our backs and in our hands. At sunset we at last reached the winter camp of a tribe, called Tecirli. They are also a nomadic tribe, but live in clay huts and not in tents for the winter. Our guide took us to the "house" of a man who seemed rather influential among the families of the tribe, and whom he knew well. This man received us most amiably. A well mannered and tactful man, he did not ask questions about the purpose of our visit or about the funny apparatus we carried with us. He at once ordered a sheep to be killed for our meal, but we said a hen would be sufficient. He invited us to enter his house and we entered a locality which was completely dark and with no windows. There were mattresses in rows along the walls and a fireplace in the middle of the room. Following the local customs, we took off our shoes and were seated in the Turkish way on the mattresses, whilst our host laid a fire. There was no chimney, no window. In a few seconds the room was filled with the most suffocating smoke. If in the previous night our ear drums had to withstand a heavy assault, it was now our eyes' turn!* Varietas delectat! *There was nothing to complain about. Fortunately, it did not take long and the fire burnt with high flames and the smoke found its way out through the gaps of the scantily built walls.*

"*Slowly the room got filled with people from the neighbourhood and we talked and talked very amicably. This went on till seven, and apparently our guide had not even mentioned yet what had brought us here. I was sitting on coals. At seven I heard our guide saying words like 'turku,' 'turk hald musiki,' etc., etc. At last I could hear that folk songs were mentioned and hoped the ice would soon be broken. And indeed, without shyness and hesitation a 15-year-old boy sang the first song, and it was again a melody that sounded Hungarian to me. I quickly prepared my instruments on the mattresses spread out on the floor and took down the song in writing by the light of the wood fire. Well, I thought, now let us begin with the recording. But this did not prove as easy as all that. My good singer was frightened he might lose his voice by singing into a machine obviously driven by a devil; this instrument, he thought, might not only take down his voice, but take it away altogether. It took me long to dispel his fright. Then we worked incessantly, undisturbed till midnight. I thought the time had then come to ask a few delicate questions, especially regarding women. Whether women sing other songs than men. Oh no, by no means, was the short but decided answer. Well, I went on, but surely they knew the same songs and it would be so nice for us to hear these songs sung by women. After some embarassment they informed us that women never sang in the presence of men. Not even a husband had the right to ask his wife for a song. I had to resign myself to this fact, since naturally I could not claim rights greater than those of a husband, and gave up all hope with a sad heart. What a pity! And to know that there in the house were the wives—more than one—of our host! Back in Ankara I told my employers that something had to be done about this question. Either they should send out women on journeys of collection or the male collectors should be accompanied by their wives, who could then deal with the women. It is an impossible situation to have to record lullabies in croacking men's voices when it was obvious that men never lulled their babies to sleep either with or withoug songs!"*

Bartók was really very disappointed with this trip, although he had been warned by his hosts that he was attempting the impossible in the time at his disposal. I must confess that his expectations of accomplishing in ten days more than he did were unrealistic. Nevertheless, he did demonstrate to some degree, though not fully enough to be definitive, the possibility of a relationship in the past between Hungarian and Turkish peasant music. In 20 of the melodies he collected he found a type, showing, to quote, "striking similarities with the downward moving construction of old Hungarian melodies." He also noted a negative finding—the absence of Arabic influence!

It was ironic that a few years later in the United States he would be transcribing melodies from women singers from a Moslem community in Hercegovina whose counterparts in Turkey he had sought so eagerly and in vain.[8] One of those singers indeed sang only Turkish and Albanian songs. At the time I was unaware of his Turkish collecting experiences, but some years afterwards I met Professor Adnan Saygün at a noteworthy conference in Indiana.

The pictures of Bartók taken on that trip to southern Anatolia are priceless, particularly two of him and Prof. Saygün in the cart, with Bartók firmly and protectively clutching the recording apparatus on his lap; and another of the same two with Haci Bekir oğlu Bekir and several city types, the accompanying scholars and local officials. The picture of Bartók sitting on a rug with a Tecirli tribesman outside a nomad tent is also memorable, as is—for a quite different reason—that of Bartók in profile standing alone with a walking cane in his hand against the stark, bleak Turkish landscape of the interior, and lowering and threatening clouds overhead.

Béla Bartók, a genius as a composer, was also an extraordinary theoretician of field collecting and a very fine, if somewhat impatient, collector himself.

NOTES

1. Béla Bartók, *Slovenske l'udove piesne,* Vol. I, pp. 17 ff.
2. Béla Bartók, *Hungarian Folk Music,* translated into English by M. D. Calvocoressi, Oxford University Press, 1931, p. 1.
3. Béla Bartók, *Rumanian Folk Music,* ed. by Benjamin Suchoff, The Hague, 1967.
4. Béla Bartók, *Miert es hogyan gyujtsunk nepzenet?* Budapest, 1936.
   Béla Bartók, *Pourquoi et comment recueilla-t-on la musique populaire?* Geneva, 1948.
   Béla Bartók, "Warum und wie sollen wir Volkmusik sammeln?" in *Béla Bartók, Weg und Werk, Schriften und Briefe,* Ed. by Bence Szabolcsi, Budapest, 1972.
5. A. Adnan Saygūn, *Béla Bartók's Folk Music Research in Turkey,* ed. by Laszlo Vikar, Budapest, 1976.
6. Béla Bartók, "Collecting Folksongs in Anatolia," *The Hungarian Quarterly,* Vol. III, No. 2, Summer, 1937, pp. 337-346.
7. Béla Bartók, "On Collecting Folk Songs in Turkey," *Tempo,* A Quarterly Review of Modern Music, No. 13, Autumn 1949, pp. 15-19.
8. Béla Bartók and Albert B. Lord, *Serbo-Croatian Folk Songs,* Columbia University Press, New York, 1951.

Heuernte – Szénagyűjtéskor – Pri hrabaní
Haymaking

BÉLA BARTÓK AND SLOVAKIA

Michal Želiar

> "... and so I could just as well be considered a Slovak composer."
>
> (From Bartók's letter to the Rumanian musicologist Octavian Beu)

How strange that we Slovaks, who at times claim the fame of people of dubious Slovak origin, forget to stake our enviable share in the life and work of such an exceptional artist as the Hungarian composer, perfomer, and musicologist Béla Bartók, a cosmopolitan figure and pacifist whose centennial is celebrated by the whole world.

Let us immediately raise a painful question: Isn't this unusual humility motivated by vestigial national prejudices and a resistance to the modernity of Bartók's music? Let us try to find an honest answer.

We know that Bartók learned his elementary music lessons from his mother Paula Bartók, *née* Voit, a native of Turec. We also know that he spent his youth in Bratislava, where music was as present as the Danube. Early on, Bartók studied with Bratislava music teachers such as Burger, Erkel, and Hyrtle, and at the age of ten created a stir with his first compositions. After graduation from high school, Bartók left for the Budapest Music Academy, whose teaching staff he eventually joined.

The Hungarian metropolis exerted its charm, and only a few educated provincials returned to their places of origin. Béla Bartók, however, often paid visits to his mother—and to Bratislava. Bratislava was more than a second home to him. Here he found his friends from high school days, the picturesque quarters around the castle, the promenades along the Danube and the tolerant ambience of a trilingual city. Indeed, the Danube and the inhabitants of Bratislava provided the inspiration for two of his compositions, "The Flow of the Danube" and "Dance orientale." Moreover, he wrote several song compositions for the local cultural club called *Toldi kör*. Later, in his honor, the club changed its name to the Béla Bartók Choir.

Yet the young, progressive composer did not confine himself to the musical tradition of Bratislava, even though this tradition was studded with names like Hummel, Haydn, Mozart, Beethoven, Liszt, and Chopin. As a young man he listened not only to the music of the concert halls but also, and even more attentively, to the folk songs of the Slovak peasants. As we read in the preface to Bartók's first collection of Slovak folk songs,

I began my musical-folklore studies in 1906 with the collecting and analysis of Hungarian material. Soon thereafter I realized, however, that, in terms of serious research, the results stemming from the Hungarian material were insufficient and that it was necessary to turn to an examination of the music of the neighboring peoples. By 1906, therefore, I had already started collecting Slovak folk songs and I continued this work—with longer intermissions—into 1918. The ensuing political and economic changes prevented me, however, from pursuing this activity further.

In 1910, Bartók completed the manuscript of "Slovak Songs" which included 400 songs, mostly from the regions of Gemer and Nitra. In 1913 and 1914, he was gathering material in the region of Hont, in 1915—1917 in Pohronie as well as Rákoskeresztúr, where he resided. Even though Bartók investigated quite disparate areas, he was repeatedly taken to task by Slovak ethnomusicologists for not "having examined the Slovak music culture in its entirety" (Professor Hudec). He was criticized for his observation that a "collector who has persisted in collecting the complete, rich 'melographic' material from two or three adjacent Slovak villages finds in his hands, albeit in a condensed form, the musical creation of the whole region."

Bartók stuck to his belief even after his collection of Slovak songs grew more comprehensive than the famous Bartoš collection (which contained 1,050 folk tunes in the 1882 and 2,100 tunes in the 1899 and 1902 editions). *The Encyclopedia of Slovakia* notes that Béla Bartók collected and recorded 3,409 melodies and 4,000 lyrics of Slovak folk songs. All foreign collectors take off their hats to these numbers.

It is likely that Bartók's avid song gathering was prompted by the affection of the Slovak intelligentsia for folk art and particularly folk music. In a 1911 letter to *Matica slovenská*, he wrote:

> It is truly admirable that, without any government subsidy, with only the help of amateur collectors, you yourselves published a beautiful collection unlike any that we Hungarians or the Croats could claim for ourselves. As far as Rumanians are concerned, they have not published any songs at all, not even in Rumania. By the time you publish these 400 songs, I shall probably have collected many more. Lately, my colleague Zoltán Kodály has also been collecting, and on top of this he speaks a good Slovak.

Bartók's familiarity with such abundant musical material could not help but influence the composer's artistic development. In his forty-three piano compositions "For Children" (1908—1909) we find twenty-one compositions inspired by Slovak folk songs. Young pianists the world over are discovering the charm of modern music from the masterful configurations of these pieces.

A student of modern philosophy, Bartók conceived of music as a social phenomenon and paid close attention to the relationships between folk songs and their creators. He was looking for the "mysterious ties between music and nature, man and cosmos, and man and freedom" (Ujfalussy). It is no accident that in the village Hrlica, in the Rimavská Sobota region, he composed his Quintet No. 77, Rhapsody for Piano Op. 1, Scherzo for Piano and Orchestra Op. 2, and that in Radvaň, in 1923, originated one of his most popular compositions, the Dance Suite.

Bartók's bonds to Slovakia were not broken by the aggravating circumstances surrounding the interminable preparations for publication of his manuscripts. By 1920 he had already negotiated the publication of his collection with *Matica slovenská*. A year later he signed a contract and turned a finished manuscript over to Professor Miloš Ruppeldt. In 1924 Viliam Figuš-Bystrý sent 820 corrected manuscript pages, including phonograph transcriptions, to the printers; and four years later he submitted the remaining 401 pages. *Matica slovenská* asked other specialists, such as Miloš Ruppeldt, Jan Valašt'an-Dolinský, and eventually Ivan Ballo, to help with the publication of the definitive edition of Bartók's Slovak folk songs collection. Yet time went by and the expected publication failed to materialize. Neither before nor after the war did the publication appear. Finally, fourteen years after World War II and Bartók's death, the collection came out under the title *Slovak Folk Songs*, Vol. I and II, in 1959 and 1969 respectively.

Why so late?

Much of the delay was surely due to the difficulties which are bound to crop up when the author himself is unable to supervise the editing of an extensive scholarly publication. But more than merely technical impediments interfered with the publication of Bartók's collection. Between the two wars, Slovakia was swept not simply by a wave of healthy national self-consciousness and of social democracy, but, increasingly, by storms of sick and chauvinistic nationalism. The latter inflicted the Slovak people with prejudices which kept them from a discerning and open-minded view of the outside world. Bartók, too, became a victim of this nationalism. In January 1938 Slovak officials refused to allow him to visit Slovakia and give a concert in Bratislava. We can judge by Bartók's subsequent response to Alois Hába's invitiation (in July, 1938) to play a concert in Prague how deeply disturbed he was by the Slovak rejection. Bartók agreed to go to Prague provided that the Slovak officials let him perform in Bratislava as well, and he complained about the "humiliation" he suffered in a place to which he felt so close.

The avalanche of World War II tumbled down on the world, and there was no time to smooth out disagreements or to heal wounds. Bartók went into exile. He had a moral right to bear a grudge against Slovakia. But in spirit he kept returning to it again and again. As we are told by his close friend and expert on his music, Professor Jenö Takács of the University of Cincinnati, "Slovakia, its music and people, figured among the memories Bartók treasured until his death in New York in 1945."

To conclude this modest piece on the occasion of Bartók's centenary, let us return to the opening quotation from the letter to Octavian Beu.

Bartók penned this letter on 10 January 1939, that is, after having been officially rejected by Slovakia. And yet despite all this he said that he could also be considered a Slovak composer, and he went on to explain:

> But what really matters, and what I have realized ever since I became a composer, is the idea of fraternal coexistence among peoples. We are bound to it in spite of all the wars and conflicts. I place my music at its service and I want to serve it as long as I have the strength in me. For this reason I do not resist any influences, whether they come from Slovak, Rumanian, Arabic, or whatever other sources. Only that the spring be clean, fresh, and healthy.

Here we encounter the spirit of a man who has a great deal to say not only to us but to the world at large.

Translated by F. W. Galan

HÁBA'S MICROTONAL THEORIES IN YUGOSLAVIA

Jelena Milojković-Djurić

The innovative concepts of the Czech composer Alois Hába in the field of microtonal music, which evolved after the First World War, were part of a widespread movement toward the development of new musical resources. Prior to Hába's experiments, the efforts of Busoni, Schönberg, Möllendorf, and Vyshnegradsky had resulted in a variety of novel subdivisions of the octave, pointing to fresh possibilities for the organization of sound. An important aspect of this movement was the interest generated by Hába's quest for a new musical language, both in his own native land and abroad; his innovations found support especially in Yugoslavia.

Hába had become independently aware of microtonal possibilities long before acquainting himself with the theories and contributions of composers elsewhere. According to his recollections, his ear was so keen that even as a child while tuning his violin, he could discern a variety of minute intervals smaller than a whole or a half step. Consequently he decided to subdivide the half steps into quarter-tone intervals, analagous to the division of a whole step into half steps. In the course of time he managed not only to play quarter-tone intervals by themselves, but also intervals such as a major third altered by an additional quarter tone, testing new and unexplored sound possibilities. [1]

There was also another untapped source that led to further elaboration of Hába's quarter-tone system: the Moravian folk song. Hába, a native of Moravia, was born in Vizovice in 1893, and as a musically endowed child was very much aware of the rich tradition of musical folklore. Hába observed that some folk melodies contained quarter-tone intervals, usually as a subtle emphasis of the melodic line enhancing the expression of the song. The diatonic flow of the melody, with the introduction of a quarter-tone interval, was enriched by a specific accentuation of the underlying text.[2] It is exactly this method that Hába chose to introduce both systematically and creatively in his theoretical studies and in his compositions. Hába understood the quarter-tone system as an expansion and continuation of the half-tone system. The new system included twenty-four tones instead of twelve. Therefore, it was possible, Hába stressed "... to form new scales for new melodic constructions and ... new harmonic relations."[3] Hába noted, however, that if a composer wished to use triads rooted in the traditional tonal system, as well as more complex tonal configurations, he had this freedom of choice. Furthermore, Hába was careful to point to the advantages of freely combining the tonal resources of both systems, since the strict use of only quarter-tone material could create a feeling of saturation.[4]

The theories of Alois Hába were presented to the Yugoslav public in an authoritative study written by Miloje Milojević and published in 1926 in Belgrade, in his first book of collected articles on music.[5] Hába himself acknowledged the study with gratitude in a paper written several years later. Hába stated that at a time when critics were constantly casting doubts on the validity of quarter-tone music and even claiming the absurdity of such a system, Milojević was the only one to devote a lengthy, objective report to this topic.[6] In the same article Hába mentioned the support of Josip Slavenski, another well-known Yugoslav composer. In 1923 Hába received from Slavenski two folk songs from Yugoslavia encompassing in their melodic line quarter-tone intervals. Slavenski himself collected and recorded these melodies.[7]

Miloje Milojević, a noted composer, educator, and musicologist, wrote his study of Alois Hába upon his return from Prague in 1925. Milojević had gone to Prague as a mature person in order to accomplish his musicological studies at Charles University under the tutelage of Zdeněk Nejedlý.[8] He stayed in Prague during the academic year 1924-1925, enrolling in three consecutive semesters. In his dissertation, "Smetana's Harmonic Style," Milojević was to establish the typical traits of Smetana's musical language by analyzing harmonic progressions formulated in Smetana's compositions. In view of the existence of an extensive body of musicological research devoted to the study of Smetana's life and compositional output, it is worth noting the favorable reception that Milojević's dissertation was accorded as an original contribution in the country of Smetana's birth.

While in Prague, Milojević keenly observed the musical scene as well as the cultural life of Prague as one of the liveliest European capitals of Europe of the day. Milojević was especially attracted to the personality of Alois Haba and the novelties of his theoretical and compositional approach. Although sufficiently open to new ideas, Milojević himself, as an already formed composer, never composed in this vein. Milojević remarked in his study that due attention should be given to Hába's work even if one did not agree with his ideas and concepts or with the necessity of dissemination of the quarter-tone system. Hába's contribution, he wrote, was a pioneering effort by a well-trained musician with profound respect for the rich heritage of the musical past. Milojević was also aware that to be vital, cultural development must not stagnate, and as evidence offered the diversity of numerous artistic movements of the period. Therefore, the contribution of the "cultural revolutionaries of music" deserved examination as a source of elements of a future musical language.[9]

In addition, Milojević warned of the dangers of passing an unjust and hasty judgment, as had often been done in the past. It would suffice to mention the unfavorable receptions of some compositions of Rameau, Gluck, Beethoven, or Wagner. Milojević also pointed to the fact that there was insufficient historical distance to allow an accurate evaluation of recent and contemporary trends.[10]

Hába's belief in the importance of a thorough knowledge of the musical heritage as a point for departure on any new path was repeatedly praised by Milojević. In many studies and articles Milojević persistently advocated the necessity of perpetuating the knowledge of the past as a means of preserving the continuity of artistic development. Similarly, Haba insisted that the future recognition of new and still undiscovered sound possibiliies would continue. Hába even anticipated the occurrence of new tonal resources. Thus the limits that the quarter- and sixth-tone system might impose would be surpassed by further efforts. The present diatonic system Hába understood "only as a part of a wider tonal range."[11]

Since the quarter-tone system was also a response to the existing crisis in music, Hába did not limit his presentation to the acoustical properties of the new system alone. Therefore he stated: "It should be understood that the new intervals and the new sound are not the essence of the new musical system." The new musical forms that would correspond to the new musical sound would also reflect the "basically different way of thinking and feeling," reflecting the spirit of the time. Hába believed that old musical forms such as the sonata, rondo, and fugue, and the stylistic characteristics inherent in the periodocity of the melody, thematic structure, and transpositions of motives and sequences, should be abandoned. Instead Hába favored the development of asymetrical melodies in a continuous and spontaneous flow. The new polyphony should make use of contrary and parallel motions in a free style which would avoid certain schematic forms of counterpoint originating in past periods.[12]

Milojević considered Hába's efforts especially valuable since he stressed that music is not a play of sounds and rhythmical patterns, but an element of truth expressing the spiritual concepts of an individual. In conclusion, Milojević did not believe that the subdivision of a diatonic scale would bring practical and positive results to the musical art. Nevertheless, he agreed with the aesthetic and artistic credo of Hába and his novel aspirations. Milojević dedicated his study to his students, as if predicting that in the course of time some of them would become Hába's disciples.

Among the Yugoslav musicians who went to Prague to study with Hába at the State Conservatory were Slavko Osterc, Dragutin Čolić, Vojislav Vučković, Ljubica Marić, Pavel Šivic, Marijan Lipovšek, and Marko Ristić. Hába himself gave a valuable account about his students in an article entitled "Young Yugoslav Composers and Quarter-Tone Music," published in 1933 in the music review *Zvuk*. Haba stated that Slavko Osterc was the first Yugoslav composer to graduate from the Division for Quarter-Tone Music at the Conservatory. Hába singled out the achievement of Dragutin Čolić who graduated in 1932. Čolić had composed a Concerto for a Quarter-Tone Piano and String Sextet. Haba praised Čolić's compositional abilities, stressing that his Concerto represented a remarkable contribution to quarter-tone music. Čolić created an original work in a free athematic style. Furthermore Haba wrote that Čolic was a well-educated musician with a profound knowledge of the contemporary developments in music. Thus Čolić was very much aware of the compositional and theoretical work of Arnold Schönberg in the field of twelve-tone music. It was Hába's opinion that Čolić was a valuable collaborator in the free athematic style and quarter-tone music.[13] Summing up his evaluation, Hába expressed the opinion that Čolić was well-suited to educate the Yugoslav public about the new compositional principles. It would be his duty to explain the mutual goals that would contribute to the renewed development of European music.[14]

Another student of Hába, Vojislav Vučković, presented the microtonal theory of his teacher in 1935 in Belgrade at the Public University Kolarac. Since its foundation in 1932 a series of lectures on music had been incorporated in its cultural program, engaging prominent personalities from the musical sphere. Vučković was invited to lecture as a promising young musician after the completion of his studies at the State Conservatory, and shortly after earning a doctorate of musical sciences at Charles University in Prague in 1934.[15]

Vučković's lecture, "On Quarter-Tone Music," was later published, and incorporated in several different editions of his collected works.[16] Vučković aimed to establish that the occurrence of quarter-tone music should not be associated only by name with its founder Alois Hába, but rather with the general development of modern music during the two first decades of the twentieth century. However, the experience gained in this process influenced the consequent evolution of musical thought. Vučković pointed out that the occurrence of quarter-tone music had parallels in other areas of human endeavor, especially with the advent of Cubism in pictorial art.[17] Hába's attempts, he wrote, were very much dictated by the wish to solve the widespread feeling of a crisis in music. Hába wanted to ensure further development by providing a theoretical explanation of new possibilities, presenting the quarter-tone system as a logical consequence and continuation of diatonic music. Hába, he continued, wanted to free composers from imposed restrictions in order to open a new creative flow of artistic imagination. Pointing to the futility of the dogmatic classification of functional tonality as the only *natural* system, Hába argued that any different comprehension of tonal resources was unjustly labeled as destructive.[18]

In his lecture Vučković tried to stress the advantages of the quarter-tone system, although he was aware that Hába's innovative efforts were not widely accepted. Part of this failure Vučković attributed to the scarcity of specially constructed instruments. Several quarter-tone instruments had been manufactured on Hába's initiative, but remained commercially unavailable. However, Vučković came to believe as a musicologist and practicing composer that the subdivision of intervals alone could not provide a solution to the crisis in music. Thus Vučković and other members of the group around Hába's Division for Quarter-Tone Music gradually started to reevaluate their position and outlook.

Interestingly enough, this change in attitude towards musical avant garde tendencies mirrored changes that were taking place on a wider scale in the late twenties and thirties throughout Europe. The economic, social, and political crises of the period influenced the aesthetic and artistic areas as well, bringing a rejection of the innovations introduced in the earlier part of the century.[19] Atonal, athematic, dodecaphonic as well as quarter-tone composing was abandoned in favor of a simpler and more accessible musical language. Although Hába's quarter-tone system did not prevail, it nevertheless represents a lasting testimony to his musical vision. His search for a new and more truthful expression inspired a number of composers in their creative endeavors.

[1] A. Hába, "Harmonické základy čtvrttonové soustavy," *Hudební Matice Umělecké Besedy* (Prague, 1922); quoted after V. Vučković, "O četvrt tonskoj muzici," in *Studije, eseji, kritike* (Belgrade: Nolit, 1968), 358-59.

[2] In 1956, in Stockholm, the author of these lines attended a public lecture by Hába on quarter-tone music. During his presentation Hába sang excerpts of some Moravian folk melodies with quarter-tone intervals.

[3] A. Hába, "Harmonické základy ... "; quoted after M. Milojević, "Ideje Aloiza Habe," *Muzičke studije i članci* (Belgrade, Geca Kon, 1926), p. 55.

[4] Ibid., 55-56.   [5] Ibid., pp. xv, 168.

[6] Alois Hába, "Mladi jugoslovenski kompozitori i četvrttonska muzika," *Zvuk*, No. 3 (Belgrade, 1933), p. 81.

[7] Ibid.

[8] Milojević was born in 1884 in Belgrade and completed his general music education in 1910 at the Music Academy in Munich, Germany.

[9] M. Milojević, "Ideje Aloiza Habe," p. 41.

[10] Ibid., p. 42.   [11] Ibid., p. 58.   [12] Ibid., 58-61.

[13] A. Hába, "Mladi jugoslovenski kompozitori i četvrttonska muzika," 82-83.

[14] Ibid., p. 83.

[15] Vučković (b. 1910) managed to make a strong impact on the cultural life of Prague and Belgrade, although he lived only until 1942. Cf. also: J. Fukač, "Die Tradition des musiksoziologischen Denkens in der Tschechoslovakei," *Die Musiksoziologie in der Tschechoslovakei* (Prague: Tschechoslovakisches Musikinformationszentrum, 1967), 12-14.

[16] *Muzika od kraja XVI do XX veka* (Belgrade, 1936); *Izbor eseja* (Belgrade, 1955); *Umetnost i umetničko delo* (Belgrade, 1962); *Studije, eseji, kritike* (Belgrade, 1968).

[17] V. Vučković, "O četvrt-tonskoj muzici," *Studije, eseji, kritike* (Belgrade, 1968), p. 358.

[18] Ibid., 363-64.

[19] E. Salzman, *Twentieth-Century Music: An Introduction* (Englewood Cliffs: Princeton-Hall, 1967), p. 78.

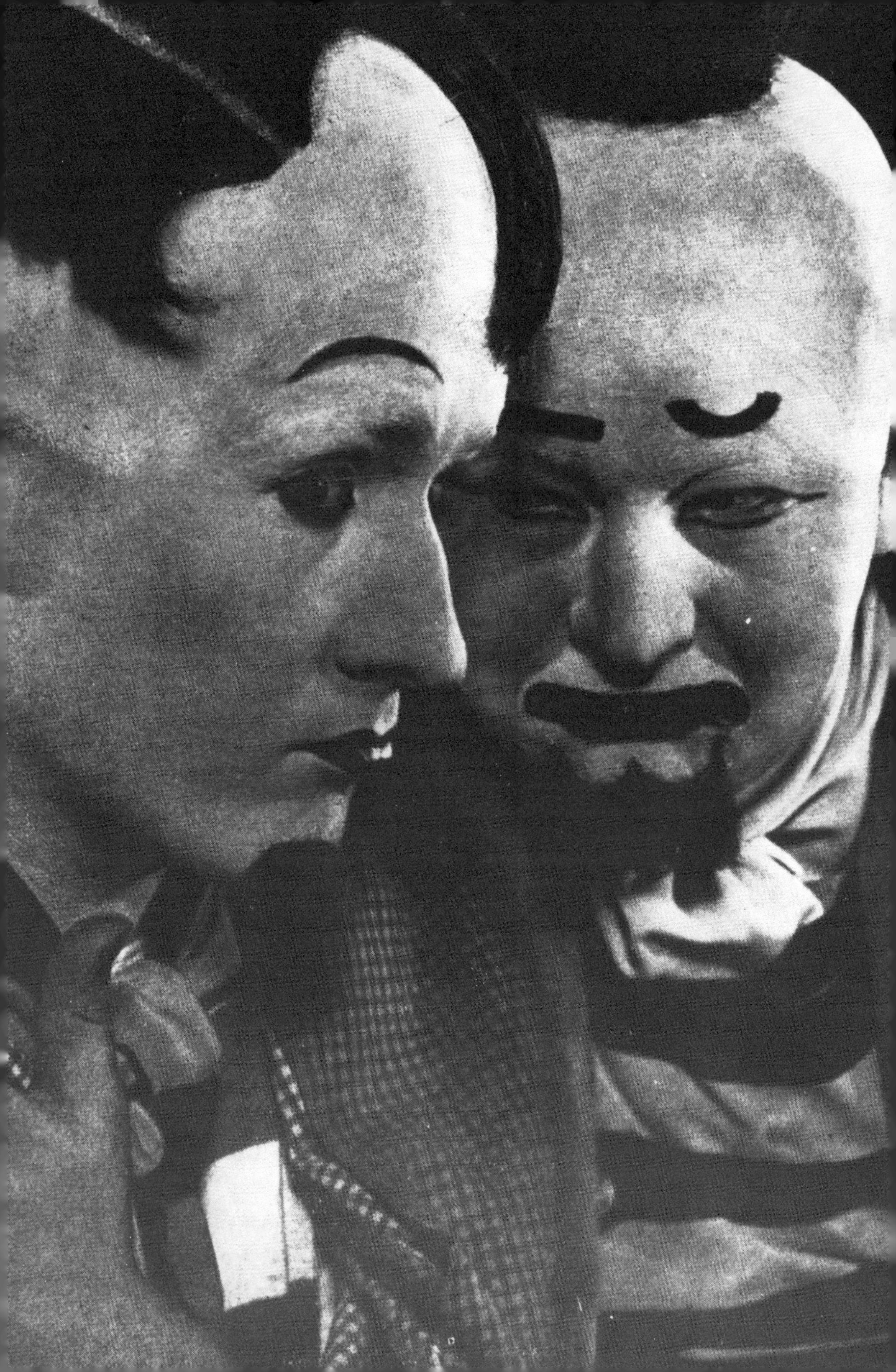

THE LIBERATED THEATRE OF VOSKOVEC AND WERICH

Jarka M. Burian
New York University

With the death of Jan Werich (31 October 1980) and Jiří Voskovec (1 July 1981) within a year of one another, the final echoes of a great era of modern Czech theatre have been stilled. There was something fitting in the most popular, best-loved author-comedians of the Czech stage of the twenties and thirties outliving their notable contemporaries: the playwright brothers Čapek; the directors K.H. Hilar, E.F. Burian, J. Honzl, and J. Frejka; the actors V. Vydra, V. Burian, and E. Kohout; and the designers V. Hofman, A. Heythum, B. Feuerstein, and F. Tröster. In surviving into the 1980's, Voskovec and Werich kept alive something of the independence and adventure of the prewar First Republic. Although they did not work importantly as a team in Czechoslovakia after 1938, and although they lived on separate sides of the Atlantic since the late 1940's, the sheer magic of their enormous appeal to all classes remained in the memory of Czechs all over the globe until the present. Nor is it likely that in death that memory will fade, for they embodied qualities central to the Czech spirit during its brightest and also darkest hours: resiliency, wit, and humanity.

It was my privilege to become acquainted with these two intellectual clowns in their later years as I was doing research on modern Czech theatre, although I first encountered them in January 1939 when, at the age of twelve, I accompanied my parents to V & W's initial, semi-improvised public performance in New York City shortly after their arrival from Czechoslovakia. In that ominous, morbid period between Munich and the final annihilation of the Czechoslovak Republic in March 1939, Voskovec and Werich (and Ježek) symbolized not only a spirit of survival but also a certain triumph over adversity by the sheer buoyancy and inventiveness of their comedy.

In the 1970's, when I met them personally, Jan Werich lived in his villa in Prague's Malá Strana (Lesser Quarter) under the lofty escarpment of Hradčany, the ancient seat of government, while Voskovec had a townhouse in New York City but was more often on the move with his fulltime professional career as an actor in theatre, film, and television. Werich's involuntary retirement (illness and politics) did not prevent him from maintaining a kind of casual salon where one might find not only long-time neighbors but also visitors from theatre and other arts, government, and commerce. His occasional public appearances were occasions for displays of mass affection and nostalgia for better times. Voskovec, who returned to the United States permanently in 1950, had a relatively more diverse and professionally more productive life. He maintained remarkable fitness and had only recently made a major move to the West Coast in order to facilitate his career and enjoy a healthier climate. The two maintained continual though intermittent communication by mail, phone, and through intermediaries. Their last brief reunion occurred in New York in 1968.

In the following study (abridged from its original publication in the Educational

Theatre Journal *in 1977), I* attempted to document the special career of these provocative, profound entertainers in relation to the shifting fortunes of their homeland, although the article could have been subtitled "The Shifting Masks of Comedy in a Changing World."

* * *

By far the most popular and, according to many, the most relevant theatre in Czechoslovakia in the period between the wars was Prague's Liberated Theatre (Osvobozené divadlo) of Voskovec and Werich. Many of its routines and songs were known by heart, recordings of its songs sold in the tens of thousands, its plays were performed by amateurs soon after they were released, and films made by Voskovec and Werich with or without other members of their company were sure-fire hits.[1] The theatre had a relatively brief but brilliant life of slightly more than eleven years. Its first performance occurred a half century ago, in the relatively easy and optimistic days of 1927, and its final curtain fell a scant month or two before the Munich agreement effectively terminated the existence of Czechoslovakia's First Republic in 1938. If ever a theatre became spokesman of a generation or rallying point of a nation, it was the Liberated Theatre during its final years, as fascism was gaining ever greater strength and arrogance in Europe. Jiří Voskovec and Jan Werich became the stuff of myth, and during the war memories of their plays and their performances contributed significantly to sustaining the morale of the occupied nation. Today, nearly forty years after the close of their Liberated Theatre and nearly thirty years after their last appearance together on stage, they are still legendary figures in Czechoslovakia, their names—or simply the initals V + W —more readily recognized than those of most theatre artists since their time.

During its brief existence their Liberated Theatre presented twenty-five full-length original productions, variations of a basic revue pattern which they developed into a flexible, distinctive form that moved toward musical comedy or, indeed, drama with musical interludes, with political satire as its core.[2] For all but one of those productions Voskovec and Werich were the sole authors and librettists; they were, moreover, the leading actors, and frequently one or both of them served as designer or director.

They made their greatest impact performing the central roles in each production. Regardless of the details of a given plot, they appeared in stylized

---

Jarka M. Burian is a Professor in the Department of Theatre at the State University of New York at Albany. He is the author of *The Scenography of Josef Svoboda* and other studies of the modern theatre in Czechoslovakia. Research for the present article was conducted mainly in Prague in 1974 – 1975 and included tape recorded interviews with its principal subjects. The research was funded by a grant awarded by the International Research and Exchanges Board. *Copyright 1977, Jarka M. Burian.*

white makeup, like eternal clowns or zanni of the *commedia*, but with the difference that their comedy could be intellectually sophisticated and they themselves were highly articulate. A good deal of their charm and comic effectiveness derived from their basic stage identities as naive, earnest, good-natured, but invincibly dense personalities, grown-up but ingenuous boys ineffectually coping with a world they could not comprehend. Twenty-two-year-old law students when they launched *Vest Pocket Revue*, they created figures "whose stupidity is boundless. It is so vast that at times it borders on wit." [3] Werich was the larger of the two, the more impulsive and elemental, yet he possessed remarkable grace in movement and facility in rapid, staccato speech. Voskovec, who was slighter in figure (though by no means small), more tentative and seemingly shy, suggested a certain self-consciousness and reserve. It was he who usually initiated and seemed to guide their verbal exchanges, he who usually made slightly pedantic distinctions in their dialogues. His voice, although not deep, was pitched slightly lower than Werich's, and his speech tempo was allegro to Werich's presto. Paradoxically, however, such seeming contrasts did not create the impression of two independent or conflicting personalities; nor was one a straight man for the other. Instead, as their editor and long-time critic Josef Träger observed, it was as if one heard "a monologue spoken by two voices at once ... [which] showed two sides of one attitude expressed by an indivisible although doubled personality." [4] What was true of their onstage performance also applied to their creativity as playwrights and librettists. Ranging from student lampoons to Aristophanic satire, their humor was the product of a dual artistry; two halves of a single creative inspriation.

Meyerhold visited Prague on a trip home from Paris in the fall of 1936. After seeing two of Voskovec and Werich's productions and spending the better part of several days and nights in their company, he inscribed the following in their theatre's guest book:

> In 1913, my friend, the late poet Apollinaire, took me to the Cirque Medrano. After what we'd seen that night, Apollinaire exclaimed: "These performers—using the means of the *commedia dell'arte*—are saving theatre for artists, actors, and directors." Since then, from time to time, I would return to the Medrano, hoping to intoxicate myself again with the hashish of improvised comedy. But Apollinaire was gone. Without him I could no longer find the artists he had shown me. I looked for them with a longing heart but the Italian "lazzi" were no more. Only tonight, October 30, 1936, I saw the "zanni" again in the persons of the unforgettable duo of Voskovec and Werich, and was once more bewitched by performers rooted in the Italian *commedia ex improviso*. Long live *commedia dell'arte*! Long live Voskovec and Werich! [5]

What distinguished their theatre and its performances? The best way to begin an answer is to refer to their own explanation of the meaning of the name of their theatre: "Liberated from what? ... Simply from all the extraneous freight that changed the pure, original nature of theatre ... to the unbearable waxworks of naturalism, symbolism, pontifical mediocrities and contorted experimenters." [6] Their consistent and heartfelt rejection of realism was perhaps most succinctly and cheekily expressed in a few lines from their very first production, *Vest Pocket Revue*:

> Realism on stage is a loathesome creature,
> Away with realism in theatre! Hurrah! [7]

Instead of realism, the ideal was fantasy, the poetic, lyrical fantasy of bright colors, masks, costumes and lights creating a special stage enchantment, as well as the fantasy of surprise, shock, and even aggression: "Not boy meets girl, boy marries girl. Fantasy, sir, *that's* theatre! Terrifying fantasy, diseased fantasy, madness.... Unbelievable things! Things that not even the smartest in the audience can anticipate." [8] Love of fantasy was wedded to an instinctive love of the theatrical, sheer delight in the game of performing; theatre was for them "a great social game." The zest for theatricality was evident in the format of most of their productions, the frequent prologues directly addressed to the audience, the stylized clown-white makeup of Voskovec and Werich, and, occasionally, the use of theatre itself as a framing element of their plots. But laughter, exuberant, liberating, even gratuitous laughter, was the essence and final cause of their art, their game, even when their satire became most seriously engaged with grim realities beyond the walls of their theatre.

Their rejection of realism, their inherent flair for theatricality, and their delight in producing laughter were nowhere more evident than in their forestage improvisations that punctuated the action of their productions. These distinctive routines began accidentally in their very first production when a piece of scenery fell and forced them to improvise a comic exchange downstage of the quickly drawn curtain while the scenery was readjusted. In their subsequent improvisations, which became a regular, keenly anticipated part of their productions, they would make a transition from incidental participation in the action to detached commentary not only on that action but, more pointedly, on the world outside the theatre. At other times, their sallies would not be focused on the real world at all, but instead would pursue in surrealistic fashion the comic absurdities implicit in language itself, or as Voskovec put it, the "satire of language on language.... On our delight in catching ourselves in the butterfly net of the abstract." [9] The Czech language, among the most heavily inflected of Indo-European tongues, especially lends itself to such butterfly nets. Peppering their dialogues were slang, multilingual punning (they were facile in German, French, Russian, and more limitedly, English), and allusions drawn from classical mythology, history, and international politics. Indeed, it is not surprising that their theatre became fondly known as one for *maturanti* (liberal arts students), for it provided a verbal feast for the alert mind. Nevertheless, it would be misleading to suggest that they played to an elite, for their productions attracted throngs from all levels except the stuffiest bourgeoisie.

Viewed in retrospect, the form of their productions can be seen evolving from loosely structured revues toward thematically unified, plotted, integrated combinations of dramatic action, musical numbers, and improvisatory routines by Voskovec and Werich. The revue form remained throughout in the pattern of different theatrical elements assembled to make a single evening's entertainment, but the shift from random parody and muscial numbers to a dramatically developed spine of action to which music and comic routines were joined is significant. Moreover, although this development might have occurred independently of external social and political circumstances, it is likely that those circumstances strongly influenced the evolution of the productions.

The essential point is that Voskovec and Werich's response to the world moved from delighted wonder or amazement at the absurdities of reality to a disturbed recognition of ills in their own society and even more alarming threats from abroad, and finally to a commitment to challenging and resisting those negative and aggressive forces. Never members of any party or allied with any ideology, dedicated to an autonomous world of theatre and the sheer delight of performing, they evolved into acute social critics and their theatre became a morale-inspiring force for democracy and national unity. Nevertheless, their fundamental purpose, from first production to last, remained comedy and laughter as the "hygiene of the soul."[10] Their productions never lost their essential identity as works of art, as worlds of imagination and fantasy. As their director Honzl put it, "Their world has a different sun and stars. A world of complete artifice. Music comes to mind."[11] Indeed, the tension between self-sufficient comic entertainment and socially engaged activism gives special interest to their mature productions and suggests the distinctive quality of their art. A survey of their productions will clarify the different forms and directions taken by that art.

Among their earliest productions were three pure revues. *Vest Pocket Revue*, *Smoking Revue* (May 1928), and *The Dice Are Cast* (January 1929) were fresh, irreverent, very casually assembled medlies of parodistic skits, the latest musical fads, and isolated songs and dances, with Voskovec and Werich basting together the elements with the slightest of plot threads. Objects of parody and satire included realistic drama, Constructivism as a way of life, the gilded youth of Prague, and stuffy Czech cultural leaders. The musical numbers were mostly based on American jazz hits, with Czech lyrics. *Smoking Revue* and *The Dice Are Cast* were self-conscious repetitions of the *Vest Pocket Revue* formula; although they had some good segments, neither was a success. Voskovec and Werich were unable to recapture the fresh spontaneity of their first work.

Four other early plays were of two types. *Having a Spree* (October 1928) was the first of their several adaptations of existing plays, in this case Johann Nestroy's *Einen Jux will er sich machen* (Thornton Wilder's source for *The Matchmaker*). Both it and the other three, *Gorila ex Machina* (November 1928), *The Diving Suit* (March 1929) and *The Trial is Adjourned* (October 1929), were also attempts, none very successful, at conventionally structured boulevard comedy. Original scripts that spoofed dime novels and detective stories, the last three can be viewed in retrospect as misguided attempts to branch off from the loose revue form and yet achieve the success of *Vest Pocket Review*. One revealing remark related to *Having a Spree* suggests their notion of self-sufficient comedy at that time: "We rank pure, non-tendentious laughter above a satiric smile." [12] The relative lack of a target for laughter may have been one of the problems of these non-revue productions. A more essential problem was that Voskovec and Werich played characters other than themselves, and the public was not interested. Both they and Honzl finally realized that traditional boulevard comedy was not their proper form, that whatever success they had previously achieved was rooted in their talents as a unique twosome playing presentational comedy that stressed their own stage personalities. And so they turned back to the revue form, but with a difference. The new, more fully evolved and structured revue, as envisaged by them, matured over a period of three years in a series of eight productions, from *Fata Morgana* in late 1929 to *A World Behind Bars* in early 1933. They called these works Jazz Revues because of the great significance of music in them and because jazz connoted for them the distinctive pulse of the postwar world.[13] The very titles of the first and last of these works suggest the thematic distance that they spanned.

Fata Morgana (December 1929) was of particular significance for Voskovec and Werich because it marked their affiliation with a number of major co-artists. It was, for example, their first substantial collaboration with the composer Ježek and the choreographer Jenčík and his dancers, who became known simply as the "Girls." It was, moreover, the first production for which they employed a professional stage designer, František Zelenka. Another affiliation was temporarily suspended during this and the next season. Jindřich Honzl departed for Brno at the end of the previous season, where he remained for two years as the chief director of drama at the National Theatre. During those two seasons, Voskovec took over direction of the Liberated Theatre's five productions, a task which he obviously performed well, but which he gladly relinquished when Honzl returned in the fall of 1931.

The Jazz Revues caught on, and a basic form became established: an entertainment in two parts with a reasonably firm plot line that incorporated at least one multi-character scene of broad farce comedy, some half-dozen song and dance numbers growing out of the main action, and two or three relatively independent forestage interludes by Voskovec and Werich. Thematically, the emphasis was on the non-erotic and the non-political, as the following lyric from *Fata Morgana* makes clear:

> You may rest assured
> We won't be vulgar
> We've forbidden ourselves forever
> The erotic element.
> Not knowing our way in politics
> Even in the slightest
> We'll avoid, willy nilly,
> Political satire. [14]

But during the years between *Fata Morgana* and *A World Behind Bars* the world-wide economic crisis made itself felt in Czechoslovakia where rapidly escalating unemployment produced social discord. The turmoil was exacerbated not only by wide-spread resurgent militarism and dictatorship in Europe but also by the rise of the Nazi Party in Germany and sympathetic fascist vibrations in Czechoslovakia. A critical socio-political event occurred in November 1931 when groups of demonstrating unemployed workers in the northern Bohemian area of Fryvaldov were fired upon by police and military units. Voskovec and Werich, along with countless other artists and intellectuals, were appalled and outraged.

Until then, the revues had concentrated on providing essentially escapist entertainment that only occasionally and incidentally noted disquieting social realities like colonialism (*Dynamite Island*, March 1930), increasing world militarism (*North Against South*, September 1930), or domestic unemployment (*Golem*, November 1931). Otherwise, the prevailing tone was of good-humored, screwball comedy usually placed in an exotic setting: the tropics (*Dynamite Island*), South America (*Don Juan and Co.*, January 1931), America during the Civil War (*North Against South*), or Renaissance Prague (*Golem*). The proceedings were dominated by Voskovec and Werich as they wove in and out of a main plot line which only gradually developed substance and coherence. A definite progression was evident toward tighter, more controlled plot construction and also toward a relatively more artistic integration of dramatic action, character delineation, musical production numbers, and the Voskovec and Werich duet sequences, culminating—as form—in *Golem*, a charming blend of romantic fable and atmosphere, relatively mature character interaction, and sustained comic invention. In *Golem*, the revue form almost gave way to a form of romantic comedy with incidental music, dance, and satiric comment. But the Fryvaldov incident occurred during the run of *Golem* and led to Voskovec and Werich's decisive turn toward much more direct involvement with the realities outside their theatre.

The subsequent production was *Caesar* (March 1932), the first of a group of vigorously satiric productions which, while maintaining the basic Jazz Revue format, reacted with a sustained, essentially negative attack on military dictatorship abroad, various forms of contemporary fascism, and the ills of a disintegrating domestic economy. The productions took a stand against a variety of contemporary evils; not until later did Voskovec and

Werich devise productions that had a positive, rallying thrust.

The engaged quality of their work in *Caesar* is captured in their remarks referring to that production."The disrupted, collapsing material world lies open before the artist and awaits his clear, divinely refreshing order. It is no longer possible to doubt that reality in its decay has ripened toward a state so critical that it would be criminal for an artist not to express his point of view. Formerly, art abandoned reality for good because it smelled. Today reality stinks and the artist must join the activists, the politicians, and the revolutionaries in order to remove the corpse." [15]

The attack in *Caesar*, aimed primarily at the machinations of European power politics, was embodied in bizarre plots and counterplots among Caesar (based on Mussolini), Brutus, Antony, Cleopatra, and others just prior to Caesar's appearance at the Senate during the Ides of March. Receiving almost equally strong satiric attention were corrupt domestic wheeling and dealing in the modern Parliament, depicted as the Roman Senate, and the grim follies of militarism and war-mongering in general, all practised at the expense of an ill-informed citizenry.

In this production, as in virtually all the Jazz Revues, Voskovec and Werich played secondary roles, characters peripheral to the main action who happen to stumble into it or be caught up by it. Usually they appeared for the first time near the end of the first act and then took the lead in a large production number that acted as a finale for the first half of the evening. In the second half they became entangled in the main action. In *Caesar* they played two plebeians, Bulva and Papullus. Near the end of the production, in a scene that updated the action to the present, they appeared in modern dress to review the current status of an ailing Europe (represented by a map showing the continent in the form of a woman). The very last scene showed the Forum being visited by a group of modern tourists, who are recognizably the characters from antiquity in modern dress. Caesar's dictatorship is ironically praised as a victory of tradition over hasty and rash progress, while Voskovec and Werich appear as news hawkers selling an "extra" edition that headlines the latest economic dilemmas of Europe.

Although the subject matter was marked by a confrontation of meaningful issues, the form remained that of the Jazz Revue, and the mixture was unsatisfactory because the theme and form were not really integrated. The satire was strong and pointed but not adequately sustained or consistent in tone largely due to the presence of elements from the non-politicized, escapist revues. In terms of a successful integration of subject, theme, and form, *Caesar* was actually a step backward from *Golem*.

The next two productions, which were transitional, can still be related to the Jazz Revue series but also anticipated the subsequent Political Revues. Neither was as effective as *Caesar*. It was as if Voskovec and Werich were not able to shape a controlled, well-organized plot to carry their recently developed, socially conscious satire and also create musical numbers that would function dramatically with that satire. *Robin the Brigand* (September 1932), a reworking of Robin Hood material, echoed many motifs from *Caesar*: militarism, demagoguery, social injustice, crises of unemployment and the economy. The problem was that thematically *Robin* was not much more than an echo, and in terms of form it managed to blend the revue components with even less success than did *Caesar*. As in every Voskovec and Werich production, to be sure, there were some outstanding comic routines and isolated moments, and at least one notable song, "Be Seeing You in Better Times," a foreshadowing of their later emphasis on collective action in adversity.[16]

A World Behind Bars (January 1933) was the only production on which Voskovec and Werich collaborated with another writer, Adolf Hofmeister. The result was a curiosity presenting a grotesque caricature of American prohibition as symptomatic evidence of the ills of contemporary capitalist democracy, which is identified with gangsterism. Such a curt description suggests a greater significance than the work actually possesses, marked as it is by a thoroughly unassimilated potpourri of slapstick farce, spoof of film melodramas, and some rather sour comments on corruption and injustice in America. It is hard to know how many of its several strands are attributable to Voskovec and Werich and how many to Hofmeister. One of the few examples of their work that directly presents a contemporary setting and action, its cartoonlike depiction of American prohibition, cops and gangsters, and nightclub life, is rather in the vein of Brecht's *Arturo Ui* or, with reference to Victorian England, *The Threepenny Opera*, but with very little of the coherence of those works.[17]

By the time of *A World Behind Bars*, the original Jazz Revue form had been profoundly altered. Musical production numbers and casually structured comic segments had become subordinate to plots, and carefree entertainment had given way to essentially negative socio-political criticism. *Golem* was the peak creation of the mature Jazz Revue, and *Caesar* the first and strongest of the new pieces that tried to integrate political satire with elements of the revue form. But the new vision had yet to find appropriate new expression.

It did so in *Ass and Shadow* (October 1933). Once again a classical source (a story by Lucian) served as a model for an assault on dictatorship and totalitariansism, this time with special emphasis on the cause-effect relationship between unemployment and other economic woes and the rise of political parties led by ruthless demogogues. The parallels to contemporary Germany and the rise to power of Hitler were so obvious as to draw official protest from the German embassy in Prague.

Much of profound significance had occurred not only in Germany but also in Czechoslovakia in 1933. In January, Hitler became Chancellor. Less than one month later the Reichstag was set on fire, and a staged trial fanned a wave of anti-Communist hysteria which helped Hitler assume dictatorial powers that spring. Later that same year the first concentration camps appeared in Germany. In Czechoslovakia unemployment reached its peak in February. One month earlier fascist groups had attempted a putsch in Brno. In October, Konrad Henlein, a German functionary living in the Czech area adjoining Germany (the Sudetenland), established a Nazi-oriented political party within Czechoslovakia to organize the Germans living in the Czech borderlands.

Voskovec and Werich drew upon many of these circumstances in writing the play, including the Reichstag fire and resultant trial, and created figures readily associable with Hitler and other fascist types. Their fantastic plot centered on two rival political parties in the fictional land of Abdera, a so-called party of the people led by the Hitler figure and a party representing capitalist industry and wealth. Their conflict is focused on the fate of an ass that had, in turn, been the bone of contention between two very ordinary citizens, played by Voskovec and Werich, who become caught up and exploited in the struggle for power between the political parties. In an effort to save themselves, they kill the ass. The two demagogues, for whom the ass has become a supreme symbol, join forces and masquerade as the ass itself in order to exploit the people and write history as they see fit. The play reaches its climax of direct contemporary relevance in their address to the people through the mouth of the ass:

> THE ASS: Fall on your knees and salute me by raising your right arms! The first Abdera is no more, the Abdera of the Ass! The second Abdera is gone, the Abdera of the Shadow! Now there arises the Third Reich! The Reich of Ass and Shadow!
> THE PEOPLE: (*Saluting and yelling*) Heilos!
> THE ASS: Only the ancient, pure Abderian race will live. Throw away your brains, forget to read and write, burn everything thought and written, and listen to the voice of the new, Third Abdera:
> LOUDSPEAKER: [the text is in German] My people of Abdera! To us belongs victory and war! We gladly sacrifice the lives of millions! Away with culture, bring on cannon and gas! Down with mankind, down with the world![18]

The situation is resolved when Dionysus, who figured in the Prologue as the narrator or author of the story and then appeared in two other identities, causes an eclipse during which the exploited people eat the ass. The play ends with a reprise of the central song, which expresses optimism and hope for the creation of a united people rather than political parties, the desire for work, and the thought that hunger must be appeased before people can be wise.

Ass and Shadow is the strongest of the trio of works that deal directly with the growing threat of fascist dictatorship in Europe in the early 1930's, *Caesar* and *Executioner and Fool* being the other two. The production combined a very clever plot with a wealth of allusions immediately applicable to the alarming realities of the day. The central metaphor of the ass as savior-dictator was an inspired stroke, gathering up in one powerful image the grotesque absurdity of what was happening just across the border. Most of the extraneous elements of the Jazz Revue were thinned out if not completely eliminated, the songs amounted to an often explicit frontal attack on personalities and incidents (one song ridiculed Europe's best-known dictators: Hitler, Mussolini, and Dolfuss), and most of the ballet sequences were directly applicable to the key moments of the action, perhaps the most outstanding being a ballet of doctors brought in to save the dying ass. Characterization also became markedly richer in this work, the chief demagogues and their cohorts forming a well-defined gallery of repellent types. But perhaps the most significant difference in the total shaping of the work occurred in the placing of the Voskovec and Werich figures at the heart of the action. It is their dispute over the ass that provides the source of the subsequent complications of the two parties and their leaders, including the analogue to the Reichstag fire and trial. The two figures, Nejezchlebos ("Don't eat bread")and Skočdopolis ("Jump into the field") become representatives of the ordinary man drawn into events beyond his control but resisting and ultimately surviving by luck and native wit. Indeed, the work is closer to a comic-satiric *play* with music than to a revue. Voskovec and Werich's reference to Aristophanes as their guide in the creation of several elements in the play was apt, for *Ass and Shadow* is a worthy descendent of his farcical, multi-element fantasies embodying socio-political satire.[19]

Between *Ass and Shadow* and its offspring, *Executioner and Fool*, appeared *The Straw Hat* (February 1934), an adaptation of Eugene Labiche's *The Italian Straw Hat*. It was frankly prompted by Voskovec and Werich's desire to get away from the heavily political slant of their recent productions. Although not without allusions to contemporary social and political events, the adaptation represented a deliberate breather and a refreshing excursion into the realm of disengaged comic fantasy in an atmosphere that held great appeal for Voskovec and Werich, that of turn-of-the-century Paris.

Executioner and Fool, which opened the following season in October 1934, was essentially a spin-off from *Ass and Shadow*, dealing with the basic themes of dictatorship and factional struggles for power. Effective as it was, it did not improve on the complex achievement of *Ass and Shadow*; in fact, it marked a certain decline in its dispersal of focus and its inclusion of non-integrated revue elements. Moreover, although theoretically central to the main line of the plot, Voskovec and Werich's roles were not integrated with the central action to the extent that they had been in *Ass and Shadow*. Nevertheless, they had some choice comic routines, including one forestage sequence which allowed for direct interplay with the audience.

The plot concerns the efforts of corrupt demagogues to exploit two unwitting "national heroes" (Voskovec and Werich) in order to assure their totalitarian grip on a highly fictive Mexico, which represents "a caricature of a rather ordinary European state." [20] A storm of controversy and actual riots in the theatre marked the production. The conservative, fascistically inclined element in Czechoslovakia had attained considerable power by this time, even though its influence in the government was limited. Neither the extreme right nor the extreme left (i.e., the Communist Party) ever seriously threatened the essentially liberal, democratic First (pre-Munich) Republic. Nevertheless, the agrarian and clerical parties, particularly their non-intellectual bourgeois followers, were aggressive and, ever fearful of the Bolshevist spectre in the East, tended to regard every attack on the fascist dictators of Western Europe as a symptom of Bolshevist-Communist sympathy if not alliance. Moreover, in this play Voskovec and Werich ridiculed the cult of national heroes and pseudo-patriotism, which also struck at some cherished ideals of the conservative elements in Czech society. Consequently, the demonstrations inside and outside the theatre were not too surprising. Werich tersely recalled the encounters, which culminated during the performance of 30 October 1934: "Stink bombs, rotten tomatoes, curses, whistles, broken windows, and a great campaign by the reactionary press against the theatre and its authors." [21]

Several statements by Voskovec and Werich at the time of *Executioner and Fool* help to define their position and attitudes at this stage of their development. The first statement originally appeared in the program for the production.

> Most of all we'd like to write wild fantasies for our theatre, crazy farces and absurd tales, because we're convinced that the stage was conceived as a platform for playing the most extraordinary scenes, at the furthest remove from what we've gotten used to calling grey reality. Unfortunately we live during a time whose daily events have become a terrifying competitor of this ideal theatre. Our fantasy isn't able to conceive scenarios whose situations and agents would stand up to the situations and leading roles of public life in 1934. Madness, bloodbaths, comedies and absurdities have become grey reality. [22]

The second passage, from a radio broadcast about one month after the premiere of *Executioner and Fool*, is essentially a sequel to the first but makes clear that V + W's fundamentally comic view of life had not been scrapped under the pressure of events. It also emphasizes the importance they placed on maintaining a political and ideological independence in the turbulent and strained mid-thirties:

> ... precisely because the horror of the absurd events that threaten civilization strips everyone of laughter—which is the most effective weapon of human feeling—it is necessary to awaken laughter and put it into the battleline on the side of culture. ... in our plays we have never served any political side and have always retained the free and

independent position of artists. . . . therefore, as artists grateful to this democracy for the freedom it provides our work, we wish to defend it against the dangers of reactionism.[23]

The question of their political and ideological position confronted V + W on more than one occasion during those days and also later, even after the war. In a country where such issues were taken seriously, Voskovec and Werich seemed to embody an attitude that characterized most of the artists and intellectuals of the time. Rationally and emotionally they leaned toward the left, which represented the most clear-cut opposition to the fascist threats as well as a persuasive critique of many of the economic and social ills of the nation. More generally, they seemed to agree with the fundamentally Marxist premise that economics determines history. Many of the most talented and productive members of the cultural community felt so strongly about these issues that they took what seemed a logical step and became members of the Communist Party. But Voskovec and Werich, whether as a result of rational analysis or, more likely, constitutional aversion to any categorical, ideological commitment except to the freedom implicit in the name of their theatre, resisted all such affiliation. Their position in regard to the classic issue of art and ideology was articulated more explicitly early in 1934 and did not change in any fundamental way thereafter: "Our mission is simple, to entertain. . . . As soon as propaganda of a certain idea intrudes into theatre, as soon as a certain ideological tendency begins to influence theatre work, it stops being theatre and loses its most distinctive mission, an artistic mission. We regard every such dutiful subservience, whether to social need or political agitation, as artistically unclean."[24]

The line between propaganda and ideological commitment on the one hand and the inherent need and obligation of art to be free to criticize and even attack is often blurred and hard to keep steady. Voskovec and Werich certainly did not withdraw to some unrealistic position above the heat of battle. Their later plays were frankly agitational, as well as very relevant and very funny, but what they agitated for was tolerance and reason, concerted, unified resistance to fascist aggression, and a democracy based on the premise that it is ultimately the interests of the people rather than those of vested minorities that should determine the criteria for social justice and general welfare.

By the time of *Executioner and Fool*, which rounded out a series of productions that began with *Caesar*, the polarization that had been developing in the country as a whole forced its way into their audiences, as the demonstrations in October 1934 made clear. The tension was increasing between V + W's wish to assert the sovereign value of laughter and the autonomy of theatre as theatre, and their part in the ongoing turmoil and conflict. This tension, in addition to the fatigue inherent in their multiple duties with the theatre and the exhausting challenge of creating new scripts, contributed to their decision to produce two conventional revues (variants of the *Vest Pocket* format), for the total time and effort expended in such productions seemed less than that involved in producing original scripts or even adaptations. Such revues also provided them with an opportunity to exercise their comic fantasy without nailing it to politically charged issues. Not that they avoided the reality of the day; rather, they were able to attack it within the revue format in an intermittent, jabbing fashion instead of having to build a sustained dramatic action that committed itself to a full confrontation. In fact, both revues, *Keep Smiling* (December 1934) and *The Wax Museum* (April 1935), were responses to the attacks that had been launched against their theatre. Both implicitly championed the right of free artistic expression, attacked censorship, and defended the theatre against charges that the irresponsible reactionary press had been leveling against them. *Keep Smiling* had as its framing action an encounter between Voskovec and Werich and the lively figures of Aristophanes and Molière, in which the masters were consulted about the prospects of satire in times of heated, often blind prejudice. And both revues hit at a number of the ongoing problems of the day, particularly those on the domestic front. It was no longer necessary to look beyond the borders to see organized manifestations of fascist, specifically Nazi, activity; Henlein's thinly disguised Nazi movement in the Sudetenland was becoming an ever increasing force agitating for autonomy of the German population along the borders. At the same time both revues also contained numerous skits and production numbers that were relatively if not completely free of tendentiousness. Among the most amusing was an extended parody in *Keep Smiling* of three Prague theatres— the conservative National Theatre, the agitational, all but officially Communist theatre of E.F. Burian, and Voskovec and Werich's own Liberated Theatre. The spoof of their own theatre involved a cast that mixed characters from *Caesar* and *Ass and Shadow*, in addition to Voskovec and Werich as themselves, and held up for laughter their penchant for anachronisms in their historicized revues, their fixed routine of providing a gloss for the action, their inveterate punning and often cerebral allusions, and their obligatory attacks on dictators.

The 1934–1935 season had been a strained and exhausting one. Voskovec and Werich had their fill of confrontations and decided to give up their theatre for the following season. Contributing to their decision was a proposed offer from France to film their production of *Golem*. They gave up the lease on the theatre they had occupied since 1929, and several members of their company, including their choreographer and his "Girls," left for other work. But the proposed film project fell through, and many people in the cultural world, including the dramatist and literary leader Karel Čapek, urged them to reopen their theatre in the fall of 1935 as, in effect, a service to the country.[25] They did so, but started much later than usual, toward the end of November, with another original, non-revue work, *The Rag Ballad*, in a smaller, rented theatre which they called, in contrast to their former Liberated Theatre, the Bound Theatre. With a smaller company and a smaller budget than usual, they deliberately keyed the production toward a tighter, more intimate, more poetic form while once again returning to the arena of political strife and contention. *Rag Ballad* was a relatively serious, lyrical study of the rebel poet François Villon, who embodied Voskovec and Werich's continued battle for social justice and for artistic freedom in the face of what they called "cultural fascism."[26] Comedy and song were not eliminated but were deemphasized and integrated into the main line of the action, which presented Villon as a defier of corrupt authority and a fighter for the rights of the under-privileged masses. Voskovec (in one of our interviews) looked back on the play, which had the longest run of all their productions, with mixed feelings. In retrospect he thought that they had lost something of their comic perspective, had allowed the production to get a bit heavy-handed and even sentimental. At the same time he recalled it as a beautiful production, the best that Honzl ever directed, with undeniable charm in the creation of a romantic past within a framework of pure theatricality.

Their next production was another, more notable attempt to break away from aggressive satire, to get back to more nearly pure theatrical values, and to mount more of a spectacle than was possible in the small theatre they had used the previous year. In these respects it was rather like *The Straw Hat*, which had also marked a sharp shift of direction. Voskovec and Werich's remarks concerning the new play and their intention with it are central to an understanding of their essential affinity for theatricalism, their stress on the autonomy of the world created by fantasy on a stage, and they thereby serve as a necessary reminder of the duality of their commitment: to pure theatre no less than to active engagement in the turmoil of their day.

> We believe deeply and faithfully in the fantastic essence of theatre and are passionate professors of theatre magic.... The original function of theatre was to create new realities and ... to feed man with the beauty and delight of fantasy.... We never want the spectator ... to "forget that he is in the theatre." ... We shall never try to fool you, hiding our masks under seeming reality.... We wear makeup and we play comedy with flats and properties and in artificial light. You know we're actors and we know you're the audience.... We respect the line [separating us] but we constantly communicate across it. Together ... we play a great social game known as theatre.[27]

It was to be their tenth anniversary season and they carefully prepared for it by moving back into their former theatre and by making an adaptation of a play that Werich had seen a year earlier in Moscow, John Fletcher's *The Spanish Curate*, which they altered by blending it with the Amphitryon legend and placing it in a combined Grecian and Baroque setting. The result was *Heaven on Earth* (September 1936), in which the central action concerned

Jupiter's visit to earth and his disenchanted recoil from it. Voskovec and Werich were attracted to the roles of two notorious swindlers—originally a curate and sexton, but in their adaptation they became rascally attendants at the Temple of Jupiter—and built up these roles in the play.

They were aiming at a literally "liberated" theatre, with the quality of Renaissance farce, but despite all their efforts and despite an elaborate production, it was not a success. For one thing, it was rather top-heavy in scenic and production elements. More important, the generally amoral, sardonic tone of the comedy did not sit well with the audience, who obviously wanted theatre fare more directly tied to the increasingly strained times they were all sharing.

With the relative failure of *Heaven on Earth*, Voskovec and Werich needed a new play quickly. Their new work, *Heads or Tails* (December 1936), returned to certain motifs last used in *Rag Ballad* and was another hit. Once again they turned to the realities of their own day, this time in an action that was a direct image of contemporary events, and that had a degree of realistic plotting that placed the work at the opposite pole from most of their previous revues. In terms of its form, *Heads or Tails* is atypical of Voskovec and Werich's works. But for the interjected song and dance numbers and the several comic interludes of the leads, the work is essentially a well-constructed social drama dealing with the economic crisis, exploited and striking workers, and a threatened *putsch* that is foiled only at the last minute. To suggest a comparison, in subject matter and tone the work is not unlike many of the socially conscious Hollywood films of the 1930's that portrayed idealized representations of the proletariat fighting big business. *Heads or Tails* added elements of fascist demagoguery and an attempted takeover of government, as well as allusions to other contemporary events such as the Spanish Civil War. Voskovec and Werich's intention, as they explained in their preface to the published version of the play, was to present some shocking contrasts of their day (the heads or tails of the title): "... the sophisticated simplicity of magnificence, the luxury of rationalized comfort, and the frightful complexity of metropolitan misery and its medieval-like horrors of filth and hunger.... [Fascism's] mystical hysteria of cruelly grand phrases and its coldly calculated methods of ruthless gangsterism ... scholars, thinkers, and poets who join hands with beggars against dictators who have nothing for it but to join with hired criminals." [28]

These themes are variations and developments from *Rag Ballad*, as is the turn toward domestic issues. Another theme from *Rag Ballad* and other earlier works is concern with the masses of ordinary men. Several of the previous works dealt with the people as gullible victims, subject to the ambition of demagogues, but the previous plays dealt with this theme indirectly or in the abstract; the people themselves were usually offstage. In *Heads or Tails*, on the other hand, the people are the central characters, striking factory workmen who, far from being gullible or victims, ultimately save the nation from a fascist plot to take over the government. Whereas the earlier political works were strongly negative in their satire, *Heads or Tails* stresses the positive strength of democratic forces. It marked a significant turn by Voskovec and Werich, which held steady in their two remaining works. Mockery and ridicule had become inadequate responses to the various threats to the integrity of their nation as well as all of Europe. The time had come to stand up *for* those elements of society worth preserving and affirming, to rally such forces, to construct a stage action that expressed inspiration and optimism. In *Heads or Tails* the revue format was not scrapped but became secondary to the socio-political subject matter of the realistically plotted main action. The result was not a sober, prosaic, uncomic production. There was still plenty of hot jazz, thematically integrated, metaphorical, story-telling ballet, and vigorous, marchlike music to lyrics that stressed militant resistance to aggression. The clownery and wit of Voskovec and Werich ran like a parallel thread to the central action, their inept, well-intentioned capers accidentally providing the key to the efforts of the workers to foil the villains.

Heavy Barbora, which opened what was to be their final season in November 1937, closely followed the pattern of *Heads or Tails* but with several important exceptions. First, although the focus was again on a national problem, the threat was not solely from domestic forces but from the increasingly naked territorial ambitions of Gemany. The reality treated by Voskovec and Werich was the patent conspiracy between Hitler and the Sudeten Nazi forces led by Henlein to force the annexation of the Czech border lands to Germany. The second important difference in *Heavy Barbora* was that Voskovec and Werich created a distanced, metaphoric action rather than a directly realistic one to embody the situation, which allowed more opportunity for humor and exotic charm than was possible in *Heads or Tails*. They set the action in the mythical land of Eidam several centuries earlier and sought an atmosphere of "old nursery rhymes or colored medieval woodcuts."[29] Eidam, which stands for Czechoslovakia, is represented as a peaceful, rural land whose main product is cheese. Its neighbor Yberlant (Germany) is conspiring with certain traitorous Eidamese to arrange a provocation that will justify the military takeover of Eidamese lands by Yberlant. Voskovec and Werich, once again centrally involved in the action, play two mercenaries in the Yberlant army who become entangled in the conspiracy; they accidentally gain possession of a small cannon (Heavy Barbora) that was to be the crucial device in the planned provocation. Ultimately they raise an alarm as the invasion begins and help the people to repel the invaders. The decisive weapon in their victory is Heavy Barbora, loaded with the hard cheeses of the Eidamese. The fundamental action is of course analogous to that of *Heads or Tails*: a massive threat to the integrity of a nation is averted by cooperative, militant resistance of the people, who again become the heroes. But this time the people are treated with more humor and presented with greater color and variety than they were in *Heads or Tails*. The distanced, exotic setting of the action also lends itself more gracefully to the musical segments of song and dance, as well as to the forestage repartee of Voskovec and Werich, than did the realistic action of *Heads or Tails*. *Heavy Barbora* is probably the most satisfying of the politically oriented quasi-revues, as *Golem* was of the Jazz Revues. The plot is particularly well constructed, sufficiently developed without the excessive complications that beset many of the previous plays. A particularly interesting aspect of this work was that the characters played by Voskovec and Werich became more actively instrumental in the plot as well as tougher, shrewder, and more enterprising than they had ever been before. This change, I believe, goes along with their move toward a more militant affirmation of values.

The wit and high-spirited optimism in the face of danger that characterized *Heavy Barbora* was sustained in *A Fist in the Eye* (April 1938), in which Voskovec and Werich recapitulated the themes of their last several productions within a mature version of their *Vest Pocket Revue* format. Almost as if they sensed that it might be their last free chance to do the type of theatre closest to them, they reverted to the form with which they began, a combination of comic sketches, bright music, song and dance, and forestage improvisations; now the combination was clearly unified by underlying motifs, the individual elements were sophisticated and integrated, and the topical relevance of the total work was squarely on target. The handwriting on the wall became unmistakable in March 1938 with Hitler's annexation of Austria, Czechoslovakia's southern neighbor. The Sudeten Germans under Henlein were making ever more flagrant demands for territorial autonomy and even for union with Germany. And there were elements of passivity and even defeatism within the country. The times called for a collective stiffening of spirit, and that is exactly what *A Fist in the Eye* provided. The basic theme was once again the significance of the common man and the idea, as expressed in the central song, that "It All Depends on Us." Voskovec and Werich once again employed the theatre as a framing element. The production began by showing the Liberated Theatre itself in a production of *Julius Caesar*. Werich interrupted the performance when he entered as a legal executor named Josef Dionysos, who was there to settle various debts of the theatre. In a discussion with Voskovec, who in effect played himself, Werich-Dionysos was revealed as a fan of the theatre who becomes caught up in the spirit of the ensemble and makes suggestions for their repertoire. He stresses that more should be made of the ordinary man throughout history: not Caesars and monumental facades, but the people who, like stage braces, support those facades. The rest of the production explores that metaphor in a series of five comic satiric sketches which, like a fist in the eye, demonstrate the reality behind the surface of celebrated events; the decisive element in history is not the "great man" but the ordinary, anonymous citizen. In scenes of comic fantasy that range from the fall of Troy, Michelangelo's sculpting of David, Columbus' discovery of America, to Czechoslovakia's day of independence in 1918, a host of anachronistic contemporary allusions are made and major points are scored against the danger of fifth-column subversion, the arrogance and obtuseness of official critics of art, the superstitious myths surrounding great discoveries, and hypocritical patriotism. The role of the little man of common sense is always underlined. The last sketch, the longest, becomes a sequel to the 1932 production of *Caesar*, "Caesar's Finale." In a very clever sequence, Werich, as a gladiator with a sore toe, fervently defends his toe against all too eager diagnoses that include recommendations of amputation. The metaphor of the Sudetenland was vividly apparent: "From here to here it's me and it's always been me, including my toe. And someday that toe is going to be glad that it's on my foot.... (*Pointing to himself*) This is simply an organism that supports my whole body. (*Yells*) And no messing around with my toe!" [30]

The larger point made in "Caesar's Finale" is that power is essentially a figment and that one Caesar more or less makes little difference. After the news of Caesar's assassination, it is revealed that it was not Caesar who was slain, but only his professional double. Caesar intends to regain his grip with renewed force, but Antony points out to him that "Caesar" is dead; no one would believe otherwise, and if they did they would start wondering who was who in the past. Caesar finally accepts this, and doesn't protest the citizens' joyful cry, "Long live the Republic!" The final production number had the entire company on stage, now in their identity as actors, not characters, joining with the audience in the last chorus of "It All Depends on Us," a song with the quality of a football fight song in swing rhythm:

> To live like people, have joy from work—
> After all, it's up to us.
> To think freely, take care of traitors
> Depends on us.
> To defend our truth and judge by truth,
> After all, it's up to us,
> Not to fear truth and believe in truth,
> To fight for truth
> And win with truth
> Depends on us.[31]

Before they closed for a brief vacation that summer, Voskovec and Werich alternated *A Fist in the Eye* with *Heavy Barbora*. It is unlikely that any theatre anywhere ever achieved a greater mass popularity and relevance than their Liberated Theatre during those pre-Munich days of growing crisis. The Liberated Theatre became, in fact, *the* national theatre. But the fall of the First Republic and the castration of Czechoslovakia followed the Munich capitulations at the end of September 1938. The dismembered, impotent Second Republic lasted until the following March, when the country became an occupied Protectorate of Germany. In the meantime, Voskovec and Werich made half-hearted attempts to stage a revised version of one of their early adaptations, *Having a Spree*. By then the government and ministries were filled by officials who could be counted on not to offend Germany. The production was to open on 11 November 1938, but on 4 November a decree from the Ministry of the Interior cancelled the theatre's license. The Liberated Theatre of Voskovec and Werich ceased to exist. Two months later Voskovec and Werich arrived by liner in New York harbor. They stayed in the Unitied States until the end of the war, when they returned separately to liberated Czechoslovakia. For a year or two they worked together again, but their Liberated Theatre was never resurrected.[32]

It is doubtful that any more appropriate tribute to their theatre and its significance was ever composed than one by Václav Holzknecht, a contemporary:

> The intoxication lasted for slightly less than twelve years: successes, battles, fame, a rapid succession of strong impressions; they achieved a theatre that was once again a tribunal of public concern, as in the time of Aristophanes. And if Achilles when confronted with the choice between a long life without glory and a short one with glory unhesitatingly chose a short and glorious life, theirs became Achilles' lot. What if their era was a short one? They created it in the time of their youth, in the peak flowering of their personalities, in the period of their greatest personal good fortune, when a man radiates the most intense light, and they were enveloped with popularity, love, and fame. Today it is completely finished. There remains but a memory of an enchanting, new, brave theatre that couldn't be repeated, imitated, or even transferred elsewhere. It was anchored in its own time and in the youth of its creators. And so it became a part of history and a legend. And those who experienced them will never forget them.[33]

Voskovec and Werich in *Ass and Shadow*.

HANDLIST OF PRODUCTIONS
THE LIBERATED THEATRE OF VOSKOVEC AND WERICH

Title	Date (No. of pers.) Theatre	Director	Designer	Choreog.	Notes
Vest Pocket Revue	19 Apr 27 (208) Úmělecká Beseda	Voskovec	Voskovec Werich	Máchov	Amateur beginning: varied sponsors
Smoking Revue	8 May 28 (88) Úmělecká Beseda	Voskovec	Voskovec		
Having a Spree (Si pořádně zařádit)	17 Oct 28 (48) Adria	Honzl	Styrsky		Based on Nestroy's *Einen Jux will er sich machen*
Gorila ex Machina	28 Nov 28 (73) Adria	Honzl	Styrsky		
The Dice are Cast (Kostky jsou vržený)	11 Jan 29 (58) Adria	Honzl	Styrsky	Máchov	
The Diving Suit (Premiéra Skafandr)	12 Mar 29 (61) Adria	Honzl	Styrsky		Successful tour of several plays at end of weak season
The Trial is Adjourned (Líčení se odručuje)	19 Oct 29 (37) U Novaku	Voskovec	Voskovec Werich		V + W sole producers; Honzl in Brno for two seasons
Fata Morgana	10 Dec 29 (117) U Nováků	Voskovec	Zelenka	Jenčík	First Jazz Revue; Ježek's music
Dynamite Island (Ostrov dynamit)	11 Mar 30 (101) U Nováků	Voskovec	Zelenka	Jenčík	
North Against South (Sever proti jihu)	1 Sep 30 (158) U Nováků	Voskovec	Zelenka	Jenčík	American Civil War, with Buffalo Bill
Don Juan and Co.	13 Jan 31 (114) U Nováků	Voskovec	Zelenka	Jenčík	Mozart's *Don Giovanni* motifs
Golem	4 Nov 31 (186) U Nováků	Honzl	Zelenka	Jenčík	
Caesar	8 Mar 32 (191) U Nováků	Honzl	Zelenka	Jenčík	
Robin Hood (Robin zbojník)	23 Sep 32 (82) U Nováků	Honzl	Zelenka	Jenčík	
A World Behind Bars (Svet za mřížemi)	24 Jan 33 (167) U Nováků	Honzl	Hofmeister	Jenčík	Script collaboration with A. Hofmeister
Ass and Shadow (Osel a stín)	13 Oct 33 (187) U Nováků	Honzl	Feuerstein	Jenčík	German Embassy protest
The Straw Hat (Slaměný klobouk)	27 Feb 34 (83) U Nováků	Honzl	Feuerstein	Jenčík	Based on Labiche's *Italian Straw Hat*

Executioner and Fool (*Kat a blázen*)	19 Oct 34 (115) U Novaků	Honzl	Feuerstein Wachsmann	Jenčik	Riots in theatre
Keep Smiling (*Vždy s úsměvem*)	31 Dec 34 (108) U Nováků	Honzl	Feuerstein Wachsmann	Jenčik	
The Wax Museum (*Panoptikum*)	9 Apr 35 (120) U Nováků	Honzl	Feuerstein Wachsmann	Jenčik	
Rag Ballad (*Balada z hadrů*)	28 Nov 35 (250) Rokoko	Honzl	Feuerstein	Máchov	The "Bound" Theatre
Heaven on Earth (*Nebe na zemi*)	23 Sep 36 (107) U Nováků	Honzl	Voskovec Werich	Máchov	Based on Fletcher's *Spanish Curate*: back in regular theatre
Heads or Tails (*Rub a líc*)	18 Dec 36 (120) U Nováků	Honzl	Voskovec	Máchov	Made into film, *World Belongs to Us*
Panorama	19 Apr 37 (85) U Nováků	Honzl		Máchov	Anthology Revue of previous hits
Heavy Barbora (*Těžká Barbora*)	5 Nov 37 (179) U Nováků	Honzl	Wachsmann	Máchov	
A Fist in the Eye (*Pěst na oko*)	8 Apr 38 (100) U Nováků	Honzl	Muzika	Máchov	In June, played in rep with *Barbora*

NOTES

[1] Voskovec and Werich made four feature-length films during off-season summers: *Greasepaint and Gasoline* (*Pudr a benzín*) 1931; *Your Money or Your Life* (*Peníze anebo život*) 1932; *Heave Ho* (*Hej rup*) 1934, and *The World Belongs to Us* (*Svět patří nám*) 1937, the last being based on one of their stage productions, *Heads or Tails* (*Rub a líc*).

[2] See the Handlist for a complete listing of their productions and other data, including the Czech titles of their works.

[3] Preface to *Vest Pocket Revue*, in *Hry Osvobozeného Divadla* (Prague, 1956), III, p. 11.

[4] Josef Träger, "Přišel Viděl Zvítězil," *Jan Werich . . . tiletý* (Prague, 1965), p. 35.

[5] Quoted in *Deset let Osvobozeného divadla* (Prague, 1937), p. 105.

[6] Preface to *Heaven on Earth*, in *Hry Osvobozeného Divadla* (Prague, 1957), IV, p. 32.

[7] Ibid., III, p. 94.

[8] *A Fist in the Eye*, in *Hry Osvobozeného Divadla*, III, p. 450.

[9] Voskovec, *Klobouk ve křoví*, p. 141.

[10] Jan Werich, "Knihkupectví aneb hříčka pro klauny," *Plamen*, I (1964), n.p.

[11] Jindřich Honzl, "Inspirované Herectví," *Deset Let Osvobozeného Divadla*, p. 47.

[12] Quoted in Träger, "Trojice Veseloherních Adaptací," *Hry Osvobozeného Divadla*, IV, p. 342.

[13] A major inspiration for their new style of revue was their viewing in Paris in the summer of 1929 of the all-black musical spectacle from New York, *Blackbirds*.

[14] *Fata Morgana a jiné hry*, p. 149. Their avoidance of political satire did not last long, but their rejection of the erotic was sustained throughout their career, probably as a result of their sense of humor.

Jan Lukas: *Jiří Voskovec in New York*

[15] Quoted in Träger, "Od Poetismu k Politické Satiře," *Hry Osvobozeného Divadla* (Prague, 1956), II, p. 414.

[16] A memorable speech by Robin expresses one of Voskovec and Werich's consistent goals: "I'm preparing a frightful, most bloody revolution, an unheard of assassination: Stupidity will be shot, Stupidity ... with a capital S, which rules the world. It will be a deafening shot, and the smoke will linger a long time." *Hry Osvobozeného Divadla*, III, p. 244.

[17] Voskovec's attitude toward Brecht's humor in relation to their own is worth noting: "He often went in the same direction as we, but he toiled at it so, like a real Bavarian—and so his attempts at laughter finally resulted only in a socially conscious grimace. We didn't belabor matters, and so [in our theatre] the same themes produced side-splitting laughter—and 'socially' it was all the more effective." *Klobouk ve křoví*, p. 272.

[18] *Hry Osvobozeného Divadla*, I, p. 132f. As a result of protests from the German Embassy, the speech in German was cut and gibberish substituted; but the intended effect was not lost.

[19] Preface to *Ass and Shadow*, in *Hry Osvobozeného Divadla*, I, p. 10.

[20] Preface to *Executioner and Fool*, in *Hry Osvobozeného Divadla*, II, p. 294.

[21] Werich, "Slovo na Závěr," *Hry Osvobozeného Divadla*, p. 526.

[22] Preface to *Executioner and Fool*, p. 293.

[23] Quoted in Jana Beránková, *Politická Satira V + W v Letech 1933–35*. Unpublished Seminar Thesis 100, Department of Theatre Science, Charles University (Prague, 1964), p. 29.

[24] Quoted in Franta Kocourek, "V + W a D34," *Rozpravy Aventína*, 9, No. 15 (May, 1934), p. 129.

[25] Karel Čapek, a letter dated 11 November 1935, in *Divadelníkem proti své vůli*, ed. Miroslav Halik (Prague, 1968), p. 92.

[26] Preface to *Rag Ballad*, in *Hry Osvobozeného Divadla*, I, p. 147.

[27] Preface to *Heaven on Earth*, p. 231f.

[28] Preface to *Heads or Tails*, in *Hry Osvobozeného Divadla*, I, p. 257.

[29] Preface to *Heavy Barbora*, in *Hry Osvobozeného Divadla*, I, p. 389.

[30] *Hry Osvobozeného Divadla*, III, p. 535.

[31] Ibid., p. 561.

[32] The previously indivisible duo split in 1947. Werich remained in Czechoslovakia, where he continued to appear on the stage, in film, and in television. He was awarded the official title of National Artist in 1963. At the time of this writing (March 1977) he is living in retirement in Prague. Voskovec, after heading his own theatre in Paris in the late 1940's, returned to the United States and has been steadily active as a leading and featured player on and off Broadway, in film, and in television, with his first name Anglicized to George. He lives in New York City. The two have recently completed a recording project: a long-playing album in which they reminisce informally (in Czech) about the past, *Relativně vzato (Relatively Speaking)*, Kampa Disc Production, New York City.

[33] Václav Holzknecht, *Jaroslav Ježek a Osvobozené Divadlo* (Prague, 1957), p. 143.

ANDRZEJ WAJDA: FILM LANGUAGE AND THE ARTIST'S TRUTH

Herbert Eagle
University of Michigan

One of the ironies in the development of East European cinema in the post-Stalin period is that a cultural medium officially considered to be a handmaiden of political and social ideology has given rise to so many innovations in aesthetic structure and style. Among the filmmakers whose pioneering work has gained international acclaim (a group which includes Yugoslavia's Makavejev, Czechoslovakia's Menzel, Forman, and Chytilova, Hungary's Jancso and Meszaros, and Poland's Kawalerowicz and Zanussi), the name of Andrzej Wajda looms large. He has made over twenty significant films from 1955 to the present and has won numerous honors (including, most recently, the 1981 Golden Palm at the Cannes Film Festival for best film—*Man of Iron*). Furthermore, using a diversity of stylistic approaches, Wajda has repeatedly pushed the norms of "socialist realist" art to their limits. It is against the background of these norms that his genius becomes most apparent.

The official requirements for "socialist realist" film might be summarized as follows: (1) that reality be depicted not *as such,* but in terms of its "revolutionary development," i.e. that social reality be depicted not *as it is,* but with a substantial admixture of what is *supposed to be* according to official ideology; (2) that the films serve the explicit, immediate needs of socialist construction by fostering the appropriate attitudes; (3) that they be didactic, clear, and relatively simple; (4) that the films' assessment of the situation, past or present, be ultimately optimistic. Socialist realist films are typically elaborated along the rational logical lines of "classical narrative cinema": spatial and temporal linearity, with actions "driven" by character motivation—a chain of intentions, causes, and effects. Such intentions are seen to have class or ideological bases, which are often made verbally explicit in the films. Characters represent their value systems clearly, and conflicts are seen in unambiguous terms.

The official socialist realist system—with its predictable conflicts, its negative types and positive heroes, and its progressive and optimistic resolutions, encouraged the production of grossly distorted representations of actual life and actual history. Documentary and *cinema verité* approaches (allowing the camera to record what actually *is*) were discouraged as vulgar "naturalism," and complex narrative structure and visual texture (including the techniques of symbolism and surrealism) were condemned as elitist formalism. But neither of these "divergent" directions in film art perished.

They were kept alive in the State Film Schools, such as the one in Lodz in Poland. Here the best work of early Soviet filmmakers (Eisenstein, Pudovkin, Dovzhenko, Dziga Vertov) was available for study, work which was innovative, complex, symbolic, as well as documentary, in ways which the Soviet socialist realist canon of the Stalin period was to forbid. Also, East European filmmakers could look back to their own native avant-garde and documentary traditions of the interwar period.

Wajda, in his long career, has drawn on both of these traditions, that of symbolism and that of documentary, in his generally successful efforts to convey truths about Polish national life—in spite of socialist realist constraints. His method has been to utilize the potentials of cinema language itself in order to make complex statements about the recent past and the present. Wajda's varied strategies are well illustrated in his most famous films: *Ashes and Diamonds* (1958), *Man of Marble* (1977) and *Man of Iron* (1981).

Ostensibly, *Ashes and Diamonds* is a film about the struggle between communists and anti-communists in post-war Poland. On the last day of World War II in Europe, two former members of the Home Army Resistance, Maciek and Andrzej (now in an anti-communist band) attempt to ambush and assassinate the local Communist Party First Secretary Szczuka, who has just returned to his provincial town from the Soviet Union. By mistake, they kill instead two innocent workers from a nearby cement factory. Szczuka and his deputy Podgorski come upon the tragedy. Szczuka tells the workers who have gathered around the bodies: "I'd be a bad Communist if I tried to comfort you as if you were children. The end of the war doesn't mean the end of our fight. The fight for Poland, the fight for what sort of country it's going to be, has only just started."[1]

That evening, in the town, Maciek and Andrzej discover their mistake and are instructed to rectify it. Maciek takes a room next to Szczuka's at the Hotel Monopol, where a banquet is to be held celebrating the end of the war, a banquet attended by members of various political factions now struggling and fawning to retain influence in the new political configuration dominated by the Communists. In its treatment of Szczuka the film stays close to the clichés typical for socialist realism. Szczuka is described as "a civil engineer, a Communist, an excellent organizer; a man who knows where he is going." The mayor of the town, Swiecki, tells the assembled gathering: "The historic victory of the Soviet Union has cleared the way for our march towards a glorious future. Another page in our history has turned over. For the first time in centuries, power belongs to the Polish people."

Meanwhile, in the hotel's bar, Maciek meets Krystyna, a beautiful girl who works as a barmaid, and has a one night affair which almost deflects him from his purpose. In the course of this brief relationship, we see another side of Maciek: romantic, confused, defiant. Sensing the possibility of a more real emotional commitment, Maciek attempts to extricate himself from his terrorist obligations, but Andrzej's appeals to Maciek's sense of loyalty and to the memory of their dead comrades succeeds in holding Maciek to the cause. In the middle of the night, he shoots and kills Szczuka on the street. He bids farewell to Krystyna at dawn, but his escape is thwarted when he accidently runs into a detachment of soldiers. They wound him and, although he eludes them, he dies wandering over a vast garbage dump, finally falling and writhing in agony. It is almost a realized socialist realist metaphor: the egotistical selfish Maciek, member of a "neo-Fascist band," dies on the "trash heap of history." However, attention to the film's interconnected visual and verbal symbolic paradigms produces quite a different meaning.

The film's title *Ashes and Diamonds* is a key to the most important nexus of interconnections. It is elaborated by a verbal text which Maciek and Krystyna read from an old tombstone, a citation from a poem by Norwid:

> "So often are you as a blazing torch,
> With flakes of burning hemp falling about you;
> Flaming, you know not if the flames freedom bring or death;
> Consuming all that you most cherish;
> If only ashes will be left and want,
> Chaos and tempest shall engulf . . .
> Or will the ashes hold the glory of a starlike diamond,
> The morning star of everlasting triumph."

Flames, raylike showers (as of burning hemp) and a diamond emerging from fire are recurrent visual images in the film. When Maciek machineguns the young factory worker who is attempting in vain to escape into a small chapel, we see a pattern of holes appear on the latter's back; flames shoot out of the holes, momentarily setting the victim's jacket ablaze. Twice Maciek lights Szczuka's cigarette for him as they pass one another casually in the hotel; they stand one on each side of the flame. When a waiter leaves a tray of vodka-filled shot glasses on the temporarily deserted bar, Maciek slides the seven glasses along the bar and begins to light them; as each glass catches fire he recites the name of a fallen Home Army comrade. Andrzej prevents him from lighting the last two glasses: "We are still alive," he says. Later, when Maciek and Krystyna burst into a small chapel in a bombed-out church, they come upon a small altar with two candles. Suddenly pulling aside the sheet, Maciek discovers the bodies of the two factory workers he killed earlier by mistake.

In the chapel also, rays emanate from Christ's head on a large fallen crucifix which swings upsidedown between Maciek and Krystyna—water drips from the rays to the ground. Finally, when Maciek shoots Szczuka, the latter stumbles toward him and falls into his arms. As Maciek holds the dying Szczuka, a cluster of fireworks shoots up into the dark sky and then falls like a shower from an exploding star. Szczuka's body falls into a puddle—the star shower (reflected in the puddle) seems to fall upward like bubbles. There is then an immediate cut to Maciek in his hotel room; he splashes water on his face and it falls from him as droplets.

The effect of these visual parallels is to identify all of these characters as mutual victims and martyrs, particular incarnations of martyred Poland, superficially opposite but essentially the same: Maciek as well as Szczuka, the anti-communist Home Army fighters as well as the communist factory workers. This equivalence is reinforced by the shots involving parallel displacement on the screen of parallel characters. Szczuka, offered two brands of cigarettes by the hotel clerk, chooses American. Offered the same choice in an identical shot moments later, Maciek chooses Hungarian. The bodies of the factory worker victims lie side-by-side; the first shot of Szczuka and his deputy Podgorski shows them walking side by side. Maciek and Andrzej drink two shots of vodka in the deserted bar, talking about their fallen comrades in the Home Army, while in the background we hear a song about the Polish soldiers who fought with the British at Monte Casino in Italy. In a later sequence, Szczuka and Podgorski listen to an old record of Spanish Civil War songs, drinking two glasses of wine, and talking about their comrades who fell in Spain.

The concept of mutual martyrdom is reinforced by the images of Christ, of crosses, and of chapels (of which there are many). The film begins with a cross atop a chapel; Andrzej is unable to open the door of the small chapel for a little girl who is bearing flowers. The chapel door does open, however, under the weight of the murdered factory worker and he falls face down into the chapel, in front of a large crucifix. Later, Maciek is juxtaposed with an inverted and shattered Christ (cf. above). The various death wounds reinforce the allusions to Christ: the visible bullet holes, Maciek's wound in the stomach, blood soaking through the white sheet behind which he is hiding, but which covers him as a shroud.

Norwid's poem had expressed the hope that martyrdom might be transformed into salvation, that out of the flames might emerge a diamond. In the film, Krystyna (Christ) is symbolically that diamond. Her potential emergence out of the flame is expressed throughout the film by a visual pattern of light within darkness. Maciek first seeks Krystyna amidst the murky grey haze of the bar; she is very blonde, fair, and dressed in a white blouse. Shafts of light dominate the film's final sequence at the Hotel Monopol, as the light of dawn streams into the dark smoke-filled bar through a window. After the murder of Szczuka, the beam of light streams into Maciek's room as he hurriedly packs. In the bar, as the drunken members of various political factions prepare, in an act of supposed patriotism, to dance a badly-played Polonaise (the Oginski A-flat), Krystyna opens a window and the dawn light streams in, a solid beam which completely engulfs her in its radiance. She becomes completely invisible in the intense ray of light—the lost diamond. Even more significantly, at the end of the film Krystyna is drawn into the grotesque Polonaise (a funeral march now replaces the Oginski on the sound track); the hypocritical characters in their insincere alliances now parade in slow motion before the camera. The hope and dream of Norwid's diamond is engulfed in the smokey haze of the postwar hypocrisy and political opportunism. These symbolic shots which close *Ashes and Diamonds* are only the culmination of a series of paradigmatic associations which deliver a meaning entirely different, and much richer, than that which would be derived from the conventional plot alone.

In his long and brilliant career as a filmmaker, Wajda has continued to exploit the nature of film language, including its potentials as an evolving system of devices and genres, to "speak" the truth, *in spite of* the rules of socialist realism and the desires of the censors. In *Man of Marble* he crafted an exposé of the cynicism of the Stalinist era in Poland and of the careerism and corruption which continue into the present. In *Man of Marble*'s "present-tense" story, a young filmmaker named Agnieszka attempts to make a documentary about a shockworker hero of the 1950's, the champion bricklayer Mateusz Birkut. Her objective is to answer the question: "Where is he now? What became of him after the early fifties when he won awards and medals for his prodigious efforts and was made into a hero?" Agnieszka's questions drive the narrative forward. To answer them, she (and the film viewer) plunge into the past, in the form of old films (documentaries about Birkut and the building of the industrial suburb of Nowa Huta; excerpts from newsreels; censored portions of old films) and in the form of interviews conducted by Agnieszka in the story's present with those who knew Birkut and worked with him. Although Birkut is Wajda's fictional creation, the documentary materials are "counterfeited" so well that an unsophisticated viewer could easily be fooled.

On a purely informational level, what Agnieszka extracts from the past is startling. Not because the essential shape of that past history is unknown to today's Poles, but rather because to see it displayed so directly on the screen (rather than through subtle hints) is a radical departure from even the liberalized artistic norms of Poland in the 1970's. Here is what Agnieszka gradually learns: the actual building of Nowa Huta was not a product of workers' romantic heroic efforts. It was a task which required exhausting labor under difficult conditions: primitive and dirty construction sites, makeshift workers' barracks, and inadequate food. Mateusz Birkut, champion bricklayer, hardly emerged spontaneously from this unromantic milieu. The idea for "creating" him came from an enterprising young filmmaker, Burski, and was facilitated through the efforts of the Party chairman at the construction site, Jodla. In this endeavor both Jodla, and to a much greater degree Burski, are motivated by the advancement of their own careers. They devise a method whereby a single bricklayer, aided by six assistants and a system of carefully prepared stacks of bricks, can lay more than 20,000 bricks in a single work shift. Only then do they seek out a young, strong, naive, and idealistic worker to become their shockworker hero; they choose the bright-faced peasant Birkut. Birkut succeeds in the task and Burski records the carefully staged and choreographed event on film. To complete his documentary newsreel *Builders of Our Happiness,* Burski exploits Birkut's relationship with a young cook and amateur gymnast at the site, Hanka Tomczyk. Burski's film celebrates the marriage of these two bright young stars (although they were not legally married) and their eventual settlement in the very apartments they have helped to build. *Builders of Our Happiness* launches Burski's career as a successful Polish filmmaker, and Mateusz Birkut's as an official culture hero.

Birkut's image and his record are displayed on huge propaganda posters; he becomes a "model" for socialist realist painting and sculpture; he appears at State functions; and he and his team are sent to other sites to teach their revolutionary bricklaying techniques. However, Birkut's efforts are not viewed favorably by all workers. Obviously, many see the creation of "shockworkers" merely as a ploy to aid in the increasing of workers' production norms. At the village of Zabinka-Mala, the workers conspire to place in the rows of prepared bricks one which is red hot. Birkut, working with automatic speed, picks up the hot brick and his hands are severely burned; his bricklaying days are ended.

It is only at this point in the story that Birkut begins to emerge as an actual rather than merely a propaganda hero. He becomes active in workers' committees and uses his reknown to badger the authorities about improving living conditions for workers. When his friend Witek is framed and arrested as the saboteur who passed the hot brick, Birkut carries his campaign to have Witek exonerated all the way to the central administration in Warsaw. When he is put off with admonitions to "trust the Party," he returns home and attempts to make a speech at a local workers' meeting, condemning the injustice. But the microphone is unplugged and Birket is drowned out by the singing of a Party humn. Disheartened and disillusioned, Birkut ends a drunken spree by hurling a brick through the glass door of the State Security office and marching in to be arrested himself. Agnieszka learns only a few things about Birkut's life beyond this point: both Birkut and his friend Witek are tried in 1952 as industrial "wreckers" and spies and convicted; released from prison in 1956, Birkut attempts to rejoin his wife Hanka, but finds that she has become the mistress of a restaurant manager in the resort town of Zakopane. He declines the manager's offer that he stay on as a front man for their operations in black-market liquor. In *Man of Marble*'s final sequences, Agnieszka learns from Birkut's "illegitimate" son Maciek Tomczyk that Mateusz Birkut died during the army's suppression of the workers' demonstrations in Gdansk in 1970.

In *Man of Marble,* Wajda does not convey Birkut's story as a continuous or chronological narrative; in fact, there are many radically different modes of narration, many versions which claim to be the truth. Here Wajda's brilliant manipulation of film language and film genre comes into play, as various sources purport to represent reality: two different kinds of documentary footage (newsreels in which Birkut appears more-or-less by chance, and Burski's pseudo-documentary *Builders of Our Happiness*); Agnieszka's interviews with those who knew Birkut; and censored archival footage of Birkut, which has been removed from newsreels. The character Mateusz Birkut is, of course, fictional, but Wajda creates his films within the larger film (the documentaries and newsreels) using not only actors, but also footage from *actual* documentaries and newsreels of the early 1950's, involving authentic speeches, demonstrations, and political figures such as the then Party leader Bierut. Wajda "matches" actual footage from documentaries and the Polish newsreels *(Polska Kronika Filmowa)* with his newly created "fictional" documentary material so skillfully as to make *all* of this material look authentic. (A typical example: Hanka Tomczyk, a "fictional" character in the story, presents a bouquet of flowers to the *actual* Party leader Bierut. In one shot we see a woman presenting a bouquet to the actual Bierut, who is facing the camera; next, in an identically toned "reverse" shot we see, as it were from over Bierut's shoulder, Hanka Tomczyk's face as she presents the flowers. Thus, Wajda matches to the newsreel his own fictional creation.)

The effect of the film's structure is to address another, equally important, theme: the ability of the film medium to recreate "reality" on its own terms, to create its own version of history—i.e. to falsify history, even while using evidently documentary materials. What Wajda does in *Man of Marble* exposes the clever strategies of filmic fabrication. He even shows (in the story) how a filmmaker like himself was drawn into the process and implicated in the operation of the propaganda apparatus. It is this message which motivates the ordering of the early segments of *Man of Marble.*

The film begins with a collage of actual documentary footage from the late 1940's and early 1950's, including "counterfeit" sequences in which the as yet unidentified Birkut appears—all of this accompanies *Man of Marble*'s opening credits. We, as viewers, are unsure of the significance or even the precise nature of what has flashed by so quickly (only after seeing the entire film might we surmise that the opening sequence was Agnieszka's suppressed film about Birkut or footage for that film). In subsequent "present-tense" scenes we learn of Agnieszka's project, watch her argue with the TV studio director about its appropriateness, and see her "lie" her way into a museum's closed-off storage area for Stalinist art to record on film a huge monumental statue of Birkut. The next segment of the film addresses the nature of "filmed reality" directly and explicitly. Agnieszka goes to the film archive to view films of Birkut unearthed for her by an archivist who at first is skeptical about Agnieszka's project but later becomes her ally.

The first footage which Agnieszka sees is from a film entitled *Birth of a City*. We see *cinema verité* footage of the construction site at Nowa Huta: bulldozers clearing flowering bushes from a hillside; the generally primitive conditions of work; mud and ramshackle barracks; even a mild protest demonstration is recorded on the film (the workers protest their meagre lunch ration of *one* small fish by clamoring for better food and pelting Party officials with the fish; among the workers are Birkut and his friend Witek). Agnieszka learns that this film was the first effort of the young film school graduate Burski. In this way, Wajda represents the efforts of young filmmakers in the early years of the Communist regime to record in their documentaries an unadorned reality—*as it was,* free from ideological preconceptions. However, as the film archivist tells Agnieszka, Burski's film was not deemed appropriate by those who controlled the arts, and his film directing career was in danger of coming to a rapid end.

Next, Agnieszka sees the work which redeemed Burski's career, *Builders of Our Happiness* (Wajda's name appears on the credits of this film as Assistant Director; Wajda, here as elsewhere, links his own actual career to that of the fictional Burski). *Builders* shows workers sallying forth from their villages and boarding trains to arrive in Nowa Huta. An impressive model of the industrial suburb is displayed. Shots of the construction site and the workers barracks are much cleaner looking now. In those barracks, we see Mateusz Birkut lying on a cot studying from a book. A shot of a classroom follows, and then one of the workers' sports club, where Birkut meets Hanka Tomczyk; next we see the visit of President Bierut to the construction site.

All of this leads up to the central sequence. Birkut and his team at work against the clock, laying 30,500 bricks in a single work shift. This sequence closes with a shot of the smiling, triumphant Birkut as he descends the scaffolding after completing his feat. The film continues with a celebratory sequence, an encomium as it were: Birkut elected a Workers' Delegate; Birkut as a model for socialist realist art (he poses for the statue we have seen Agnieszka "unearth" earlier); Birkut at the opening of the Second National Art Exhibit (heroic socialist realist works are counterposed to the "degenerate" sculpture of Henry Moore); a large parade and demonstration features Mateusz and Hanka as well as posters of Bierut and Stalin. We also see our young hero and heroine moving into their new apartment, "their own handiwork," and return for final shots of the large demonstration and gymnastics exhibition in which Hanka participates.

After *Builders of Our Happiness,* Agnieszka views one additional piece of footage; a sequence she herself has discovered in an old newsreel. It shows the wall of a workers' apartment building covered with banners several stories high honoring various shockworkers. But the one depicting Birkut is being hauled down and replaced. "Any idea why?" she asks the archivist. "I don't know. Saint's lives are not my department," answers the latter dryly. Through the character of the archivist, Wajda explicitly labels the typical socialist realist documentary he has so skillfully recreated as a monumental, worshipful, fairy tale.

Having juxtaposed a *cinema verité* view of the building of Nowa Huta (Burski's *Birth of a City*) with the socialist realist paean (Burski's *Builders of Our Happiness*), Wajda turns his attention to revealing how films like the latter were made. For this, he has Agnieszka track down Burski, who (now in his fifties) has become Poland's premier director and is just returning from a foreign film festival where he has won yet another prize (once again, the resemblance to Wajda's own biography is striking). Agnieszka charms Burski into giving an interview and he reveals to her how *Builders* was made: how he dreamed up the idea in order to save his career; how Jodla was convinced that the film would make his construction project famous; how the bricks were set up in advance; how the bricklayers were groomed and shaved by barbers brought in from Krakow; how the crowds and "extras" were assembled. The whole enterprise is capped by an incident which is emblematic: at the end of the record-breaking shift, Birkut nearly collapses as he stumbles down the scaffolding. Burski makes the exhausted Birkut repeat this descent, complete with upright bearing, a tired but undaunted smile, and a wave of the hand—so that it can be captured properly for the camera.

Throughout *Man of Marble*, Wajda utilizes the structures described above. *Cinema verité* sequences capture events as they are, haphazardly and without ideological censorship (e.g. a later sequence of an older Birkut, now back in his village after release from prison, leading his village in casting votes for the Gomulka regime—although obviously without particular enthusiasm). Other sequences are clearly fabricated along socialist realist lines: for example, the sequence of Witek's trial for industrial sabotage. Witek and three co-defendants openly admit to being part of a Western espionage ring trying to wreck Poland's socialist economy. The carefully staged trial sequence is, however, ruined by Birkut's behavior when he is called as a witness against Witek. Birkut, who himself has been arrested in connection with the brick-throwing assault on the police station (he is indicted as the leader of another spy ring, code-named "Gypsy Band"), testifies that his operation and that headed by Witek were in close collaboration, and that he knew in advance about the hot brick which crippled his hands. This assertion is so obvious in its intent to make a mockery of "voluntary confessions" (so popular during this Stalinist period) that it encourages Witek to publicly recant his own confession. Witek's sudden outburst ruins the carefully staged trial (it is being filmed for the newsreels). This is what makes the film sequence unusable for its intended "socialist realist" purpose; the archivist discovers this censored footage at a crucial point in Agnieszka's search.

Within *Man of Marble,* the *cinema verité* and socialist realist documentary pieces are always in black and white. On the contrary, the recollections of the eye-witnesses whom Agnieszka interviews are always in color and in a style associated with Western cinema (dynamic compositions, more camera movement, use of "zooms" and other lens effects). These color flashback sequences are purely fictional; such fictional sequences, with which we are very familiar in narrative cinema, involve a "suspension of disbelief." What we see is regarded not as being through the eye of any actual camera, but rather through an omnicient, interpretive "author's" eye—here obviously Wajda's own. (This is the aesthetic position of Western cinema—exemplified by such critical terminology as the *auteur* theory). However, Wajda so places his fictionally-treated segments within *Man of Marble* that they are accorded greater truth value than either type of documentary footage.

Thus, the fictionally-treated flashback of Burski's actual making of *Builders of Our Happiness* logically usurps the previous "documentary" views of the Nowa Huta construction project, showing how these documentaries were made. The fictional creation of an artist of truth is shown to be *more true* than any "documents."

As in *Ashes and Diamonds,* Wajda adds his own stylistic marks as author-filmmaker: the heightening of certain features (particular objects, shapes, or visual compositions) and their elevation through repeated occurrence to the status of symbolic paradigms. In *Man of Marble,* several symbolic objects and images are used to signify the decline of Birkut's "official" political behavior and the increasing intensity of his moral rebellion. Birkut's record-breaking feat was officially symbolized by "the last brick," awarded to him as a trophy. Later, at the point when his rejection of the Party becomes explicit, Birkut wraps the prize brick in paper and hurls it through the glass door of the police station. In an immediately preceding sequence, Birkut uses another award (a prize watch) to pay for his drinking bout at the "Three Fish" tavern. The linkage with fish is an oblique reference to Christian lore and might be seen to signify the ascendancy of Christian ethics over Communist political morality: the underfed workers protest by throwing fish, and Birkut recruits his "Gypsy Band" of social outcasts at the "Three Fish." Later, at Witek's trial, the brick, the fish, and the espionage ring code-named "Gypsy Band" are all cited as evidence of Birkut's political heresy and rebellion (the political rebellion is thus linked to a religious and moral one by Wajda's symbolic paradigms).

Birkut's fresh physiognomy and increasingly assertive bearing as the story progresses are matched by Agnieszka, physically as well as thematically. As Birkut presses his defense of Witek with a series of authorities, so Agnieszka, long-legged and dressed in jeans, marches into battle against the television director who wants to stop her project. Very characteristic is a repeated shot of Agnieszka striding down the long corridor of the television studio only to be intercepted by the director—who admonishes her for dealing with sensitive material and ultimately tells her that her project must be abandoned. This determined march is photographed with deep focus, so that the corridor appears to be a long tunnel leading out of the duplicitous past. It occurs at the end of the film as a symbol of the ongoing struggle for truth, and gives the film a surreal rather than a realistically motivated closure. Agnieszka returns to the television studio from Gdansk, where she has located Birkut's son Maciek Tomczyk and learned of the circumstances of Birkut's death. The film cuts suddenly, without logical elucidation, from the Gdansk sequences to a shot of Agnieszka and the young Tomczyk striding assertively through the long corridor of the television studio (as if to imply that together they will force the authorities to speak the truth). This last shot continues for several *minutes* as the film's closing credits roll by: the corridor becomes impossibly, unrealistically, long, as Agnieszka and Maciek break through several sets of double doors. Since Maciek Tomczyk is played by the same actor who played Birkut in the earlier sequences (Jerzy Radziwilowicz), Wajda achieves here a symbolic unification of his idealistic, energetic, principled young protagonists and asserts their ultimate triumph over the morally corrupt hierarchies and bureaucracies of the Party.

In the 1981 sequel *Man of Iron,* Wajda creates a moving tribute to the workers who died in clashes with the police and army in Gdansk in 1970 (a tribute which gains special poignancy in the light of the martial law imposed at the end of 1981). He also chronicles the growth of the dissident democratic movement at the Gdansk shipyards and its moment of triumph in the recognition of *Solidarity* in the summer of 1980. Using actual documentary footage of the strikers, their leaders (including Lech Walesa), and of the major Party figures who negotiated with the strikers, Wajda deftly blends this material with a continuation of the fictional stories of Agnieszka and Maciek Tomczyk. In a bold stroke, Wajda convinced two of the leading figures in the *actual* historical events then taking place (Walesa and First Party Secretary of Gdansk Fiszbach) to participate as actors in segments of the fictional story! (Something which has never, to my knowledge, been done in film before.) Early in *Man of Iron,* we see documentary footage of Walesa speaking to the assembled shipyard workers; later, he appears in the sequence of Maciek and Agnieszka's church wedding, "democratically" giving each of them a flower and offering, as their "witness," to help them if they have trouble in years to come. In the film's triumphant finale, Maciek (who, in the fictional story, is also one of the strike's principal leaders) is seen embracing Walesa as the latter walks to the podium to sign the historic document recognizing the free union. Fiszbach (who appears early in the film making an actual television speech in which he asserts that the Gdansk workers are *not* antisocialist or counter-revolutionary) is later interviewed in a television studio sequence which includes some of the fictional characters in the film.

In *Man of Iron* Wajda also cleverly "turns" the plot and characters of *Man of Marble* so that he can tell the story of the student and labor demonstrations in Gdansk in 1968 and 1970 and of the subsequent growth of a free underground labor movement. We learn how Mateusz Birkut becomes a shipyard worker in Gdansk, where his "illegitimate" son Maciek Tomczyk is an engineering student. During the student strike of 1968, Birkut refuses to help organize the workers in a sympathy strike (he feels the students are merely facilitating a meaningless "palace coup"). Maciek, in anger over the workers' refusal, two years later stands aloof while workers march in the streets of Gdansk, where they face police clubs, tanks, and bullets. In despair over the turn of events, Mateusz Birkut walks into a hail of bullets to his death.

The tragic absence of solidarity between workers and intellectuals, which results in his own father's death, is the first step in forging the "man of iron," Maciek Tomczyk. In his student dormitory, he smashes a television set (!) on which Gierek is speaking. He is committed to a mental institution and upon release gives up his studies to become a welder at the shipyards. We then see him as an underground labor organizer and activist, conducting symbolic protests, arrested for putting up illegal posters, fired from a series of jobs. It is at this point that the events which form the story of *Man of Iron* link up with those of *Man of Marble*. Agnieszka finds Maciek in Gdansk and brings him to Warsaw to convince the television director to allow her to complete her film (here Wajda uses the same shot which provided the finale of *Man of Marble*). Instead, the project is entirely shelved and when Agnieszka insists she will make the film anyway, *some* way, she is expelled. She returns to Gdansk with Maciek, helps him set up a photographic exhibit commemorating the police repression of 1970, gives up her career as a filmmaker to become an underground political activist, and ultimately marries Maciek. The film traces their tribulations together: arrests, searches, harassment by the secret police—but ends with their moment of triumph during the stirring events of the summer of 1980.

As in *Man of Marble,* Wajda's film narration is neither direct nor chronological. Mirroring the structure of the earlier work, Wajda uses as vehicle a filmmaker and television reporter, Winkiel, who is given the job of gathering material for a film on Maciek Tomczyk. Only Winkiel is not a young idealist like Agnieszka; he is a weak-willed "hack" who, although he helped in an earlier effort to make a story about Birkut, is now a cynical alcoholic, easily bullied and manipulated by the secret police. The task he is given is to gather documentary material for a smear campaign against Tomcyzk.

Thus, it is through Winkiel's eyes that we witness the historic events of 1980, and through his interviews with Maciek's former student friend (now a television technician), his coworkers in the free labor union movement, and his wife Agnieszka (now being "detained" by the police) that we piece together the flashback stories. The documentary events of the film's present tense (the summer of 1980) are cut into the film as Winkiel encounters them, sometimes by chance. Documentary footage from the past is introduced by the former-student, now a television technician, who is sympathetic to Maciek's cause. He is somehow (and Wajda *was* somehow) in possession of actual footage of the workers' demonstrations and police brutality in Gdansk in 1970.

Whereas we were made to see that the "documentary" films in *Man of Marble,* representing official documentaries and newsreels, distorted events by including material out of context and staging rather than recording history, the more extensive documentary footage in *Man of Iron* asserts its accuracy and truth. Wajda, unlike the fictional Burski who created *Builders of Our Happiness,* makes no effort to mask the construction of his film. A written title at the outset announces that the film's main story is fictional, although documentary footage has been used in many places. Nor does Wajda attempt to hide the fiction-to-documentary match cuts. The fictional segments (including those with Walesa) are presented in smooth-textured, sharp, color images; the *actual* documentary footage, although also in color, has images which are very grainy. Besides, the contemporary events themselves (e.g. the workers' discussions with the Communist Party negotiating team or Walesa's speeches) are so well-known to Polish audiences that there is little possibility of confusing fact with fiction. However, the film's fiction is received by audiences as having high truth value by its honest integration with filmic traces of actual history. It is as if Wajda has said: here is an attempt to reflect the typical personal stories of struggle which accompanied the great historic confrontation of recent months.

The story of Winkiel's journey is also a mirroring of a real transformation. The weak and cynical fence-sitter is transformed by what he witnesses into a courageous artist who dares to proclaim the truth. Having gained admittance to the shipyards—and as the historical confrontation nears its climax—Winkiel calls the television executive who is his employer (actually also a secret police operative) to formally "resign" from the project. Winkiel's transformation has been prefigured minutes earlier in a sequence where Wajda employs his powerful methods of symbolic underscoring. Winkiel is summoned to meet his secret police contact in a gymnasium filled with hanging dummies (which the police use to train for beating demonstrators with truncheons). As Winkiel is threatened with his own former misdeeds, he breaks into a rage, grabs a club, and begins to savagely and uncontrollably beat one of the dummies. The sequence recalls and amplifies the documentary footage of police beating prisoners during the riots in Gdansk in 1970. We witness Winkiel's emotional realization that to accede to his "employers" demands is to become an accomplice in all of the violence to humanity perpetrated by the state, and we sense that Winkiel's transformation is near. Wajda's symbolic paradigms, so important in his work from the outset, are employed with great power again here.

It is almost a cliché in the history of narrative film that such films are "supposed" to represent reality and reflect truth. Throughout his career, Wajda has explored the subtle complexities of that artistic process.

Epilogue. Wajda has frequently remarked upon the special role of the artist in Polish culture: the political conscience of a nation during long periods when politics could not be openly and honestly discussed. He has also noted that Polish artists have fulfilled themselves not only in their art but in their participation in history. As this article goes to press in February 1982, Andrzej Wajda (one of the first to be detained when martial law was declared) has violated the "terms" of his release by signing an open letter from more than 100 Polish intellectuals and artists petitioning the Polish parliament for an end to martial law and the release of interned members of Solidarity.

NOTE

1. This, and all subsequent citations, are taken from the English translation of the filmscript: *Ashes and Diamonds, Kanal, A Generation: Three Films by Andrzej Wajda* (New York: Simon and Schuster, 1973).

THE SWELL SEASON COMES TO AN END: SAD AUTUMN BLUES

Josef Škvorecký

> *We shall never meet again*
> *and you will go dancing with other lads*
> *in the mountains.*
> *We shall never meet again*
> *and other loves will make your head ache....*
>
> *Josef Krátký, 7b*

That was the end of it. At least for the rest of the summer. The alderman sent his wayward daughters to Count Czernin's estate where his brother was bailiff. The brother's wife was a regular contributor to a religious magazine for young girls and thus the alderman's daughters were in the safest of hands, or so he thought. At the end of August, however, Zdeněk suddenly vanished from Kostelec. He got ten days off from the factory and was putting it about that he was going to visit his ailing mother in Prague again, but I wasn't among those who believed him. About halfway through August, I felt a faint glimmer of hope because by sheer chance I went from Rounov in the same train in an empty compartment with Marie Dreslerová and she seemed to have forgotten all about that little scene she'd informed the alderman about over the phone. But when I called her next day, her brother said she had gone to her grandmother's for the harvest. All those girls seemed to have strong bonds with their native soil. But there wasn't much time to brood over it, because the sups were coming up in the last week of August. Brynych had one in Latin, and he failed. I was also getting ready to say farewell to the eighth form, but the day I was to take my sup Mr. Bivoj came down with an attack of colicitis from eating too many gooseberries and Mr. Stařec took his place. Stařec set me a problem that he almost couldn't solve himself, though in the end he did manage, and I passed. Alena also passed her sup in exactly the same way, but I had no opportunity to talk to her because the alderman brought her to the exam himself, and when Mr. Stařec passed her with a C, the alderman led her away again and the next day he sent her to take sixth form in the Eliška Krásnohorská Girls' Secondary School in Prague, where a sister of his was a teacher. He came from a many-branched family and Alena was boarded with the sister, who had two sons, both of them theological students. Catholic.

The week school began Fonda got us a job in the Beránek café and his father arranged the necessary permission from the school principal Mr. Junák. We had to play music for listening to, because dancing was no longer allowed, out of mourning for the fallen soldiers of the Reich. We played for dances too, however; every Saturday afternoon in Provodov, about five kilometres up in the hills, where the power of the Reich was not so much in evidence.

* * *

And so we were swinging *Chinatown* in the Baránek when Irena walked in. I made a huge flub and couldn't find my place again. Lexa, who was next to me, said, "Get with it, man," very quietly and in the middle of the chorus, Benno suddenly intervened with an unplanned solo and saved the situation.

I wasn't even aware the song was over. Irena fascinated me because Alena was out of sight and she had never really been too much in my mind, except for those two or three days at the end of July. Irena *was* in my mind, despite the way she's treated me, despite the things I'd discovered about her, despite what I saw in front of me now. I carried her about in my heart, or somewhere. Irena. She was sitting at a table with Franta Kočandrle, who should have been with Marie Dreslerová, except that Marie was nowhere to be seen. So it wasn't hard to guess what had happened. Irena was a bitch. She had dumped Zdeněk, justifiably, on the whole, but she wouldn't forgive me that twisted ankle, which had healed perfectly in a week or so anyway. If she had to seek the comfort of male company, then at least she could have done it with someone who was available. But no. She had to steal Kočandrle away from poor Marie.

Then we played *Down by the Old Mill Stream,* and I lost my place again half-way through the solo, so that when we finished Benno said, "Gentlemen, shall we take ten small ones so Smiřický here can get over the arrival of her highness, the alderman's daughter?"

Fonda announced the break over the microphone, in different words, of course, and Kočandrle went off to the bathroom.

I was beside Irena like greased lightning.

"Hi," she said rather cooly.

I got straight to the point. "Irena, you are going with Kočandrle now?"

"What's to stop me?"

"But it's not very nice of you. After all, Kočandrle's going with Molly."

"Not any more he isn't."

"I can see that. Are you still angry with me?"

"What do you think? I'd rather you stayed out of my sight."

"Be logical, Irena, please. I only wanted to help you. Surely you don't think I let you fall off those rocks on purpose?"

"I'm not talking about rocks."

"Then what are you talking about?"

She cast a very unfriendly glance at me. "Look. Helenka Teichmanová, Jarmilka Dovolilová, Laďa Hornychová and so on—I can't remember the whole crowd—I could forgive you all that. And the Weber sisters, even though they are my distant cousins. But to swear you love me and then try to debauch my own sister—well, there's a limit to everything, do you know that, Dannykins?"

Dannykins, Dannykins! All at once I almost felt disappointment. I had thought her sister Alena was quite a girl. Evidently she wasn't.

"So Alena didn't keep it to herself. But I can explain it to you Al—Irena," I said by way of introducing a classic argument, the essence of which I was still unsure of.

"Alena! That's a good one. She never tells me about her scuff-abouts."

That was Alena's word. Or it could have been Irena's. Those two shared almost everything. Except that Alena had a shiny nose and she had character, whereas only Irena's eyes were shiny and she was a bitch.

"Who was it then? Your father?"

"Jirka Fibír, if you want to know. He saw you from the kitchen. He also saw Father bundle you away before you got a chance to despoil her."

She said it very acidly. It annoyed me.

"Do you suppose your father will bundle you away from Kočandrle in time? Or is it too late already?"

As soon as I said it I regretted it, but it was out.

"You're disgusting," said Irena. "Go away. I never—never, understand? —ever want to see you again."

"Look, Irena, I didn't mean. . . ."

But just then the freshly relieved Kočandrle returned from the toilets and he could see from Irena's expression what the essence of the problem was. He stared at me as though he were taking my measure. "Isn't it about time we went back to playing? What are you paid for here, anyway?"

So I glared back at him as though I were taking his measure, and then left without a word.

We played the *St. James' Infirmary*. That is, Fonda announced it as *A Sad Song*, and then in German for Mr. Ceeh, who was sitting in the corner of the café in a *Flugabwehr* uniform, as *Traurigere Lied,* because he had almost flunked out in German. There was a big tenor solo in the middle, and I played it with such feeling that even Mr. Ceeh stopped talking about his heroic feats in catching blackmarketeers and appeared to be listening.

* * *

Next Wednesday I went to Bíloves for mineral water and on a bench on the lower path in the Montace woods I ran into Přema with Vahař and Benda talking to Leopold Váňa. They were arguing about something. I sat down beside them just as Váňa was saying, "Right! The dictatorship of the proletariat."

"We don't want another dictatorship," said Benda. "We got one already."

Benda was the shyest person in town. He had probably never even talked to a girl in his life. Once, in the amusement park, we goaded him into chatting one up, but all he could manage was to ask her what the time was. She told him, he thanked her and that was that. Except for his sisters, she was probably the only girl he'd ever talked to in his life.

"The dictatorship of the proletariat is real democracy," said Leopold Váňa.

"How can a dictatorship be democracy, you twit?" said Benda. "Explain it to me."

"It's a democracy in relation to the proletariat," said Leopold Váňa. "To workers like you."

"I'm no proletarian," said Benda. "I'm a skilled machinist."

"You belong to the working class. And the dictatorship of the proletariat is a dictatorship in relation to the bourgeoisie."

"That means you, don't it?" said Přema.

"But I have grasped the historic role of the working class," said Leopold Váňa. "After the war we're going to establish socialism. The bourgeoisie are going to have to clear out."

"My old man's a socialist too," said Vahař. "A Czech Socialist."

"Czech Socialists are bourgeois socialists," said Leopold Váňa. "Objectively they help maintain the rule of the bourgeoisie."

"Then how come the Krauts are locking them up?" said Přema. "You said that Nazism is the open dictatorship of the bourgeoisie. They locked Lexa's old man up, and he was an MP for the Czech Socialists."

"Because the bourgeoisie is chauvinistic, whereas the proletariat is international."

"Just a minute, stupid," said Přema. "So like that means the bourgeoisie are against the Germans, but the workers —"

Leopold Váňa, however, was not listening. He had a head full of steam. "The majority of the Czech bourgeoisie is collaborating with the Germans. The workers are sticking their necks —"

"Is that a fact?" Benda interrupted him. "In the factory it's the workers who are breaking their asses working hard so they'll earn their schnapps coupons."

"Also a lot of the better sort of people are locked up," said Vahař. "School teachers, butchers, people from Sokol. And Jews, of course. They're almost all bourgeois."

"They're only paying for the corruption of a system they themselves helped to create," said Leopold Váňa. "But after the war they'll all be pushed aside. I don't mean the Jews, I mean all those gentlemen factory owners and governors and aldermen —"

"Be seeing you," I said. "I have to go for mineral water."

"Hang on, Danny, this is interesting," said Přema.

"No, I have to go."

"Let him go," said Leopold Váňa. He didn't like me, instinctively perhaps. "All he cares about is blowing his horn."

"That's right," I said. "Be seeing you."

I walked quickly away through the woods. Not that it didn't interest me, but Váňa rubbed me the wrong way. As I walked along I remembered how Father always used to say after the news: "God defend us from Bolshevism. That would be out of the frying pan into the fire." But it may all have been exaggeration, how was I to know? Aunt Pavla Kohnová, the sister of Uncle Kohn, who married my mother's pretty youngest sister Molly, was also a Communist. And also rich, like Leopold Váňa. But she wasn't obnoxious. She went to demonstrations with a sun-umbrella and she always managed to bop some policeman over the helmet with it so she wouldn't harm him, and they always ran her in. But every time it happened she would pay her bail, then write an article about her brutal arrest. Uncle Kohn said that Aunt Pavla gave the party all the money she had inherited, and what she had now was mostly borrowed from him. He said he had nothing against the Communists, that they defended the poor and that as a secretary of the Czecho-Jewish Association and an unpaid administrator of a soccer club he had very close ties to the poor. But he said that if Aunt Pavla didn't stop knocking about with that whore-monger Fučík, he wouldn't lend her another cent. For some reason Uncle Kohn had it in for Fučík, either because he was so virtuous, or, more likely, because it was the same Fučík who almost broke up his marriage with Aunt Molly. Aunt Molly was twenty years younger than Uncle Kohn, and Fučík was about fifteen years younger. If it really *was* the same Fučík, Uncle Kohn never told us, but it could well have been, and probably was. He got on Uncle Kohn's nerves and he was always bringing him up in conversation. He and Aunt Molly had a reconciliation. When the Germans came, Aunt Pavla fled to Russia. We thought they'd give her a job there and that we might eventually hear her speaking over Radio Moscow or something. Radio Moscow my eye. We got a letter from her on lined paper and the return address was *Lager* something or other. Father said that meant concentration camp. That was before the war against Poland broke out. She wanted Father to send her a Czech-Russian dictionary. My father must have had something going with her too, because when he sent it to her, I could see that he was crying. Aunt Pavla was pretty too; she used to go round in men's trousers and smoke pink cigarettes from foot-long holders. We never heard whether she received the dictionary or not. Then war broke out and the Russians joined up with the Germans and marched into Poland from the other side. Perhaps Father was just talking through his hat, but whenever someone started carrying on like Leopold Váňa had just done, I couldn't help thinking of

Aunt Pavla, and I could never feel too enthusiastic for that dictatorship, even though Leopold Váňa claimed it was an even more democratic democracy than the one the alderman and his Father Masaryk believed in. And I also liked Aunt Pavla. She couldn't have been very old. Twenty-five at the most.

I walked out of the woods and when I go to the river I turned towards the spring where people were pumping free mineral water. And once more the Lord remembered me. There was only one girl at the pump and that girl was Marie Dreslerová. She was dressed in a pale blue raincoat and her hair had just been washed so that it fell down her back in richly golden cascades like the St. John's Falls on the Vltava River.

"I'll give it a pump if you want, goldie," I said.

She turned her blue eyes on me. "There's no need. I'm finished."

"Then pour it out, and I'll pump it again. I want to do something for you."

She looked at me again and said, "Hm."

She was always saying that.

"What's that supposed to mean? That you're thinking it over?"

"I've already thought it over. You can help me carry the water back, if you want."

She had two handbags with three bottles in each one. I had the same amount.

"You're taking a long time to think it over," she said.

"No I'm not. It's just that it seems so little to me. Is that all you drink at home?"

"I can go and borrow more bottles in the spa, if you'd like."

"They don't have any," I said quickly.

"You seem pretty well informed."

"On the whole. For example, I know that if I ask you for a date, there's nothing to stop you from saying 'yes'."

She searched me with her blue eyes. She was apparently very intelligent. At least in that field.

"You mean because I've split up with Franta?"

"Exactly," I said. "But I'll make up for him entirely. I'm a lot better than Kočandrle."

A fresh inquisition from those beautiful forget-me-not eyes, and then she said again, "Hm."

"Are you thinking it over?"

"I'm not sure. That 'Hm' means that in any case you write better essays than Kočandrle."

My fame as a writer had clearly reached all the girls in the Kostelec grammar school.

"But you had a sup in math," she said.

"But I passed it."

"A sup is a sup."

"I'll arrange for someone to help you in math, I said. "Like Vaníčková. She gets straight As. And besides essays I'll do your German homework for you. And Latin."

"Didn't you have a sup in Latin last year?"

"The year before last. I've improved a lot since. I can handle the sixth form material."

It was beautiful shooting the breeze with Marie Dreslerová. An autumn fog was rolling off the river and a leaf dropped off a chestnut tree and landed on her shoulder. She brushed it off.

"It's autumn already," she said. "That's sad."

"What's sad about autumn?" I asked.

"Everything," she said.

* * *

Carrying her mineral water, of course, made any other activity impossible. Not even Clarke Gable could have made a pass at her with twelve full bottles in his hands. We strolled slowly along the lower path; the leaves floated down from the trees and tiny rust and red leaflets lodged in Marie's golden curls. She wore a belt around her raincoat made of the same material, and it made her waistline look very pretty. And she wore a black band around her sleeve, and black stockings.

"What are you in mourning for, Marie? I asked, when I'd got my second wind.

"That's —" and she hesitated for quite a while before she said, "I'm wearing it for Kočandrle." She was obviously talking hot air.

"You're joking."

"No, it's true."

"But Kočandrle's still alive."

"He's dead as far as I'm concerned."

In those black stockings her legs were, let's face it, the most beautiful in Kostelec. It's what I always told her.

"You're only wearing them because of your legs."

"What do you mean?"

"Your legs look pretty in black stockings. I mean prettier than usual."

"That's you all over," she said. "Not a serious thought in your head, ever."

"Kočandrle is some thing to get serious about?" I said. "He's an ass."

"He is," she said, "and I don't have a thought of him in my head."

"Then why are you wearing black stockings?"

"Because I want my legs to look prettier."

"It works," I said with utter conviction. Then we dropped the subject of her black stockings and I never did learn their secret.

"Everything works for me," she said. "Except Kočandrle."

Oh dear, I thought. And I said, "I work best of all for you."

On the other side of the bushes the bench where Přema, Benda and Vahař were still debating with Leopold Váňa came into view. Leopold Váňa was just saying angrily, "Lexa's father has always been a servant of the bourgeoisie, and it was his fault that they —" and Přema interrupted him, even more angrily.

"But he joined the reistence."

And Leopold Váňa said, "He was just *playing* at resisting. In real —" and then he saw Marie and forgot his great message.

Leopold Váňa had made a try for Marie before Franta Kočandrle's successful attempt. His family had a villa two houses away from the Dreslers. But I suppose he wasn't her type. I managed to get farther with her than he had, and the distance I had gone with Marie made the distance I had gone with Irena look like a world distance record. As soon as she saw Leopold Váňa, Marie lifted her nose and walked past the bench like Nefretiti arisen from the dead. I trotted after her like an Egyptian slave, with my arms stretched so far out of their sockets that they seemed to be held only by the sleeves of my jacket. Leopold Váňa tried to greet her in some fashion, but Marie ignored him. Přema, Benda and Vahař didn't even attempt a greeting, but they loyally looked in the same direction as Leopold Váňa, and all eight eyes described a slow arc as Marie walked past, all following her behind as it bobbed along above those very pretty legs in their black stockings, until finally the bushes hid the watchers.

"I work best for you, Marie," I repeated, to remind her.

"Much too much," she said. "So you think that Kočandrle is all there is keeping you and me apart?"

"I haven't heard of anyone else."

"There can be more separating boys and girls," she sermonized, "than just boys."

"I'd like to know what."

"Girls," she said. "Have you forgotten last winter? What I saw when I looked out auntie's window?"

"I haven't forgotten that, but I was hoping you had."

"I'd sort of forgotten about it," said Marie, "but I don't know whether or not my memory might not be refreshed."

"Couldn't you might go on kind of forgetting about it?" I asked.

"Hm," she said

"Does that mean you're still thinking it over?"

"Exactly," she said. "When I see you suffering under that load of bottles, maybe I'll forget about it altogether."

* * *

Then it started to rain, lightly at first, only enough to make me wet, then harder, but still not enough to penetrate Marie's raincoat. Finally, it began to pour and threatened to soak through and shrink the new dress she was wearing under her raincoat. Fortunately we were close to the Pitterman's cottage, and I knew that Rosťa hid the key in a pine tree behind the outhouse, in a knot hole.

Normally, Marie wouldn't have gone in with me, but she was worried about her dress. It was almost dark inside, because of the black thunderclouds. I had to light a carbide lamp and Marie took off her raincoat and there she was in her new dress, which was absolutely stunning. Her skirt was pleated and white, and her breasts were contained in a beautifully tight-fitting pale blue middy with anchor designs on it. I knew that Marie had the most beautiful legs and breasts in Kostelec, but I never suspected they were so sensational. When she turned round, there was a sailor's collar at the back.

She looked around the cottage. Against one wall Rosťa had a messy couch strewn with things, including grubby underwear with yellow stains in the crotch. I was delighted. Rosťa was one of the candidates for Marie's affections, and though his chances were small, they were still extant. After this still-life on the couch, I expected they would drop even further. And after Kočandrle's betrayal, my chances were once more on the rise.

Marie stepped up to an easel. Whatever it was Rosťa was working on at the moment was hidden by a dirty rag.

"I'll make some tea, all right?" I said. "I know where it is."

"That would hit the spot," said Marie.

I opened a cupboard and found a great surprise.

"He's got some rum here. Would you like rum in your tea?"

"That would be even better. I'm cold," said Marie, and she continued snooping about Rosťa's lair. Rosťa had already painted all the girls in Kostelec, except perhaps for the hunch-back Vaníčková, and he'd even done Dadka Habrová in the nude. But Marie had never let him paint her, although she was the one he would most have liked to do. She was the object of his yearnings.

Meanwhile Marie had gone to the table and very gingerly picked up two filthy cups.

"It's a pig-sty in here," she said.

"I'll wash them."

"That's women's work," said Marie. "You make the tea. With rum."

So I made the tea and she opened the door, caught some rainwater in the cups and washed them out with her fingers. Her nails were blood-red.

* * *

Then we sat on the couch, sipping the hot drink and she was unaware that she had two-thirds of a cup of pure rum in her tea. After a few sips her eyes began to glow like lanterns.

"Marie," I said, "you are absolutely the most beautiful girl in all Kostelec."

"Kostelec isn't exactly a jackpot," she said.

"In the whole German Reich. In all Europe," I said. "In the whole world. In the entire universe."

"Is that all?" she said disappointedly.

"I don't know what there is after that," I said.

"Neither do I."

"So how should I know if you don't?"

"I suppose you're right," she said, "even though you ought to know. You're the one who writes all those essay assignments. You're the one with the imagination."

"You're greater than my imagination, Marie."

"You made this kind of strong," she said. "Let's switch cups."

"What for, Marie? You've only got a spoonful in there."

I hadn't even put a spoonful in my cup. I wanted to keep my head clear for the time when her head would be full.

"Show me. This one is a real headspinner," and she took my cup from my hand. There was nothing left to do but take hers.

She took a sip.

"You're a cheat!" she cried, staring at me with her illuminated blue eyes. "You've put nothing in it at all."

"What do you mean?"

"You wanted to get me drunk," she said. "I can see what you're up to."

"I did not."

"You did so."

"I did not."

"You did so."

"I did not. I only wanted to save the rum. It's not mine."

She looked at me with those very merry blue eyes and burst out laughing. So she was a little tipsy after all. Even with those few sips. She said, "As a punishment you have to drink it all yourself. Right to the bottom."

"No, Marie!" I was frightened.

"Admit you wanted to get me drunk."

"Well—all right, so I did. But only because in your normal state you're like an icicle."

"Me? Like an icicle?"

"At least as far as I know. Maybe Kočandrle knows more."

"Kočandrle can go—spit on himself, for all I care," said Marie. "And start drinking. Right to the bottom."

I drank it.

It took effect immediately.

I took Marie around the waist.

"Hey, leave me alone!" she screeched and jumped out of the way. I couldn't see where she had gone, but I could hear her rummaging about, and then her voice said, "There's still a half a bottle left."

"Only half?"

"That's enough," she said. "Since you've finished my share, I'll make my own."

I heard a gurgling.

"Pour me out some too, Marie."

I heard the rum gurgling into my cup.

Suddenly Marie was standing in front of me in her white pleated skirt with her breasts peaking magnificently out of the pale blue blouse and eagerly, with a kind of dissatisfaction, she looked around.

"I wonder what else he could have here?"

"All he's got is rum."

"Aha," said Marie. "I know."

She stepped up to the easel and pulled the paint-stained rag off it.

And any advantage I might have had over Rosťa because of his stained underwear vanished.

I recognized the picture, even though I'd never seen it before. He may have been painting it for me, as a surprise for my birthday. A fine surprise. The composition was the same as that painting of the martyr with his skin stripped down to his waist, the one we'd seen in the rectory when we were helping out the Venerable Father Meloun. Except that the martyr was clearly me, an exact likeness, something Rosťa was very good at, and my skin was being stripped off not by mercenaries, but by those twenty-three girls from Kostelec, all of them completely naked, including the two Weber sisters from Linz. All of them looked exactly as they did in real life, I mean their faces, for I had no way of judging the rest. Marie was the second from the edge, right next to Irena. So he had painted her after all. But I hadn't realized that Rosťa was a pronographer.

Marie burst out laughing. She laughed so hard she doubled over, and then leaned back and the pleated skirt flipped immodestly over her knees. And they say she was the most pious girl in Kostelec. What were the impious ones like, then? I grabbed the bottle and, without her seeing me, took a swig.

"Goodness me," laughed Marie. "Wait till I spread this round."

"Who will you tell?"

"I don't know, but someone." She leaned over to get a closer look. "That's Jaruna Dovolilová," she said, pointing, "and that's Eva Bojanovská. And that's Irena."

"And that's you," I said, attempting to point, but instead I staggered to one side.

"Me!" she giggled, and took a swig from her cup. "I don't have such huge breasts, and I'm blonde down below, too."

"Is that a fact?" I said with interest, and stood up. That is, I thought I was standing up, but in fact I fell down.

Marie looked around at me. "My God, you're completely slopped."

"That I am," I said. "Because of you."

"What do you mean 'because of me'?" she inquired, as though she didn't know.

"Because," I said. "Because because because."

"What's that mean, 'because because because'?"

"It means because because because."

"Because because because you're drunk."

"No! Because because because I love you."

"Because because because you're going to lie down."

"Because because because you're coming on Saturday to the dance in Provodova."

"Because because because maybe I'll come," said Marie. "Because because because you're going to stand up now, like this," and she helped me to my feet, "and because because because Marie is going to help you into beddy-bye."

"Because because because Marie is going to beddy-bye *with* me."

"Because because because Marie is *not* going to beddy-bye with you." My head was reeling. "Because because because you're terribly drunk."

"No I'm not!"

"Because because," she said, "because you are."

She picked Rosta's underwear up delicately with two fingers. "Because somebody has made kaka here and because Molly tidied it up because Dannykins is drunk and has to go to sleep. Isn't it true that Dannykins has to go to sleep now?"

"It's true," I said. "Because he has to. Because he's sloshed. Because he doesn't want to."

"But because he's sloshed because he has to," said Marie, that beautiful blonde girl from Kostelec.

She put something under my head, perhaps Rosta's sweatsuit, pulled a smelly blanket over me, but through the smell I caught the aroma of her hair. Girls can always stand more than boys; when a fellow gets totally smashed, there's always some girl around, or was then, to lead him to bed and cover him up and turn out the light, oh mother of men, mother of moths, mother of everything . . . of life oh so hard. . . .

Marie extinguished the carbide lamp. Outside the gentle patter of rain. I felt wonderful. I felt wonderful in that cottage, in that beautiful town of Kostelec, so long ago. . . . Marie was a fine . . . girl . . . so long ago. . . .

I was in limbo

* * *

I woke up next morning and it was still raining. The sound of rain was mingled with a different sound. For a long time I couldn't figure out what it was, until finally it hit me, and I was alarmed. Someone was snoring. Surely it couldn't be —

I turned over. It was Rosťa. He was lying next to me on the wide couch, emitting loud and terrifying sounds.

I lifted myself up and fell back with a groan. That rum of his must have been first class.

The snoring stopped. Rosťa opened his eyes.

"Top of the morning, you sot," he said.

"Oh God, man," I said, "if that was methyl alcohol, then you'll have me on your conscience. Ow!"

I grabbed my head.

"Don't look a stolen horse in the mouth," said Rosťa. There was something amiss in that proverb, but my head was hurting too much for me to dwell on it.

"Ow ow ow!" I roared. "And you'll have her on your conscience too. If the prettiest girl in Kostelec goes blind —"

"Who were you here with, you rotter?"

That brought me up short. I couldn't very well tell Rosťa that it had been Marie, even though I'd only got drunk with her. Or more precisely, I'd got drunk under her watchful eye.

"Guess," I said. "She's over there on that fresco of yours."

Rosťa squinted at the unveiled immoralities and said, "Irena?"

I said nothing, which in its own way was a reply. But he said, "Oh wait a minute. Couldn't have been her. She's taken up with that asshole Kočandrle."

"But he's going with that bitch Marie," I said, to cover he tracks.

"The bitch Irena has scoffed him off her."

In fact I'd dropped him a hint, but fortunately he failed to notice it.

"Ow! Have you got an aspirin here?"

Rosťa stood up and went over to the table. I said, "Do you think it makes any difference to that bitch Irena that she's going with that asshole Kočandrle at the moment?"

Rosťa turned to me with a bottle of aspirin in his hand. "So Irena *was* here with you. Well, she is a super-bitch," he said, handing me the aspirins. "I tell you, all girls are whores."

"They certainly are."

"So you shafted her at last," said Rosťa.

That took me aback. Rosťa was a fine fellow, but he might easily get pissed somewhere, or a girl might get him into a confessional mood, for he wasn't entirely resistent to their wiles, and Irena could eventually discover I was spreading stories about her that, unfortunately, were only lies.

"I would have, man," I said, "if it hadn't been for that bloody methyl alcohol of yours."

"So it was a wash-out, eh?"

"What do you expect, man? One swig of that stuff and you're planked right out."

"Come off it man. That was genuine pre-war Meinl Rum," said Rosťa. "Don't blame the rum for your incompetence."

"And I suppose you're competent?"

"I am."

"And what about Marie. Have you shafted her?"

Rosťa shook his head sadly. "Not her, man. She's a stubborn one, she is. I haven't even got to paint her yet."

"There, you see, stupid? And all you'd have to do would be to drag her in here when it was raining, paint her and there you'd have it."

I stood up. My brain was screaming in protest.

"It's not that simple," said Rosťa. "Anyway, not with Molly."

"But you've painted her all the same," I said, pointing to the naked Marie on that votive picture, with the enormous breasts and the black mount of Venus.

"That's just kind of a Freudian fantasy," said Rosťa.

"So I see," I said. "And quite a bit wide of the mark. Her tits are nowhere that big."

"I know. I was just mad at her when I painted them."

I went up to the canvas and studied the naked Marie. Despite my rickey brain, I recalled the beautiful late afternoon of yesterday, the fog, the chestnut leaves, Marie's pleated skirt, the rain, and the blonde waterfall of golden curls. The rain was still coming down. And also what she had told me. It was really a question of realism, the same question Rosťa had argued about with Mr. Balaš, the art teacher.

"You know what else, man?" I said. "I doubt whether a natural blonde like her would be brunette down there."

Saying it made me feel utterly blissful.

Rosťa came up beside me and also studied Marie's little garden, at least as he had depicted it in the painting. After a while he said, "You may be right. I guess it wouldn't be. Man," he said dreamily, "when I think that she might have that fantastic gold colour down there too. . . ."

Suddenly it struck me with alarm that I'd spent the night away from home and hadn't told my parents a thing. My two bags with the six bottles of mineral water were over in the corner, and there was a clock on the wall above them. A quarter to seven! My God! Mother must have died of fright.

"Shit!" I cried. "I didn't tell the parents a thing yesterday."

* * *

I ran home in the rain. The shit is really going to hit the fan, I thought. I flew up the stairs to the third floor and rang the bell.

Mother answered the door. She frowned at me, but otherwise she seemed unconcerned.

"You should be ashamed of yourself, Danny," she said sternly.

I felt a pang of fear.

"Mother, look, I can explain. I —" but I didn't know how much she already knew, and what made her so calm, given the circumstances.

"You're much too young to go around getting drunk like that."

So that was it. But who could have —

"And gambling."

Somebody had told a white lie. Who? Of course —

"I didn't want it to happen, Mother, but it just kind of —"

"You're not used to alcohol. You have to be careful."

"I was, only —"

"Honza Dresler said you just drank a glass of grog and —"

"Honza Dresler?"

"Yes. Molly Dreslerová phoned and said that Honza Dresler wanted to tell me that you passed out in Pitterman's cottage."

Molly! So she was really a good girl after all, and not a bitch. It was true she had tattled on me to the alderman last winter, but you could hardly blame her, since she had a date with me and then saw me with her own eyes scuffing about with someone else. And she was thinking of me. A message from Honza Dresler. And she was also very smart.

"I won't do it again, mother," I said.

"Don't talk foolishness," said mother. "But do try to drink in moderation. Drinking yourself unconscious—why you've got no call to do that. You're young, good looking, intelligent —"

* * *

At school I only caught sight of Marie during a break, walking up and down the corridor with Blanka Poznerová under the watchful eye of Mrs. Řivnáčová, and when she saw me, she stifled a laugh with her hand and began to giggle. I grinned at her too and it didn't bother me in the least to have her laughing at me. I must have been quite hilarious after all that rum, but the fact was she had covered for me at home and her kind consideration had kept me from getting into hot water with the parents.

I went to the washroom where about a hundred people were smoking home-grown tobacco and Leopold Váňa was instructing Lexa and Jiří Horák, the Kôstelec billiard champ, in communism.

"In the Reich, the bourgeoisie hold the power," he said frowningly smoking a cigar he had evidently stolen from his father.

"Rot!" said Jiří Horák. "The Nazi's hold the power. And they ain't no bourgeoisie, at least not if I know anything about it. Take Kühl, for instance," he said, holding up the local Reichskommissar as an example of them all. "Before the war he worked for the railway as a watchman, just like my Dad, but they chucked him out of work for drinking on the job and embezzling company money."

"And besides that, he informed on my father," said Lexa. "The only decent German in Kostelec is Mr. Kleinander, and I'll admit he's a bourgeois. He's chief accountant."

"Get me right," said Leopold Váňa. "I'm looking at this in general terms. Naturally the details —"

A terrible stench rolled in from the direction of the toilets. "My God," Lexa said, "It's like a barrel of fecal matter exploding. The Mánes's undoubtedly had boiled cabbage for supper again last night. Benno!" he called toward the toilets, "next time bring some eau de cologne with you. Why should we have to suffer for your gluttony?"

"Fuck off," said Benno's voice behind the doors.

The bell rang and we all left the washroom.

* * *

It was still raining but I felt good. The last lesson of the day was maths with Mr. Bivoj, and he always has us an oral test. His method, I reckoned, was derived from the Grand Guignol. He always called on the dullest girl in the class first, in this case Ladislava Hornychová, set her a problem and then let her talk. She never managed to say very much, and Mr. Bivoj said nothing either. He always kept silent for precisely two minutes, whereupon he would ask quietly, but with icy irony, "That's it?" Ladislava Hornychová would reply, equally calmly, "I'm afraid I don't know," and then Mr. Bivoj would say, "Sit down," and with a great flourish write what was evidently an "F" in his black notebook. Next he would call up the dullest boy, which was usually me or the class poet, Josef Krátký. This time it was me, and my performance was like a silent film that lasted two minutes, then I broke the silence with, "I'm sorry I don't know." Then I was given an 'F,' sat down, and Mr. Bivoj asked Lubuše Maršíková to come forward

Thus he made his way around the entire classroom and was able to knock us all out with a single problem. That's how well he knew his job. There were twenty-one of us in the class, the rain was drumming on the windowpanes, wisps of foggy mist were floating quickly past the castle tower, and I felt great. Mr. Bivoj made it as far as Jarda Bukavec, who was tops in mathematics, but even better at chess and Mr. Bivoj liked him but at the same time was jealous of him because before Jarda had begun to play chess, Bivoj had been the best player in Kostelec. Now Jarda Bukavec lost to Bivoj only in math classes, where he deliberately flubbed the test for the class's sake, so that Bivoj would be in a good mood and set us easier problems. Today, however, Jarda genuinely couldn't do anything with the problem, Mr. Bivoj wrote a large "F" into his notebook with great relish, and the bell rang. No one was bothered too much by getting an 'F' from Bivoj, because the mark had been devalued by the large number he handed out.

* * *

As soon as I got home, and as soon as father left for his bank, and mother to visit Mrs. Moutelíková, I dialed the Dresler's number. Molly's brother answered the phone.

"Molly's doing her homework," he said.

"So don't be a stick and call her."

"Dad says she's not to leave her room. She got an 'F' in composition."

"Come off it, they never give 'Fs' in composition."

"She had four major spelling mistakes," said Honza. You lose a point for every big one, and then the essay looked like a five-year-old wrote it, so you figure it out."

"Is your Dad home?"

"No."

"Look, you're not going to refuse a friend, are you?"

"Well, OK, I'll tell her."

A few moments later I heard her voice. "Danny?"

"Yes."

"Danny you were wonderfully drunk. Are you feeling all right now?"

"I feel fantastic, Marie, thanks to you."

"Sure, thanks to me. I was the one who poured the rum into you."

"Doesn't make a difference. I tried to pour it into you."

"I know. But my intentions were honourable."

"So were mine."

"That depends on how you look at it," she said. "I did it just for fun."

"But it was really nice of you, Marie."

"Well, I'm not so sure about that," she said uncertainly. "It's a sin, after all."

"No. I mean telephoning my parents."

"Oh that. Well —"

"Well what?"

"That was just a kind of penance for that telephone call I made last winter—you know, Dannykins?" she said.

A wave of tender love filled me right down to the ultimate pores of my soul. I had almost forgotten how pious she was, easy enough to do, with her. But she was pious, that was obvious.

"It wasn't very nice of me," she said.

"Except that I deserved it. If I love you, I oughtn't to lay a finger on anyone else."

"You mean cast an eye," she corrected me.

"Really, I'll never do it again," I said with the best of intentions. "Marie, are you coming to the dance in Provodov on Saturday?"

"Yes, I am," she said.

I started rapidly to climb the winding heavenly staircase, till I found myself in the sixth.

"Let's go together, OK? We start playing at three, so if we leave at one —"

"I've already got a ride. Blanka Poznerová is taking me there by car."

I stopped short of seventh heaven. "Well—couldn't I catch a ride out with you then?"

"There are five of us girls going. There's no room for you."

I sank back to third heaven, but I was still in heaven.

"But you are coming, aren't you, Marie?"

"You know I am, Danny," she said in her sweetest voice. Kočandrle by now had probably been forgotten. I'd have to strike while the iron —

"Father's coming," she whispered into the phone. "I have to go, otherwise we can forget about Saturday. Bye bye, Dannykins."

And she hung up with a click.

* * *

So I walked to Provodov with the band. We dragged a cart loaded up with our instruments and were followed by a crowd of zoot-suiters and their dolls from Kostelec, and they helped us push, so that in fact it wasn't difficult. The girls were mostly wearing scruffy boots and carried their dancing shoes in shopping bags. When the wind blew and lifted their raincoats, you could see their dancing dresses. They had all had their hair done for the occasion, and wore coloured kerchiefs to keep the wind from making a mess of their perms.

We dragged ourselves up the gentle slope of the hill and beneath us in the valley, Kostelec glistened in the rain. Grey and black clouds hung over the town and a mist was rising from the woods. It was almost four kilometers to Provodov, which was in fact a large highland village, a church with a red onion tower in the centre and right next to the church a huge pub called "The Acorn." Tonda Novák, the pub-keeper's son, was an afficianado of swing and he was the one who had set it all up for us with his father. Behind the tap room there was a large hall where they used to have tea dances and perform amateur plays before the Germans had banned dancing altogether. But the Germans were stupid and only came round to check up on the ban on Saturday evenings and Sunday afternoons, so we played on Saturdays till six, and then hurried back down to Kostelec to play dinner music in the evening at the Beránek café. In winter we made the trip back on sleighs. Just to make sure, Mr. Nosek, the local constable, would sit in front by the bar window and let us know if anyone were coming to check up.

The hall was already quite full when Brynych gave the countdown and we started in on our signature tune, *The Casa Loma Stomp.* By that time everyone knew it was just our signature tune, so no one danced. We played standing up because we all knew it by heart, and I looked round the hall. Naturally there was no sign of Marie yet. I reckoned they would come in about an hour. Blanka Poznerová had been brought up to do that sort of thing. She arrived late wherever she went. The Pozners owned the biggest factory in Kostelec, a huge rubber plant, and Blanka went to Prague every week by car to Jirásek's dancing classes. They had a car with a chauffeur. They would probably arrive about four, which would still leave me two hours.

So for the time being I could play with pleasant anticipation. I looked round the hall. Helena Teichmanová was there with Kábrt, Prdlas, the king of the zoot-suiters with some painted doll who was probably from Hradec, Ladislava Hornychová was there with Pepík Kučera and Dadka Habrová in a strapless dress, bare from the tits up, with Jarka Mokrý, who was probably carrying on behind Zuzana's back with her. In short, everyone was there. At least fifteen or sixteen of my twenty-three sheep. We chopped our way through that quick stomp, Venca Štern was laying on a kind of glissando trombone solo over our heads when the door opened and in from the taproom stepped Irena in a yellowish-green dress of Georgette and behind her the fool Kočandrle in a black double-breasted suit with red stripes. And right after them came Leopold Váňa and Rosťa Pitterman.

This aroused rather mixed feelings in me. Irena with Kočandrle—that was all right. I always enjoyed showing off in front of Irena on the tenor, even though she was as deaf as a stump as far as jazz went. And today I would do the same for Marie. When she saw Irena with Kočandrle, she would certainly wind herself around me like a vine. And I around her like three vine, naturally. I'd tell the boys to play a few numbers without me; Benno always knew how to fill up the holes when I wasn't soloing, and so did Fonda. Instead of our usual Bob Crosby Dixieland, they'd simply play normal dixie.

But Rosťa represented a complication. I hadn't invited him, but of course you didn't have to. He was always where the girls were. Like me. I was a fool not to think of it, to try and arrange some way to forestall him. God knows how. I was certain he'd make a play for Marie. Maybe I should have paid Piksla, a well-known Kostelec prostitute, to model for him in his cottage in the nude. Except that Rosťa probably wouldn't have given her the time of day. He wasn't interested in that kind of nude study.

But I had to do something. We finished our signature tune and started in on *Some of These Days.* Here in Provodov Fonda announced it by its real name, in English, and not as *Einmal, einmal mein Schatz,* as he did in the Beránek.

The first out on the floor, naturally, were Rosťa and Dadka Habrová. The devil knows how Rosťa had managed to spirit her away from Jarka right at the start, and they were jiving so energetically it seemed that the dress would come right off her. Soon, however, there was such a crowd on the dance floor that I lost track of them. Kočandrle, of course, was dancing with Irena. The fool looked as though he had a ramrod up his back, but Irena cut the ice around him, her Georgette skirt swinging so high around her legs I could see her garters. Irena, the bitch. It was my turn to solo, and I sobbed out the line that went *Some of these days, you'll miss me honey...* Irena certainly didn't look as though she'd ever miss me, but for the time being I wasn't missing her either, as I roared out triumphantly in the middle range, where the tenor sounds best ... *you'll be sorry when I'm gone away* ... and then I merely waited around with that pleasant feeling until the doors would open and Marie's golden mane would appear. I decorated my solo with ironic little curlicues as I had never done before, then sat down and Benno came in fast and magnificently, with a mute in the bell of his trumpet, and it seemed to me that he was making fun of Irena for me. He croaked like a frog, but just slightly out of rhythm, and I blew little fill-in riffs just under his diabolical wailing, and then we rounded it up tutti and fotissimo. Right after that we played *Swingin' the Blues* and *Bob Cats*. And *Tiger Rag*. Then I went for a leak. Mr. Novák gave us two percent beer free of charge, and you could drink ten pints of the stuff and the effect would not have been nearly as powerful as that cup of rum at the cottage. On the other hand, you had to relieve yourself more frequently.

Leopold Váňa was standing in the corridor with Jířa Horák and again he was pumping it into him like a missionary. I found it odd that he would bother to come here at all, since he evidently had no interest in horn-blowing. But this was a place where souls assembled.

"You're right, Jířa," shouted Leopold Váňa when I stepped up to him and he realized that it was just me. "It's a nation-wide struggle of resistance. But we have to try and turn it into a movement of class consciousness."

"Well, isn't the thing to beat the Germans?" said the billiards champ.

"Sure, that's part of it," said Leopold Váňa, "but the main thing is —"

Rosťa walked by and called out, "Danny, Marie's coming."

"Is that so? How do you know?" I said, as though it were news to me.

"Zuzana Princová told me. They're both coming in Blanka Poznerová's car."

"Is that so? And who's she coming with?"

Rosťa pulled me a little to one side away from the preacher, who had stopped sermonizing and started listening to what we were saying. Excitedly, Rosťa said, "That's just it, man, she's coming alone. Just with the other girls."

"I see."

"That gives me a chance, man."

I knew very well that it did. That was no news to me. Except the thought didn't excite me as much as it did him.

"Danny, would you do me a favour?"

"Sure," I said, rather unenthusiastically.

"You guys play that number *Everybody Loves my Baby*, right?"

"Right."

"That's a charleston," Rosťa whispered like a conspirator. "Nobody knows how to do that here except me. I can still remember how from the 'Spring Sun' review. I'll tell Marie I'm going to teach her how, then I'll come up to you and request it for her, you arrange it with the band, and I'll teach her the charleston."

"Just what fantastic results do you expect from that?"

"Well, you know—I'll teach her how, right? Get her into the mood. She's probably bored to death after being with Kočandrle all that time, so I have to present myself to her in a favourable light, so to speak. And I know how to charleston real well. And no one else in Kostelec can do it."

I remembered the underwear shorts on the couch in his cottage and I wondered whether the charleston would be much help to him. My hopes rose slightly.

"Well, OK, if that's what you want," I said.

We went to piss and then returned to the hall.

And there, at a table right by the door, sat Marie with Zdeněk Pivoňka.

* * *

I shuffled over to the podium and Rosťa shuffled over to Zuzana Princová. We started off with a blues, which you could dance the slow fox-trot to, and both girls, Marie and Irena, eagerly came onto the dance floor with their switcheroo lovers. And both of them put on a great show, casting indifferently murderous glances at each other while winding themselves like lianas around those two fools, while both fools, Kočandrle and Pivoňka, danced to beat the band.

Oh God! Oh dear God! I sobbed in my soul, and honked on the tenor like the whistling of a sad Mississippi riverboat. The branches of an appletree were waving outside the window of the pub and the autumn wind brought another rainstorm to Provodov. We finished *Joe Turner,* Fonda noticed the raindrops and announced a slow foxtrot, *Heaven Cries for Me.* It really was crying. Weeping, really bawling, as Alena, now in exile at a girls' school in Prague, once said.

"The rain is dancing round us," sang Lexa, who occasionally acted as our crooner, *"it's just the fog turned into drops,"* . . . and Benno and I played the blues breaks, although they weren't in the notes, so moved were

we by that autumn rainfall, "*. . . but I know that it ain't true . . .* sang Lexa, slipping into dialect to avoid taking the lyrics too seriously, and I caught sight of Marie's garters as she executed a giant pirouette, utterly happy that she had managed to get revenge on Irena and Kočandrle at one blow. . . . *"It's heaven cryin' over me,"* sang Lexa, and in the final pause, he let his voice break like Oldřich Nový when he sang *Only for Today* in that movie, Kristián, and Benno and I barked out a friendly, bluesy argument over that terribly long pause.

* * *

Things were not looking too friendly on the dance floor. They were waiting for the next number and both girls were chattering away with their respective fools, laughing and carrying on, and Rosťa watched them gloomily from an empty table in the corner. He had let Leopold Váňa go off with Zuzanka Princová.

"Swingers Congress," announced Fonda, and we set into a slow swing number and the girls danced it almost as though it were a Cossack dance. And so we dragged it out, that is I did, with my heart full of blues, through another two foxtrots, and then we took a break and Zdeněk went to the bathroom.

I caught Rosťa's sad eyes and got an idea. In this particular struggle Rosťa had suddenly turned from a rival into an ally because I'd rather she went with anyone but that Zdeněk Pivonka. . . . Wasn't it enough for the bastard to keep me away from Irena for two years now? Did he have to start the same thing with Marie? Rosťa must have felt the same.

"Fonda," I said, "let's play *Everybody*, OK?"

"Fine with me."

"But right now, OK?"

"Why right now?"

"I'll explain later. Hurry."

Fonda asked no more questions and gave the sign. He understood that a girl was involved and cases like that took absolute precedence, even over a break. Brynych rattled off the charleston rhythm on the wood and over the neck of my tenor I could see that Rosťa had grasped what was happening and was standing up. He walked briskly over to Marie. And we jumped right into it. . . *Everybody loves my baby . . .* sharp and fast, and in my mind's eye I saw Kristýna's white legs in that wire cage . . . *but my baby don't love nobody but me. . . .* Hardly anyone had expected us to take such a short break, and a lot of fellows had gone to the washroom so the dance floor was almost empty. And it emptied entirely when people saw what Rosťa was starting to do with a slightly dazed Marie.

She may have been dazed but she didn't stay that way for long. Marie learned fast. Where dancing and like frivolities were concerned, she was quicker to learn than she was in school. In a few moments her legs, in that white pleated skirt and black stockings, and more beautiful than Kristýna's legs, began to flash up and down and Rosťa danced the charleston as though he were mounted on a spring, so charged with love was he. Those few couples who had come onto the dance floor to dance the foxtrot stopped and watched Marie and Rosťa. *Everybody wants my baby but my baby don't want nobody....* I sang along in my mind, and I blasted out staccatto notes to match their steps... *but me....*

Sure. And all at once, out of nowhere and quite brazenly, Zdeněk appeared on the dance floor, tapped the cavorting Rosťa on the shoulder and said something, obviously "May I?" and in a second he started to bob up and down as though he were on a spring, while Rosťa stopped, as though his spring had snapped and then, quite wilted, he shuffled back to his table, for Marie, the viper, had turned her smiling face to Zdeněk and was flashing her legs so high that her garter buckles were signaling in all directions... *'cause when my baby kisses me on my rosy cheeks*... and truly her cheeks were burning, like genuine little roses, her pale blue eyes were as bright as they had been two nights ago with the rum and that thick golden hair was flying about her head, beautifully washed, shampooed, curled or whatever she did with it.... *I just let those kisses be and don't wash my face for weeks.... Oh! Everybody loves my baby....* I blew so aggressively that the strap broke and I had to carry the full weight of the sax on my right thumb... *everybody loves my baby*... we played the last chorus, Zdeněk must have done a somersault on the dance floor or something... *and my baby loves... everybody....* Marie's black legs in their dancing shoes flashed up and down as though they were on wires... *but me... oh!... but me....*

* * *

Well, in short, Zdeněk was king of the dance floor and by popular demand we had to repeat that stupid charleston three times because everyone wanted to learn it and Zdeněk very willingly played the role of instructor, demonstrating it with Marie, the crowd followed them, hundreds of legs flashed up and down beyond the neck of my tenor, I blew into it in a fury and in my mind the words of that stupid song became completely confused.

Only Irena was not dancing the charleston and sat tensely the whole time at the table with Kočandrle. That made me feel good, and as I watched them, I had the very strong impression that they were arguing. That made me feel even better.

After the glut of charlestoning, Zdeněk felt the urge and left for the washroom and Marie went to sit down. To give ourselves and the dancers a rest, we played *I'm Going to Lock up Today*. I signalled to Benno to carry on without me and in a flash I was beside Marie.

"Marie, may I?"

She looked at me from the pocket mirror in which she was studying her own beauty, which she had enhanced with some intoxicatingly fragrant powder.

"I'm absolutely bushed, Danny."

"But it's only a slow foxtrot, Marie."

She looked at me. Her breasts were rising and falling more rapidly than usual.

"Please, Marie, I'm going to have to go and play again in a minute and I've been dying for a chance to dance with you. Come on."

"Well, since you put it so nicely."

She stood up and I pressed myself against her sweet breasts, felt the pressure of her sweet thighs as she moved them to the rhythm of the foxtrot . . . *"I'm going to lock up today in my treasure-chest of dreams,"* sang Lexa through his nose, imitating Václav Irmanov, *". . . then it will stay right here with me. . . ."*

* * *

"Marie," I said into her little white ear. She was wearing a blue baptismal earring in it because she was pious. "You said you were coming alone, only with some other girls."

"I thought I was, Danny, I really did."

"Then how come you came with Pivonka?"

She said nothing, and I executed a perfect, but melancholy about turn, just as the dance master Toman had taught us to, and she leaned into me with her breasts, which were soft and at the same time firm, qualities that no other material in the world possesses in that relation. . . .

"You promised, and then you went back on your word."

"It's hard, Danny . . . there are things. . . ."

Right. Things. It didn't look good.

"What things?" I wanted to know, although I knew very well.

". . . then the light of all my grey days . . ." sang Lexa . . . *"that still burn in the dark. . . ."*

"Oh, you know," said Marie.

Yes, I knew, I knew.

"Have you started going with Zdeněk?"

"Hm."

"What's that mean, 'Hm'?" I asked, very bitterly.

"Oh, you know."

We were silent for a while and I felt only her breasts and those long, slender legs. . . .

". . . I'm going to lock up today," sang Lexa, *"in a lock-me-up heart . . . and keep it there forever. . . ."*

Sure. I will forever, but Marie?
Perhaps she will as well. Who knows?
Suddenly I lost my temper.
"Sure, I know, Marie. I know very well."
She felt that I was angry and said quietly, "Maybe you don't know."
"Oh yes I do. I'm not that stupid. You still love Kočandrle."
"Kočandrle? Tickle me so I'll laugh."
"I'd like to but you wouldn't let me."
"You're right, I wouldn't."
"But you'd let Zdeněk, wouldn't you, and you don't love him either."
"Don't be disgusting, Danny."
"So I'm disgusting, am I?"
"You're starting to be."

I gained control of myself and felt the anger subsiding somewhat, so we were silent for a while. Then I said, still angry but more desperate now, "You started going with Pivonka to make Kočandrle jealous."

"Oh, my!" said Marie.
"And I'm just a temporary amusement, aren't I?"
"Well, when you say things like that —"
"I'm just your plaything, aren't I?"
"No, you're not. But you are annoying."
"Me? Annoying? My God!"
"But you are."
"Because I'm right."
"You're not right at all," she said, but in such a way that I knew I'd hit the nail on the head. A very big nail.

"... and then this day will never end. ..." sang Lexa.

"May I?" said someone behind me in a dripping voice that sounded like liquid air.

I looked around. Of course, Kočandrle himself. I looked Marie in the eye and went on dancing, but Marie avoided my eyes and wanted to stop.

"Danny, please don't be angry with me, but ..." she whispered urgently in my ear, and then slipped out of my grasp. If she had started to pretend to be in a huff I would probably, angry and desperate as I was, have tried to keep leading her across the dance floor and left Kočandrle standing there like a fool, or following after us like a bigger fool. But Marie had whispered, "Don't be angry," and I couldn't be, not with her. Ever. I only felt terribly, terribly sorry. Even much later, when years had passed, terribly quickly. ...

I let her go. Kočandrle pushed in to take my place.

"... *I remember oh, so fondly* ..." sang Lexa. For a moment I stood there like a fool on the dance floor, and then I turned around and saw the full extent of the catastrophe. Pivonka, that thick-lipped idiot, with Irena in his arms. She was showing off again, Zdeněk was spinning her around in great circles, around and around, and Irena was smiling as though nothing had happened between her fall from the Five Fingers Rock and this second fall.

Oh God! Oh damn! Someone bumped into me and a sharp female heel sank into my calf. Oh God! I turned around, groped my way among the couples on the dance floor and went quickly to the washroom to bawl.

In the corridor, Leopold Váňa was hectoring away at Rosťa. "We have to try and make it clear to our people that . . ."

I went into the washroom and had a long, melancholy piss. My tears slid down into the urinal. Vigorous runnels of rain flowed down the dirty, fly-stained window.

* * *

Then we played a whole set of blues. *Blues in the Dark.* If I had played last Saturday in a way that made even Mr. Ceeh sit up and listen, I don't know how I played now. *Can't cheatin' make me love you* . . . I played with deep feeling . . . *be mean and you drive me away.* . . . Except that it didn't fit my situation. No matter how cruelly the girls treated me, I loved them all the same. Or whatever it was. Or perhaps I was just young. Or it was the rain. The fog. This sad autumn. The war that brought everything to such a bad end.

I played, not looking at the music, Benno behind me on his muted trumpet wailed and cried and Lexa howled in dizzying heights on his clarinet . . . *did you ever dream, lucky baby.* . . . Benno's trumpet was talking, Haryk leaned over his guitar, seeming almost to embrace it, playing sharp, lamenting chords . . . *and wake up cold in hand.* . . . The terribly sad, beautiful music took me into its consoling embrace, the boys and girls were whirling and dancing in front of me, Venca Štern's trombone sounded like a bell, like a knell of love . . . of whatever . . . of youth. . . .

The doors opened, and constable Nosek of the local constabulary appeared and gave us the all clear sign. He looked around. From the table in the corner where Jířa Horák was sitting, Leopold Váňa got up and walked over to Mr. Nosek. Mr. Nosek shouted something in his ear. It must have been hard to hear because we were making a terrible, wailing racket. Leopold Váňa looked startled and blanched or something. Then he gaped at us, at the band, as white as death and walked across the hall, skirting the dance floor. Lexa started in on his blues solo, and he played it beautifully in the heavenly register. In the stratosphere . . . *did you ever, ever dream, lucky baby.* . . . Leopold Váňa picked his way across the hall and around our podium and climbed onto it from behind, came right up to me and then stood there between me and Lexa. Perhaps he was waiting for us to finish . . . *you gonna long for me baby.* . . . Lexa was playing, blowing high in the unattainable heights of that terrible autumn sadness . . . *one of these cold rainy days* . . . then he finished and it was Fonda's turn to solo, a Count Basie-type of solo that sounded like rain drops on a tin roof. Leopold Váňa said something to Lexa, Lexa seemed to rise halfway out of his chair and Leopold Váňa disappeared.

"What's up?" I asked Lexa in a pause in the music.

"They shot my old man," said Lexa, and he was really and truly, oh God, pale and he stood up and vanished somewhere behind the podium and it was my turn to solo, and everything was spinning . . . everything comes to an end . . . this was the end of everything . . . they're going to shoot them all . . . our youth . . . those bourgeois. . . . *Did you ever dream, lucky baby* . . . I wailed in pain, into the emptiness, with no one to hear me . . . *and wake up . . . cold . . . in the dark. . . .*

Augsburg College
George Sverdrup Library
Minneapolis, Minnesota 55454